TRUE and HOLY

TRUE and HOLY

Christian Scripture and Other Religions

Leo D. Lefebure

ORBIS BOOKS

Maryknoll, New York 10545

ORBIS BOOKS
Maryknoll, New York 10545

Fathers and Brothers
MARYKNOLL™

Founded in 1970, Orbis Books endeavors to publish works that enlighten the mind, nourish the spirit, and challenge the conscience. The publishing arm of the Maryknoll Fathers and Brothers, Orbis seeks to explore the global dimensions of the Christian faith and mission, to invite dialogue with diverse cultures and religious traditions, and to serve the cause of reconciliation and peace. The books published reflect the views of their authors and do not represent the official position of the Maryknoll Society. To learn more about Maryknoll and Orbis Books, please visit our website at www.maryknollsociety.org.

The Scripture quotations contained herein are from the New Revised Standard Version Bible, copyright © 1989 by the Division of Christian Education of the National Council of the Churches of Christ in the U.S.A. and are used by permission. All rights reserved.

Library of Congress Cataloging-in-Publication Data

Lefebure, Leo D., 1952-
    True and holy : Christian scripture and other religions / by Leo D. Lefebure.
        pages cm
    Includes bibliographical references and index.
    ISBN 978-1-62698-053-2 (pbk.)
    1. Bible—Criticism, interpretation, etc. 2. Christianity and other religions. I. Title.
    BS511.3.L435   2013
    261.2—dc23
                                                    2013023840

To Sheila Reynolds Trainor
In friendship and esteem

Table of Contents

Acknowledgments

I would like to thank all those with whom I have participated in interreligious conversations through many years, especially the many persons in a number of countries with whom I have discussed the issues in this work. I especially thank those who hosted me during a sabbatical year at Ukrainian Catholic University in Lviv, St. Thomas Aquinas Institute in Kyiv (Kiev), St. Pius College in Mumbai, St. Xavier School in Delhi, the Centre for Catholic Studies of the Chinese University of Hong Kong, and the community of Rissho Kosei-kai in Tokyo. Portions of this work were delivered in lectures at Synagogue Ohr Kodesh in Chevy Chase, Maryland, for The Foundation for Jewish Studies Distinguished Scholar Lecture Series; at the Third International Muslim–Christian Conference at Bethlehem University; at Ukrainian Catholic University in Lviv; at the Institute of Philosophy of the National Academy of Sciences of Ukraine in Kyiv; at the Center for Studies of History and Culture of Eastern European Jews of the National University Kyiv—Mohyla Academy; at St. Thomas Aquinas Institute in Kyiv; at Taras Shevchenko National University of Kyiv; at National University Kyiv—Mohyla Academy; and at Mykhailo Drahomanov Kyiv National University. I also delivered lectures on these topics at St. Pius College and St. Andrew's College in Mumbai, at Vidyajyoti School of Theology in Delhi, at meetings of the priests of the dioceses of Vasai and Mumbai, and at the conference of Ecclesiological Investigations in Assisi in 2012: "Where We Dwell in Common": Pathways for Dialogue in the 21st Century. I also spoke on these topics at the Centre for Catholic Studies of the Chinese University of Hong Kong, at Gakurin Seminary and the Buddhist Discussion Group in Tokyo, and at Trinity College Dublin. To all those who listened and contributed to improving these discussions, I am profoundly grateful.

"Not as Competitors but as Pilgrims in Search of the Truth"

> The Catholic Church rejects nothing of those things which are true and holy in these religions. It regards with respect those ways of acting and living and those precepts and teachings which, though often at variance with what it holds and expounds, frequently reflect a ray of that truth which enlightens everyone. (*Nostra Aetate* 2; Tanner 1990, 2:969)

Followers of Jesus Christ have been involved in relationships with other religious traditions from the very beginning. At times these relationships have been respectful and generous, but all too often they have been conflictual and hostile. In every context, interreligious relationships have profoundly influenced Christian self-understanding, either for better or for worse. In diverse ways the biblical precedents and models have profoundly shaped the history of Christian relations with followers of other religious paths. Christians relate to followers of other religious paths in light of biblical perspectives, and the quality of Christian interreligious relationships in turn influences the manner in which Christians read the Bible in regard to other religious traditions. In situations of hostility, Christians can easily find biblical precedents and commands for criticizing, demeaning, or even destroying religious others. For example, Christians have frequently constructed their identity in sharp negative opposition to Jews and Muslims, who were historically often seen as allies of the Antichrist. Similarly, Christians have often held hostile attitudes toward Buddhists and Hindus, deriding them as idolaters. However, in a more respectful, generous atmosphere, Christians can read the Bible in cordial dialogue with other religious traditions, looking for common values and shared beliefs and goals.

This diversity begins in the Bible itself, with its varying and conflicting viewpoints on how to engage religious difference. In the pages of the Bible, Christians find harsh condemnations of those who worship alien gods or follow different religious practices. The Bible fiercely denounces idolatry, and Elijah even commanded that all the prophets of Baal be slaughtered (1 Kgs. 18:39-40). Both Testaments of the Bible offer sharp criticisms of Jews and Jewish leaders;

1

in later periods of history Christians repeatedly interpreted these passages to justify and reinforce hostile relations with generation after generation of Jews.

Christians also find biblical examples of respectful, cordial relationships among people from different religious backgrounds. The biblical wisdom teachers engaged in conversations with the wise of other lands, offering a model for more respectful, generous relationships, as in the friendly conversation and exchange of gifts between King Solomon and the Queen of Sheba (1 Kgs. 10:1-13). The editors of the book of Proverbs incorporated an adaptation of an Egyptian sapiential book, the *Wisdom of Amenemope*, into Proverbs 22:17-24:22. In the Acts of the Apostles, the apostle Paul offers a model of how to relate to those who honor multiple gods when he speaks at the Areopagus in Athens. While rejecting the multiple gods of the Athenians, Paul nonetheless seeks common ground with his audience and suggests they are already in some way in touch with the one God, albeit as "unknown" (Acts 17:22-31). Christians of each generation decide which aspects of the biblical heritage to follow and which to leave in the background.

From the origins of Christianity to the present, scriptural interpretation has been a battlefield of animated conflict between competing perspectives, and the tension between these two approaches to the Bible and other religions runs throughout Christian history and continues to the present. A hermeneutics of hostility interprets interreligious relationships in light of the sharp scriptural condemnations of different religious perspectives, all too often with deadly consequences. Most of the history of Christianity has been characterized by intense hostility toward followers of other religious paths. This heritage of hostility weighs heavily on present-day relationships and is by no means ended.

Even though all too often in history a hermeneutics of hostility has prevailed, in recent decades Catholics and many other Christians have been going through a major shift in relations with other religious traditions and in biblical interpretation. In publicly expressing the respect of the Catholic Church for what is true and holy in other religions, and specifically for Hindus, Buddhists, Muslims, and Jews, the Second Vatican Council expressed and encouraged a revolutionary conversion of mind and heart, of attitudes and actions. For Catholics, this Council was a major milestone in this transformation, launching a new era for Catholic relationships to followers of other religions. In *Nostra Aetate* (Declaration on the Church's Relation to Non-Christian Religions), the council noted values that Catholics share with Hindus, Buddhists, Muslims, and Jews. After asserting that the Catholic Church rejects nothing that is true and holy in these traditions, the council urged all religious persons to work together for the realization of common values:

> It [the Council] therefore calls upon all its sons and daughters with prudence and charity, through dialogues and cooperation with the followers of other religions, bearing witness to the Christian faith and way of life, to recognize, preserve and promote those spiritual and

moral good things as well as the socio-cultural values which are to be found among them. (*Nostra Aetate* 2; Tanner 1990, 2:969)

The Second Vatican Council was by no means the first or the only moment in changing Catholic attitudes toward the Bible in relation to other religions, but in this area it endorsed and encouraged a fundamental and important change that was already under way. In recent years, Catholics have debated the degree to which the Second Vatican Council represents continuity with the earlier tradition and the degree to which there are new developments. In looking forward to the third millennium of Christian faith, Pope John Paul II reflected on a number of unprecedented pronouncements of this council:

No Council had ever spoken so clearly about Christian unity, about dialogue with non-Christian religions, about the specific meaning of the Old Covenant and of Israel, about the dignity of each person's conscience, about the principle of religious liberty, about the different cultural traditions within which the Church carries out her missionary mandate, and about the means of social communication. (*Tertio Millennio Adveniente* §19)

Edward Idris Cardinal Cassidy later described *Nostra Aetate* as "a completely new approach to interreligious dialogue on the part of the church. Rather than stress and condemn what is to be found there that is not compatible with Christian teaching and understanding, dialogue and cooperation are proposed" (2005, 130). For Catholics and many other Christians, there has been a revolution, a conversion of heart, conscience, and mind, in the area of interpreting the Bible in relation to other religious traditions. There are many sides to this transformation. Many Christians throughout the centuries have worked constructively for harmonious relations with other religious traditions. While the shift in Christian attitudes is particularly dramatic in relation to Jews and Judaism, the transformation is not restricted to Jewish–Christian relations but embraces every interreligious relationship. By explicitly mentioning Hindus, Buddhists, Muslims, and Jews, *Nostra Aetate* acknowledged the importance of these traditions and encouraged further exploration in each of these relationships.

In settings where Christian relationships with other religious traditions are amicable, interpretations of the Bible can focus on shared perspectives, values, and ideals, with a respectful recognition of differences. In these situations, a hermeneutics of respect and generosity, while acknowledging important differences, can emphasize common beliefs and principles and promote mutual understanding and respect. As Christian relations with other traditions have changed in recent decades, many Christians have also entered an epochal transformation in interpreting scripture in relation to other religious traditions; many aspects of this process remain in discernment. Jews and Christians explore the intertwining and the distinctions between their traditions, seeking to overcome centuries of enmity and to shape more cordial relations. Despite the often negative images in the media, in many settings Christians and Muslims now meet to discuss the relation between their scriptures and their beliefs. Some Christians have entered deeply into Hindu and Buddhist meditation practices and have come to read the Bible in distinctive ways.

Respect and generosity cannot mean unlimited acceptance; critique remains an indispensable aspect of interreligious relations. In recent years, some of the most intense interreligious discussions have addressed questions of human rights and religious liberty. In conflict-ridden situations, one of the most pressing challenges in interreligious relations is how to respond to injustice and violence without imitating it in an unending cycle of violent recrimination. How to interpret the Bible in situations of injustice is a pressing challenge. In relation to this issue, Mahatma Gandhi is one of the most influential figures in shaping Christian understanding of Jesus' teaching of nonviolent response to injury.

This work will explore the ongoing transformation from a widespread biblical hermeneutics of hostility to a growing hermeneutics of respect, generosity, and friendship in relation to the four religious communities named in *Nostra Aetate*: Jewish, Islamic, Hindu, and Buddhist. In each relationship there are tensions and challenges; in each relationship there have been important developments in recent decades. I will begin by exploring the precedents, problems, and principles for engaging religious difference in the Bible, and the hermeneutical issues involved in Christians interpreting their scriptures in relation to other religious traditions. Succeeding chapters will examine the specific issues involved in interpreting the Bible in relations with Jews, Muslims, Hindus, and Buddhists. The final chapter will reflect on the experience of conversion from a hermeneutics of hostility to a hermeneutics of generosity in light of the philosophical theology of Bernard Lonergan and the mimetic theory of René Girard.

In May 2013, Jean-Louis Cardinal Tauran addressed an assembly of European Catholic bishops in London, which addressed the question of Muslim–Christian relations. He commented on interreligious relations with particular reference to Muslims: "Believers know that 'man does not just live off bread.' They are aware of the fact that they have to make their own personal contribution in their everyday lives and they must do so together, not as competitors but as pilgrims in search of the truth" (Rolandi 2013, n.p.).

CHAPTER ONE

Engaging Religious Difference: Respect, Hospitality, and Charity

The Hope for Dialogue of Friendship

Jorge Mario Cardinal Bergoglio, the archbishop of Buenos Aires who would later become Pope Francis, engaged in a number of conversations with his friend Rabbi Abraham Skorka, which they presented to the world in their joint publication, *On Heaven and Earth*. Bergoglio describes the attitude required for dialogue:

> Dialogue is born from a respectful attitude toward the other person, from a conviction that the other person has something good to say. It supposes that we can make room in our heart for their point of view, their opinion and their proposals. Dialogue entails a warm reception and not a preemptive condemnation. To dialogue, one must know how to lower the defenses, to open the doors of one's home and to offer warmth. (2013, xiv)

Bergoglio acknowledges that maintaining such a respectful, open attitude can be difficult or impossible in some situations, noting that for many of his fellow Argentineans, "I think that we succumb to attitudes that do not permit us to dialogue: domination, not knowing how to listen, annoyance in our speech, preconceived judgments and so many others" (2013, xiv). He mentions various barriers to dialogue: "misinformation, gossip, prejudices, defamation, and slander" (xiv).

Most traditional Christian interpretations of the Bible in relation to other religious traditions and their followers have not proceeded from the respectful, warm, welcoming attitude commended by Cardinal Bergoglio. Instead, to a large degree, the attitudes that Bergoglio identifies as preventing dialogue have dominated the history of Christian attitudes toward other religious traditions. All too often, Christians regarded followers of other religious paths with hostility, and they interpreted the Bible in ways that presumed "a preemptive condemnation" of them.

Regarding situations of conflict, Jesus advises his hearers: "Why do you see the speck in your neighbor's eye, but do not notice the log in your own eye? Or how can you say to your neighbor, 'Let me take the speck out of your eye', while the log is in your own eye? You hypocrite, first take the log out of your own eye, and then you will see clearly to take the speck out of your neighbor's eye" (Matt. 7:3-4).[1] Without explicitly mentioning Jesus' teaching, Bergoglio describes his own approach to difficulties in relationships in similar terms:

> When I have a problem with someone, it helps me to have the same attitude that the Egyptian monks had at the beginning of Christianity. They accused themselves so they could find a solution; they put themselves in the defendant's seat to see what things were not working well inside of themselves. I do it to observe how things are not working well inside of me. This attitude gives me the freedom to, later, be able to forgive the fault of the other person. The mistake of the other person does not need to be emphasized too much because I have my own mistakes and both of us have failures. (2013, 214)

Bergoglio also stresses that a fundamental attitude of mutual affection and respect for the identity of one's partner should envelope interreligious dialogue:

> With Rabbi Skorka I never had to compromise my Catholic identity, just like he never had to with his Jewish identity, and this was not only out of the respect that we have for each other, but also because of how we understand interreligious dialogue. The challenge consisted in walking the path of respect and affection, walking in the presence of God and striving to be faultless. (2013, xv-xvi)

When Cardinal Bergoglio was elected to the papacy on March 13, 2013, he took the name of Pope Francis in honor of Francis of Assisi, who has often been invoked in recent years as a model of interreligious respect. Shortly afterward, Pope Francis reaffirmed his commitment to interreligious dialogue as a major theme of his pontificate. Jean-Louis Cardinal Tauran, the president of the Pontifical Council for Interreligious Dialogue, comments on the pope's behalf in the message of the Holy See addressed to Buddhists for their feast of Vesakh in 2013: "Pope Francis, at the very beginning of his ministry, has reaffirmed the necessity of dialogue of friendship among followers of different religions" (2013, 2).

Bergoglio's conversations with Rabbi Skorka and his hope for a "dialogue of friendship" express and build on a fundamental conversion that has taken place in the attitudes of Catholics and many other Christians, not only toward Judaism but toward all other religious traditions in recent decades. During the time of the preparations for the Second Vatican Council, Pope John XXIII met on June 13, 1960, with a French Jewish historian, Jules Isaac, who had carefully studied the New Testament's references to Jews and the later history of

---

1. Unless otherwise noted, all biblical translations will be from *The New Oxford Annotated Bible* (New Revised Standard Version).

Catholic teaching regarding Jews and Judaism. Isaac presented to Pope John a request that the upcoming ecumenical council correct the untrue and unjust statements about Jews in traditional Catholic teaching. At the center of Isaac's proposal was a confidence that a more accurate understanding of the Bible could help to heal the rift between Jews and Catholics. After the audience, Pope John entrusted responsibility for developing a statement in this area to Augustin Cardinal Bea, a German Jesuit scripture scholar. Interpretation of the Bible played an integral role in the transformation of interreligious relations. Even though Pope John died in June 1963, prior to any statement on interreligious relations from Vatican II, his spirit shaped the deliberations of the council in this area.

Also in the background of Bergoglio's attitude toward interreligious dialogue lies the stirring call to self-examination, renewal, and dialogue of Pope Paul VI in his first encyclical, *Ecclesiam Suam*, promulgated on August 6, 1964. Pope Paul proposes three fundamental policies of his pontificate, first summoning the church to a greater depth of self-knowledge, and, second, in light of this self-examination, acknowledging the faults and failings of the church and the necessity of reform and renewal. Finally, Pope Paul envisages that the outcome of this movement of self-knowledge and renewal will be dialogue with all people of good will, seeking more harmonious relations amid the ominous threats to international peace.

Pope Paul notes that self-examination requires *metanoia,* a conversion of heart and mind, of attitudes and actions: "Herein lies the secret of the Church's renewal, its *metanoia,* to use the Greek term, its practice of perfection" (*Ecclesiam Suam* §51). At the core of this *metanoia,* Paul explains, are the values of poverty and charity: "The zeal for the spirit of poverty is vitally necessary if we are to realize the many failures and mistakes we have made in the past, and learn the principle on which we must now base our way of life and how best to proclaim the religion of Christ" (§54). Complementing the spirit of poverty is the virtue of charity: "Charity is the key to everything. It sets all to rights. There is nothing which charity cannot achieve and renew. Charity 'beareth all things, believeth all things, hopeth all things, endureth all things (1 Cor. 13:7)'" (§56).

For Pope Paul, charity is the motivating force in dialogue: "To this internal drive of charity which seeks expression in the external gift of charity, We will apply the word 'dialogue'" (§64). He describes the attitude necessary for dialogue:

> Confidence is also necessary; confidence not only in the power of one's own words, but also in the good will of both parties to the dialogue. Hence dialogue promotes intimacy and friendship on both sides. It unites them in a mutual adherence to the Good, and thus excludes all self-seeking. . . . In a dialogue conducted with this kind of foresight, truth is wedded to charity and understanding to love. (§§81, 82)

Paul acknowledges that dialogue "will be a slow process of thought, but it will result in the discovery of elements of truth in the opinion of others and make us want to express our teaching with great fairness" (§83). Prior to the

Second Vatican Council issuing any statement regarding other religions, Pope Paul directed the church's attention to respectful relations with other religious traditions:

> We would mention first the Jewish people, who still retain the religion of the Old Testament, and who are indeed worthy of our respect and love. Then we have those worshipers who adhere to other monotheistic systems of religion, especially the Moslem religion. We do well to admire these people for all that is good and true in their worship of God. And finally we have the followers of the great Afro-Asiatic religions. (§107)

Quietly reversing centuries of papal teaching, Pope Paul expresses his hopes for interreligious dialogue, recognizing the goodness in other religions and the importance of working together:

> But we do not wish to turn a blind eye to the spiritual and moral values of the various non-Christian religions, for we desire to join with them in promoting and defending common ideals in the spheres of religious liberty, human brotherhood, education, culture, social welfare, and civic order. Dialogue is possible in all these great projects, which are our concern as much as theirs, and we will not fail to offer opportunities for discussion in the event of such an offer being favorably received in genuine, mutual respect. (§108)

In this same time period, after many difficult discussions and debates, the council presented principles and attitudes for interreligious relations in *Lumen Gentium, Nostra Aetate, Dignitatis Humanae,* and *Gaudium et Spes.* These principles for dialogue shape the current horizon of Catholic interpretation of the Bible in relation to other religious traditions. One of the greatest challenges to establishing respectful interreligious relations today is the long history of animosity and violence, to which Christians, including Catholics, have contributed greatly. Many of the greatest difficulties in interreligious relations today arise from the resentments and grievances born of a history of hostility and often fueled by an adversarial interpretation of the Bible against other religious paths.

Biblical Interpretation and Interreligious Relations

Interpreting the Bible in relation to other religions is among the most far-reaching and challenging tasks facing the Christian community today. The history of Christian interpretations of the Bible includes many diverse strands and concerns, including countless conflicts over methodology and hermeneutics and many conflicting conclusions concerning proper belief and practice. Both as individuals and as communities, we understand ourselves in relation to those with whom we differ. How we interpret and negotiate differences in relationships is among the most important factors shaping our identity. Further, relations with other religious traditions powerfully shape the horizon of Christian interpretation of the Bible. Running through all discussions of the Bible are at least implicit attitudes and assumptions regarding other religious traditions. Whether or not these attitudes and assumptions are the object of explicit reflection, they are among the most powerful factors shaping the way Christians understand the biblical texts and relate to other religious bodies.

Boundaries in interreligious relations, as in other areas of life, are important but relative. Scriptures do not remain comfortably within the boundaries of their respective traditions. Once released to the attention of the world's religious communities, they follow trajectories beyond their original context, intersecting with the sacred texts of other traditions, challenging and being challenged by other traditions, and often as a result appearing in new guises. These relations can move in various ways. The sacred texts and teachings from one tradition may clash with those of other traditions, but they may also resonate deeply. Sometimes the perspectives of one tradition find a welcome in another, where they may be embraced and incorporated into the other tradition in ways that appear surprising and revealing to followers of the original tradition.

Every interpretation of scripture in relation to another religion is located in a specific context that opens up a particular angle of vision. Interpreters and the communities to which they belong have specific histories that shape their perspectives and contributions; and so there is always a local, contextual dimension in interpreting the Bible in interreligious perspective. Allow me to use myself as an example: I am a native of Chicago, Illinois, born in the middle of the twentieth century; and I am a Roman Catholic priest of the Archdiocese of Chicago. I was a young student during the years of the Second Vatican Council. Just a few years after the council ended in 1965, I was given a high school religion class assignment to interview a leader from another religious tradition. I made an appointment and met the rabbi of a synagogue near my home in Chicago. This was my first interreligious conversation. I have been involved in various dialogues with Jews, Muslims, Hindus, and Buddhists for many years. I teach Christian theology in dialogue with other religious traditions at Georgetown University, which as a Catholic, Jesuit university places great importance on interreligious understanding as a university-wide priority.

In the early twenty-first century, Christians encounter both inviting opportunities and daunting challenges in relating the Bible to other religious traditions. On the one hand, there are extraordinary openings for exchange. In many settings today, including many communities in the United States, Christians enjoy cordial relations with followers of other religious paths; and there are numerous opportunities for interreligious studies and conversations. Christians have ready access to more information about the Bible, its complex relation to its ancient interreligious context, the history of its interpretation, and also more knowledge readily available about other religious traditions and their scriptures than ever before.

In the United States and elsewhere, many Christians read the Bible in dialogue and cooperation with followers of other religious paths. In 2000, leaders from multiple Jewish traditions issued a public statement, *Dabru Emet* ("Speak the Truth"), acknowledging the positive changes in Christian views of Jews and Judaism in recent decades and inviting a deeper conversation. Tikva Frymer-Kensky and other scholars involved in *Dabru Emet* developed this proposal by reflecting on themes of Christian theology and inviting Christians to respond to their thoughts in *Christianity in Jewish Terms* (2000). More recently, Jewish scholars led by Amy-Jill Levine and Marc Zvi Brettler have commented on each book of the New Testament in relation to the Jewish tradition in *The Jewish Annotated New Testament* (2011). Muslims and Christians have explored the Bible and the Qur'an together in various forums, including the Building Bridges to Solidarity Seminar convened by the Archbishop of Canterbury in Doha, Qatar in 2003 (Ipgrave 2005). The annual meeting of the Society of Biblical Literature now includes discussions of the Qur'an and biblical literature. In 2007, 138 Islamic leaders from a wide range of traditions issued *A Common Word between Us and You*, an unprecedented appeal inviting Christians to dialogue based on the common teaching of love of God and neighbor found in the scriptures of all three Abrahamic religions. The Scriptural Reasoning project brings together Jews, Christians, and Muslims to study their respective scriptures in relation to each other (Ford and Pecknold 2006).

Increasingly, religious practitioners comment on the scriptures of traditions other than their own. The Fourteenth Dalai Lama and Ravi Ravindra have reflected publicly on Jesus and the Gospels in light of their respective Buddhist and Hindu traditions. Abhishiktananda (originally Henri Le Saux), Bede Griffiths, J. K. Kadowaki, Robert Kennedy, and John Keenan interpret the Bible in relation to the wisdom of the Hindu and Buddhist traditions. Catherine Cornille edits a series of books, *Christian Commentaries on Non-Christian Sacred Texts,* in which Christian authors reflect on the sacred texts of other traditions in light of the Bible and the Christian tradition.

While much has changed for the better in interreligious relations, there remain many serious challenges and obstacles to interreligious understanding in the United States and elsewhere, and interpreting the Bible in relation to other religions is often problematic. Despite the vigorous efforts to improve Jewish–Christian relations, in some contexts anti-Jewish attitudes continue to pose a challenge. Many harsh, negative stereotypes about Muslims circulate in the public media and among many Christians; many Christians interpret the Bible in an adversarial relation to Muslims and Islam. Some Christians continue to condemn Buddhists and Hindus as idolaters, applying to them the biblical polemic against idols.

In all too many places across the world today, cordial interreligious conversations seem completely impossible because religious freedom is violated, trust is lacking, and the obstacles to respectful interreligious exchange appear overwhelming. In many situations the problem is not a lack of familiarity, but rather deep-seated, hostile perceptions of other religious communities shaped by mistrust, anger, and resentment over perceived injuries past or present. In contexts where people inherit a past filled with hostility and where interreligious relationships continue to be highly conflicted, the Bible can tragically serve as an arsenal offering weapons of war with which to attack opponents. Viewed through a lens of hostility, the Bible can be interpreted as harshly condemning other religious perspectives, leaving no room whatsoever for dialogue. Most of the history of Christian interpretation of the Bible in relation to other religions has been dominated by a hermeneutics of hostility, which sees every other religious tradition as an enemy and which looks to the Bible as a resource for condemning other religions and their followers.

In light of the history of religiously motivated conflicts, Christopher Hitchens and others have charged that religions in general and the Bible in particular are responsible for causing conflict and violence. Followers of one tradition frequently blame another religion for wrongs they or their forebears have suffered. The list of conflicts seems endless. Precisely because religions call forth strong commitments, they can be extremely destructive when religious fervor is channeled toward animosity. In adversarial interreligious relationships, what Gerd Lüdemann calls "the dark side of the Bible" can contribute powerfully to the animosity and intensity of the conflict. John J. Collins comments wryly that "the devil does not have to work very hard to find biblical precedents for the legitimation of violence" (2004, 1-2).

In assessing these charges, it is important to examine the role that religion actually plays in particular conflicts in their respective contexts, and this varies considerably from one region to another. The 2006 United Nations statement *The Alliance of Civilizations: Report of the High-Level Group*, co-sponsored by the prime ministers of Turkey and Spain, warns against assuming that contemporary conflicts are essentially religious: "The exploitation of religion by ideologies intent on swaying people to their causes has led to the misguided perception that religion itself is a root cause of intercultural conflict" (3.8). The authors comment further: "Extremism, on the other hand, advocates radical measures in pursuit of political goals. It is not, by nature, religious, and can also be found in secular movements" (3.10). As Scott Appleby has shown, religions are ambiguous; often the heart of a conflict involves political power, economic position, and social privilege; but religions can serve as powerful identity markers between the competing communities. This dilemma poses the challenge of what is meant by religion and what role it plays in human life.

Christians past and present have approached the Bible's relationship to other religions from different perspectives and with different attitudes. Biblical interpretations shaped by hostility have repeatedly buttressed interreligious animosity and in some settings even physical violence. Indeed, much of traditional biblical hermeneutics takes an adversarial relationship with other religions for granted. However, biblical interpretations shaped by a respectful, generous attitude with the intention to improve interreligious relations can shed new light on old problems. Even situations of deep-seated conflict can be approached in a new manner. Mahatma Gandhi interpreted the teachings of Jesus in relation to the practice of *ahimsa* (nonviolence) in the Jain and Hindu traditions, and he demonstrated in practice on an unprecedented level that the nonviolent teaching of Jesus could be effective in transforming social and political conflicts (Gandhi 1991, 3-74). Gandhi had many limitations, which became evident especially in his debate over the caste system with Dalit leader B. R. Ambedkar; nonetheless, it was through Gandhi that many Christians came to understand Jesus and the practical ramifications of his teachings on nonviolence in new ways. It is one of the greatest ironies in the history of biblical interpretation that it took a Hindu to teach Christians how effective the teachings of Jesus on nonviolence could be. Recently the Iranian-Canadian philosopher Ramin Jahanbegloo has described what he calls the "Gandhian Moment" extending across religious boundaries. Despite the limitations of the Mahatma himself, Gandhi's example demonstrates how far-reaching the influence of interreligious cross-fertilization on scriptural interpretation can be.

Conflicts of religious belief and practice need not be barriers to dialogue if they are addressed in a respectful manner. John Paul Lederach urges recognition that "conflict is normal in human relationships, and conflict is a motor of change" (2003, 5). He recommends the goal not of conflict resolution but rather of conflict transformation: "*Transformation* provides a clear and important vision because it brings into focus the horizon toward which we journey—the building of healthy relationships and communities, locally and globally. This goal requires real change in our current ways of thinking" (5). Lederach's definition of conflict transformation offers a way to consider the possibilities inherent in interreligious differences: "Conflict transformation is to *envision and respond* to the *ebb and flow* of social conflict as *life-giving opportunities* for creating *constructive change processes* that *reduce violence, increase justice* in *direct interaction and social structures,* and respond to real-life problems in *human relationships*" (14; emphasis in original). This approach looks at the long-term movements and patterns in relationships, and places specific moments of conflict in a broad perspective that is always developing and changing for better or for worse: "A transformational approach seeks to understand the particular episode of conflict not in isolation, but as embedded in the greater pattern" (16). Both for better and for worse, one of the most important elements in the long-term patterns of Christian interreligious conflicts has been the interpretation of the Bible.

Religious boundaries are always under negotiation, often in dispute, and frequently shifting. In interreligious relations, "inside" and "outside" are relative terms: a belief or practice that was outside at one period may move deeply within the tradition, and what was accepted within a tradition at one stage may come to be rejected later on. The early church vigorously rejected the gods of Rome and Greece as demons. Nonetheless, one of the most important terms for papal identity comes from ancient Roman religion. The title commonly used by popes on buildings and monuments across Rome is "Pontifex Maximus" ("Greatest Bridge-Builder"), a religious title in the early Roman Republic that was appropriated by Julius Caesar, Caesar Augustus, and succeeding Roman emperors, but as far as we know, was never claimed by the apostle Peter. The ancient title takes on ever new roles in new horizons. When Pope Benedict XVI entered the world of electronic social networking in December 2012, he appeared on Twitter as "@pontifex."

Because what is outside can enter deeply within a religion, interreligious relations can profoundly affect the internal dynamics of a tradition. Raimon Panikkar comments that an interreligious conversation can lead to an intrareligious dialogue, "an inner dialogue within myself, an encounter in the depth of my personal religiousness, having met another religious experience on that very intimate level. In other words, if *interreligious* dialogue is to be real dialogue, an *intrareligious* dialogue must accompany it" (1978, 40). Encounters with other religious voices and perspectives can have a profound impact on Christian self-understanding and the interpretation of the Bible.

Religion

In recent decades, many have questioned even how to understand the term "religion." In *Nostra Aetate,* the Second Vatican Council uses the term *religiones* without pausing to define it, and some scholars have argued that it is problematic to identify "religion" as a distinct sphere prior to Western modernity. William T. Cavanaugh agrees with scholars who claim that "the category 'religion' has been invented in the modern West and in colonial contexts according to the specific configurations of political power" (2009, 3). According to Cavanaugh, there is no overarching definition of religion: "what counts as religion and what does not in any given context depends on different configurations of power and authority" (9).

Ludwig Wittgenstein famously questioned the universal need for univocal definitions. He observed that while one could expect an informed person to state the elevation of Mount Blanc, someone who knows the sound of a clarinet may well find it difficult to put that knowledge into words (1968, 36). Following the lead of Wittgenstein, James C. Livingston, like many other scholars, renounces the quest for any univocal definition of an alleged essence in favor of a set of "family resemblances" based on relationship to the sacred (Wittgenstein 1965, 17; 1968, 31-32; Livingston 2009, 7).

According to *Cassell's Latin Dictionary,* the Latin word *religio* can refer to a quality of persons, viz., "scrupulousness, conscientious exactness"; it can also mean "respect for what is sacred" or "superstition"; it can also refer to an object of worship, "a holy thing or place" (511). The history of the Latin word *religio* in European discourse since late antiquity has been profoundly shaped by Christian history. In an imperial decree issued around the time of the First Council of Constantinople in 381, Emperor Theodosius I used the word *religio* for the first time to refer "to normative belief, specifically belief that has descended from the apostles themselves and is now executed by a Roman emperor" (Unterseher 2009, 18). Theodosius understood *vera religio* ("true religion") to be the form of Christianity taught by the Councils of Nicaea and Constantinople; however, traditional Roman religions were not as yet prohibited. Wilfred Cantwell Smith points out that during the same period Jerome used the term *religio* in the sense of ritual, and Augustine wrote on *De Vera Religione,* which Cantwell Smith translates as *On Proper Piety* or *On Genuine Worship* (1991, 28-29).

Beginning in the sixteenth century, European thinkers began to puzzle over the meaning of religion in light of the bitter confessional conflicts between Catholics and Protestants. Ivan Strenski has traced the modern quest for a definition of religion, emphasizing the close connection between Christian interpretation of the Bible through historical criticism and the modern study of other religious traditions. Friedrich Schleiermacher famously defined religion as "neither thinking nor acting, but intuition and feeling" (2000, 22). He added, "Praxis is an art, speculation is a science, religion is the sensibility and taste for the infinite" (23). Schleiermacher sought a common element in a wide variety of different forms. Later in his career he defined piety as "the consciousness of being absolutely dependent, or, which is the same thing, of being in relation with God" ([1928] 1976, 12). Paul Tillich defined faith as "the state of being ultimately concerned" (1958, 1).

In his wide-ranging, magisterial survey, *Religion in Human Evolution*, Robert Bellah proposes a simplified definition based on Emile Durkheim: "Religion is a system of beliefs and practices relative to the sacred that unite those who adhere to them in a moral community" (Bellah 2011, 1). Bellah follows Durkheim a step further in seeing the sacred as "something set apart or forbidden. Durkheim's definition might be widened to define the sacred as a realm of nonordinary reality" (1).

Despite vast diversity, a number of recent scholars insist that there is a common thread running through religions past and present. Psychologist Antoine Vergote notes the difficulties in finding a definition of religion but nonetheless maintains, "I trust the wisdom of cultural language which employs the word 'religion' without difficulty. I also believe that comparison between religious worlds is possible, regardless of the fact that similar words—God, spirit, sacrifice, etc.—do not everywhere carry the same meaning" (1996, 14). For Vergote, "religion is the entirety of the linguistic expressions, emotions, actions and signs that refer to a supernatural being or supernatural beings. 'Supernatural' is here taken to mean that which belongs neither to the powers of nature nor to human agency, but transcends these domains" (16).

Similarly, sociologist Rodney Stark argues that religion consists of "explanations of the meaning of existence based on supernatural assumptions and including statements about the nature of the supernatural" (2001, 15). Another sociologist, Martin Riesebrodt, surveys the debate over the use of the term "religion" and argues that premodern cultures did have a coherent understanding that bears a clear resemblance to what contemporary scholars mean by religion. "Human beings can understand each other despite cultural differences. We are not simply foreign to each other; we have the ability to overcome foreignness through communication" (2010, 19). Riesebrodt proposes an action–theory approach to address the difficulties in traditional conceptions: "According to this definition, religion is a complex of practices that are based on the premise of the existence of superhuman powers, whether personal or impersonal, that are generally invisible" (74-75). While acknowledging that the functions of religions vary tremendously across traditions, Riesebrodt nonetheless insists: "Religion's promise, by contrast, remains astonishingly constant in different historical periods and cultures. Religions promise to ward off misfortune, to help cope with crises, and to provide salvation" (xiii). This theory does not claim that there is any single, universal essence of religion: "It does not seek to prove that all religions are 'ultimately' the same, but rather to make it possible to compare them in relation to a structure of meaning that underlies them" (xiii). The approach of Riesebrodt offers a helpful response to the role of religion in differing contexts.

Biblical Precedents and Principles

Both the problems of and the opportunities for relating the Bible to other religions begin in the scriptures themselves. Diversity is rooted in the content and structure of the Christian Bible, which offers many competing precedents for interreligious relations. The word "Bible" comes from *ta biblia* in Greek, which is plural: "the books." The Bible presents a multitude of different voices that range over many centuries. In ever-changing contexts, later scriptural authors take up the challenge of earlier biblical texts, sometimes agreeing with previous biblical writers and continuing an ongoing trajectory but on other occasions rejecting earlier perspectives and setting a new course. There is both continuity and change. Thus, we should not be surprised to find more than one biblical model for encountering other religious traditions. Other religious traditions also bring their own wide variety of approaches to religious diversity.

Because interreligious relations shape the biblical heritage in diverse ways, Christians find in the Bible a variety of precedents, problems, and principles for engaging religious difference, some hostile and some respectful. Across the ancient Mediterranean world and Mesopotamia, all religious traditions were influenced by the constant movements of peoples, merchants, and armies. Ancient Israelite religion, biblical Judaism, and early Christianity had complex and ambivalent relationships to their environments, resisting some aspects of the neighboring religious environment but also borrowing heavily from their respective neighbors. As a result, the Bible offers multiple and conflicting precedents for engaging other religious traditions, ranging from appreciative borrowing to forthright demands for destruction and mass killing. The ambiguity is deep-seated and long-lasting: while biblical traditions struggled fiercely against competing religious traditions, they also appropriated many elements from other traditions. There are analogues in ancient religions for almost every aspect of ancient Israelite religion; there are also stern condemnations of other religions and their practices.

The Canons and the Names of the Testaments of the Bible
The challenge of interpreting the Bible in relation to other religions is complicated by the fact that there is no consensus on what constitutes the canon of the Christian Bible or on how to name the two testaments. In early Christianity the process of deciding what books should constitute the biblical canon was long and extremely complex, with multiple practices in different locations

(McDonald 2007, 190-429). The first debates over the Christian canon involved conflicts over Jewish and Christian identities and relations. One of the major figures stimulating discussion of a Christian canon was Marcion of Pontus in the middle of the second century. By rejecting the Jewish scriptures from the canon of the Christian Bible and by accepting only his own edited versions of the Pauline letters and the Gospel of Luke into his canon, Marcion sharply distinguished Christianity from Judaism and provoked other Christians to ponder what books should be included in the Bible.

Debates over the Christian canon continued through the centuries, and there is no agreement among the Christian communities today on what constitutes the Bible. Protestant Christians accept only the books in the Hebrew Bible as the First Testament of the Bible. Catholics, following the Council of Trent in the sixteenth century, accept not only these texts but also a number of other ancient Jewish books from the Septuagint as also constituting the First Testament. Protestants often view these books from the Septuagint that are not in the Hebrew Bible as "Apocryphal" or "Deuterocanonical." The Byzantine Orthodox Churches, the Oriental Orthodox Churches, and the Assyrian Church of the East accept a varying range of books in the First Testament of their respective Bibles, generally including more books than the canon of the Catholic Church. There was long debate over whether the book of Revelation should be accepted into the canon of the Bible; and to this day, the Byzantine Orthodox Churches do not read this book during the liturgy (Wienrich 2005, xx). I accept the Catholic canon of the Bible, while being aware of the differences among the various Christian canons.

In recent decades, many Christians have become aware that the term "Old Testament" has been traditionally understood to imply that the covenant of God with Israel has been broken off and superseded by the "New Testament." Most traditional Christian theology was supersessionist, maintaining that God had rejected the Jewish people because they had violated the covenant by rejecting Jesus; the Christian Church saw itself as the "true Israel," the authentic heir to the biblical promises that God made to Israel. To avoid the danger of supersessionism in present discussions, many Christians are exploring different terminology for the two testaments. Some speak of the First Testament of the Christian Bible. Some Christians use the term "Hebrew Bible" for the First Testament; however, the Hebrew Bible is not the same as the First Testaments of the Catholic or the Eastern Christian communities, which include other works as well. Other terms that have been proposed for the First Testament are the "Prior Testament," "Former Covenant," and "Prime Testament" (Cunningham 2003, 11, 16). There is no widely accepted substitute term for the "New Testament," but some have experimented with the terms "Common Testament," "Shared Testament," "Apostolic Writings," "Christian Testament," and "Second Testament." Philip Cunningham notes that this question cannot be resolved simply by historical or exegetical research, since it is intimately related to the development of a positive, post-supersessionist theology of Judaism (12). In this matter no term has escaped criticism, and no new usage has become universally accepted in the Christian communities at the present time.

Belief in One God

The emergence of a monotheistic faith and worldview in the biblical traditions is one of the most important developments for interpreting and engaging religious diversity. Monotheistic faith provides an all-encompassing framework for interpreting all of creation and human history, including other religions, in relation to the one God. Rodney Stark suggests that, in terms of social effects, "perhaps no other single innovation had so much impact on history" as monotheism (2001, 1).

However, the biblical heritage in this area is complex and multisided, and not all biblical texts are strictly monotheistic. The Decalogue (Exod. 20:2-6) can be read as demanding henotheism, devotion to one God, without denying the existence of other gods. Mark S. Smith (2002) has argued that early Israelites shared the polytheistic Canaanite religious culture of their neighbors and came to belief in one God only after a long process of identity formation through differentiation from the surrounding traditions.

Egyptologist Jan Assmann has argued that in the fourteenth century B.C.E., the Egyptian Pharaoh Akhenaten made a distinction that was the decisive precedent for what he calls "the Mosaic distinction": "the idea of an exclusive and emphatic Truth that sets God apart from everything that is not God and therefore must not be worshipped, and that sets religion apart from what comes to be shunned as superstition, paganism, or heresy" (2008, 3). With Akhenaten, "counter-religion" appears for the first time in history with its hallmarks of radically rejecting earlier tradition and violent intolerance. Assmann stresses the oppositional character of monotheistic faith defining itself over against its opposite: "Monotheism always appears as a counter-religion. There is no natural or evolutionary way leading from the error of idolatry to the truth of monotheism. This truth can come only from outside, by way of revelation" (1997, 7). Thus, for the first time, conversion becomes central to religion: "Conversion presupposes and constructs an opposition between 'old' and 'new' in religion" (1997, 7). "Conversion defines itself as the result of an overcoming and a liberation from one's own past which is no longer one's own" (1997, 7). The Mosaic distinction does not deny the existence of other gods but rather presupposes them. This sets the context for Assmann's understanding of biblical faith in God: "The biblical concept of God is not about absolute but relational oneness" (2008, 4).

Assmann notes two ways in which the Mosaic distinction has functioned. First, it defines the difference between Israel's "true religion" and Egypt's "idolatry." Israelites are called to remember where they came from so that they do not go back there. Assmann sees biblical monotheism as preserving the memory of Egypt as a counter-image to be rejected; he points out that in later Jewish services, the narrative of the idolatry of the golden calf was read on the Day of Atonement as the primordial temptation to be rejected (1997, 212). This led to mutual polemics in later times, when Jews attacked Egyptian idolaters as mad and the Egyptian priest Manetho wrote a history in the third century B.C.E., presenting Moses as a rebellious Egyptian priest who led a colony of lepers (4).

Second, Assmann describes the function of "deconstructive memory."

Here discoveries of Egyptian truth put in question the Mosaic distinction. Assmann finds this especially in the European Enlightenment, when deists and pantheists combated the Mosaic distinction in various forms of "cosmotheism," in which Nature itself is exalted as the highest ideal. Spinoza puts in question the distinction between God and nature (*deus sive natura*), which leads to a new appraisal of Egypt: "The Egyptians were spinozists and 'cosmotheists.' Ancient cosmotheism as a basis for intercultural translation was rediscovered" (1997, 8). This approach allows for intercultural translation: since all the gods are expressions of Nature, they can all be honored as roughly equivalent (45). Thus Assmann identifies two very different approaches to memory and monotheism: "The first form of memory functions as a means of cultural identity formation and reproduction, whereas the second form functions as a technique of intercultural translation" (8).

P. Kyle McCarter (1997) dates the development of monotheism to period of the Babylonian exile in the sixth century B.C.E., after the First Temple had been destroyed during the Babylonian conquest of Jerusalem. In this traumatic context of loss, Jews came to believe that the God of Israel was the only God, the creator of the entire universe. Robert Gnuse speculates that it was precisely the pain of exile that prompted Jews to develop belief in a transcendent God: "Had the Jews remained in Palestine, they probably never would have attained pure monotheism, for they never would have experienced a crisis sufficiently great to generate such an intellectual leap" (1997, 214). The creation account in Genesis 1:1-2:4a, which many scholars believe was composed in this setting, provides a cosmic setting for all the narratives, commandments, prophecies, proverbs, and poems that follow.

Belief in one God who creates the entire universe can play various roles in interreligious relations. Monotheistic faith can give rise to attacks on other beliefs as idolatrous and can fuel religious conflicts. Since there is to be devotion to only one God, all other gods can be seen as idols, and their followers can be seen as dangerous threats. The prophet Elijah's victorious competition with the priests of Baal on Mount Carmel ended in his slaughtering them all, thereby demonstrating the superior power of the God of Israel against alien gods (1 Kgs. 18:20-40). Assmann maintains that in the Hebrew Bible, the violent language against other gods is directed internally against the threat of reversion to polytheism: "At the root of the pronounced anti-Canaanism of Deuteronomy and its language of violence lies the pathos of conversion; the passion of a life-changing commitment, the fear of relapse, and the resolve to exterminate the pagan within" (2008, 124). In the later history of Christianity, monotheistic faith has often given rise to hostile views of other religions as idolatrous, including Hinduism and Buddhism.

Jonathan Kirsch provocatively charges that monotheism is a perennial source of interreligious violence against "paganism" because monotheists can never accept their polytheistic neighbors: "Precisely because the monotheist regards the polytheist with such fear and loathing, peaceful coexistence between the two theologies is possible only from the pagan's point of view and never for the true believer in the Only True God" (2005, 12). In a more careful and nuanced exploration, Stark documents the profound ambiguity of belief in one God: monotheism can call forth rational exploration of the universe and it can also give rise to religious wars. Stark emphasizes "the ability of monotheism to unite and mobilize humans on behalf of great undertakings, and to also plunge them into bitter and often bloody conflict. These are, of course, aspects of the same phenomenon as seen from within a group or from outside" (2001, 33).

Monotheistic faith is ambiguous. What is most significant for interreligious relations is the fundamental attitude of respect or of hostility. Faith in one God can serve as a framework for envisioning a common human community. The opening section of *Nostra Aetate* asserts that "all peoples are one community" (*una enim communitas sunt omnes gentes*) because all have a common origin and a common vocation to salvation, and because God's providence extends to all (§1). In opposition to those who posit irreconcilable conflicts between civilizations because of religious differences, the council asserts that belief in the one God, who is the beginning and end of all things and who cares for all, is a basis from which Catholics can approach every other religious tradition. This approach, as developed by Vatican II, can acknowledge and respect religious and cultural differences but interprets them ultimately in the context of a single cosmos created and cared for by the one God. In *Nostra Aetate*, belief in one God provides a basis for recognizing the activity of God in all creation and the presence of God in all religions. This perspective can offer an invitation to dialogue with even the most diverse interlocutors. Since there is only one God, everyone has already experienced God and nonbiblical authors can in some way reflect awareness of the one true God.

Among the world's religious communities, belief in one God can be seen as a point of contact between Christians and some other religious traditions and a point of contrast with others. However, the meaning of monotheism is not universally identical. Jews, Christians, Muslims, Sikhs, Zoroastrians, Baha'is, as well as many Hindus, identify themselves as monotheists; but frequently they understand this belief in different ways. Some proclaim that belief in one God unites the Abrahamic religions; but even here there are significant differences in the way Jews, Christians, and Muslims understand the meaning of "oneness" in God, especially because of Christian faith in the Trinity.

Jewish scholar Jon Levenson states frankly his doubts that Christians are monotheistic. After quoting the Nicene Creed, he comments: "Now to call this theology, affirmed by hundreds of millions of Christians—Roman Catholic, Eastern Orthodox, and Protestant—simply 'monotheistic,' as Judaism and Islam are monotheistic, is, if not wrong, at least seriously misleading" (2012, 177). Levenson notes that Moses Maimonides viewed Christianity as a form of idolatry (179). However, the Jewish tradition is itself not monolithic, and Jewish monotheism can also take various forms, some of which have allowed for some form of plurality in divinity.[2]

2. Neil Gillman reflects on how in Judaism God both is and is not *echad* ("one") (2000, 17–32). In rather different ways Daniel Boyarin (2004) and Moshe Idel (2007) have explored how historically many Jews have believed in some form of plurality in divinity, while con-

Another Jewish scholar, Alon Goshen-Gottstein, takes a different approach, which opens up a fruitful avenue for Christian reflection on other religions. He notes that the Jewish statement regarding Christians, *Dabru Emet*, asserts, "Jews and Christians worship the same God" (2012, 51). Acknowledging that this assertion is not immediately self-evident to Jews, Goshen-Gottstein explores the assumptions and decisions behind it. His method is not to look to the classic historical foundations of the two religions for adjudication of this question. Instead, he boldly proposes, "The path that I would personally give greatest weight to is the path that recognizes God not through doctrine, but through the signs of God's presence in the lives of the faithful" (74). He explains, "Recognizing the divine presence in the lives of believers is a powerful strategy for recognizing the same God, and thereby opening up possibilities for spiritual and theological inspiration between Christians and Jews" (75). He closes his discussion with hope: "God's presence is the common quest of Christians and Jews. In looking towards the future, seeking God's presence, Judaism may not only cure its own deficiencies, but also find a healing for the painful history of its relationship with Christianity" (75). Goshen-Gottstein's example offers a strategy for handling religious difference: one can recognize irresolvable conflicts on the doctrinal level while looking hopefully for signs of God's presence in other traditions.

From the Muslim tradition, Reza Shah-Kazemi reflects on the question of whether Muslims and Christians worship the same God. While one option is for Muslims to dismiss Christians as polytheists because of their faith in the Trinity, Shah-Kazemi proposes another approach: "For his part, the Muslim theologian can likewise affirm with Christians a common belief in the transcendent unity of God without this affirmation in any way implying acceptance of the Trinity" (2012, 146).

Even though Christians have sometimes condemned Hinduism as polytheistic, many Hindus are monotheists, believing in one God behind all the manifold Indian deities; and many Hindus accept Jesus as in some way a manifestation of God, though the meaning of this belief is often very different from Christian perspectives. One of the most important differences between Buddhists and the monotheistic traditions is that Buddhists do not believe in a transcendent God who creates the universe. Here again, the meaning of the word "God" requires careful attention, and this topic can be the focus for fruitful discussion. At the first Gethsemani Encounter in 1996, His Holiness, the Fourteenth Dalai Lama, remarked to the assembly: "I can accept God as infinite love, but not God as Creator." This fundamental difference does not mean that Buddhist–Christian dialogue is impossible, but it does pose a significant challenge to be explored. In each relationship, the meaning of oneness and the meaning of God are challenges to be examined.

---

tinuing to affirm belief in one God. Arthur Green (2006) explores the meaning of plurality in divinity in the Jewish mystical tradition of Kabbalah.

Creation

Closely related to the development of monotheism is the belief that God created the universe. The opening chapters of Genesis provide Jews and Christians with a narrative context for interpreting the cosmos and all of human history. The first creation account in Genesis describes the earth as a "formless void" at the beginning with darkness covering the face of the deep (1:2). This suggests a divine shaping of existing, amorphous material. The second creation account in Genesis also suggests that God shapes a yet unformed world (Gen. 2:4b-9). Catherine Keller reflects on these texts in light of a process theology inspired by Alfred North Whitehead, in which God does not create the universe out of nothing but rather lures creation by providing the initial aims for each entity. Noting that creation *ex nihilo* is not found in the text of Genesis, she comments: "The bible narrates instead various versions of a more mysterious process: that of creation from the deep, known as the watery chaos" (2008, 47). Keller finds that this perspective resonates deeply with the philosophy of Whitehead, who sees God as shaping the flow of creativity throughout the universe, but not as creating out of nothing.

In the Hellenistic period, centuries after the creation accounts in Genesis were composed, Jews developed the belief in creation out of nothing (*ex nihilo*), which makes its first appearance in a narrative context of interreligious violence. In the early second century B.C.E., during the violent persecution of Jews under the Seleucid ruler Antiochus IV Epiphanes, the Second Book of Maccabees interpreted God's making the world in the strict sense of creation out of nothing. According to the dramatic narrative, a bold Jewish mother tells her endangered son not to fear his human persecutors: "I beg you, child, to look at the heaven and the earth and see everything that is in them, and recognize that God did not make them out of things that existed. In the same way the human race came into being" (2 Macc. 7:28).

Belief in creation out of nothing has been decisive for most of the Christian tradition. Later Christian theologians developed the implications of "radical monotheism," based on belief in creation out of nothing, maintaining a fundamental distinction between God, who alone is worthy of worship, and all other reality, which is not to be worshiped. H. Richard Niebuhr comments: "Radical monotheism dethrones all absolutes short of the principle of being itself. At the same time it references every relative existent. Its two great mottos are: 'I am the Lord thy God; thou shalt have no other gods before me' and 'Whatever is, is good'" (1970, 37). For traditional Christianity, God is the beginning and end of all things, both transcendent and immanent; to worship anything other than God is idolatry. The belief that God created the world out of nothing has multiple philosophical and theological implications, which would interest Jewish, Christian, and Muslim thinkers of later ages. David Burrell proposes creation out of nothing as a fundamental belief uniting Jews, Christians, and Muslims both in the Middle Ages and today (2011).

It is characteristic of Christian faith to hold that all things are created through the Word (John 1:1-4), that is, through Christ (1 Cor. 8:6; Col. 1:15-

20). This perspective interprets creation in a distinctively Christian light, though Daniel Boyarin has argued that there are close analogues to the binitarian perspectives in some forms of early Judaism: "Prior (and even well into) the rabbinic period, most (or at any rate many) non-Christian Jews did see the Logos (or his female ego, Sophia) as a central part of their doctrines about God" (2004, 38).

According to Genesis 1:26-27, God created humans in the image and likeness of God. This principle offers one of the most important perspectives for engaging religious diversity and fostering interreligious relations. Jonathan Sacks, Chief Rabbi of the Commonwealth, stresses that this belief affirms the dignity of every human being, and he reflects on the implications for interpreting differences. Recognizing the ambiguity of the Bible and the difficulty of scriptural interpretation in relation to other traditions, he takes the affirmation of the image of God in every human being as a normative point of reference for judging every other perspective in the Bible. Sacks eloquently expresses the hermeneutical challenge facing every religious tradition today: "The test of faith is whether I can make space for difference. Can I recognize God's image in someone else who is not in my image, whose language, faith, ideas, are different from mine? If I cannot, then I have made God in my image instead of allowing him to remake me in his" (2002, 201).

The violence of our past challenges every religious tradition to reflect critically on its sacred texts and rituals, discerning what leads to further hatred and division and what leads to healing. Sacks notes that every great religious tradition has "abrasive" aspects that lead to "narrow particularism, suspicion of strangers, and intolerance"; each tradition also has more generous principles that can lead to shaping new communities across old boundaries of animosity. We are responsible for which aspects we use to interpret and critique the others and which we place in the center of our religious practice (2002, 207-8). Sacks emphasizes the simple ethical imperative implied by this view as summing up the goal of Jewish life: "Judaism contains mysteries, but its ultimate purpose is not mysterious at all. It is to honour the image of God in other people, and thus turn the world into a home for the divine presence" (2005, 4).

The second creation account in Genesis 2:4b-25 describes the harmony of life in the Garden of Eden before the disobedience of first humans. With the violation of this harmony in Genesis 3, the tragedy of human life begins. The first humans seek to become like God, discover fear and shame, and begin to scapegoat others to avoid their responsibility (Gen. 3:1-13). The dynamics of this chapter will be reenacted in many forms and in many contexts. As René Girard has explored, the pattern of scapegoating others will tragically shape much of the history of Christian interreligious relations (1992, 1-11); each tradition can blame another for its troubles.

Primordial Narratives: Genesis 4-11
After the account of the creation and fall of the first humans, Genesis recounts the primordial history of humans during the earliest times, offering later generations of Jews and Christians examples and images that can foster either

interreligious conflict or respectful conversation. The Qur'an takes up many of these images and presents many of these figures in its own way.

As the narrative in Genesis continues, human rivalry quickly develops into violent conflict. Cain murders his brother Abel because of jealousy over divine favor (Gen. 4:3-8). God then questions Cain about his brother and places a curse upon Cain, who becomes a fugitive. God places a mark on him to protect him from anyone who tries to kill him; then Cain founds the first city, which he names Enoch, after his son (Gen. 4:9-17). The curse of Cain offers a powerful model that will shape later interreligious relations: Augustine and generations of later Christians will interpret the curse of Cain as applying to all Jews who do not accept Jesus Christ and become Christian; they are to be punished but not killed. More recently, Girard interprets this account as bringing into the open the truth that there is primal violence hidden in the foundations of human culture.

The succeeding chapters of Genesis describe sin increasing in extent and power until God sends the destructive power of the flood, wiping out human sinners. This catastrophe is followed by a covenant between God and all creation. After the terrible devastation of the flood, God establishes a covenant with Noah and his family, who according to the biblical narrative are the ancestors of all future humans. God makes this covenant not with humans alone but with all creation (Gen. 9:1-17). In the so-called Noachide covenant, traditional Judaism finds a framework for affirming God's positive relationship to Gentiles who were not incorporated into the Mosaic covenant. Jon Levenson comments: "If the message is universalism, the Jewish and Christian Bibles have figures on whom to focus—Adam and Noah, the universal fathers of the human race, as the biblical narrative would have it" (2012, 181). The Qur'an also tells of the flood, with the additional account of another son of Noah, Canaan, who was reportedly drowned in the flood (Qur'an 11:43). Brian Brown explores the "other son" of Noah in an effort to bridge the gap between the Bible and the Qur'an (2007).

Like the initial harmony of the Garden of Eden, the harmony of the Noachide covenant does not last very long. The narrative continues immediately with the drunkenness of Noah, who is discovered and seen by his son Ham (Gen. 9:20-23). There follows Noah's curse on Canaan, the son of Ham (Gen. 9:24-25). It is not immediately clear in the narrative why Noah curses Canaan, since Canaan is not the offender but only the son of Ham, who had committed the offense: "Cursed be Canaan; lowest of slaves shall he be to his brothers" (Gen. 9:25). In Genesis the curse comes from Noah, not from God. Nonetheless, later Christians transposed this curse into the so-called curse of Ham, applied to all descendants in all generations without end, and used it as the primary biblical justification in the United States for enslaving Africans as the putative descendants of Ham. Appealing to the curse of Ham in Genesis 9:25-27, Christians enslaved countless Africans, including Muslims and followers of traditional African religions, with Genesis 9:25-27 as a bulwark.

The primeval history culminates in the narrative of the tower of Babel, which dramatically exemplifies the proud ambitions of humans and the subsequent impossibility of communication (Gen. 11:5-8). Genesis sharply condemns the pretensions of the builders of the tower of Babel, furnishing Jews and Christians with a model for condemning prideful idolatry, which could be applied to followers of other religious paths. Again the Qur'an presents a similar narrative (2:100-103). In recent years, George Steiner (1998) and Paul Ricoeur (2006) have seen the tower of Babel as an image of our situation: we need to communicate across boundaries but are condemned to misunderstand those from other communities. In this situation, both Steiner and Ricoeur conclude that we are called to translate across borders.

Abraham

With the call of Abram in Genesis 12, the narrative of Genesis narrows its focus from all humanity to a particular family. Abraham, as he is later named (Gen. 17:5), is an important but disputed figure for Jews, Christians, and Muslims, all of whom claim to be his descendants in faith. Abraham's relationships and actions set a number of precedents, which move in different directions. One of important precedents that Abraham sets for interreligious relations is to offer hospitality to his heavenly visitors; in response, he receives the blessing of a promised son (Gen. 18:1-10). The paradigm of sacred hospitality toward the stranger comes down through the centuries as one of the most powerful models for interreligious encounters.

Not all of Abraham's relationships are peaceful. He lives in a time of violence. When his nephew Lot is captured by the enemy, Abraham leads a military expedition to defeat the foe (Gen. 14:12-16). After Abraham's victory, "King Melchizedek of Salem brought out bread and wine; he was priest of God most High" (Gen. 14:18). Melchizedek blesses Abram (Gen. 14:19-20). Abraham shares one-tenth of his goods with Melchizedek, but Abraham refuses to accept anything from the king of Sodom (Gen. 14:20-24). Melchizedek is a mysterious figure, since there is no account of his origins or his later career. He appears for one moment in the life of Abraham, offers bread, wine, and a blessing, and disappears, only to reappear in the enthronement Psalm 110:4 and in the later Jewish and Christian traditions (Heb. 7:1-17). The narrative of Melchizedek offers the hopeful account that some relations with outsiders can bring blessings to Abraham. For later generations of Jews and Christians, Melchizedek offers a model of a righteous Gentile ruler who knows and worships the one God. In some settings, later Jewish leaders would view even a nontheistic leader on the model of Melchizedek. When Jews in the late twentieth century prepared for a visit to the Dalai Lama in India, they pondered how they should relate to him, debating whether he should be honored as Melchizedek. After much discussion, they agreed that this was the most appropriate approach (Kamenetz 1995, 42, 43, 188). The model of Melchizedek opened a path for respectful conversations with a religious leader whose cosmology differs profoundly from anything in the biblical heritage.

Abraham's hospitality has its limits, however, and not all relations are harmonious. The family relationships involving Abraham, Sarah, Hagar, Ishmael, and Isaac are profoundly troubled, foreshadowing problems in later Abrahamic interreligious relations to the present day (Gen. 11:26-25:18). Abraham and Sarah, frustrated at being childless, press Hagar, their Egyptian slave girl, into sexual service in the hope of producing an heir. But when the Egyptian slave conceives, the animosity between Hagar and her mistress is so intense that Hagar flees into the wilderness, where she is instructed to return to the troubled household. She is told that her son Ishmael "shall be a wild ass of a man, with his hand against everyone, and everyone's hand against him; and he shall live at odds with all his kin" (Gen. 16:12). This image will shape negative Christian perceptions of Muslims as "Ishmaelites" in centuries to come.

Later, Isaac plays with his older half-brother Ishmael, provoking the anxieties of Sarah over having to divide the family inheritance between them (Gen. 21:9-10). God instructs Abraham to follow Sarah's directions and cast Hagar and Ishmael out of the home, but God adds that Ishmael will also be ancestor of a nation (Gen. 21:12-13). Abraham drives Hagar and Ishmael out of the household without adequate provisions, but God provides a well in the wilderness (Gen. 21:14-19). Ishmael will return only after the death of Abraham to join with Isaac in apparent harmony as they bury their common father (Gen 25:9). It is a tragic irony that the site venerated as Abraham's tomb in Hebron, where Ishmael and Isaac reportedly came together in harmony, is today a bitter place of contention between Israelis and Palestinians.

Jews, Christians, and Muslims approach the stories of Abraham in very different ways. Again we find ambiguity, which can be approached from multiple directions. Terence Fretheim notes the complexity of Abraham's relations with outsiders, distinguishing three forms of relationship in the text of Genesis. Some outsiders appear as a gift and both offer and receive a blessing in a relation of mutual harmony. However, other outsiders pose a threat to Abraham's family. In a third type of relation, outsiders present a challenge in that families across the entire world are to be blessed through Abraham. Fretheim finds that this promise poses a question: "How will this family fare in taking up this responsibility?" (2007, xiii). Each of these types of relationship will shape later history.

The troubled relations within Abraham's family influenced the self-understandings of the later traditions in different manners, as Jews, Christians, and Muslims interpret the conflicts involving Abraham, Sarah and Hagar, Ishmael and Isaac in various ways. Since the time of Jesus, Jews and Christians have both claimed to be the heirs of Abraham, often in bitter disputes; and Muslims subsequently asserted their claim as well. In recent years, some have proposed Abraham as a figure uniting Jews, Christians, and Muslims; but he can also be seen as a figure dividing the traditions that claim him. Jon Levenson notes the strikingly different ways in which Jews, Christians, and Muslims have remembered Abraham and insists that there is no way to harmonize the different claims. Bruce Chilton reflects on the troubling violent legacy of child sacrifice in *Abraham's Curse*: "For Genesis, Abraham is a brutal father, whose reckless disregard for the life of his family had to be tamed by God so that he could learn compassion" (2008, 221). Chilton stresses that the lesson learned by each of the Abrahamic traditions is the imperative to renounce the sacrifice of human lives: "The distinctive voices of the Torah, Jesus Christ, and the Prophet Muhammad agree that Moriah is behind us, never to be visited again" (224).

Louis Massignon, an influential Catholic scholar of Islam, looked to Abraham as an example of sacred hospitality and a sign of hope for the future: "The guest is the representative of God. The hospitality of Abraham is a sign announcing the final consummation of the assembly of all nations blessed in Abraham, in this Holy Land which should not be monopolized by any one" (1987, 121).

God Acting in History

One of the most pervasive themes in many of the biblical narratives is that God acts in history on behalf of God's people and demands fidelity in return. While some earlier scholars saw this belief as unique to the Hebrew Bible, Bertil Albrektson demonstrated that this pattern was commonly used throughout the ancient world, though the Hebrew Bible gives a distinctive interpretation to this widely held belief. Much of this tradition of the Bible presents a hermeneutics of hostility regarding other religious traditions with no possibility of compromise. One of the oldest and most enduring biblical approaches to other religious traditions is to view them as enemies and to invoke God's wrath upon them in the traditions of sacred combat studied by Gerhard von Rad (1991), Susan Niditch (1993), and Gerd Lüdemann (1997). The book of Exodus presents God as a divine warrior who was directly involved in military combat on earth (Exod. 15:3). According to Exodus, God intervened on behalf of the Israelites against the Egyptians so that both sides would know God's power: "The Egyptians shall know that I am the Lord, when I stretch out my hand against Egypt and bring the Israelites out from among them" (Exod. 7:5). God reportedly kills countless Egyptians, not only the military warriors of Pharaoh (Exod. 14:28) but young boys who have the misfortune to be firstborn sons (Exod. 12:29-30). As Thomas Dozeman has documented (1996), the exodus became a central symbol for Jews and Christians, inspiring a long tradition of wars deemed sacred. Many Christians coming to regions such as the Americas or to South Africa saw themselves as the new Israelites coming to the promised land, whose inhabitants were deemed to have no inherent rights to it. Biblical hymns repeatedly celebrate the power of God in war (Deut. 33:2-3; Num. 10:35-36; Ps. 24; Isa. 35; Hab. 3:3-60). According to this tradition, when ancient Israelites marched out to fight their earthly opponents, God went to war on their behalf (Judg. 5:19-20; Isa. 24:21).

According to the violent strand of the biblical witness, loyalty to the God of Israel motivates and justifies aggressive interreligious conflicts. The Pentateuch commands that Israelites who sacrifice to alien gods are to be executed and that foreigners who tempt or who could potentially tempt Israelites to do likewise are to be put to death (Num. 25:1-18; Deut. 17:2-7). Israel's ideology of the holy war demands the complete destruction of the enemy, including even nonhuman forms of life (Niditch 1993, 28-55). According to Deuteronomy, God commands the Israelites to slaughter all those already living in the promised land:

> But as for the towns of these peoples that the Lord your God is giving you as an inheritance, you must not let anything that breathes remain alive. You shall annihilate them—the Hittites and the Amorites, the Canaanites and the Perizzites, the Hivites and the Jebusites—just as the Lord your God has commanded, so that they may not teach you to do all the abhorrent things that they do for their gods, and you thus sin against the Lord your God. (Deut. 20:16-18)

According to this brutal model for interreligious encounter, God demands the complete massacre of those who worship other gods to preserve the purity of worship of the people of Israel. Deuteronomy presents the fundamental principle that God inflicts punishments for wickedness not only on the perpetrators but on children to the third and fourth generation, but God bestows mercy on the virtuous and their descendants to the thousandth generation:

> You shall not make for yourself an idol, whether in the form of anything that is in heaven above, or that is on the earth beneath, or that is in the water under the earth. You shall not bow down to them or worship them; for I the Lord your God am a jealous God, punishing children for the iniquity of parents, to the third and fourth generation of those who reject me, but showing steadfast love to the thousandth generation of those who love me and keep my commandments. (Deut. 5:9-10)

The historical books of the Bible, from Joshua through Judges and 1-2 Samuel to 1-2 Kings, present a theology of history inspired by Deuteronomy, interpreting military defeat as God's punishment upon Israelites for their infidelity, especially their worship of other gods. The Bible does not see God as always fighting for the people of ancient Israel. Biblical prophets reversed the usual expectations of the theology of the holy war in a dramatic way to rebuke Israel. Amos, Jeremiah, and Ezekiel sharply condemned ancient Israelites, often for imitating their religious neighbors, and interpreted their defeats in war as God using the foes of ancient Israel to punish them for their sins (Amos 2:4-8; Jer. 4:5-31; Ezek. 39:22-24).

The Deuteronomic theology of God acting in history would long shape Christian interpretations of the military victories and defeats in relation to other religious communities, especially Muslims, and would have a long influence on Christian interpretations of proper relations with other religious traditions. Christians would often view the religious images of those outside the Abrahamic fold, such as Hindus, Buddhists, and indigenous traditions around the world, as idols to be denounced.

The prophetic heritage of ancient Israel is one of the most important points of contact among Jews, Christians, and Muslims, since each tradition claims to be the legitimate heir to the legacy of the prophets of Israel, though each understands this heritage in a different way. Biblical prophets could be brutal in applying the principles of the holy war to their opponents, as in Elijah's slay-ing of the prophets of Baal on Mount Carmel (1 Kgs. 18:39-40). The prophets' fierce critique of idols would have ominous implications for interreligious relations, as many later Christians would apply the prophetic critique of idols to the figures of the Hindu and Buddhist traditions and of indigenous religions around the world. Some European Christians coming to America understood themselves to be the biblical Israelites on an errand in the wilderness and correspondingly saw the Native Americans of the First Nations as idolaters who had no rights to the lands where they had long dwelled.

There are other sides to the prophetic heritage, however. The prophets' concern for social justice has had great influence in all three Abrahamic traditions, providing a basis for common concern and action in the world today. Alongside the theology of holy war, there also emerged from ancient Israel a prophetic vision of a more peaceful community of nations. The prophet Isaiah issued a moving call for peace, for beating swords into ploughshares and transforming spears into pruning hooks (Isa. 2:4). Isaiah presented the hope that the wolf will live with the lamb, that nations will live in peace, and that the poor and oppressed will find justice (Isa. 11:1-9).

Some books of prophets forcefully acknowledge the broader horizon of God's concern for other nations. The book of Jonah presents God's concern for the people of Nineveh in contrast to Jonah's desire for destruction. When Jonah wants to see the repentant city destroyed, God chides him (Jonah 4:1-11). The book of Jonah offers a satirical rebuttal to the brutality of the model of sacred combat. The final part of the book of Isaiah proclaims the universal care of God and foretells a day when all peoples will be welcome in Jerusalem (Isa 60:3-16).

Amos broadens the horizon of God's acting in history and also transforms the meaning of the Day of the Lord. Instead of being the day when God would defeat Israel's enemies, the Day of the Lord for Amos becomes the day of reckoning and judgment for unfaithful Israelites: "Alas for you who desire the day of the Lord! Why do you want the day of the Lord? It is darkness, not light" (Amos 5:18). According to Amos, God challenges the people of Israel to recognize God's care for other nations. But the ominous implication is that because all have received God's goodness, all will be held accountable on the day of judgment:

Are you not like the Ethiopians to me,
O people of Israel? says the Lord.
Did I not bring Israel up from the land of Egypt,
and the Philistines from Caphtor
and the Arameans from Kir? (Amos 9:7)

Apocalyptic Literature
The apocalyptic tradition vigorously affirms divine justice in a world of unjust suffering, promising that those who do not find justice in this world will be vindicated in the next. Apocalyptic works generally address communities in light

of an experienced or expected threat from forces of evil; apocalyptic authors warn ominously that the time for repentance is running out and predict a decisive intervention by God on behalf of the faithful. The book of Daniel draws on the ancient mythological imagery of holy war to interpret contemporary rulers, especially the Seleucid Antiochus IV Epiphanes, as evil enemies of God, continuing the tradition of sacred combat, where heavenly powers do battle against the earthly forces of evil. Daniel portrays Israel's earthly enemies in symbolic form as fearsome beasts emerging from the sea and challenging the heavenly powers (Dan. 7:2-27). Daniel expects God to break into the normal course of history and send heavenly assistance in the form of one like a Son of Man, a figure resembling a human being, who will destroy the powers of evil and establish God's kingdom (Dan. 7:9-27).

The apocalyptic trajectory had a tremendous influence in shaping Christian thought about interreligious encounter for centuries. By interpreting contemporary events in light of archetypal patterns, the apocalyptic tradition gave decisive precedents that shaped the way that Christians interpreted successive interreligious conflicts. Whenever Christians are being persecuted or are facing danger, they can look to apocalyptic literature as a ground for eschatological hope. However, a sense of being persecuted can fuel a long-lasting cycle of hostile interpretation and action. While the apocalyptic tradition presents hope for ultimate justice for those suffering in this world, it can also be interpreted in ways that demonize opponents and increase unjust suffering for others. Christians in tense interreligious situations often interpreted events in apocalyptic terms, viewing their adversaries as allies of the demonic forces of evil. While in the book of Daniel the decisive action comes from heavenly figures, in later centuries, Christians sometimes launched their own violent attacks on Jewish and Muslim communities in the expectation that the events of the end-time would commence in the near future (Whalen 2009, 42-99).

The Wisdom Tradition

In addition to the historical and prophetic traditions, the Bible also presents the wisdom tradition, represented especially by the books of Proverbs, Ecclesiastes, Job, and a number of Psalms, as well as by the later deuterocanonical books of Ben Sira and the Wisdom of Solomon. The wisdom teachers of the Bible participated in a cosmopolitan hermeneutical circle, acknowledging an international, interreligious, and intercultural community of discourse. Since the wisdom implanted by God in creation is universal and universally accessible, sages from different religious backgrounds can find points of contact and exchange. The cordial exchange of gifts between the Queen of Sheba and King Solomon stands as a symbol of the respectful mutual relationship (1 Kgs. 10:1-13), though in the chapter immediately following, Solomon is sharply criticized for marrying foreign women and being too open to honoring other gods (1 Kgs. 11:1-13). In the Hebrew Bible, the wisdom tradition presents a hermeneutic of generosity, an amicable exchange of perspectives in the cosmopolitan search for wisdom involving Israelite, Egyptian, and Mesopotamian participants.

The sages of ancient Israel reflected on the patterns in ordinary human experience and expressed their insights in proverbs, poems, and riddles. Rather than claiming any special prophetic call or apocalyptic vision, they sought discernment and understanding in everyday life. In principle, wisdom is open to all those who seek diligently for understanding through discipline. For later generations, the biblical search for wisdom provides a point of contact for interreligious encounters, including conversations with Buddhists or Daoists who seek wisdom but do not believe in a transcendent, creating God. The wisdom tradition offers a precedent for a hermeneutics of friendship, which assumes that other cultures are already in contact with the Wisdom of the God of Israel.

Pope John XXIII addressed his final encyclical, *Pacem in Terris,* to all people of good will. In order to reach the widest possible audience, Pope John appealed to the wisdom Psalms that sing of the goodness of God in creation and to the Wisdom of Solomon (§§3, 83). In *Dialogue and Proclamation,* the Pontifical Council for Interreligious Dialogue cites the biblical wisdom tradition in this regard as a precedent for contemporary interreligious openness:

> In the Wisdom literature also, which bears witness to cultural exchanges between Israel and its neighbours, the action of God in the whole universe is clearly affirmed. It goes beyond the boundaries of the Chosen People to touch both the history of nations and the lives of individuals. (§20)

Nonetheless, the wisdom tradition is not uncritical of other religions. The later wisdom books are very critical of religious practices in the Hellenistic period, and the Wisdom of Solomon issues a fierce polemic against the gods of the nations. The Wisdom of Solomon assumes a wide audience, addressing rulers throughout the ancient world: "Love justice, you who rule on earth" (1:1), and it assumes a common horizon of conversation. It is also extremely critical of idols, interpreting the many gods as simply human beings who are honored:

> For a father, consumed with grief at an untimely bereavement,
> made an image of his child, who had been suddenly taken from him;
> he now honored as a god what was once a dead human being,
> and handed on to his dependents secret rites and initiations. (Wis. 14:15)

Matters become more severe as the Wisdom of Solomon describes horrible rituals:

> For whether they kill children in their initiations, or celebrate secret
>   mysteries,
> they no longer keep either their lives or their marriages pure,
> but they either treacherously kill one another, or grieve one another
>   by adultery,
> and all is a raging riot of blood and murder, theft and deceit,
>   corruption,

faithlessness, tumult, perjury,
confusion over what is good, forgetfulness of favors,
defiling of souls, sexual perversion,
disorder in marriages, adultery, and debauchery.
For the worship of idols not to be named
is the beginning and cause and end of every evil. (Wis. 14:23-27)

For those who practice such deeds, the Wisdom of Solomon threatens harsh retribution:

But just penalties will overtake them on two counts:
Because they thought wrongly about God in devoting themselves to
    idols,
And because in deceit they swore unrighteously through contempt
    for holiness. (Wis. 14:30)

The perspectives of the wisdom tradition were extremely influential in shaping the early Christian community's interpretation of Greek and Roman religions, both in the rejection of the gods and in the appropriation of Hellenistic philosophy.

The New Testament

The New Testament inherits all the trajectories of the earlier Jewish tradition and reinterprets them in relation to the life, ministry, death, and resurrection of Jesus Christ. The themes of monotheism, creation, the primeval narratives, God acting in history, prophecy, apocalyptic, and wisdom all find new meanings and applications in relation to Jesus Christ; he is acclaimed as prophet and sage, as apocalyptic seer, as the Word and Wisdom of God through whom all things are created, as the Son of God. Yet he is also proclaimed as more than a prophet or wisdom teacher or apocalyptic seer; the apostle Thomas hails him as "my Lord and my God" (John 20:28). Like the First Testament of the Bible, the New Testament offers models that can serve as a basis for either hostility or respect in interreligious relations.

In the Sermon on the Mount, Jesus offers precedents for how to handle conflict. In sharp contrast to the heritage of the holy war, Jesus instructs his followers in situations of struggle: "Love your enemies and pray for those who persecute you" (Matt. 5:44). He advises them to turn the other cheek, give the extra garment, and go the extra mile (Matt. 5:39-41). Jesus relates in a positive manner to people from different religious backgrounds, granting the request of a persistent Syro-Phoenician woman (Mark 7:24-30), praising the faith of a Roman centurion (Matt. 8:5-13), and engaging a Samaritan woman in conversation (John 4:7-26). The Samaritan woman then proposes to her neighbors that Jesus may be the Messiah, and some come to faith through her testimony, which is then confirmed by their experience of Jesus (John 4:29, 39-42). In the parable of the Good Samaritan, Jesus applies the command to love one's neighbor to those of a different religious community (Luke 10:29-37). The command to love one's neighbor offers an all-embracing horizon for interreligious hermeneutics. Augustine will place *caritas* at the center of his biblical herme-neutics, and Pope Paul VI proposes charity as the virtue encompassing the call to dialogue.

In the Acts of the Apostles, Paul sharply criticizes the images of the Greek gods in Athens, but he nonetheless quotes ancient Greek authors as having some knowledge of God, which offers a point of contact with his audience at the Areopagus (17:22-31). This account offers a model both for critique of idols and also for a hermeneutic of respect and generosity.

The New Testament's presentation of Jesus Christ as the one through whom all things are created and are (1 Cor. 8:6; Col. 1:15-20; John 1:1-4) pro-vides both a point of distinction from other religions and also a context for finding points of contact with other traditions. Raimon Panikkar develops the interpretation of Jesus Christ as the cosmic Wisdom or Logos of God as a basis for finding Christ throughout all experience, including in other religious tradi-tions (1993; 2004). The Gospel of John contains sayings of Jesus that have been understood as exclusivist (12:48; 14:6). Nonetheless, according to the prologue of John, "The light shines in the darkness, and the darkness did not overcome it" (1:5). This can be understood as a primordial revelation of God prior to the Word becoming flesh in John 1:14. C. H. Dodd argues that the revelation of God in Jesus Christ is not an exclusive limiting of God's presence but rather a manifestation of what the cosmic Logos is always and everywhere doing: "The life of Jesus there *is* the history of the Logos, as incarnate, and this must be, upon the stage of limited time, the same thing as the history of the Logos in perpetual relations with man and the world" (1965, 285). The Johannine Jesus says: "I have other sheep that do not belong to this fold. I must bring them also, and they will listen to my voice" (John 10:16), and the evangelist mentions "the dispersed children of God" beyond the Jewish nation (John 11:52). Dodd sug-gests that these include people throughout the world who do not have contact with Jesus (282).

In the Acts of the Apostles, the apostle Paul addresses the Athenians at the Areopagus:

> For as I went through the city and looked carefully at the objects of your worship, I found among them an altar with the inscription, "to an unknown god." What therefore you worship as unknown, this I pro-claim to you. . . . [I]ndeed [God] is not far from each one of us. For "In him we live and move and have our being," as even some of your own poets have said, "For we too are his offspring." (Acts 17:23, 27-28)

This speech would be one of the most important biblical precedents for later Christians encountering religious traditions around the world, including those that are not monotheistic.

Some passages in the New Testament have traditionally served as the basis for hostility toward other religious traditions. As we will see in the next chap-ter, the accounts of Jesus' conflicts with the Jewish leaders of his day, which come to a climax in the passion narrative, had a long, deleterious effect on later Jewish–Christian relations. The book of Revelation's application of the imagery of the holy war to the conflict with Rome would also have a long history of effects, reinforcing hostility with other religious communities.

One of the most influential images of the New Testament for later interreligious relations is the Antichrist. While this figure would later become a major apocalyptic figure, the First Letter of John uses the term "antichrist" for those who reject the proper understanding of Jesus:

> Children, it is the last hour! As you have heard that antichrist is coming, so now many antichrists have come. From this we know that it is the last hour. . . . Who is the liar but the one who denies that Jesus is the Christ? This is the antichrist, the one who denies the Father and the Son. (1 John 2:18, 22)

In the original context of 1 John, the term "antichrist" refers to someone who denies that Jesus is the Christ who has come in the flesh; it is a term for the opposing side of a christological debate. The figure is not yet the preternatural, apocalyptic ally of the devil that would appear in the later tradition. Later Christians would view Jews and Muslims as allies of the Antichrist. Applying the biblical model to his context, the Christian apocalyptic writer Lactantius in the fourth century viewed Jews as allies of the Antichrist. Later, in the seventh century, Pseudo-Methodius set the pattern for countless other Christians by interpreting Muslims as allies of the Antichrist.

The mention of the Son of Destruction in 2 Thessalonians would also have a major influence on interreligious relations. The letter warns of a coming "lawless one," described as "the son of destruction" (2:3; NRSV: "the one destined for destruction"; KJV: "son of perdition"), who will play an important role in the events of the end-time. In the later tradition, the Antichrist and the Son of Destruction would become common images for Christian views of Jews and Muslims.

The multiple models of the Bible can be interpreted either as fostering hostility toward other religious traditions or as encouraging respect and cooperation. The diversity of biblical models for relating to followers of other religious traditions makes all the more pressing the question of how the Bible is to be interpreted.

CHAPTER TWO

Hermeneutics

From the beginning of Christianity, followers of Jesus Christ have debated how to interpret the scriptures. The Gospel of Luke presents Jesus at the beginning of his public ministry reading from the scroll of Isaiah 61:1-2 in the synagogue in Nazareth and applying the text to himself: "Today this scripture has been fulfilled in your hearing" (Luke 4:21). Almost immediately a bitter dispute ensues in the assembly (4:23-30). At the end of the Gospel, Luke presents the narrative of the risen Lord appearing unrecognized to his disciples on the road to Emmaus. As the mysterious stranger interprets Moses and the prophets in relation to the recent events concerning Jesus of Nazareth, the disciples feel their hearts burning within them (Luke 24:25-32). This evocative narrative illustrates the route whereby early followers of Jesus came to read the familiar Jewish scriptures in new ways in light of Jesus Christ. One of the places in which followers of Jesus will find him is in the transformed interpretation of scripture. The Gospel of Luke blesses the new manner of interpreting the scriptures by tracing it back to the risen Lord himself.

Luke says that as the two disciples listened to the stranger interpret the scriptures, "the eyes of them both were opened, and they recognized him" (Luke 24:31). Tom Wright notes that the Greek words in this passage are almost exactly the same as those used in Genesis for Adam and Eve after they ate the forbidden fruit: "their eyes were opened, and they knew that they were naked" (Gen. 3:7). Wright draws the connection: "Luke is hinting that with Jesus' resurrection the curse of the Fall has been undone" (Wright 2004, 34). Biblical hermeneutics can be an integral part of the path leading from sin to healing and new life.

However, the multiple and conflicting biblical models for interreligious interactions pose many hermeneutical challenges, and there has never been unanimous agreement among Christians on how to interpret the Bible. Traditionally, hermeneutics refers to the interpretation of texts, especially of sacred texts in cases where the texts are difficult to understand. Hermeneutics becomes self-conscious when there is a problem in interpreting, when there is a break or a major shift in a tradition, or when different traditions encounter each other. In recent decades, the term "hermeneutics" is also used more broadly to refer to all interpretation of texts and human action. The hermeneutics of scripture begins with the interpretation of the Bible, but it opens out onto all the questions of human identity for both individuals and communities. But the passage through interpretation is not smooth. From ancient times to the present, hermeneutics has been a field of constant struggle, where interpretations clash. In Greek mythology, Hermes, from whom "hermeneutics" takes its name, is the bearer of messages between humans and gods. He is the patron of those who cross boundaries, but he is also a thief and a trickster.

Patristic Hermeneutics

Early Christians developed their styles of interpreting the Bible in light of multiple challenges in relating both to the Jewish community and to the Greek and Roman world. They were appreciative of some elements in these traditions and critical of others. By the first century B.C.E., Jewish and Greco-Roman thinkers had already developed allegorical methods to address difficulties of interpretation and to probe the allegedly deeper significance of classical texts.

In the second half of the sixth century B.C.E., Theagenes of Rhegium defended Homer by interpreting the fighting among the Homeric gods as an allegory of natural elements, where heat is opposed to cold; Anaxagoras interpreted the gods psychologically, with Zeus symbolizing intelligence and Athene technical prowess (Simonetti 1994, 5-6). Prodicus of Ceos viewed the Homeric gods as symbols of natural substances, with Demeter representing bread, Poseidon standing for water, and Dionysus for wine. Cynic philosophers interpreted Homer as expressing their views. Stoic interpreters used allegorical interpretation to eliminate anything that was unseemly from Greek myths and also to bring the traditional polytheism into harmony with their own monotheism. Later, Plotinus saw in the Odyssey an allegory of the soul making the long, difficult voyage to its true home.

In the first century C.E., Philo of Alexandria followed the lead of earlier Jewish interpreters in applying Greek methods of allegorical interpretation to the Jewish scriptures, bringing them into harmony with the best of Greek philosophical thought. Philo's belief that Moses had anticipated Plato in important teachings established a framework for harmonizing Jewish and Greek thought. For Philo, the Temple in Jerusalem is a symbol of the world, with the parts of the Temple representing various parts and the vestments of the high priest symbolizing elements of nature (Simonetti 1994, 7). Adam represents intelligence and Eve sensitivity.

Early Christian writers appropriated many of the methods of interpretation from Jewish and Greek writers, but they applied these in the context of developing Christian identity. There were places of overlap with Jewish and Greek hermeneutics, but increasingly there were points of conflict and distinctive emphases as well. Christians interpreted passages from the Jewish scriptures as symbolically referring to Jesus Christ, often sparking debates with Jews who rejected such interpretations.

Continuing the polemics of Jewish authors against the deities of the Gentiles, Christians rejected the gods of ancient world. The translation of one psalm from Hebrew to Greek had enormous influence and importance in shaping Christian attitudes. The Hebrew text of Psalm 96:5 states, "The gods of nations are idols." In about 250 B.C.E., the Septuagint (LXX) translated this line into Greek as: "The gods of the nations are demons [*daimonia*]" (LXX Ps 95:5) (L. T. Johnson 2009, 2). In accordance with this translation, early Christians viewed the Greco-Roman gods as demons, and some interpreted their similarities to Christian beliefs and practices as instances of demonic plagiarism. Nonetheless, the situation was complex, since Christians also borrowed heavily from the Greco-Roman milieu, especially their forms of philosophical thought, which were heavily religious.

Allegorical hermeneutics provides a way of interpreting difficult texts symbolically, sometimes deflecting any literal meaning or application. Allegorical interpretation had multiple implications for Christians in interreligious relations. It provided a polemical method for rejecting Jewish interpretations of the Hebrew Bible that did not recognize Jesus as the Christ, the Son of God. Christian allegorists often viewed Jews as literalists who could not understand the symbolic, spiritual meanings of their own scriptures. In relating to the Jewish community, Christians developed a polemical interpretation of the Bible, claiming that they were the true heirs to the legacy of ancient Israel. Allegorical interpretation also offered an important method for rejecting a literal interpretation of biblical texts viewed as offensive, such as those calling for violence against entire populations.

Early Christians appropriated the method of allegorical interpretation from earlier Jewish, Greek, and Roman interpreters in the context of the struggle over the proper interpretation of the Bible and Greek myths. In different ways, Origen and Augustine, two of the most influential scriptural interpreters in all of Christian history, proposed hermeneutical principles that can form the basis for a critical discernment of the appropriateness of biblical interpretations.

Origen

Origen (ca. 183–ca. 254), who began his career in Alexandria, Egypt, and later moved to Caesarea in Palestine, immersed himself in the study of the Hebrew language so that he could better understand the Jewish scriptures. He also studied Hellenistic philosophy in depth, especially the Platonic tradition. From his studies, he became sharply critical of Jewish interpretations of scripture, critical of the Greek and Roman gods, and critical also of much of Hellenistic philosophy. Nonetheless, like Justin Martyr and Clement of Alexandria, Origen acknowledges that Plato and other ancient Greek thinkers knew some religious truths: "God revealed to them these things and all other truths which they stated rightly" (*Contra Celsum* 6.3; 1980, p. 317). Even though Greek and Roman thinkers had some knowledge of God, Origen denies that they were able to put this into practice and genuinely worship the one God.

Crucial to Origen's hermeneutics is his distinction between the letter and the spirit, based on his interpretation of 2 Corinthians 3:6: "for the letter kills, but the Spirit gives life." In some biblical texts, Origen does not believe that the literal meaning is what God intended at all. Origen tells us that God places "impossibilities and incongruities" in the biblical text "in order that the very interruption of the narrative might as it were present a barrier to the reader and lead him to refuse to proceed along the pathway of the ordinary meaning" (*On First Principles* 4.2.9; 1973, 285). By renouncing the direct path of literal reading and going through the narrow footpath of spiritual interpretation, readers of the Bible can come to "the immense breadth of the divine wisdom" (4.2.9). The impossibility of the literal sense beckons the reader to attend to the spiritual meaning. Origen often subdivides the spiritual sense into the moral (or psychic) and the spiritual, though sometimes he mentions only the twofold distinction between the literal and the spiritual.

As one criterion for discerning what is meant literally in the Bible, Origen appeals to what a person of intelligence would consider to be a reasonable statement (4.3.1). "It is quite easy for any one who wills to collect from the holy scriptures instances that are recorded as actual events, but which it would be inappropriate and unreasonable to believe could possibly have happened in history" (4.3.2). He explains: "For we recognize that the letter is often impossible and inconsistent with itself, that is, that things not only irrational but even impossible are occasionally described by it" (4.3.4). His conclusion is: "For our contention with regard to the whole of divine scripture is, that it all has a spiritual meaning, but not all a bodily meaning; for the bodily meaning is often proved to be an impossibility" (4.3.5).

Origen interprets the commands to kill all the inhabitants of the promised land not as prescriptions for a literal holy war of conquest of the land but rather as allegorical commands to kill one's own evil emotions and intentions; the real struggle is within the human person. Commenting on the preparation for battle in the book of Joshua, Origen exhorts his audience: "Let us go forth to war so that we may destroy the chief city of this world, malice, and destroy the proud walls of sin" (*Homilies on Joshua* 5.2). Origen explains that the struggle is within: "You require nothing from without, beyond your self; within you is the battle that you are about to wage; on the inside is the evil edifice that must be overthrown; your enemy proceeds from your own heart" (5.2). Origen cites Jesus' warning that all evils come from within the human person (Matt. 15:19) as confirmation of his interpretation.

Origen comments pointedly: "Unless those physical wars bore the figure of spiritual wars, I do not think that the books of Jewish history would ever have been handed down by the Apostles to the disciples of Christ, who came to teach peace, that they may be read in the churches" (15.1). Origen appeals to the criterion of the intention of Christ, who offers peace (John 14:27), and also to the writings of Paul, who describes the followers of Jesus as suffering injury but not avenging themselves (Rom. 12:19; 1 Cor. 6:7; Origen, *Homilies on Joshua* 15.1). Thus, to guide his biblical hermeneutics Origen combines the intentionality of Jesus Christ to offer peace with the criterion of what is worthy of God and of human reason. If the literal meaning of a text violates these criteria, then the text must be interpreted spiritually and symbolically.

Origen's hermeneutical method is remarkably similar to Gandhi's interpretation of the violent commands that Krishna, the avatar of Vishnu, issues to Arjuna in the Bhagavad Gita. Gandhi argues that the Gita is referring not to military combat but rather to the inner battle:

> I felt that it was not a historical work, but that, under the guise of physical warfare, it described the duel that perpetually went on in the hearts of mankind, and that physical warfare was brought in merely to make the description of the internal duel more alluring. This preliminary intuition became more confirmed on a closer study of religion and the Gita. (2000, 16)

In the later tradition, Origen was of immense influence for giving a systematic reflection on biblical interpretation, but he was also quite controversial and would be condemned centuries later. Origen located criteria for biblical hermeneutics in the intentionality of Jesus Christ to bring peace and in the worthiness of an interpretation to God and to human reason. These would echo through the centuries.

Augustine of Hippo

For Latin Christians throughout the Middle Ages and beyond, Augustine of Hippo (354–430) was often the most influential guide to interpreting the Bible. To read the Bible properly, Augustine believes it is essential to make distinctions in order to interpret the Bible according to the intention of the divine author. He begins *De Doctrina Christiana* by making a distinction between *res* ("reality") and *signum* ("sign") (1.2.2). We come to know realities through signs; but if we do not know the reality at all, the sign cannot communicate effectively to us. In relation to God, we find ourselves in a dilemma that we cannot resolve on our own. God is strictly incomprehensible, and to make matters worse, we are alienated from God by sin. We are trapped in ignorance and sin, and there is no way we can come to know God in such a way as to be saved.

However, God comes to our aid: God is love, and divine love (*caritas*) gives us the signs in the Bible that guide us to know love. Thus through God's grace the impasse is overcome, and the hermeneutical circle of sign and reality becomes fruitful: the reality of divine love is both the communicator and the communicated. This establishes Augustine's fundamental interpretive principle for scripture; scripture teaches nothing but *caritas*, the twofold love of God and neighbor:

> So if it seems to you that you have understood the divine scriptures, or any part of them, in such a way that by this understanding you do not build up this twin love of God and neighbor, then you have not yet understood them. If, on the other hand you have made judgments about them that are helpful for building up this love, but for all that have not said what the author you have been reading actually meant in that place, then your mistake is not pernicious, and you certainly cannot be accused of lying. (*De Doctrina Christiana* 1.36.40)

Augustine later summarizes his hermeneutical principle for the Bible: "Scripture, though, commands nothing but charity, or love, and censures nothing but cupidity, or greed, and that is the way it gives shape and form to human morals" (3.10.15). This principle offers a basis for reading the Bible critically, assessing texts in relation to the central teaching of charity.

As we will see in the next chapter, Augustine both defends the continued existence of the Jewish people and strongly criticizes their way of interpreting the Bible. Augustine engages the other religions of his acquaintance in *The City of God*, where he is very harsh in judging the gods of other nations as idols to be rejected and condemned.

In different ways, Origen and Augustine propose hermeneutical principles that resist the literal implementation of the Bible's violent commands to destroy followers of other religions. For the next millennium of Christian history, an atmosphere of hostility generally proved to be very influential in shaping the hermeneutics of the Bible. Especially in relation to the Jewish and Islamic traditions, through much of history, a hermeneutics of hostility largely dominated Christian belief, life, and practice. Nonetheless, Origen holds up the intention of Jesus Christ to bring peace as a hermeneutical criterion, and Augustine similarly holds up *caritas* as the central significance of the Bible and demands that any interpretation cohere with charity. These criteria offer an alternative vision as a basis for a critical review of the history of biblical interpretation in relation to other religions.

Modern Hermeneutics: Suspicion and Trust

Throughout the modern period, Christian theology and hermeneutics have been intimately related, if not identified. Modern hermeneutics arises from an awareness of distance and rupture between the past and the present. Modern hermeneutics was born in a situation of questioning and perplexity over the interpretation of scripture in a changing world and in the wake of the bitter wars of religion in Europe in the sixteenth and seventeenth centuries. The European Enlightenment sought to break with tradition on multiple levels, rejecting traditional religious authorities partly because of the religiously motivated violence of the wars of religion of the sixteenth and seventeenth centuries. Modern hermeneutical theories often offer strategies for the critique, reinterpretation, and retrieval of a tradition that has become suspect.

As scholars developed the historical-critical method in the seventeenth and eighteenth centuries, they rejected the allegorical methods of interpretation and sought to be objective and neutral regarding the investigation of the Bible. However, investigators inevitably reveal their own assumptions and biases, including their attitudes toward other religions. Historical criticism can provide a basis for academic exploration of the interreligious context of biblical texts, but it does not necessarily insulate scholars from hostile attitudes toward other religions.

Immanuel Kant

In the modern period, hermeneutics has often been suspicious about every aspect of knowledge and tradition. Immanuel Kant pondered the famous question, "What Is Enlightenment?" The answer he proposes is: "Sapere aude! 'Have courage to use your own reason!'—that is the motto of enlightenment" (1975, 3). Acutely aware of the violence of the wars of religion, Kant is suspicious of following traditional religious authorities and believes that the critical search for wisdom, instructed by moral duty, is incumbent upon each autonomous individual. Kant ushers in a new era of hermeneutics not only by suspecting the traditional religious authorities but above all by warning that illusion is systemic and transcendental. In a very different way from Origen and Augustine, Kant proposes a method of interpretation that demands critical discernment and that places limits on what should be acknowledged as divine revelation.

For Kant, illusion operates on various levels. In *Critique of Pure Reason,* Kant cautions that we fall into illusion and deceive ourselves whenever we reach beyond our limits. In particular, attempts rationally to prove the existence of God extend beyond the limits of the competence of human reason. Nonetheless, Kant sees reason's search for the unconditional as well founded, though in need of limitation and guidance. He sets limits to what reason can know with certainty in order to make room for a chastened but reasonable religious faith. In *Critique of Practical Reason,* he reinterprets the ideas of God, the soul, and immortality as postulates of practical reason. Then, in *Critique of Judgment,* Kant reflects on aesthetics and teleology. In addition to theoretical concepts and the imperative of moral duty, Kant argues that we have aesthetic ideas that make claims upon us even though these are not concepts that give knowledge in the normal sense. Kant describes the challenge of an aesthetic idea: "[B]y an aesthetic idea I mean a presentation of the imagination which prompts much thought, but to which no determinate thought whatsoever, i.e., no [determinate] *concept,* can be adequate, so that no language can express it completely and allow us to grasp it" (1987, 182). An aesthetic idea gives much to ponder without any concept ever being equal to it; no conceptual reflection fully captures a major aesthetic idea. This sets up a role for philosophy in pondering aesthetic ideas without pretending to exhaust their meaning. This approach has very important ramifications for approaching religious symbols, which Paul Ricoeur would later explore.

After writing three epochal *Critiques,* Kant turned to the concrete and the historical issues of religiosity in *Religion within the Boundaries of Mere Reason.* Here again he finds deep-seated illusions; but, nonetheless, he trusts what he takes to be the fundamental message of religion, if it is interpreted properly. To understand the texture, tragedy, and possibilities for human existence, Kant turns principally to the concrete language of the Bible but also to other scriptures as well. He cites the wisdom of ancient India to correct the unwarranted optimism of the modern Western Enlightenment (2010, 45). Kant is profoundly skeptical about the claims of modern European culture that history brings progress, and he cites ancient Indian wisdom as a counter-witness.

For Kant, ancient *Dichtung* ("poetry" or "fiction") can correct the illusions of the modern West.

For Kant, the core of true religion is to see one's moral duty as coming from God. In addition to the universal experience of moral duty, Kant acknowledges the possibility of divine revelation and the legitimacy in principle of a biblical theology based on revelation. However, he warns that if we take religious language beyond its proper limits, we end in the illusions of fanaticism, superstition, and magic. Kant is profoundly aware of the problem of religiously motivated violence, as exemplified in the wars of religion in Europe. He hopes that a philosophical hermeneutics of religious claims can serve as a type of police action, forbidding religious claims that violate human dignity. According to Kant, the categorical imperative is strictly universal, setting a framework that every claim of divine revelation must respect. For Kant, the philosophical theologian must scrutinize the claims of the biblical theologian and object whenever human dignity is violated. Thus, Kant proposes that when Abraham was confronted with the command to kill his son, he ought to have replied: "That I ought not to kill my good son is quite certain. But that you, this apparition, are god—of that I am not certain, and never can be, not even if this voice rings down to me from (visible) heaven" (quoted by Bielefeldt 2001, 172). For Kant, this limit is essential to forestall the violence of fanaticism and to shape a commonwealth of ends and to foster universal peace (1975, 85-135).

To protect a reasonable faith from the violent dangers of superstition and fanaticism, Kant offers a philosophical meditation on aspects of human experience, inspired by biblical texts such as the fall of the first humans in Genesis 3 and the Servant of the Lord in Isaiah 52-53. Without quoting the text of Genesis 3 directly, he reflects on its wisdom in his notion of radical evil, directly challenging the optimism of the Enlightenment. Then, in light of his understanding of sin, he ponders the meaning of grace in the archetype of humanity well-pleasing to God, a reflection inspired by the poems of the Servant of the Lord in the book of Isaiah. Then he reinterprets the notion of the religious community as the commonwealth of ends. Kant offers a powerful combination of suspicion and retrieval in interpreting traditional religious language; his reflections mark a major turning point in Western thought about reason and religion.

Friedrich Schleiermacher

Friedrich Schleiermacher, who was deeply influenced by Kant even though he rejected Kant's moral approach to religion, is frequently seen as the founder of modern hermeneutics. Schleiermacher sets forth a number of hermeneutical principles that have been very influential. In *On Religion: Speeches to Its Cultured Despisers*, he famously pleaded with the Enlightenment critics of religion: "If you only knew how to read between the lines!" (1988, 101). He holds that hermeneutics consists of both grammatical and psychological interpretation, maintaining that each of these skills is an art that no exact rules can dictate (1977, 100). He also distinguishes two approaches to interpretation. The easier approach assumes that understanding is normal and thinks that misunderstandings are only occasional problems. Schleiermacher, however, advocates the more rigorous approach that assumes that "misunderstanding occurs as a matter of course, and so understanding must be willed and sought at every point" (1977, 110). He goes on to explain: "It is common experience that one notices no distinction until . . . [the] beginning of a misunderstanding. Therefore, this more rigorous practice presupposes that the speaker and hearer differ in their use of language in their ways of formulating thoughts, although to be sure there is an underlying unity between them" (1977, 110).

This warning has special importance for the interpretation of the scriptures in relation to other religions. In interreligious conversations, participants can assume they understand their interlocutors, but even when there are shared vocabularies and images, the underlying assumptions often differ profoundly. Schleiermacher's more rigorous form of hermeneutics challenges Christians to question the assumption that they immediately understand their religious neighbors.

Compared to most of the earlier Christian tradition, Schleiermacher expresses an attitude of respect and generosity toward other religions. In the proto-phenomenological approach of his speeches, *On Religion*, Schleiermacher honors all intuitions of the universe. By approaching religion as "the sensibility and taste for the infinite," he places the concept of God in a position of secondary importance in relation to an allegedly universal awareness and intuition; this approach could open a path for dialogue with non-dualistic traditions in Hinduism and Buddhism (2000, 23). In this work Schleiermacher is not committed to any single concept of the universe and hopes that a multitude of intuitions can be helpful: "I have at all times presupposed the plurality of religions and their most distinct diversity as something necessary and unavoidable. . . . Thus I have presupposed the multiplicity of religions, and I likewise find them rooted in the essence of religion" (2000, 96, 97).

Later, in his mature reflections on Christian dogmatic theology, Schleiermacher assesses Christian faith as the most relatively adequate expression of God-consciousness, but he does not view other approaches as completely wrong. He offers his dogmatic reflections "only for Christians; and so this account is only for those who live within the pale of Christianity" (1976, 60). He denies any attempt to prove the truth of Christianity: "We entirely renounce all attempt to prove the truth or necessity of Christianity; and we presuppose, on the contrary, that every Christian, before he enters at all upon inquiries of this kind, has already the inward certainty that his religion cannot take any other form than this" (1976, 60). Presumably, Schleiermacher allows that other religious traditions bring their own "inward certainty." Schleiermacher's confidence that the Christian religion "cannot take any other form" becomes open to question in interreligious conversations, where Christians have often found their religion taking on new forms.

While many later scholars have criticized Schleiermacher's notion of psychological interpretation, his hermeneutics of suspicion on our immediate understanding has proved extremely influential. In recent years, Ramon Panikkar's exploration of the experience of Jesus Christ in *Christophany* does not explicitly cite Schleiermacher but bears many resemblances.

Hans-Georg Gadamer

Hans-Georg Gadamer proposes a post-Romantic hermeneutics that questions the validity of psychological interpretation and focuses on language more than on the subjectivity of the author. Gadamer's hermeneutics addresses the difficulties of understanding the other. Nicholas Davey notes that, for Gadamer, "Difficulty sets us at a distance. It places us between expectation and outcome. In Latin, *dis* + *facultas* conveys a sense of reversal, of meeting an obstacle that throws one back on oneself. The negative nuances of the term are not at odds with claims of philosophical hermeneutics. Gadamer speaks of how distance is the condition of understanding [*Truth and Method*, 298]. Hermeneutics, he claims, is rooted in the in-between" (Davey 2006, 163).

Gadamer sees classic works as contemporary with each age that ponders them. A great work of art undergoes what Gadamer called a *Verwandlung ins Gebilde*, a "transformation into structure," which frees it from the particular circumstances of its origin and allows it to live its own life (1989, 110-21). It has the temporality of a festival that is completely present in each occurrence: "It has its being only in becoming and return" (1989, 123). Classic texts move beyond the boundaries of their original period and their culture, addressing and challenging all the world's communities.

Each religious tradition has an entire network of assumptions that is largely taken for granted because it seems "natural." When we meet people from another religious tradition, we encounter assumptions and beliefs that often differ profoundly from our own. While misunderstanding seems unavoidable, especially at the beginning, these encounters can be tremendous opportunities for learning if we continue the conversation attentively and learn from our mistakes. Gadamer proposes that our prejudices dominate us as long as we are unaware of them (1989, 299); a different perspective can make us aware of our prejudices and hold them up for scrutiny:

> Understanding begins . . . when something addresses us. This is the first condition of hermeneutics. . . . The essence of the *question* is to open up possibilities and keep them open. . . . In fact, our own prejudice is properly brought into play by being put at risk. Only by being given full play is it able to experience the other's claim to truth and make it possible for him to have full play himself. (1989, 299)

For Gadamer, hermeneutical understanding takes place in a conversation in which the goal is not winning an argument but finding the truth. This demands that the interpreter be open to transformation in a to-and-fro process that cannot be completely predicted or controlled. Understanding another perspective transforms us: "A person who thinks must ask himself questions. . . . This is the reason why understanding is always more than merely re-creating someone else's meaning. Questioning opens up possibilities of meaning, and thus what is meaningful passes into one's own thinking on the subject" (1989, 375).

Gadamer rejects the pretensions of the European Enlightenment to eliminate prejudices; prejudices are part of our finitude. He describes the hope for a fusion of horizons that occurs when we enter a broader horizon in which we can see further aspects of life. Gadamer insists "that a hermeneutical situation is determined by the prejudices that we bring with us. They constitute, then, the horizon of a particular present, for they represent that beyond which it is impossible to see" (1989, 306). Gadamer observes that encountering classic works of the past challenges our prejudices: "In fact the horizon of the present is continually in the process of being formed because we are continually having to test all our prejudices. An important part of this testing occurs in encountering the past and in understanding the tradition from which we come" (1989, 306).

When we encounter representatives and texts of other religious traditions past or present, our prejudices and our understanding of our tradition are challenged. Tension is not to be feared or avoided; it can be generative of understanding. Gadamer advises: "Every encounter with tradition that takes place within historical consciousness involves the experience of a tension between the text and the present. The hermeneutic task consists in not covering up this tension by attempting a naïve assimilation of the two but in consciously bringing it out. This is why it is part of the hermeneutic approach to project a historical horizon that is different from the horizon of the present" (1989, 306). When understanding occurs, there is what Gadamer calls a fusion of horizons, and we can see a broader range of experience: "In the process of understanding, a real fusing of horizons occurs" (1989, 307).

Gadamer warns that the course of a true conversation is unpredictable: "Every experience worthy of the name thwarts an expectation" (1989, 356). A genuine conversation can bring about a transformation and the formation of a new community. With reference to parties in a conversation, Gadamer proposes that

> in a successful conversation they both come under the influence of the truth of the object and are thus bound to one another in a new community. To reach an understanding in a dialogue is not merely a matter of putting oneself forward and successfully asserting one's own point of view, but being transformed into a communion in which we do not remain what we were. (1989, 379)

In a similar vein, Martin Buber emphasizes the importance of "the between" in dialogical relationships. He acknowledges that each dialogue partner is unavoidably partial and must be aware of being limited by the other. Nonetheless, unpredictable disclosures can occur:

> The experience of being limited is included in what I refer to; but so too is the experience of overcoming it together. This cannot be completed on the level of *Weltanschauung*, but on that of reality. Neither needs to give up his point of view; only, in that unexpectedly they do something and unexpectedly something happens to them which

is called a covenant, they enter a realm where the law of the point of view no longer holds. (Buber 1968, 6)

Gadamer's remarks can be applied to interreligious conversations. If, as Cardinal Bergoglio proposes, dialogue means being open to the other person's point of view and proposals, then neither side can control the flow of a genuine dialogue. In the exchanges between the parties to the dialogue, unpredictable transformations can occur. Without surrendering their fundamental convictions, the parties can come to a new awareness in a broader horizon.

Paul Ricoeur

Continuing the hermeneutical tradition in dialogue with ideology critiques, Paul Ricoeur has offered some of the most penetrating reflections on hermeneutics, religion, translation, and dialogue of recent years. Deeply influenced by Kant's philosophy of limits and hermeneutics of religious language, Ricoeur argues that symbols are essential for religious discourse; in particular, the experience of evil is never expressed directly but always appears in symbols, images, or metaphors, or in later theoretical reflections on such symbols. For Ricoeur, the symbolic level is prior to explicit theological or philosophical reflection. Drawing upon Kant's claim that aesthetic ideas prompt much thought, Ricoeur asserts, "The symbol gives rise to thought" (1967, 347). Ricoeur transposes Kant's view of aesthetic ideas to the interpretation of religious symbols.

For Ricoeur, the human will does not consciously create symbols but rather discovers symbols and then interprets them. In interpreting the symbols we learn who we are and what possibilities may appear on the future horizon. Ricoeur sees a symbol as having a double meaning that must be interpreted, and so, for him, "to interpret is to understand a double meaning" (1970, 8). Ricoeur adapts Freud's notion of "overdetermination" to refer to the multiple or plurivocal signification of the symbol (1970, 19). From his intensive study of Freud, Ricoeur developed a healthy suspicion of our initial conceptions of our identity. The Cartesian hope for immediate certitude through introspection dies: our initial self-awareness is not to be trusted. To learn who we are, we must take a long journey that leads through the interpretation of signs, leading to the hoped-for gift of a new sense of identity. In subsequent works on interpretation theory, metaphor, and narrative, Ricoeur explores how metaphors create meaning through the simultaneous assertion of "is" and "is not," and how narratives both in fiction and history construct a sense of the self in time.

In light of the hermeneutics of suspicion of Marx, Nietzsche, and Freud, Ricoeur warns that our initial self-understanding is liable to be systemically distorted. He argues persuasively that both as individuals and as communities, we come to appropriate our identities not through introspection but rather through negotiating the conflict of interpretations, rereading ancient texts and wagering new self-understandings in dialogue with others. Critique is necessary but leaves a desert if not complemented by a renewed appreciation of the symbolic call of the scriptures. From Freud, Ricoeur learns to be suspicious of the surface meaning of symbols, yet he does not remain in suspicion but moves on to a retrieval on the other side of suspicion, in a second naiveté: "Herme-neutics seems to me to be animated by this double motivation: willingness to suspect, willingness to listen; vow of rigor, vow of obedience. In our time we have not finished doing away with *idols* and we have barely begun to listen to *symbols*" (1970, 27). Ricoeur advises us to approach classic expressions with both suspicion and trust, seeking a second naiveté on the other side of critique: "Beyond the desert of criticism, we wish to be called again" (1967, 349).

Ricoeur acknowledges, however, a major problem in this project. Our present communicative situation resembles the account of the tower of Babel in Genesis, where humans cannot understand each other: "This is how we are, this is how we exist, scattered and confounded, and called to what? Well . . . to translation!" (2006, 19). Marianne Moyaert reflects on the significance of Ricoeur's philosophy of translation and hermeneutics of identity for interreli-gious relations, stressing Ricoeur's focus on the "between" as central to identity and to interreligious relations: "He is a philosopher of mediation and, in view of religious plurality, his question is: How can we bring people who belong to different traditions together? How can we tear down some of the walls between different 'language' communities? How can we overcome the threat of incom-municability?" (2010, 75)

Ricoeur observes that many contemporaries see otherness as a threat and seek a secure identity by withdrawing into traditional parameters and seeking a permanent essence (1996, 4). An insecure identity seeks protection from the manifold dangers of others who are different. Ricoeur distrusts constructions of identity that defensively close out others in the quest for security, calling this "the temptation of identity" (Moyaert 2010, 76).

A traditional Italian saying warns: "*Traduttore traditore!*" ("A translator is a traitor!") Even though perfect translation is an impossible ideal, Ricoeur notes that if we wish to travel and trade, we need messengers who can translate (2006, 21). Because translation occurs, it must be possible (2006, 15). Transla-tion for Ricoeur becomes a paradigm for all human relations with those who are different from us. He cites George Steiner's statement in *After Babel*: "After Babel, 'to understand is to translate'" (Ricoeur 2006, 24). Just as the story of Babel in Genesis comes after the fratricide of Cain killing Abel, so Ricoeur interprets our situation as seeking healing after violence: "Despite fratricides, we campaign for universal fraternity. Despite the heterogeneity of idioms there are bilinguals, polyglots, interpreters and translators" (2006, 18).

On a hopeful note, Ricoeur observes that, despite the fragmented state of humanity, we still speak of humankind or humanity in the singular. Ricoeur hopes that the entwining of memories and the exchange of narratives among different peoples and religions can lead to a healing of the wounds of history. Ricoeur calls the hope for translation "linguistic hospitality" (2006, 10). He proposes linguistic hospitality as a model for interreligious communication: "It is this which serves as a model for other forms of hospitality that I think resemble it: confessions, religions, are they not languages that are foreign to one another, with their lexicon, their grammar, their rhetoric, their stylistics which we must learn in order to make our way into them?" (2006, 23-24).

Richard Kearney comments on the implications of linguistic hospitality for Ricoeur: "For it is only when we translate our own wounds into the language of stranger and retranslate the wounds of strangers into our own language that healing and reconciliation can take place. This is ultimately what Ricoeur intends when he describes the ethics of translation as an interlinguistic hospitality" (Kearney 2006, xx).

David Tracy

David Tracy has reflected on the challenge of interpreting religious classics in conversation with followers of other religious traditions. Drawing on the work of both Gadamer and Ricoeur, Tracy explores the meaning of cultural and religious classics. Tracy develops the implications of Gadamer's view of experience and hermeneutics for the conversation about religious classics in interreligious dialogue. Tracy warns that genuine conversation is very difficult because it demands interlocutors to be freed from the domination of their personal and collective egos, from the desire always to win and be right (Grant and Tracy 2005, 151-81). Genuine conversation is a search for the true, whether the discussion occurs orally with a living partner or with a text from centuries past or with the inner dialogue partner inside each person. The search for truth demands that one be ready to revise earlier interpretations and change judgments and decisions. Genuine conversations, guided by eros for the truth, are unpredictable because one can never know where they will lead. Conversations leave their participants changed, transformed, understanding their experience in a new light. As Gadamer had proposed, Tracy believes that tradition and earlier personal experience do not lock persons into fixed positions but open people to be ready for the unexpected. The scriptures and classics of the world's religious traditions are still living voices that challenge, provoke, irritate, and transform interlocutors today. While we question the past, the classics of the past question us as well.

Francis X. Clooney

The director of the Center for the Study of World Religions at Harvard University, Francis X. Clooney, has proposed a hermeneutical model of comparative theology that has been very influential. Clooney rejects the search for a general theory of religion and refuses to begin with abstract consideration of general issues such as the religious a priori. Instead, he plunges *in medias res*, into the middle of things. In *Seeing through Texts*, he thrusts the reader immediately into a poem by a Hindu saint from southern India, Shatakopan (probably eighth century C.E.). In the poem, a young woman goes to a temple to honor Vishnu-Narayana (1996, 1-4). People do this all the time, and they go home. They see the image of God, which Hindus call *darshan*, and return to their normal lives. This young woman, however, is smitten by the power of God and falls hopelessly in love. Return to her "normal" state is impossible. This concrete image serves as a warning to all who would enter temples out of curiosity—while we may think that we can enter for a brief time and then return to life as normal, we can never be sure of that. We may be forever changed.

Clooney's method is self-involving in ways that are unpredictable. When he was an undergraduate, he went to a lecture by a Jesuit from the Philippines, who urged the audience to have "hearts as large as the world" (1998, ix). The young Clooney took the challenge seriously and went to Nepal to teach high school as part of his training as a Jesuit. He later studied Indology at the University of Chicago, where he read a single poem in Tamil and became enthralled by an entire body of literature. The possibility of being transformed by a visit or a conversation or a reading of a text runs throughout Clooney's method. This means that there is no pretense of establishing a completely objective stance. Clooney embarks on the voyage as a Catholic theologian open to inquiry. He is a member of a believing community with specific doctrinal and liturgical commitments, and he encounters other religious traditions from this stance.

Clooney is influenced by Gadamer's and Tracy's accounts of genuine conversation: we risk our self-understanding by allowing the questions of the text to address us, even if they are different from our own questions. Clooney borrows Jacques Derrida's method of collage—taking texts that are very different from each other and pasting them together and prodding the reader to allow them to interpret each other in the act of reading. In doing comparative theology, Clooney takes texts and images from one tradition and inserts them into a new context, where they reveal new possibilities. He calls his text "bibliobiographical"; that is, it is largely about texts, but also about how his biography has been changed by his reading of these texts. Clooney calls this process *collectio*—a Latin term that literally means "reading together." Comparative theology can involve a *collectio*, a reading of two or more traditions together with openness to intellectual and personal transformation. The approach is modest and incremental, not seeking bold novelties or all-encompassing theories but rather exploring what is old in both traditions in the hope that the act of comparing will lead to new awareness.

A Biblical Hermeneutic of Hospitality

The Bible's hermeneutic of hospitality offers a basis for respectful encounters with other religious traditions. Pierre-François de Béthune, a Benedictine monastic leader with extensive experience in interreligious relations, reflects on the biblical models for hospitality and their analogies in other traditions: "In every culture, hospitality is a sacred duty. It may be an expression of refinement in certain civilizations, but its basic motivation is always religious. The stranger shares certain attributes with God, the mysterious stranger who visits his people" (2002, 4). De Béthune follows the example of the *First Letter of Clement*, which holds up the biblical models of hospitality through which Abraham, Lot, and Rahab received salvation: "*It was through faith and hospitality that Abraham received the son of the Promise. . . . Through hospitality and piety, Lot was rescued from Sodom* (2 Peter 2:7). *. . . Through faith and hospitality Rahab was saved* (Heb 11:11, 31). *The Lord himself guarantees the rights of aliens and immigrants* (Deut 24:14)" (*1 Clem.* 10:7; 11:1; 12:1; de Béthune 2002, 4).

De Béthune applies these biblical precedents for hospitality to the present: "Not by faith alone, but also by a hospitality that had its origin in faith. Today, more than ever, it is important that our faith is linked to hospitality, to welcoming the stranger in our midst" (2002, vii). The word translated as "hospitality" in the *First Letter of Clement* is *philoxenia*, literally the "love of [or friendship with] the *xenos.*" The Greek word *xenos* is ambiguous. It can refer to a guest deserving of ritual welcome; it can mean a friend with whom one has a hereditary treaty of hospitality; it can also mean a stranger, an unfamiliar foreigner who is perceived as a danger. When the *xenos* appears to be a menace, the virtue of *philoxenia* serves as the antidote to xenophobia.

De Béthune notes the analogous ambiguity of the Indo-European root *host*: "From this same word for host come *hospitality* and *hostility* and *hostages.* The arrival of a stranger is always something ambivalent. He can be a Trojan horse" (2002, 7). De Béthune observes that religious traditions can interpret the stranger as profane and polluting and defiling, but they can also view strangers as sacred messengers from God: "In this way we pass from hate to love in the name of religion, but sadly also from love to hate" (2002, 21). Hospitality involves a risk, but it is deeply rooted in the teaching of Jesus to love one's enemies: "In fact to receive a guest (Lat. *Hospes*) always supposes a capacity for loving one's enemy (Lat. *Hostis*)" (2002, 7). To receive a stranger as a guest requires an ability to welcome difference. While the Bible and the Christian tradition are both ambiguous regarding interreligious relations, there are grounds in the biblical heritage and the Christian hermeneutical tradition for shaping respectful, generous relations with followers of other religious paths.

Metanoia and Interreligious Interpretation

In the history of interpretation of the Bible in relation to other religious traditions, all too often a hermeneutics of hostility has shaped the horizon. Pope Paul VI's call for self-examination and *metanoia* leading to interreligious dialogue resounds through the decades. In the Catholic tradition, *metanoia* and conversion involve a number of elements. There is a critical review of the past, examining both failings and strengths, followed by a quest for forgiveness and a search for reconciliation. Despite the important differences, Christians find multiple points of contact with other traditions. The quest for justice in society, which flows from the biblical traditions, runs across religious traditions today. The Christian mystical tradition of reading the Bible in relation to union with God invites exploration in dialogue with non-dual traditions of other religions.

The encounter with the voices of other religious traditions can challenge long-held assumptions, shed new light on biblical perspectives, and open up possibilities for a renewed community of the world's religious traditions. Conversion involves more than forgiveness, for it leads into a deeper experience of God's life and invites believers to deeper union with God and with other humans, shaping new forms of community.

CHAPTER THREE

Christian Interpretations of Scripture in Relation to Jews and Judaism

Christianity's connection with Jews and Judaism is its most intimate interreligious relation, but it has tragically been extremely conflicted and problematic. As a result, reviewing the history of interpretations of the Bible in relation to Jews and Judaism can be both profoundly illuminating and deeply troubling for Christians. Nowhere can Christians gain greater insight into the roots of their tradition, including the identity of Jesus Christ; but nowhere are the tragic implications of hostile biblical interpretation more glaringly evident. In no other interreligious relationship has the transformation from hostility to generosity been so dramatic and far-reaching in such a short span of time.

In his 1937 encyclical *Mit brennender Sorge,* Pope Pius XI condemned Nazism as "an aggressive paganism" (§13); nonetheless, he also implicated the Jewish people as a whole in responsibility for the death of Jesus. Pius described Christ as taking "His human nature from a people that was to crucify Him" (§16); this assertion repeats the age-old Catholic teaching, informed by a traditional reading of the New Testament (e.g., Matt. 27:25), that the entire Jewish people was responsible for Jesus' crucifixion. After World War II, Catholics and many other Christians recoiled from such generalizing judgments about the entire Jewish people.

Because the heritage of Israel is internal to Christian faith and practice, the relation of Christians to Jews and Judaism is not simply an external liaison. Fifty years after *Mit brennender Sorge,* the interreligious climate had changed. When Pope John Paul II visited the Great Synagogue of Rome in 1986, he described the relation between Jews and Catholics in strikingly different tones from Pius XI, commenting that Christianity has an intrinsic relationship to Judaism:

> The Church of Christ discovers her "bond" with Judaism by "searching into her own mystery" (cf. *Nostra Aetate* 4). The Jewish religion is not "extrinsic" to us, but in a certain way is "intrinsic" to our own religion. With Judaism therefore we have a relationship which we do not have with any other religion. You are our dearly beloved brothers and, in a certain way, it could be said that you are our elder brothers. (1986, 4)

For Christians, the boundary between Judaism and Christianity is not a hard and fast separation. Between the Jewish and Christian traditions of interpreting the Bible, there is continuity and discontinuity, similarity and difference, agreement and disagreement. Precisely because the relationship involves so much proximity, Christians have historically had great difficulty handling the discontinuity, differences, and disagreements responsibly. Christianity's most intimate interreligious relationship has traditionally been its most difficult. Christians have chronically disputed with Jews regarding the interpretation of the Hebrew Bible and the significance of Judaism in God's plan of salvation.

Christianity's acceptance of the scriptures of ancient Israel into the Christian Bible is both a shared heritage and a controversial point of differing interpretations. No other interreligious dialogue has so many intimate ramifications for Christian self-understanding in relation to the biblical heritage. Changes in biblical interpretation in relation to Jews and Judaism have implications for every other Christian interreligious relationship. After centuries of hostile interpretation of the Bible in relation to Jews and Judaism, there have been intense efforts in recent decades to interpret the Bible in ways more respectful of Jews and the Jewish heritage. While much has happened to improve relations, serious challenges remain.

From the early church to the twentieth century, time and time again hostile interpretations of scripture shaped negative Christian attitudes and policies toward Jews. Christian interpretations of the Bible in relation to Jews and Judaism shaped Christians' own self-understanding; and Christians frequently engaged in oppositional bonding, defining their own identity in opposition to the "evil" Jews, who were seen as enemies of God and Christianity. Traditionally, Christians usually believed that Judaism had come to an end as a living tradition and had been superseded by Christianity, which could henceforth claim to be the "true Israel." Philip Cunningham comments: "For nearly two millennia the prevailing supersessionist model was not seriously critiqued. In this context, supersessionism can be defined as a network of related theological claims predicated on the assertion that the Jewish people had been replaced by Christians as the people of God (or at best relegated to a very subordinate status) because God's wrath was upon them for their alleged rejection of Christ" (2012, 144). As a result, Christians inherit a long, tragic history of animosity toward Judaism that stretches back through many centuries.

There has been much debate concerning the proper terminology for traditional Christian animosity toward Jews, with no unanimous consensus or practice at the present time. Many scholars, including Eric Gritsch (2012) and Robert Michael (2006, 2008), use the term variously spelled "anti-Semitism," "Anti-Semitism" or "Antisemitism" to refer to all forms of animosity toward Jews, including both Christian and Nazi expressions as variations of a single underlying problem. Others, however, make a distinction between anti-Judaism and anti-Semitism, proposing that the term "anti-Semitism" be used to refer to the distinctively modern hatred of Jews that is based on pseudo-scientific interpretations of race.

The modern development of anti-Semitism dates from the middle of the nineteenth century, when there emerged a new form of animosity against Jews based on a racist perversion of science. In 1855, the French Count Arthur de Gobineau published a four-volume work, *The Inequality of Human Races*. With a distorted, pseudo-biology, he argued that the white, "Aryan" race is the highest and finest form of human life, and he characterized the Jews as a separate, inferior race. He claimed that the great danger to racial purity is interbreeding, which he thought had already severely damaged the Latin and Semitic peoples. According to de Gobineau, only the Germans are a truly pure Aryan race. This ideology provided a very different basis for animosity toward the Jews from traditional Christianity and had great influence on the Nazis' later notions of racial superiority and indiscriminate hatred of persons with Jewish ancestry. In contrast to traditional Christian efforts to convert Jews, the modern, pseudo-scientific, racist anti-Semitism did not acknowledge any difference based on what Jews did religiously; de Gobineau and his later Nazi heirs viewed Jews as a lower race because of their genealogical ancestry.

The Commission on Religious Relations with Jews of the Catholic Church makes a distinction, as expressed in *We Remember: A Reflection on the Shoah*:

> Thus we cannot ignore the distinction which exists between anti-Semitism, based on theories contrary to the constant teaching of the Church on the unity of the human race and on the equal dignity of all races and peoples, and the long-standing sentiments of mistrust and hostility that we call anti-Judaism, of which, unfortunately, Christians also have been guilty. (§4)

Traditional Christian animosity toward Jews was based to a large degree on hostile theological interpretations of the Bible; its ideological basis was profoundly different from modern racist anti-Semitism. In approaching the questions of biblical interpretation, many scholars contend that "Christian anti-Judaism" is the more appropriate term to refer to traditional Christian hostility toward Jews. They maintain that the term "anti-Semitism" should be used to refer to the specifically modern racist development. For example, William R. Farmer writes to other biblical scholars: "As distinct from the term Anti-Semitism, Anti-Judaism is a specifically Christian, theologically driven attitude toward Jews, including concepts of the divine rejection and punishment of Jews, as well as Christian supersessionism and triumphalism" (quoted by Carter 1998, 49). Not all scholars, however, accept this distinction; a number continue to use "anti-Semitism" to include traditional Christian animosity toward Jews (e.g., Leibig 1983, 223-27; Nicholls 1995; Carroll 2001; Crossan 1996).

The term "anti-Judaism" is itself subject to debate and can be understood in various ways (Taylor 1995). The question of what constitutes anti-Judaism is complicated by the existence of competing forms of Judaism in the ancient world, many of which were quite antagonistic to each other (L. T. Johnson 1989). Jews past and present can be quite critical of other Jews without being "anti-Semitic" or "anti-Jewish." One of the most important developments of recent New Testament scholarship is to read the New Testament debates as intra-Jewish quarrels (Boyarin 2012). In this discussion, I will reserve "anti-Semitism" for modern movements that defame Jews in light of racial theories, and I will use "anti-Judaism" for traditional Christian animosity. I will respect the usage of other authors when quoting their works.

Assessing the New Testament

One of the most pressing challenges is to discern whether the New Testament itself is anti-Jewish.

The Apostle Paul
The earliest follower of Jesus to have left a written record of interpreting scripture is the apostle Paul. The letters of Paul, which are the oldest of all Christian writings, have had an enormous impact on Christian perceptions of Jews and Judaism. Much of the Christian tradition understood Paul as rejecting his Jewish past and as presenting a very critical assessment of the Jewish people and their allegedly legalistic religion. Jews have often regarded Paul as responsible for many of the difficulties between Christians and Jews. Paul's letters include a number of statements that reflect conflicts with other Jews, and in some passages Paul is highly critical of Jews who do not accept Jesus. His letters make a contrast between the Torah and the redemption that Paul experienced in the death and resurrection of Jesus Christ. Later generations of Christians often assumed that Paul had left Judaism and become a Christian in a world that had already experienced the division between Jews and Christians.

Roman Catholics and Protestants traditionally interpreted Paul through the lens of the theology of Augustine, and Protestants generally read Paul in light of the experience and theology of Martin Luther as well. Both Augustine and Luther went through severe personal crises in which they felt they could not fulfill the moral demands of Christianity; both experienced divine grace as releasing them from the struggle; both shaped their mature theologies in light of their respective experiences of divine grace freely given to undeserving sinners. As a result, generations of Christians understood Paul as rejecting the alleged legalism of Judaism; many Christians thought that Paul viewed the Torah in a very negative way. During the Reformation, Roman Catholics and Protestants quarreled over how Paul was to be understood. But for both sides, Paul's remarks about the Torah, often understood as "the Law," were often thought to express a fundamental rejection of Judaism and of all Jews who did not accept Jesus as Lord and Messiah. Christians generally viewed the descriptions of Paul's experience of Jesus on the road to Damascus in the Acts of the Apostles (9:1-19; 22:4-16; 26:9-18) as a conversion from the old, superseded religion, Judaism, to the new, true religion, Christianity.

In lectures originally delivered in 1963 and 1964, the Swedish Lutheran scripture scholar Krister Stendahl strongly challenged this age-old tradition of interpretation and launched a new era of scholarship on Paul (1989, 2). Stendahl argues that Paul did not go through a conversion from one religion to another but rather received a mission to bring the message of God acting in Jesus Christ to the Gentiles. On the question of Paul's identity, Stendahl maintains that "it is obvious that Paul remains a Jew as he fulfills his role as an Apostle to the Gentiles" (11). He considers the question of whether such a mission to the Gentiles should be seen as conflicting with Judaism; reflecting on Paul's comments in Romans 9-11, Stendahl comments:

> It is tempting to suggest that in important respects Paul's thought here approximates an idea well documented in later Jewish thought from Maimonides to Franz Rosenzweig. Christianity—and in the case of Maimonides, also Islam—is seen as the conduit of Torah, for the declaration of both monotheism and the moral order to the Gentiles. The differences are obvious, but the similarity should not be missed: Paul's reference to God's mysterious plan is an affirmation of a God-willed coexistence between Judaism and Christianity in which the missionary urge to convert Israel is held in check. (1989, 4)

Stendahl argues that in his discussions regarding the Torah, Paul was concerned only with the question of what obligations Gentile followers of Jesus had to accept; according to Stendahl, Paul did not pronounce any opinion on what practices Jewish followers of Jesus should observe (1989, 2). In a vigorous rebuke to his own Lutheran tradition, Stendahl charges that reading Paul through the experience of Luther or Calvin has led to most of the misunderstandings of Paul (12). While scholars have not accepted all of Stendahl's proposal, his fundamental argument that Paul did not abandon Judaism was an important step in refocusing the direction of the debates in Pauline scholarship (Dunn 2005).

From various angles, more recent scholars have stressed the continuing Jewish identity of Paul long after he had accepted Jesus as Lord and Messiah. Stanley Stowers proposes a new interpretation of the Epistle to the Romans, imagining how readers innocent of the later history of Christian interpretations would have understood it. Stowers acknowledges the powerful influence of Augustine's interpretation on the later Western psyche, but he denies that this is what Paul or his first readers would have understood. Stowers agrees with Stendahl that Paul remained a Jew after accepting Jesus as the Christ: "He neither converted to another religion replacing Judaism nor radically revised Judaism as a personal religion of faith" (Stowers 1994, 327). Stowers closes his discussion by evoking a Pauline Christianity very different from Augustine's interpretation: "Paul's letters reveal a kind of Christianity that existed before Christianity became a religion of an intrinsically sick human nature and its cure" (1994, 329). The noted Catholic scripture scholar Raymond E. Brown endorsed Stendahl's approach and posed the question whether, if Paul had had a son after he became a follower of Jesus, Paul would have had his son circumcised (R. Brown 1997, 438-39).

Recent scholarship generally maintains that in the time of Paul there was no complete separation or division between Jews and Christians. Paul remained a Jew throughout his life, long after he had accepted Jesus as Lord and Christ. Jörg Frey comments, "The common picture, inspired by the Lukan report of the turning point in Paul's life (Acts 9), of *the 'conversion' of the Jew Saul into the Christian Paul* is consequently *factually incorrect*" (2012, 57). John G. Gager pointedly asserts a series of theses concerning Paul:

> He is not the father of Christian anti-Judaism.
> He was not the inventor of the rejection-replacement theory.
> He did not repudiate the law of Moses.
> He did not argue that God had rejected Israel.
> His enemies were not Jews outside the Jesus-movement but
>   competing apostles within.
> He did not expect Jews to find their salvation through Jesus Christ.
>   (2000, 10)

One of the most important factors in hermeneutics is the composition of the interpretive community, and one of the most important developments of recent decades is the involvement of Jewish scholars as active participants in New Testament scholarship. Historically, Christians and Jews have largely read their respective Bibles in opposition to each other. Today Jewish and Christian scholars collaborate together as colleagues, studying both Testaments of the Christian Bible and increasingly reading the New Testament writings as Jewish texts. For example, Jewish scholar Daniel Boyarin sets out to "reclaim Paul as an important Jewish thinker. On my reading of the Pauline corpus, Paul lived and died convinced that he was a Jew living out Judaism" (1994, 2). Recently another Jewish scholar, Pamela Eisenbaum, has forcefully argued the thesis that Paul remained a Jew and should not be considered a "Christian" because that category did not yet exist (2009, 3-4). Eisenbaum presents Paul as a model for approaching religious pluralism: "Reconciling non-Jews to God also meant reconciling non-Jews to Jews, not because they were necessarily hostile to each other but because, if all people were potentially children of God, Jews and Gentiles must now be considered part of the same family; this entailed a new level of interaction and intimacy" (4).

Much of the later Western Christian discussion of sin and grace, both Roman Catholic and Protestant, has revolved around interpretations of Augustine, especially Augustine's reading of Paul. Thus, the recent changes in interpreting Paul pose a major challenge to Western Christian understandings of Paul on questions of sin, grace, and justification. In 2009, the International Conference of Christians and Jews met in Berlin and recalled the historic gathering in the summer of 1947, when sixty-five Jews and Christians from nineteen countries, met in Seelisberg, Switzerland, to develop better relations and chart a new path for the future. These leaders jointly condemned anti-Semitism as a sin against God and humankind, and they set forth ten points that called Christian churches radically to transform their attitudes and behavior toward Judaism and the Jewish community. In 2009, the International Conference of Christians and Jews reaffirmed the importance of developing Jewish–Christian relationships by issuing a new statement: *A Time for Recommitment: Jewish Christian Dialogue 70 Years after War and Shoah* (often referred to informally as "The Berlin Statement"). Endorsing the approach to Paul as a Jew and sharply rejecting the earlier tradition of interpretation, *A Time for Recommitment* challenges Christians to combat anti-Semitism "by recognizing Paul's profound identity as a Jew of his day, and interpreting his writings within the contextual framework of first-century Judaism" (§15). The question of whether and to what degree Paul departs from the Jewish traditions of his day in his theology of salvation continues to be debated, with major scholars taking conflicting positions.

Paul's example of interpreting Jewish scripture had a massive influence on later Christian interpreters of the Bible. According to Paul, the scriptures were written "for our sake" (1 Cor. 9:10; Rom. 4:23-24), and thus his concern is always for the present significance of biblical texts. In a passage that set an important precedent for the history of Christian biblical interpretation, Paul offers a spiritual, symbolic interpretation of the exodus, claiming that "the spiritual rock" that accompanied the Israelites on their journey out of Egypt and gave them "spiritual water" was Christ. The main focus of Paul's interpretation is on the present application:

> I do not want you to be unaware, brothers and sisters, that our ancestors were all under the cloud, and all passed through the sea, and all were baptized into Moses in the cloud and in the sea, and all ate the same spiritual food, and all drank the same spiritual drink. For they drank from the spiritual rock that followed them, and the rock was Christ. Nevertheless, God was not pleased with most of them, and they were struck down in the wilderness. Now these things occurred as examples for us, so that we might not desire evil as they did. (1 Cor. 10:1-6)

Paul warns sternly against idolatry, lest his readers fall into the same temptations as the Israelites in the wilderness and be similarly punished (Exod. 32:1-6; see also Num. 25:1-9; 1 Cor. 10:9-11). Raymond F. Collins comments on Paul's approach to the question of identity in this passage: "Notwithstanding their ethnicity Paul has virtually coöpted the Gentile Christians of Corinth into the Jewish community. He begins his exposition with a mention of 'all our ancestors.' The Israelites of the generation in the wilderness are the ancestors of the Corinthian Christians" (1999, 365). Using various forms of spiritual, symbolic interpretation, many generations of later Christians followed Paul's example in reading all the events of the First Testament symbolically in light of the experience of Jesus Christ and in relation to contemporary Christian life.

In his later correspondence with Corinth, Paul distinguishes the letter from the spirit:

The letter kills, but the Spirit gives life. Now if the ministry of death, chiseled in letters on stone tablets, came in glory so that the people of Israel could not gaze at Moses' face because of the glory of his face, a glory now set aside, how much more will the ministry of the Spirit come in glory? . . . But their minds were hardened. Indeed, to this very day, when they hear the reading of the old covenant, that same veil is still there, since only in Christ is it set aside. Indeed, to this very day whenever Moses is read, a veil lies over their minds; but when one turns to the Lord, the veil is removed. (2 Cor. 3:6-8, 14-16)

Later generations of Christians would find in these passages the basis for rejecting the biblical hermeneutics of the Jewish people (de Lubac 1998). Christians repeatedly excoriated Jews for clinging to the letter that "kills," and they proposed a wide range of distinctively Christian spiritual interpretations that were claimed to "give life" (Reventlow 2009–10, 1:118-209). However, recent biblical scholars take a different view of Paul's meaning in the context of his time. Regarding 2 Corinthians 3:6-16, Jan Lambrecht explains Paul's comments as expressing his Jewish Christian identity: "The old covenant is the ministration of death and condemnation; because of the absence of the Spirit it is only engraved on tablets of stone. No Jew who was not a Christian would speak in this way. It is a Jewish Christian who looks back on his non-Christian Jewish past" (1999, 61). Jewish scholar Alan J. Avery-Peck comments on the Jewish character of Paul's critique of the Jewish tradition in 2 Corinthians:

Even the places in which Paul differs from Jewish thinking—his negative attitude toward the law; his distinctive use of the concept of Satan (11:14)—suggest that he consistently thinks within a Jewish framework. It is one more irony of this letter that in order to deny the validity of the 'old' covenant of the flesh that God made with the Jews, Paul depends for proof on those biblical writings that embody that covenant, through which he loudly and proudly proclaims his own Jewish heritage. (2011, 316)

In his letter to the Galatians, Paul argues against those who demand that Gentile followers of Jesus observe the Mosaic Law; to support his position he interprets the Genesis account of Abraham's family allegorically. Paul urges his readers to follow the precedent of Abraham in sending away the slave woman and her son:

Now this is an allegory: these two women are two covenants. One woman, in fact, is Hagar, from Mount Sinai, bearing children for slavery. Now Hagar is Mount Sinai in Arabia and corresponds to the present Jerusalem, for she is in slavery with her children. But the other woman corresponds to the Jerusalem above; she is free, and she is our mother. . . . Now you, my friends, are children of the promise, like

Isaac. But just as at that time the child who was born according to the flesh persecuted the child who was born according to the Spirit, so it is now also. But what does the scripture say? Drive out the slave and her child; for the child of the slave will not share the inheritance with the child of the free woman. So then, friends, we are children, not of the slave but of the free woman. (Gal. 4:24-31)

The later Christian tradition generally understood this passage to refer to two separate religions: "the present Jerusalem" (Hagar) was thought to represent Judaism and "the Jerusalem above" (Sarah) was thought to represent Christianity. This interpretation formed an integral part of the broader view of Paul as fundamentally rejecting the Jewish tradition. Here again, contemporary scholars argue that in this passage, as elsewhere, Paul does not view Judaism as another religion. Rejecting the traditional interpretation of this text, Frank J. Matera follows the lead of J. Louis Martyn and reframes the discussion to make it clear that Paul is not talking about two different religions:

Paul talks about the children of two different apostolates: his circumcision-free apostolate and the circumcision-apostolate of the agitators. An important aspect of this approach is Martyn's insight that Paul is not referring to the religions of Judaism and Christianity in the Hagar-Sarah allegory but to Jewish Christians who insist upon the Law and Gentile Christians of a Pauline persuasion who do not. In other words, this passage reflects a struggle between two factions of early Christianity rather than opposition between Christianity and Judaism. (Matera 2007, 173)

On this understanding, Paul does not seek to drive out Jews or Jewish Christians as such. Rather, he is focusing on those in Galatia who reject the agreement in Jerusalem (Gal. 2:3-10) and demand that Gentile Christians observe the full Mosaic Law (R. Brown 1997, 473 n. 19).

Paul cites the Jewish scriptures in his reflections on Jews who have not accepted Jesus as the Messiah in Romans 9-11. In Romans 11:26-27, Paul cites Isaiah 59:20-21: "Out of Zion will come the Deliverer; he will banish ungodliness from Jacob." Paul then immediately adds a quotation from Isaiah 27:9: "And this is my covenant with them, when I take away their sins." From this Paul concludes that "all Israel will be saved" (Rom. 11:26), trusting that "the gifts and the calling of God are irrevocable" (Rom. 11:29); God's mercy embraces the disobedience of Jews and Gentiles alike (Rom. 11:30-32). In recent years, as Christians have sought to move beyond the long history of hostility to Jews, Paul's discussion in Romans 9-11 has been of decisive importance, including at the Second Vatican Council (*Nostra Aetate* §4).

The result of these shifts in interpretation is that the field of Pauline interpretation is no longer a basis for anti-Jewish attitudes but rather is an area for joint Jewish–Christian reflection on both continuity and discontinuity in Paul's relation to the Jewish tradition he inherited. This does not mean that all difficulties have been resolved. As Philip Cunningham notes, Vatican II and much recent biblical interpretation have stressed the positive side of Paul's comments on Jews and Judaism, but he cautions that *Nostra Aetate* passes over in silence Paul's more critical comments (2012, 142-43).

The Gospels

There have been analogous developments in the interpretation of the canonical Gospels. Many difficult questions of interpretation surround the Gospels' descriptions of Jesus in relation to other Jews. Many scholars now hold that the canonical Gospels, like the Pauline letters, were composed prior to the clear differentiation and separation of Jews and Christians into two distinct religions (Boyarin 2012; Becker and Reed 2007). Most of the first followers of Jesus were Jews who accepted Jesus as Lord and Messiah; they did not see themselves as leaving the religion of Judaism in order to join another religion of Christianity. As in the case of the letters of Paul, the Gospels are Jewish texts that demonstrate both continuity and discontinuity with the received Jewish traditions of the first century. However, there are many questions and much ambiguity.

In the Gospels, Jesus repeatedly engages in fierce polemics against Jewish leaders, including the scribes, the Pharisees, and the Sadducees. When Jewish leaders challenge Jesus for allowing his disciples to eat without washing their hands, he calls them "Hypocrites!" and severely chastises them (Matt. 15:3-9; Mark 7:1-8). Jesus cautions his disciples against the "yeast" of the Pharisees and Sadducees, meaning their evil corruption (Matt. 16:5-12). Jesus warns the crowds in Jerusalem against the example of the scribes and Pharisees, again accusing them of hypocrisy; they are "blind guides" (Matt. 23:16, 24). Jesus angrily foretells the suffering that will come upon the scribes and Pharisees:

> You snakes, you brood of vipers! How can you escape being sentenced to hell? Therefore I send you prophets, sages, and scribes, some of whom you will kill and crucify, and some you will flog in your synagogues and pursue from town to town, so that upon you may come all the righteous blood shed on earth, from the blood of righteous Abel to the blood of Zechariah son of Barachiah, whom you murdered between the sanctuary and the altar. (Matt. 23:33-36)

In light of Jesus' fierce debates with Jewish leaders, Christians traditionally often characterized Jews in general as untrustworthy hypocrites and legalists. In recent decades Christians have increasingly come to see these arguments as reflecting the intense inner-Jewish debates that were typical of the first century and beyond. When Jesus disagrees vigorously with other Jews about the practice of the Torah, this does not make him anti-Jewish. Rather, it firmly roots him in the Jewish tradition of halakhic debate. We know from the Dead Sea Scrolls that the polemics of one group of Jews against another could be extremely vehement in the first century C.E.

Christians have also more and more come to see the Gospels not as literal transcripts but rather as literary documents composed in the latter part of the first century, when there were fierce debates between followers of Jesus, on the one hand, and Jewish leaders who rejected their claims, on the other. Often the conflict narratives concerning Jesus are addressing issues of concern to the later generation and may not reflect events in the lifetime of Jesus himself.

Historically, Christians often viewed all Jews and Judaism quite harshly in light of the conflicts between Jesus and other Jews of his day. The most serious charge of all came from the climactic scene in Matthew, where the Jewish leaders and crowd in Jerusalem are presented as persuading a reluctant Pontius Pilate to have Jesus crucified (Matt. 27:25). Later Christians widely interpreted this scene to mean that all Jews who did not believe in Jesus were rejected by God, and their covenant broken off. Some held that the history of Israel came to an end at this point.

With the recognition that throughout the first century these conflicts were not yet between two completely separate religions, the context of the contemporary debate over these narratives has changed dramatically. Nonetheless, there remains the question of whether and to what degree the canonical Gospels and the Acts of the Apostles promote anti-Judaism. The long history of hostile interpretation poses the question of whether the Gospels themselves are anti-Jewish or whether the problem comes with later Christian interpretations. Scholarly opinion is divided on this question. George M. Smiga surveys the extensive scholarship regarding "Anti-Judaism in the Gospels," proposing several categories of analysis: prophetic polemic, subordinating polemic, and abrogating anti-Judaism (1992, 18-23). For Smiga, "prophetic polemic" is an internal critique within the Jewish tradition, which seeks to renew Jewish life and practice. This had long been familiar to ancient Israel and is not anti-Jewish. "Subordinating polemic" retains central features of Jewish life and practice, but it subordinates these to what has happened in Jesus Christ, especially his death and resurrection. Neither of these options involves a fundamental rejection of Judaism or the Jewish people.

Smiga reserves the term "anti-Judaism" in the full sense for the final option, which he calls "abrogating anti-Judaism," because it involves the abrogation of the Jewish religion. This perspective views the Jewish people as rejected by God and sees Judaism as completely replaced by Christianity: "God has instead ordained a 'new' Israel which replaces and eliminates the 'old' Israel" (1992, 21).

Smiga finds that the canonical Gospels are ambiguous and open to plural interpretations. He suggests that the Gospel of Mark's critique of the temple in Jerusalem can be plausibly interpreted as representing each of the options: prophetic polemic, subordinating polemic, or abrogating anti-Judaism (1992, 44). Similarly, Smiga believes that the parable of the wicked tenants (Mark 12:1-12) could be reasonably understood within each of his categories, but personally he argues that Mark was "professing a kind of subordinating polemic" (49). Smiga reads the Gospel of Mark as remaining within the horizon of Jewish life and thus as not anti-Jewish:

> Yet for all the themes of rejection and reformulation, Mark never clearly states that Israel's status has been taken away. . . . Therefore, it

seems wisest to understand Mark's evaluative claims regarding Judaism by taking the gospel at its word—and no more. Central aspects of Jewish life will have to be subordinated to Christ and the new community. Israel, however, is not abrogated. (1992, 51).

Similarly, Robert A. Guelich sees Mark's portrait of Jesus as remaining within Judaism; Jesus' criticisms of religious authorities represent a form of "prophetic anti-Judaism," similar to the biblical prophets, Qumran, and John the Baptist: "While definitely offering a challenge to the religious authorities, Jesus hardly represented a break with Judaism in Mark" (1993, 99).

Smiga stresses the Jewish character of Matthew's Gospel and the deep concern for the Torah. While he acknowledges that some texts of the Gospel could be understood as "abrogating anti-Judaism," he finds that the Gospel is ambivalent regarding Judaism but remaining within the Jewish community: "I am persuaded that this tension is best explained by reading Matthew's polemic as part of an intra-Jewish debate over the direction of the Jewish tradition after 70 CE" (1992, 90). Smiga concludes paradoxically that Matthew is not "anti-Jewish," but that the Gospel does nonetheless propose an "abrogating polemic":

> What is emphasized by "abrogating polemic" is Matthew's exclusive stance. There is reason to believe that any teaching which would not correspond to the absolute validity of Matthew's claims would be rejected. . . . The phrase "abrogating polemic" captures the absolute nature of Matthew's claims without forcing us to see the polemic as an attack on Judaism. (1992, 95)

Smiga acknowledges that later Christians "who were increasingly more Gentile" did interpret Matthew in anti-Jewish ways (1992, 95). Scot McKnight acknowledges that Matthew was traditionally understood in anti-Semitic ways, but he argues that "Matthew's Gospel, however harsh and unpleasant to modern sensitivities, is not anti-Semitic. It is, on the contrary, a compassionate but vigorous appeal to nonmessianic Judaism to respond to the Messiah" (1993, 77); according to McKnight, Matthew "is no more anti-Semitic than Amos or Jeremiah" (78).

Turning to Luke-Acts, Smiga finds a conflict of perspectives within the scholarly community: "The approach of Luke-Acts to Jews and Judaism is complex and often pulls in different directions. Flattering images and evaluations commingle with harsh programmatic statements" (1992, 97). Again, Smiga's conclusion is that reasonable interpreters can disagree. He notes that the influential work of Jacob Jervell "presents Luke-Acts as one of the most favorable works of the New Testament toward Jews and Judaism. In this view the repentant portion of empirical Israel becomes the essential link through which salvation is open to the Gentiles" (Smiga 1992, 105). However, Smiga also notes the opposing judgment of J. T. Sanders: "When Sanders' approach is adopted, Luke-Acts contains one of the most negative evaluations of Jews and Judaism within the New Testament. . . . Sanders pushes this point so far as to argue that Jews can only be valid Christians to the extent that they admit that real Christianity has left Judaism and its understanding of the law behind" (Smiga 1992, 113-14). While finding merits in both approaches, Smiga agrees more with those who see Luke-Acts as critical of Jews and Judaism: "In the end, then, I am persuaded that Luke-Acts presents a disjunctive picture of salvation history wherein the Jews have been rejected at the same time as the Christian church claims Jewish roots" (1992, 133).

David L. Tiede notes the anti-Semitic tradition of interpreting Luke-Acts, but he denies that this is reflective of its original context: "When viewed within the social world of formative Christianity and Judaism, Luke-Acts will appear to be a claimant to the heritage of Israel alongside others. In its historical setting, it is impossible for this narrative to be anti-Jewish, at least not anti-Jewish in the way it will later be used by a dominant culture of gentile Christianity" (1993, 104).

Smiga finds that the Gospel of John lends itself to multiple and conflicting interpretations. The use of the term *hoi iudaioi* in John is extremely controversial and highly debated. Traditionally translated as "the Jews," this term often has an extremely hostile connotation in John, where *hoi iudaioi* are often the adversaries of Jesus who seek his death. Smiga notes that Malcolm Lowe has proposed that the term be translated as a geographical reference to "the Judeans," referring to those in the south of Israel in contrast to Galileans or Samaritans. Urban C. von Wahlde takes *hoi iudaioi* as referring not to the entire people but specifically to the religious leaders, especially those with whom Jesus is in conflict (Smiga 1992, 163-67).

While Smiga (1992, 171) accepts von Wahlde's proposal, he nonetheless notes problems with it. Smiga warns that "arguments which intend to limit the referent of 'the Jews' invariably tend to slip into an ever-widening extension until the reference approximates all Jewish people" (168). Even if the original referent of the term was limited to the Judeans or the religious authorities, Smiga explains: "The sense of the gospel usage, therefore, is to place on the side of darkness all those who do not believe in Jesus and accept the teaching of the Johannine community. Clearly included among these are all Jewish people who do not believe in Jesus" (169). The implication is quite negative overall: "A limited anti-Jewish polemic grows into a universal one" (171).

Smiga places John's anti-Jewish polemic in the larger context of the Gospel's attack on "all who do not accept the Johannine Jesus regardless of their heritage or origins" (1992, 172). Smiga concludes: "Although the gospel of John looks with sectarian eyes beyond 'the Jews' to the greater darkness of the unbelieving 'world,' unbelieving Jews cannot be said to stand in the light. They stand with those who are rejected and condemned and testify to the abrogating anti-Judaism of the Fourth Gospel" (173).

Smiga's survey is helpful in demonstrating the variety of possible interpretations. In effect, Smiga is forced to admit the inadequacy of the threefold set of categories that he proposes. This admission in turn raises a question about the project of applying contemporary evaluative conceptual labels to such multisided and ambiguous narratives as the canonical Gospels. It is not an easy task to label the complex and conflicting first-century Gospels according to the normative criteria of the present. The Gospels have clearly given rise to anti-Jewish readings, but in their original context their language can be read in various ways. Smiga's reflections illustrate the challenge of interpreting the canonical Gospels in relation to the tradition of anti-Judaism.

Jewish scholar Amy-Jill Levine questions the helpfulness of Smiga's project, agreeing with Gerd Lüdemann "that the labels, and qualifications, and then more qualifications, are more distracting than helpful" (Levine 1999, 15, citing Lüdemann 1997, 80-81). Nonetheless, she proceeds to use Smiga's terms to analyze Matthew in light of the question of whether it is anti-Jewish or not. While she concludes that Matthew is indeed anti-Jewish, she also notes that the Gospel can be understood in different ways, depending on which passages are placed in the foreground. Citing the courageous example of Christians sheltering Jews during the Shoah, Levine notes that they did not follow the multitude of sermons preached against Jews based on Matthew 23 or 27, but rather "opened their Bibles to Matt. 25:31-46," and accepted the challenge of Jesus' parable of the Last Judgment that whatever is done to the least is done to him (1999, 36). To a large degree, the interpretation of the Bible in inter-religious relations hinges on which biblical texts are placed in the forefront of attention and which are relegated to lesser prominence. Scriptural texts can be compared to musical scores that can be performed in various ways (Leithart 2009, viii, 141-72).

One of the most problematic texts comes in the climax of the argument in the Gospel of John, when Jesus pointedly asserts to "the Jews": "You are from your father the devil, and you choose to do your father's desires. He was a murderer from the beginning and does not stand in the truth, because there is no truth in him. . . . Whoever is from God hears the words of God. The reason you do not hear them is that you are not from God" (John 8:44, 47-48). Regarding the context, Jewish scholar Adele Reinhartz comments on the Jewish character of the Gospel: "The Fourth Gospel has an overall Jewish 'feel.' . . . Jesus and most of the other characters in the Gospel are Jews, and they participate fully in the Jewish world of early first-century Palestine" (2002, 102). Many scholars point out that in its original context, the dispute can be seen as a family quarrel that has become extremely heated (Ashton 1991, 151).

Nonetheless, the harshness of the accusation remains problematic. Raymond Brown rejects the translation of *oi iudaioi* as "Judeans" because the term is used for Galileans in John 6:41, 52 (1979, 41). While the term often refers to the religious authorities, Brown warns, "John deliberately uses the same term for the Jewish authorities of Jesus' time and for the hostile inhabitants of the synagogue in his own time" (41). He adds the harsh judgment: "This makes John guilty of offensive and dangerous generalizing" (41 n. 65).

In 1995 Joseph Cardinal Bernardin visited the Holy Land together with Jewish leaders from the Chicago area, and he delivered a lecture at Hebrew University in Jerusalem entitled "Antisemitism: The Historical Legacy and the Continuing Challenge for Christians." Cardinal Bernardin frankly acknowledges the harshness of the rhetoric in the Gospel of John, and he repeats and concurs with the judgment of Catholic biblical scholar Raymond Brown: "It would be incredible for a twentieth-century Christian to share or justify the Johannine contention that 'the Jews' are the children of the Devil, an affirmation which is placed on the lips of Jesus (John 8:44)" (Bernardin 1995, 13). This is a remarkable development: a cardinal archbishop of the Roman Catholic Church is publicly and candidly acknowledging the profound problem in the language of the Gospel of John and stating that the traditional understanding of this verse cannot be taken as authoritative for Christians today.

Book of Revelation

Christians have often read the book of Revelation as condemning Jews, especially because of its castigation of "the synagogue of Satan" (2:9; 3:9). In the opening vision, the prophet sees one like the Son of Man (1:13) and receives messages to be delivered to various churches. The message addressed to the church in Smyrna asserts: "I know your affliction and your poverty, even though you are rich. I know the slander on the part of those who say that they are Jews and are not, but are a synagogue of Satan" (Rev. 2:9). While in later contexts this last phrase lent itself to anti-Jewish interpretations, Adela Yarbro Collins comments on the original context:

> The attack on the Jews in the same context (vs 9) is an indication that some Christians in Smyrna were probably accused before the Roman governor by Jews. According to Eusebius, Jewish citizens of Smyrna assisted the Roman authorities in convicting and executing some Christians in about 160, including the bishop, Polycarp. Thus the statement that the Jews of Smyrna *are a synagogue of Satan* is a remark born out of strife and controversy. It is not an expression of anti-Semitism. The title "Jew" is respected; in fact, it is claimed for the followers of Christ. (1979, 17)

Wilfred Harringon comments on the two occurrences of the phrase "the synagogue of Satan": "The sad overkill of polemic! . . . As at Smyrna opposition came from Jews . . . 'synagogue of Satan' refers to a body of ethnic Jews who reject the claim of Christians to be the true Israel" (2008, 58, 70). Even though the book of Revelation insists on justice and ultimate vindication for victims of persecution, later Christian interpreters often read it in contexts of sharp hostility to Jews and Muslims and used it as a basis for persecuting others.

Judeo-Christianity and the Patristic Heritage

The revised reading of the New Testament texts as Jewish documents is part of a much broader shift in historical scholarship on Christian origins and Jewish–Christian relations in antiquity. During the early centuries of the Common Era, followers of Jesus engaged in a series of far-reaching debates over the Bible and its interpretation. Traditionally, Christians understood these debates in the context of what was generally seen as competition between the two completely separate religions of Judaism and Christianity. Until recently, it was generally assumed that Christianity had definitively and clearly separated from Judaism in its early years—sometimes this was thought to have occurred in the ministry of Jesus himself, sometimes in the time of Paul or at the destruction of Jerusalem in 70 C.E. Sometimes it was thought that the decisive moment in the "parting of the ways" came when the rabbis met in council at Javneh in 90 C.E. and reportedly excommunicated anyone who acclaimed Jesus as Messiah. Still others looked to the end of the Second Jewish Revolt against the Roman Empire in 135 C.E. as the decisive date for the separation.

Recent scholars cast doubt on these assumptions and argue that there was a much longer period of what has been called "Judeo-Christianity," in which Jewish and Christian identities overlapped (Dunn 1999; Boyarin 2004; Becker and Reed 2007; Skarsaune 2002; Skarsaune and Hvalvik 2007). For centuries, many believers considered themselves to be Jewish followers of Jesus (Broadhead 2010). While students of early Christianity like Jean Daniélou have long been aware of Jewish Christians, scholars frequently viewed Jewish Christians as a relatively unimportant and marginal movement. Recent studies have suggested that Jewish Christian practice was far more widespread and long-lasting than had previously been thought (Jackson-McCabe 2007). For Jewish Christians or Christian Jews, there was no contradiction between being Jewish and following the path of Jesus. As John Gager argues, "they insisted that there was no need to choose between being Christians or Jews. Indeed, for them it was an altogether false choice" (2007, 370).

There were, to be sure, numerous Jews who were not in any way followers of Jesus, but increasingly Jewish scholars like Israel Jacob Yuval have recognized how important relations with Christians were for the formation of rabbinic Judaism. There were Christians such as Marcion and some Gnostics who radically opposed Judaism, rejected the Hebrew Bible, and denied that the God of Israel was the God of Jesus Christ (Frend 1984, 193-218). However, most Christians refused to follow Marcion or the Gnostics; the vast majority of Christians read the Jewish scriptures, usually in the form of the Septuagint, as what came to be the First Testament of the Christian Bible. This set up a fierce, multisided debate over the interpretation of the Jewish heritage. During the first centuries of the Common Era, there developed a complex, overlapping, and troubled network of relationships between Jews and Christians, including Jewish Christians or Christian Jews. This provides a new context for understanding early Christian arguments against Jews and Jewish practices.

As time went on, the leaders of the emerging Christian church as well as the leaders of emerging rabbinic Judaism came to view the existence of the Jewish Christian community as a serious error and a grave threat. From opposite viewpoints, both the Jewish and the Christian elite leaders argued that Jews who honored Jesus as the Christ while continuing to practice Judaism were inconsistent. Daniel Boyarin interprets the situation as analogous to Chicanos along the Mexican-American border who maintain: "We didn't cross the border; the border crossed us" (2004, 2). Jewish and Christian identities and histories for a number of centuries in antiquity were far more intertwined than we traditionally believed.

In this context the polemics could be intense. Gager notes that, according to the sociology of conflict, "the rule holds that the closer the relationship between two parties the greater the potential for conflict. In other words, whenever we encounter polemical language or the rhetoric of separation, we should look close to home for its source" (2007, 370). Jews who believed in Jesus claimed to be the true Christians and the true Jews; because of this claim, they posed a threat to those Jews and Christians who sought to draw clear boundary lines between these communities. Many scholars, including Marcel Simon (1964) and Robert Wilken (1983), have interpreted harsh Christian anti-Jewish rhetoric as a response to challenges from the Jewish community and competition in proselytization.

Eventually, the Jewish and Christian communities came to define their respective identities in distinction from and usually in harsh opposition to each other. As the Jewish and Christian traditions separated, Christians denounced Jews; as Peter Schäfer (2007) has shown, some passages in the Talmud portrayed Jesus in very negative terms. As a result, hostile attitudes toward Jews largely dominated Christian interpretations of the Bible for most of the later history of the tradition. Within this complex world, rhetoric was often heated, and harsh charges made in Christian texts would have a long-lasting negative influence on Jewish–Christian relations.

Christians often turned to symbolic, allegorical interpretation as a tool to denounce Jews. Paul's interpretation of Hagar and Sarah in Galatians 4:21-31 offered early Christian thinkers a scriptural precedent for allegorical interpretation. Paul's interpretation of Hagar and Sarah was not cited frequently in anti-Jewish writings during the second century c.e.; but beginning with Cyprian of Carthage in the mid-third century, it became the basis for numerous patristic reflections on the relation between Jews and Christians.

Interpreting the Torah

The *Epistle of Barnabas*, written in the late first or second century c.e., harshly criticizes traditional Jewish interpretations of Torah, paving the way for centuries of Christian disparagement of Jewish biblical exegesis. Barnabas maintains that even though Jews received a revelation from God through Moses, they did not understand it because they interpreted it literally and thus missed its spiritual significance: "Moses received the covenant, but the people were not worthy" (14:4). Barnabas strongly attacks Jewish religious practice and urges his readers to choose the "way of light" (18:1; 19:1). Discussing prophecies, fasting, sacrifices, the Sabbath, the scapegoat, dietary laws, and circumcision, Barnabas repeatedly accuses Jews of misunderstanding the meaning of the revelation of the Torah.

According to Reidar Hvalik, Barnabas has two central concerns regarding (1) the interpretation of scripture and (2) the two peoples and the two Ways:

A closer examination of his interpretation of Scripture reveals what he is aiming at: he seeks to show that only the Christians are able to understand the intended meaning of the texts (cf. 8:7; 10:12). This indicates that the Jews have totally misinterpreted and misunderstood God's commandments; consequently their religious observance is quite in opposition to God's will. (1996, 324)

Barnabas concludes that only Christians interpret scripture correctly and thus only Christians are heirs to the promises of the covenant. Hvalik argues that Barnabas regards both Judaism and Judaizers as threats, proposing that the most likely internal challenge came from Gentile Judaizers who wanted to practice the Mosaic Law within the Christian community (1996, 328).

Similarly, in debating with a second-century Jewish leader, Trypho, Justin Martyr understands the Mosaic precepts as "types, symbols, and prophecies of what would happen to Christ and those who were foreknown as those who would believe in him, and, similarly of the deeds of Christ himself" (*Dialogue with Trypho* 42.4; p. 64). In Justin's typology, the lamb of the Passover represents Christ (40.1; p. 61), the bells on the robes of the Israelite priests prefigure the apostles (42.1; p. 63), and the offering of flour in Leviticus 14:10 foreshadows the Eucharist (41.1; p. 62.). Justin sees no reason for continuing the practice of the Mosaic Law after the coming of Christ, since it is now obsolete: "The law promulgated at Horeb is already obsolete, and was intended for you Jews only, whereas the law of which I speak is simply for all men. Now a later law in opposition to an older law abrogates the older; so, too, does a later covenant void an earlier one" (11.2; p. 20).

Justin tells Trypho that some of the precepts of the Law of Moses "were occasioned by the hardness of your people's hearts" (45.3; p. 68). Justin is the first author recorded to interpret circumcision as a punitive measure, a sign that Jews were to be set apart from other nations and punished (16.2; p. 27; Stylianopoulos 1975, 138). In contrast to Paul, who affirmed the essential goodness of the Torah (Rom. 7:12, 16), Justin sees the Law "through penal spectacles" (Unterseher 2009, 113). Justin concludes that Christians alone possess the right of interpreting the Jewish scriptures, since they now belong to Christians. Justin tells Trypho that the words of David, Isaiah, Zechariah, and Moses "are contained in your Scriptures, or rather not yours, but ours. For we believe and obey them, whereas you, though you read them, do not grasp their spirit" (29.2; 44; see also de Lubac 1998, 242). This set the tone for Christian attitudes toward Jewish biblical interpretation for centuries.

Irenaeus of Lyons includes the experience of Israel within an all-embracing narrative of salvation from creation to the final recapitulation of all things in Christ. According to Irenaeus, God gave the Mosaic Law to Israel as training for a child to prepare them for Christ. For its time, the Mosaic Law was appropriate, but Irenaeus sees its commands as now abolished by Jesus Christ (*Adversus Haereses* 15.2; Unterseher 2009, 114). Irenaeus sees some aspects of the Law as punishment for Israel's sin of worshiping the golden calf (4.15.1; Exodus 32), but he emphasizes the educative value of this punishment (4.16.5).

Tertullian defends the Mosaic Law against Marcion (*Adversus Marcionem*), arguing that the Law itself is good and that the gospel does not contradict the Mosaic Law but enlarges it (*Adv. Marc.* 4.11; Unterseher 2009, 114-15). Tertullian stresses that Jesus did not contradict the Old Testament (*Adv. Marc.* 4.12); by fully expressing the meaning of the rituals of ancient Israel, Jesus caused them to be superseded (*Adversus Judaeos* 6). For Tertullian, the coming of John the Baptist marks the fundamental divide in salvation history, the point of separation between "old things and new, a line at which Judaism should cease and Christianity should begin" (*Adv. Marc.* 4.33; quoted by Unterseher 2009, 115). Tertullian sees no reason for Jews to continue to observe the rituals of the Law. Like Justin, Tertullian interprets circumcision as a punitive measure marking out Jews to be forbidden to enter Jerusalem; both Justin and Tertullian are aware that Roman emperor Hadrian prohibited Jews from entering the holy city (*Adv. Jud.* 3; Unterseher 2009, 115-16). Tertullian can see no basis for Jews continuing their ritual practices after the coming of Christ.

Melito of Sardis: Deicide

In the late second century, Melito of Sardis interpreted the events of the history of ancient Israel, especially the exodus, as types (*typoi*) of Jesus Christ and the church. He understood these types on the model of a preliminary sketch made by a sculptor. Once the sculpture has been completed, the preliminary sketch is of no further value. Melito writes:

> When the thing comes about of which the sketch was a type,
> that which was to be, of which the type bore the likeness,
> then the type is destroyed, it has become useless,
> it yields up the image to what is truly real.
> What was once valuable becomes worthless,
> when what is of true value appears.
> (*On Pascha* 37; trans. Stewart-Sykes 2001, 46)

According to Melito, the Jewish people had value only until the church came:

> So the type was valuable in advance of the reality, and the illustration was wonderful before its elucidation. So the people were valuable before the church arose, and the law was wonderful before the illumination of the Gospel.
>
> But when the church arose and the Gospel came to be, the type, depleted, gave up meaning to the truth, and the law, fulfilled, gave up meaning to the gospel. . . . And today those things of value are worthless, since the things of true worth have been revealed. (*On Pascha* 41-42, 43; trans. Stewart-Sykes 2001, 47, 48)

The worst charge against the Jews was not that they misunderstood the Torah; it was that they attempted to murder God in the coming of Jesus Christ. In an extremely influential reflection on the Paschal Mystery, Melito weaves biblical images of the passion of Christ into a damning judgment on all Jews:

But you cast the vote of opposition against your Lord, whom the gentiles worshipped, at whom the uncircumcised marveled, whom the
foreigners glorified, over whom even Pilate washed his hands; for
you killed him at the great feast. Therefore the feast of unleavened
bread is bitter for you. . . . You killed the Lord in the middle of Jerusalem. . . .God has been murdered. The King of Israel has been destroyed
by an Israelite right hand. O mystifying murder! O mystifying injustice. . . . Therefore, Israel, You did not shudder at the presence of the
Lord; So you have trembled, embattled by foes. (*On Pascha* 92-93,
96-97, 99; trans. Stewart-Sykes 2001, 62-63, 64)

Melito proposes a high Christology similar to that of the Gospel of John,
and he uses the term *hoi iudaioi*, usually translated as "the Jews," in a hostile manner that is also similar to the Fourth Gospel. Melito does not mention
Roman responsibility for Jesus' death at all, blaming only "the Jews." From the
time of Melito of Sardis in the late second century onward, Christians repeatedly accused Jews of deicide, the attempted murder of God. This charge would
echo through the ages into the present. Amy-Jill Levine recalls that at age seven
she was told by a Christian playmate: "You killed our Lord" (1999, 12).

Critiques of the Jews

To a hostile interpreter, the Hebrew Bible offers much material in its repeated
criticisms of ancient Israelites and Jews, and Christians interpreted many passages in Tanakh, the Jewish Bible, as maligning the Jewish people of all times
and places. In the Torah, Moses repeatedly has difficulties with the Israelites
on the long journey through the wilderness to the promised land. The book of
Exodus tells us that no sooner had the people of Israel accepted the covenant
at Mount Sinai than they broke it by fashioning the golden calf (Exod. 32:1-6).
In later centuries, the prophets of ancient Israel fiercely criticized their people,
including kings and Temple authorities. Jeremiah and Ezekiel interpret the
destruction of the First Temple by the Babylonians as God's just punishment
on the sins of the Jewish people. Tragically, Christians often took these harsh
judgments as literally applying to all Jews of all times and places—Jews were
seen as a stiff-necked people who constantly disobeyed God and repeatedly
broke the demands of the covenant. Christians interpreted what they called the
"Old Testament" as recounting Jewish misunderstanding and infidelity generation after generation; this history of rebellion against God was seen to climax
in the Jewish people's rejection of Jesus of Nazareth.

Allegorical interpretation became one of the points of contention between
Jews and Christians, since most Jews rejected Christian allegorizing. Origen
(ca. 184-ca. 254) argues against the pagan critic Celsus that, since the Bible
itself contains allegories such as Galatians 4, this style of interpretation was
willed by God (*Contra Celsum* 4.43-49; trans. Chadwick 1980, 220-24). Origen's
allegorical approach to the Bible rejects all literal Jewish interpretations: "For
the Jews, owing to their hardness of heart and their desire to appear wise in
their own sight, have refused to believe in our Lord and Savior because they

suppose that the prophecies that relate to him must be understood literally" (*On First Principles* 4.2.1; trans. Butterworth 1973, 269). This method of interpretation often involved bitter polemics, including accusations ad hominem. In rebutting the Jewish interlocutor proposed by Celsus, Origen goes on to criticize Jews in general: "But it is just like a Jew, I think, and consistent with their bitterness, when he reviles Jesus without giving any plausible argument" (*Contra Celsum* 2.29; Chadwick 1980, 91-92). Like Melito, Origen blames the Jews collectively for the death of Jesus, charging that "they refused to acknowledge the presence of our Lord Jesus Christ; nay, contrary to all right and justice, that is contrary to the faith of prophecy, they nailed him to the cross for assuming for himself the name of Christ" (*On First Principles* 4.2.1; Butterworth 1973, 270).

The Syriac Tradition

The Syriac tradition of Christianity remained close to its Jewish roots. For centuries, Syriac, which is closely related to Aramaic, the language of Jesus, was a major language for Christian literature, and Syriac-speaking Christians spread to Mesopotamia, India, Central Asia, and China. Christine C. Shepardson notes that "early Syriac Christianity was particularly Jewish in character, producing a long-lived hybrid 'Jewish-Christianity'" (2001, 502). Despite the Jewish roots of Syriac Christianity, there were nonetheless disputes, which again pose the question of whether Syriac Christian writers were anti-Jewish.

The Syriac monk Aphrahat (ca. 270-ca. 345) engaged in extended debate with his Jewish contemporaries over the meaning of the Jewish scriptures. Aphrahat summarizes the prophets of Israel as accusers of the Jewish people:

> Moses their leader testified concerning them, saying to them, "You have been rebellious from the day that I knew you" (Deut. 9:24). Furthermore, he reiterated in the hymn of testimony, "Your vine [is] from the vine of Sodom and from the planting of Gomorrah. Your grapes are bitter grapes, and your clusters are bitter for you" (Deut. 32:32). . . . And through Isaiah, the Holy One testified, saying, "I have planted a vineyard and have worked it. But instead of grapes, it brought forth wild grapes' (Is. 5:2). Again Jeremiah the prophet also said concerning the congregation of the people, 'I have planted you as a shoot which was entirely a true seed, but you have changed and rebelled against me as an alien vine" (Jer. 2:21). Ezekiel testified about the vine: "fire has consumed the twig, its middle is dried up, and it is not again useful for anything' (Ezek. 15:4). (*On Circumcision* 11, quoted by Neusner 1993, 369)

However, even in his criticisms, Aphrahat remains deeply rooted in the Jewish tradition. What makes his example all the more telling, as Jewish scholar Jacob Neusner observes, is that "what is striking is the utter absence of anti-Semitism from Aphrahat's thought. While much provoked, he exhibits scarcely a trace of the pervasive hatred of 'the Jews' characteristic of the Greek-speaking churches of the Roman orient, indeed of his contemporary John Chrysostom" (Neusner 1993, 367).

Another major Syriac author, Ephrem the Syrian (ca. 306-373), was concerned about Christians in Edessa who followed Jewish practices and attended the synagogue. He has harsh words for the Jews in Edessa, but nonetheless his writings reflect generally cordial relations between Jews and Christians. Hans Drivjers proposes that Christians in Edessa "were friends with Jews (cf. the *Doctrina Addai*), visited the synagogue, prayed with Jews and observed Jewish religious practice. Some of them may have been Jewish converts" (Drivjers 1993, 361).

Like Aphrahat, Ephrem represents the Syriac tradition that remained in close contact with Christianity's Semitic roots. Elena Narinskaya argues "that Ephrem's familiarity with Judaism is thoroughly grounded in the close interplay of the Jewish and Christian communities at that time. This emphasizes Ephrem's predisposition to, rather than any resentment of, his Jewish heritage, especially in the area of biblical exegesis" (2010, 5). Narinskaya proposes Ephrem the Syrian as an example of a Christian Jewish sage. Narinskaya points out that Ephrem draws on a detailed knowledge of Judaism and Jewish exegetical practices including wordplay, parallelism, analogy, polarization, antithesis, and testimonia (83-88).

There is a vigorous debate over how to characterize Ephrem's relationship to Jews and Judaism. While noting that some earlier scholars have interpreted him as being "anti-Jewish" or "anti-Semitic," Narinskaya rejects these characterizations (2010, 13-27): "There is no indication in Ephrem's writings to suggest that he was ever interested in racial theories and the like" (27). Regarding the charge of anti-Judaism, she comments that "this study suggests considering Ephrem's so-called anti-Jewish remarks in some of his hymns and prose works as directed homiletically at his fellow Christians and their beliefs, and not at the Jews in a spirit of confrontation and condemnation" (27). She proposes that Ephrem's critical remarks about Jews are directed at other Christians whom he sees as heretics. The context is the struggle within the Syriac church of his time, which was wrestling with issues of identity (291).

Narinskaya maintains that Ephrem never sees the Jewish people as being replaced by Christians; rather, she proposes: "I suggest the understanding of Ephrem as the author who extends Jewish boundaries (to include Gentiles). He furthers the living tradition of Judaism or a common Jewish-Christian tradition into the revelation of Christ. . . . Thus, he is supplementing the tradition, not replacing it" (2010, 42). When Ephrem cites the Jewish scriptures to criticize particular behavior of contemporary Jews, Narinskaya argues that this is not a generic indictment of all Jews: "This makes Ephrem a pro-Judaic writer working within the framework of the Semitic mindset" (45).

Even though critical of Jewish failings, Ephrem clearly respects the Jewish people. For Ephrem, the decisive moment came when Israel rejected God by worshiping the golden calf at Mount Sinai (Exod. 32:1-6). Narinskaya explains that, according to Ephrem, "This led to catastrophe for Israel as a nation, which resulted, according to Ephrem's presentation, in the loss of the ability of the people to see God. Consequently Israel did not see Christ and did not recognize Him. Thus, the loss of the ability to see God resulted in Israel losing its path of divine choice and virtue" (2010, 288). She adds poignantly, "What is important to emphasise is that this tragedy is taken by Ephrem as his personal tragedy, as well as the tragedy of the nation" (288).

Ephrem sees Christ as the focal point of both Testaments of the Bible and interprets the Jewish scriptures as witnesses to Christ: "He [Christ] is in the rod of Moses and in the hyssop of Aaron and in the diadem of David. The prophets have His likeness, but the apostles have His gospel" (*Hymns on Virginity* 8.4; 1989, 298). Ephrem addresses Christ as the Tree of Life: "Revelations gazed at You; similes awaited You; symbols expected You; likenesses longed for You; parables took refuge in you" (*Hymns on Virginity* 8.6; 1989, 298). Ephrem believes that the Passover refers to Christ and that the Jewish priesthood ended with Christ. He places responsibility for the death of Jesus on the Jewish people as a whole: "Jealous of You is the People that is aware that You will teach the peoples. By means of death they silenced You. Your death itself became endowed with speech; it instructs and teaches the universe" (*Hymns on Virginity* 8.22; 1989, 300).

Narinskaya argues that Ephrem's unique contribution is his combination of rabbinic techniques with christological interpretations of Jewish scriptures and rites such as the Passover celebration (2010, 299). He combines "high esteem for 'the chosen people' as demonstrated in his exegetical writings, and the disappointment with the contemporary Jews still denying Christ" (302). It is significant that, even as Narinskaya strives to present Ephrem's view of Jews and Judaism in the most positive light, she nonetheless must deal with his strong critique of them.

Not all scholars accept Narinskaya's defense of Ephrem. In sharp contrast, Christine C. Shepardson offers a much harsher judgment of Ephrem's rhetoric, describing it as "vitriolic anti-Jewish language" in the context of the post-Nicene christological struggles against "those in his congregation who would literally Judaize" (2008, 157), as well as other subordinationist, "Arian" opponents. Shepardson notes that Ephrem attacks Jews and Judaizers as an integral part of his struggle to establish boundaries of orthodox, Nicene Christianity. Ephrem also opposes Christians who continue to participate in Passover celebrations in the synagogues. The refrain of Hymn 19 of Ephrem's *Hymns of Unleavened Bread* is "Glory be to Christ through whose body the unleavened bread of the People became obsolete, together with the People itself" (Shepardson 2008, 32). Ephrem states that Jews stink of garlic and onions; their unleavened bread is a deadly drug, the opposite of the eucharistic drug of life. Ephrem cites the cry of the crowd that Jesus' blood be on them and their children (Matt. 27:25), and he cautions his audience to beware of Jews with their hands contaminated by blood and unleavened bread (*Hymns of Unleavened Bread* 19.25-28; Shepardson 2008, 34). When Jews invite Christians to their services in synagogues, Ephrem sees them luring Christians into danger, and he warns that "the evil People that wants our death, enticing, gives us death in food" (*Hymns of Unleavened Bread* 19.5; Shepardson 2008, 35).

Rejection of Judeo-Christianity: John Chrysostom and Jerome

Many members of Christian congregations in the late fourth and early fifth centuries continued to frequent the synagogue and combined Jewish customs and practices with Christian observance. The continuing practice of Jewish Christians evoked sharp criticism as time went on. John Chrysostom (345-407) expresses some of the harshest but most eloquent attacks on Jews in all of Christian literature. As Robert Wilken (1983) has shown, the fierce rhetoric of John Chrysostom against Judaism is directed to members of his Christian congregation in Antioch around the year 400 c.e. who were coming to church but also attending the synagogue. Chrysostom sees this as a threat to Christian identity and launches a virulent attack, charging that the Jews are the most miserable of all people, wolves who threaten the flock of Christ. He claims that the synagogue is a place of drunken parties where prostitutes and thieves gather.

Chrysostom compares Jews to brute animals who are "unfit for work" but "fit for killing." In a horrifying application of the conclusion of Jesus' parable in Luke 19:11-27, Chrysostom asserts: "Although such beasts are unfit for work, they are fit for killing. And this is what happened to the Jews: while they were making themselves unfit for work, they grew fit for slaughter. This is why Christ said: 'But as for these my enemies, who did not want me to be king over them, bring them here and slay them' (Lk 19:27)" (*Discourses against Judaizing Christians* 2.6; 1979, 8). Chrysostom's rhetoric was extreme. Fortunately, in the later Christian tradition the judgment of Augustine that Jews should be allowed to live would carry more authority.

Marcel Simon comments on the audience and context of John Chrysostom's sermons in Antioch:

> They are not aimed at the Jews at all. It is the Judaizing Christians of Antioch who are addressed. Thus the arguments they offer are really for internal consumption.... It is the devices of the Jews and the drawing power of the Synagogue that they are designed to meet.... They did not spring from any reflection on scripture, but were prompted by living example. They developed through contact with strong and lively Jewish communities. There could be no Judaizers if there were no Jews. (1964, 145)

Jerome (ca. 347-420) fiercely opposed Origen's style of biblical hermeneutics, but like Origen he immersed himself in the study of Hebrew so that he could read the First Testament in its original language. Prior to Jerome, translations of the First Testament into Latin were based on the Greek Septuagint, which Augustine and many others thought to be an inspired translation. Jerome for the first time translated the Hebrew Bible directly from Hebrew into Latin, and the resulting Vulgate Bible shaped the way Latin Christians understood these texts for centuries. Jerome did not think the deuterocanonical works were inspired, but he translated some of them into Latin.

Jerome saw Judas Iscariot as a representative symbol for all Jews, whom he characterized as malicious, blind, and ungrateful (Hood 1995, 16). Jerome did not see Jews as playing any positive role in history after the coming of Christ and viewed their continuing existence as a community as an affront to God. Jerome interpreted the Antichrist in an anti-Jewish manner, predicting that he will be born as a Jew from a virgin, in a parody of Jesus, and he wondered if the time of the Antichrist was drawing near (McGinn 1994, 75). The association of Jews and the Antichrist would have a long history in later ages.

Jerome was familiar with Nazarene Jewish Christians, though it is not clear if he had direct personal contact with them. He was aware that they were in synagogues throughout the East, that they were cursed by the Pharisees, that they had a Gospel in Hebrew, and that they combined faith in Jesus Christ with observance of the Mosaic Law (Pritz 1988, 55). Like John Chrysostom, Jerome firmly opposed the practice of Jewish Christianity and summarized bluntly what became the official attitude of the church: "As long as the Nazoreans want to be both Jews and Christians, they are neither Jews nor Christians" (*Epistle* 112.13, quoted by Strecker 1993, 32). After much debate and conflict, both Christian bishops and Jewish rabbis would agree with Jerome.

Augustine of Hippo

Augustine of Hippo (354-430) proposed one of the most influential interpretations of scripture in relation to the Jewish people in the history of Western Christianity. As we have seen, Augustine developed a very influential form of symbolic interpretation of the Bible, which hinged on the criterion of whether an interpretation supported charity or cupidity. Like earlier authors, Augustine charges that Jews read the Bible in a carnal, material manner and thus misunderstand its promises: "The Jews, it is true, worship the one omnipotent God, but they expect from him only temporal and visible goods. Being too secure they were unwilling to observe in their own Scriptures the indications of a new people of God arising out of humble estate, and so they remained in 'the old man'" (*On True Religion* 5.9; trans. Burleigh 1964, 11). While he criticized Jews for their literal-mindedness in reading the Bible, he nonetheless saw them as playing a vital and continuing role in history.

Augustine proposes a thoroughly Christocentric interpretation of the Bible according to which the entire "Old Testament" can be understood figuratively to apply to Jesus Christ. According to Augustine, the events in the Old Testament did occur historically, but their full significance is seen only in relation to Christ. Thus, all the events of the exodus and the Passover lamb all find their true meaning by pointing beyond themselves to Jesus Christ (*De Doctrina Christiana* 2.40.61; trans. Hill 1996, 160; Unterseher 2009, 102). "So they [students of the divine scriptures] should remember how those who celebrated the Passover at that time as a shadow and image of things to come" (2.41.62; Hill, 161).

Augustine understands Jeremiah's command to circumcise the foreskin of the heart (Jer. 4:4) as applying to the spiritual interpretation of the Bible

(Unterseher 2009, 102). Nonetheless, arguing against the Manicheans, Augustine insists that Christians cannot omit the Jewish scriptures because they refer to Christ. Thus, there is what Lisa Unterseher calls a "double movement": "The figurative meaning of the Old Testament is understood only with the coming of Christ. Yet, Christ's advent cannot be understood apart from the foreshadowings found in the Old Testament" (2009, 103). According to Augustine, the Old Testament presents promises which find fulfillment in the New Testament (*City of God* 18.11; trans. Dyson 1998, 834). Augustine believes that because the covenant has now passed to the Christian church, Christians are the true Jews; he also thinks that the Mosaic Law had been written in stone, but the new covenant of the gospel is in the heart (*De Spiritu et Litera* 17.29).

Even though Jews failed to understand their own scriptures, Augustine nonetheless saw them as invaluable though unwitting witnesses to Jesus Christ because they demonstrated to pagans that Christians did not invent the biblical prophecies of Christ (Harkins 2008). Augustine praised Jews for following the Mosaic Law before the coming of Jesus Christ, and he recognized that the first generation of Jesus' followers continued to practice the Mosaic Law, but after the destruction of the Temple, there was no place for continuing such practices.

Early in his career Augustine set a major precedent for the later tradition by interpreting all Jews in light of the curse of Cain. Augustine saw Abel as a type of Christ, offering faithful praise of God in his blood offering. Augustine saw Cain as a type of the Jews, bound to the earth. As the elder brother Cain killed his younger brother, so Augustine saw the elder brother, the Jews, killing Christ, the head of the "younger" people, the Gentiles (*Against Faustus* 12.9; Fredriksen 2008, 264). When Cain is being punished for the murder of his brother, in Genesis 4:15, God responds to Cain's worry that anyone who meets him may kill him: "Then the Lord said to him [Cain], 'Not so! Whoever kills Cain will suffer a sevenfold vengeance.' And the Lord put a mark on Cain, so that no one who came upon him would kill him." The mark of Cain is a lasting sign of guilt, but it is primarily intended to protect the life of Cain. Augustine applies both senses of the mark of Cain to all Jews through the ages: they are to be protected but also kept in a subordinate position (Unterseher 2009, 8). For Augustine, the curse of Cain corresponds (1) to the persistent and distinctive identity of Jews and (2) to their ubiquity throughout the world. God protects the Jews but scatters them (Fredriksen 2008, 265).

Later in his career, in *City of God* Augustine quietly drops the reference to Cain and turns instead to Vulgate Psalm 58:12-13 [59:10-11]: "As for my God, his mercy will go before me; my God has shown me this in the case of my enemies. Do not slay them, lest at some time they forget your Law; scatter them by your might" (*City of God* 18.46; Fredriksen 2008, 348). Augustine cites Paul in Romans 11:11, noting that the failure of Jews to accept Jesus has meant salvation for Gentiles. Augustine explains that Jews should not be slain "for fear that they might forget the Law of God and thus fail to give convincing testimony on this point"; on the other hand, he adds that it was not enough for the Psalmist to say "do not slay them . . . with-out adding, 'Scatter them.'" For if they lived with that testimony of the Scriptures only in their own land, and not everywhere, then the Church, which is everywhere, would not have them available among all the nations as witnesses to the prophecies given beforehand about Christ. (*City of God* 18:46; Fredriksen 2008, 348)

In large measure Augustine's views were responsible for shaping the long-last-ing policy of the Catholic Church that Jews were to be allowed to live, albeit in subordinate circumstances (Fredriksen 2008).

Supersessionism in the Patristic Heritage
In his magisterial survey of patristic and medieval exegesis, written in the years following the end of the Shoah, Henri de Lubac surveys the long history of patristic and medieval Christian exegesis and recapitulates the Christian claims to have displaced the Jews. Personally, de Lubac was very courageous in resisting the Nazi occupation of France during World War II. He supported the French resistance, and he openly condemned anti-Semitism. Nonetheless, in his theological work, de Lubac reprises the supersessionist rhetoric of early church writers, triumphantly proclaiming that, after the events of the death and resurrection of Jesus Christ and Pentecost, "the Church took the place of Israel. . . . She is Abraham's posterity, the only one in possession of his heritage" (1998, 241). De Lubac confidently expresses the victorious claim of the Chris-tian tradition: "The book [the Bible] is now in their [the Christians'] hands. It belongs by right to these new people, because they are the people of Christ. . . . The great transition has taken place" (241).

De Lubac repeats without dissent the patristic and medieval view that Jews have been completely displaced by Christians; the Christian Church "now possesses, in her living reality, 'the truth of figurative expressions.' She is the 'just Remnant' announced by Isaiah. She is that 'people of the New Covenant' promised by Jeremiah, that Israel 'raised from the dead' which is contemplated in a vision by Ezekiel, that 'people of the secrets of the Most High' prophesied by the Book of Daniel" (1998, 241). "Her head men, the twelve Apostles, are the twelve true sons of Jacob" (241). De Lubac quotes approvingly Gregory of Nazianzus, who proclaims: "That which is ancient has passed away, everything has become new! The letter gives way, the Spirit surpasses it; the shadows lift, Truth makes its entry" (de Lubac 1998, 259). With no sign of disagreement, de Lubac notes that medieval Christians viewed Jews solely in the role of librar-ians who present to Christians a book that they themselves cannot under-stand: "The Synagogue, which has become blind and sterile, is merely her [the Church's] librarian" (242).

Referring to 2 Corinthians, de Lubac notes the importance of "the Pauline symbol of the veil that covered the face of Moses, that veil of the letter which formerly hid the secret of the spirit, which finds its expression through the facial features" (1998, 251). De Lubac also cites interpretations of Zechariah entering the temple "at the hour of incense," that is, the evening; Christians understood that this was "because, as the sun set then behind the temple, even so was night falling on the Jewish religion. The day of the law was growing dim, in order to give way to the dawn of the Gospel" (251).

Traditionally, Christians criticized Jewish interpretations for clinging to the letter and missing the spiritual sense, and de Lubac comments that for the medieval Christian tradition, Jesus Christ "*kills* the shadows and images in terms of their literal meaning" (1998, 239; emphasis in original). When the Psalmist predicts that "the night will be illumined like day," Christians understood this to refer to the coming of Jesus (238).

The Early Middle Ages

The anti-Jewish interpretations of the Bible that appear in the early church fathers shaped Christian life throughout the Middle Ages and beyond. In particular, the charge that the Jews of each age were responsible for killing Christ echoed through the ages. Regardless of whether Christians could read the biblical passages or the church fathers for themselves, they heard texts and sermons critical of Jews proclaimed in their liturgies year after year, century after century. Tragically, often Christian celebrations of the death of Jesus on Good Friday would lead to attacks on Jews. Veneration for the cross of Christ often led to vengeance against his murderers, who were understood to be the contemporary Jewish community.

Pope Gregory I had a major influence on the policies of the medieval Catholic Church toward Jews. Gregory interpreted the parable of Lazarus and the rich man (Luke 16:19-31) in an anti-Jewish manner, with the poor, wounded Lazarus representing the Gentiles and the rich man representing the proud Jewish people:

> Whom, dearest brothers and sisters, whom does this rich man clothed in purple and fine linen who feasted sumptuously each day indicate, other than the Jewish people who, having the visible trappings of a fine life, put the delights of the law they had received to the use of their own splendor rather than any good purpose? . . . But the wounded Lazarus *longed to be fed by the crumbs which fell from the rich man's table* [Luke 16:21], and no-one gave him any, because that proud people disdained to admit any gentile to knowledge of the law. It viewed the teaching of the law as a matter not of charity but of self-regard, puffing itself up, as it were, on account of the riches it had been given. (*Homiliae xl in Evangelia* 40.2; Moorhead 2005, 75)

Gregory accepted Augustine's principle that the Jews were not to be killed, and he repeatedly intervened to protect Jews from violence. In 598 Jews in Rome complained to Gregory about alleged injustice done to the Jews in Palermo. Gregory wrote to the bishop of Palermo: "Just as the Jews should not have license in their synagogues to arrogate anything beyond that permitted by law, so too in those things granted them they should experience no infringement of their rights" (*Epistolae* 8.25; Novikoff 2010, 65). The opening words of this bull, *Sicut Judaeis,* would live on in the later Catholic tradition, and the bull was reissued multiple times in later periods (Novikoff, 66). In the letter Gregory tries to balance the competing claims in light of the legal precedents, instructing the bishop: "Therefore, if the complaint is based on the truth, your Fraternity ought to examine the import of the law for them diligently, and you should protect and preserve whatever has been decreed about this matter, in such a way that neither you appear to be doing something unjust, nor do they seem to be suffering from prejudice" (*Epistolae* 8.25; trans. Martyn, 2004, 2:521).

Gregory referred to Jews frequently in his biblical commentaries and in his *Moralia* on Job. Gregory saw the Jewish people as blind because of their sins; thus age after age they failed to recognize Jesus. He saw the Jews as carnal because they clung to the literal sense of the Bible and missed its spiritual significance. He believed that the devil lived among them and that they were linked to the Antichrist until the end of time, when they would be converted (Novikoff 2010, 66). His dual precedent of legally protecting Jewish life and of actively seeking their conversion would shape Latin Christian practice for centuries.

In the Carolingian period, Rabanus Maurus (ca. 780-856) interprets the unclean animals in Leviticus as symbolic of sinful conditions, and he interprets the prohibitions concerning eating unclean animals as symbolic: "If indeed 'man does not live by bread alone, but in every word which proceeds from the mouth,' then just as bread is the nourishment of the body, so also the Law of God is the nourishment of the soul" (*Expositionum in Leviticum* 3.1; quoted by Firey 2010, 209). He concludes that Jews are unclean because they "ruminate upon the words of the Law but do not divide the hoof, that is, because they do not receive the two Testaments, and do not place the steps of their faith on the Father and the Son" (3.1; in Firey 2010, 209). Rabanus continues: "The camel is the Jews, swollen with pride, just as were the Scribes and Pharisees, to whom the Lord said, 'straining out a gnat and swallowing a camel.' Therefore the Scribes and Pharisees eat while ruminating, because they glory in meditation upon the letter of the law. . . their knowledge is unclean" (3.1; in Firey, 209).

In the early Middle Ages, the celebration of Good Friday often became the prelude to attacks on Jewish communities. In the ninth century, in Toulouse, the custom began of striking a Jew on the face on Good Friday as punishment for the crucifixion of Jesus. In Beziers, France, Christians would listen to a sermon by the bishop on Palm Sunday and would then proceed to stone the houses of Jews; this custom lasted in that location until 1160. For the first millennium of Christian history, attacks on Jews were, for the most part, rhetorical rather than physical.

Isidore of Seville (ca. 560-636) associated all those outside the church, including the Jewish people, with the Antichrist, and later Agobard of Lyons (ca. 779-840) specified more precisely in a letter to Emperor Louis the Pious that Jews were all antichrists (Gabriele 2007, 64). As the year 1000 approached, there were bitter expressions of anti-Jewish sentiment that poisoned the atmosphere in the eleventh century and beyond. About 950, the abbot Adso of Montier-en-Der (d. 992) wrote "The Letter on the Origin and Time of the Antichrist," which predicts that the Antichrist will be a Jew of the tribe of Dan, fulfilling the prophecy of Dan being a snake, an adder (Gen. 49:17). According to Adso, at the time of the Antichrist's conception, the devil will enter his mother's womb in a perverse parody of the Holy Spirit's role in the conception of Jesus, "so that with the devil's cooperation she will conceive through a man and what will be born from her will be totally wicked, totally evil, totally lost. For this reason that man is called the 'Son of Perdition' (2 Thess. 2:3), because he will destroy the human race as far as he can" (in McGinn 1979b, 91).

According to Adso, after being born in Babylon, the Antichrist will go together with evil spirits and magicians to Jerusalem where he will circumcise himself and where Jews will flock to him. Adso warns that the Antichrist will torture and kill all Christians whom he cannot dominate. Weaving together predictions from multiple biblical books, Adso predicts a dire conflict. "Even though he is a man, he [Antichrist] will still be the source of all sins and the son of Perdition, that is, the son of the devil, not through nature but through imitation because he will fulfill the devil's will in everything" (McGinn 1979b, 93). The Antichrist will torture and dominate the people of God for three and a half years, but then, as Paul predicts, "The Lord Jesus will kill him with the breath of his mouth" (2 Thess. 2:8; McGinn 1979b, 96). The letter powerfully fostered animosity toward Jews throughout Europe. Jews would long be associated with the Antichrist.

The High Middle Ages

In Claremont, France, in 1095, Pope Urban II called for European Christians to take up arms to rescue the Holy Land from Islamic forces. Even though the pope reportedly made no mention of attacking Jews, many Christians noted that nearby Jews were also enemies of God. In Normandy, as Crusaders were preparing to fight the Saracens in the distant Holy Land, they asked why they should attack Muslims who were so far away while sparing the Jews who were close at hand (Golb 1998, 117-19). In Romans 11:25-27, Paul had hoped that both Gentiles and Jews would accept Jesus Christ before the end-time. Apocalyptic excitement contributed to an atmosphere in which Jews were offered a choice of conversion to Christianity or death (Gabriele 2007, 68-74). One of the main leaders of violence against Jews, Count Emicho of Flonheim, apparently believed the eschatological end-time had begun and saw himself as the apocalyptic Last Emperor.

Crusaders began their attacks on Jews in the spring of 1096, especially around Holy Week, when the death of Christ was observed. A Jewish chronicler recalls that it was on the fifteenth day of the month of Nisan, the first day of Passover, that Peter the Hermit arrived in Trier as an emissary of the French Crusaders and demanded support. That year Peter preached a Good Friday Sermon in Cologne that so inflamed the congregation that it went forth as a mob seeking Jews to punish (Carroll 2001, 246-50). Many church leaders opposed the attacks; Bishop Cosmas in Prague, Bishop Adalbert II in Worms, Bishop John in Speyer, and Archbishop Ruthard in Mainz did their best to protect the Jews in their areas. Catholic leaders in Hungary refused to allow Emicho and his troops to enter. The emperor Henry IV ordered Jews to be protected, but despite these efforts the First Crusade marks the beginning of a markedly higher scale of physical violence against Jewish communities.

About a century later, Pope Innocent III marks another turning point in Jewish–Catholic relations, for he viewed Jews as a source of pollution and a threat to the purity of Catholics (Tolan 2012, 4). In 1208, a papal bull of Pope Innocent to Count Hervé IV de Donzy of Nevers, France, regarding the Jews bears the title of its opening words: *Ut esset Cain* ("As Cain was [wandering and fleeing on earth]"). Innocent interprets the situation of thirteenth-century Jews in Europe in light of the curse of Cain. Just as Cain was not to be killed, so Innocent directs that Jews are not to be killed; but just as Cain had to be punished for his crime, so Jews must be kept in a subordinate status because of their murderous crime of killing Christ (Tolan 2012, 7). In accordance with this biblical precedent, Innocent condemns activities such as Jews nursing Christian children, hiring Christian servants, or lending money to Christians; all these actions threatened to reverse the Jews' subservient position in society and thus were suspect according to Innocent. Innocent reprimanded Christian rulers in France for not keeping the Jews firmly in the subordinate position that they deserved. He also applied the blood curse of Matthew 27:25 to the Jews of his day (Tolan 2012, 7).

In the thirteenth century, there developed a body of Catholic canon law that both protected the continued existence of Jews as a community and also kept Jews segregated and in a subordinate position in society. At the request of Jews who sought papal protection, Pope Calixtus II (1119–1124) promulgated a "Constitution for the Jews" with the same title as Gregory I's bull: *Sicut Iudaeis*. This document protects Jews from injury as long as they do not plot against Christians, but it also chastises them for not accepting Christ (Hood 1995, 29-30). In 1234, Pope Gregory IX incorporated this Constitution into his collection of canon law, the *Decretales*. This document, based on Augustine and Gregory I, set the main outlines of papal policy for centuries.

Thomas Aquinas

Thomas Aquinas, like his predecessors and contemporaries, assumed that the Bible has multiple senses, but he transformed exegesis by insisting that theological arguments must be based on the literal sense of the Bible, thereby setting limits to the use of allegorical interpretations in theology: "Thus in Holy Writ no confusion results, for all the senses are founded on one—the literal—from which alone can any argument be drawn, and not from those intended in allegory (*Summa Theologica* [ST] 1.1.10.1; 1947, 7). Aquinas holds that God can signify meanings "not by words only (as man also can do) but also by things themselves" (ST 1.1.10; 1947, 7). Thus, through the working of God's intentionality, the prescriptions of the Mosaic Law and the persons and events of ancient Israelite history can signify Jesus Christ and events in the New Testament.

Within the spiritual sense, Aquinas accepts the traditional distinction of allegorical, anagogical, and moral meanings. He accepts the principle of allegory from the Letter to the Hebrews (10:1), which teaches that the Old Law is the figure of the New Law; he finds the principle for anagogical reference in the *Celestial Hierarchy* of Pseudo-Dionysius the Areopagite (1): "the New Law itself is a figure of future glory"; he finds the moral sense in the actions of Christ in the New Testament: "Again, in the New Law, whatever our Head has done is a type of what we ought to do" (ST 1.10.1; 1947, 7):

> Therefore, so far as the things of the Old Law signify the things of the New Law, there is the allegorical sense; so far as the things done in Christ, or so far as the things which signify Christ, are types of what we ought to do, there is the moral sense. But so far as they signify what relates to eternal glory, there is the anagogical sense. Since the literal sense is that which the author intends and since the author of Holy Writ is God, Who by one act comprehends all things by His intellect, it is not unfitting, as Augustine says (*Confessions* 12), if, even according to the literal sense, one word in Holy Writ should have several senses. (ST 1.1.10; 1947, 7)

Aquinas believes that "nothing necessary to faith is contained under the spiritual sense which is not elsewhere put forward by the Scripture in its literal sense" (ST 1.1.10.1; 1947, 7). Aquinas includes metaphors, which he calls the "parabolical sense," in the literal sense: "The parabolical sense is contained in the literal, for by words things are signified properly and figuratively. Nor is the figure itself, but that which is figured, the literal sense. When Scripture speaks of God's arm, the literal sense is not that God has such a member, but only what is signified by this member, namely, operative power" (ST 1.1.10.3; 1947, 7).

Aquinas views Jews in light of the different stages in the economy of salvation. From the covenant at Mount Sinai until the coming of Jesus Christ, Jews were the people in covenant with God. Like his medieval contemporaries, Aquinas looked at the events in the history of Israel recounted in the Bible as symbolic anticipations of Jesus Christ and the church. The Mosaic Law contains a hidden sense that teaches moral and religious knowledge of Christ; Aquinas explored this meaning at length in his "Treatise on the Old Law" in the *Summa Theologica* 1-2.98-105.

Aquinas interprets the Mosaic Law in response to the challenge of Moses Maimonides' Jewish interpretation in *Guide of the Perplexed* and in dialogue with Aristotle's *Politics*. The result is that, for Aquinas, Moses emerges as a type of philosopher-king viewed through the lens of Roman legal concepts and interpreted both as a purveyor of wise legislation and as a type of Christ's future coming (Hood 1995, 40-41). Aquinas searched for the literal sense of the Mosaic Law in relation to the concrete historical context of ancient Israel, and he also probed its deeper mystical significance in relation to Christ and the church.

Based on his reading of the Pentateuch, Aquinas thought that ancient Israelites were idolatrous, cruel, and avaricious and thus needed guidance. He commented that the Mosaic Law allowed lending money at interest to foreigners (Deut. 23:19, 20) not to approve of the practice in itself, "but only to tolerate it on account of the proneness of the Jews to avarice" (ST 1-2.105.3.3; 1947, 1100). He interpreted the function of the Mosaic Law on different levels, depending on the audience: "For the obstinate, the Law was given as a whip. . . . For the proficient who are called 'ordinary,' the Law was a pedagogue. . . . For the perfect, the ritual commandments functioned as mystical signs, while the moral precepts assured them that their actions were upright" (*Commentary on Romans* 5.6; Hood 1995, 42).

In contrast to patristic authors, Aquinas believed every prescription of the Law had a literal, historical meaning; but he subordinated the Law of Moses to Christ. Based on his understanding of Paul, Aquinas believed that the Mosaic Law could not produce righteousness because its prohibitions increased desire (Hood 1995, 43). Aquinas accepted much of Moses Maimonides' positive appreciation of the Law in its literal sense. However, where Maimonides celebrated the religious truth and moral virtue offered by the Law, Aquinas saw these as just a starting point, preconditions for the coming of Christ, who alone would bring salvation. Where Maimonides acknowledged that some ceremonial commandments of the Law were unclear, Aquinas interpreted this situation in terms of symbolism: "for all precepts relating to the worship of God are necessarily symbolic . . . and this is why their rational basis is not entirely clear" (ST 1-2.101.1 ad 4; Hood 1995, 50). Such commandments could refer to the interior state of the worshiper, but Aquinas viewed the unclear commandments as primarily symbolizing Christ (Hood 1995, 51). The sacrifices of the Law symbolize above all the passion and death of Jesus Christ. These Jewish sacrifices had no power of their own to save from sin, but they could symbolize Christ and thus become a means of justification through faith in Christ (ST 1-2.103.2; Hood 1995, 55). Because the Jewish rituals had a symbolic meaning, they could mediate saving faith in Christ. Aquinas believed that the patriarchs and some other figures of the Old Testament believed that Christ would come and thus had faith in Christ and his saving work (Hood 1995, 55).

Aquinas noted that relations with foreigners can be peaceful or hostile (ST 1-2.105.3), and he considered the question of whether the Mosaic Law's precepts regarding foreigners were suitable. He observed the universal invitation: "The Law excluded the men of no nation from the worship of God and from things pertaining to the welfare of the soul" (ST 1-2.105.3.1; 1947, 1100). Aquinas noted the Law's provisions for incorporating foreigners into fellowship with the Israelites and their form of worship. However, he was also aware of the troublesome command in Deuteronomy 20 to kill an entire population, and he posed the objection that "men are much more akin to us than trees. But we should show greater care and love for these things that are nearest to us. . . . Therefore, the Lord unsuitably commanded (Deut. 20:13-19) that all the inhabitants of a captured hostile city were to be slain, but that the fruit trees should not be cut down" (ST 1-2.105.3.ad 4; 1947, 1099). In response to the objection, Aquinas maintained that execution of the entire population in the neighboring cities was an appropriate punishment for sin manifesting the divine justice: "But in the neighboring cities which had been promised to them [the Israelites], all were ordered to be slain, on account of their former crimes, to punish which God sent the Israelites as executor of Divine justice: for it is written (Deut. 9:5): *Because they have done wickedly, they are destroyed at thy coming in.*—The fruit trees were commanded to be left untouched, for the use of the people themselves, to whom the city with its territory was destined to be subjected" (ST 1-2.105.3.4; 1947, 1101).

Thomas Aquinas shares the common medieval judgment that Judaism lost its legitimacy at the time of the crucifixion of Jesus. The moral precepts of the Old Law continued to be still valid, but after the coming of Christ the ceremonial precepts lost their validity (ST 1-2.103.3; 1947, 1084-85). Jesus gave Jews a choice: those who accepted him found salvation, but those who rejected him became cursed infidels, condemned to homelessness and wandering. Aquinas believed that pride and self-interest led the Pharisees and Temple priests to reject Jesus, who threatened their authority with the people. Aquinas describes the reasons for the hostility of Jewish leaders toward Jesus after the resurrection of Lazarus in the Gospel of John: "The root of their problem was that they feared the losses that would follow. . . . First, their loss of spiritual leadership . . . for they believed that no one who believed in Christ would obey them. . . . Secondly, he [the Evangelist] mentions their ambition for temporal possessions" (*Commentary on John* 11:7; 2010, 2:252, 253). Thomas believes that some Jewish leaders recognized that Jesus was the savior but they dissuaded the crowds from believing this. He thought that Judas acted out of greed, the Jewish leaders out of envy, and Pilate out of worldly fear (ST 3.47.3.ad 3; Hood 1995,71). Aquinas believes that Jesus' prayer to God on the cross asking forgiveness for his executioners applied only to those who were genuinely ignorant. However, the leaders were culpable of the crime of deicide. Thomas believes that because of their rejection of Jesus Christ, Jews are guilty of mortal sin and cast into exile; by continuing to observe the Mosaic Law, Jews assert that the Christ is still to come and thus lose their status as the "true Israel."

Nonetheless, Thomas also ponders Paul's hope in Romans 9–11 that Jews will one day accept Jesus Christ. Steven Boguslawski argues that in his commentary on Romans, especially on chapters 9–11, Thomas Aquinas moves beyond the anti-Judaism of his contemporaries and follows Paul in upholding "the inherent dignity of the Jews as God's chosen people and their vital role in salvation history" (2008, 128). Aquinas follows Paul in seeing a providential role in the Jews' rejection of Jesus Christ, since it leads to the inclusion of Gentiles in the plan of salvation. Boguslawski points out that, for Thomas as for Paul, both Jews and Gentiles are sinners deserving of condemnation; those who are elected by God are recipients of unmerited grace due to the will of God (64). Thus, there is no basis for one community to boast against the other: "For Aquinas, God loves the elect more because he wills more good for them, and these chosen are taken from among Jews and Gentiles alike. Divine election effectively relativizes the status of Jew and Gentile, making them equal in their present call, justification, and glorification" (65). Boguslawski summarizes Aquinas's central theological convictions, based on Romans 9–11: "[I]t is God who predestines and elects; it is God who grants Jew and Gentile their privileged status; it is God who saves 'all Israel' once the 'fullness of the Gentiles' has entered into salvation, and it is God to whom the synagogue and the church are accountable" (129). Boguslawski concludes that in his commentary on Romans 9–11, "Thomas is not anti-Jewish: he remains faithful to the plot line established by Paul" (129). Thus, Boguslawski proposes Thomas Aquinas as a positive precedent for contemporary efforts to improve Jewish–Christian relations by reflecting on Paul.

Later Middle Ages

In the late thirteenth century in Normandy, a noted debater named Paul Christian, a former Jew who had become a Christian, disputed with Jews, insisting that Jews were downtrodden and despised because of the wounds they had inflicted on Christ (Golb 1998, 505). Paul cites the Jewish prophecies of the Messiah, as well as Midrashic and Talmudic commentary, and argues that the prophecies were fulfilled in Christ (501). Paul maintains that Jeremiah's foretelling of a new covenant (Jer. 31:31) has been similarly fulfilled in Christ. In each case a Jew named Abraham rejects his arguments (501-6).

For most Christians, the most influential interpretations of scripture in relation to Jews came not in the learned commentaries, which relatively few could read, but in the sermons and religious dramas that brought the biblical accounts to life. In particular, Passion Plays presented the sufferings of Jesus in dramatic form that inflamed the viewers against contemporary Jews. Jews were often portrayed wearing conical hats and horns, giving them a diabolical appearance. Not all church authorities approved, and often Catholic hierarchs intervened to prevent physical violence against Jews. Nonetheless, in many times and places Holy Week celebrations and Passion Plays focused hostile attention on the Jews. The effect was that Christians formed their own identity in sharp contrast to the hated Jews. Repeatedly, vicious pogroms were the result. Often Christians separated Jesus from the Jewish people and viewed Judaism as a negative contrast to the teachings and actions of Jesus. Jews became projection screens for Christian anger and guilt and served as scapegoats for a wide variety of issues (Little 1991, 276-97; Roth 1991, 298-309).

Despite the sad history of persecutions of Jews by Christians, there were contexts in which Jews and Christians lived in relative harmony and there was intellectual exchange. Muslim-ruled Cordoba in Spain has often been cited, but there were Christian-ruled places as well, including the Sicily of Roger II and northern France in the eleventh, twelfth, and thirteenth centuries. The great Jewish exegete Rashi lived in northern France during the time of the First Crusade. Despite the violence against Jews in the Rhineland during this period, Rashi apparently lived undisturbed by the conflicts elsewhere (Reventlow 2009-10, 219).

While most European Christian interpreters of the Bible in the Middle Ages read the Old Testament in Latin or Greek translation, there were a few Christian exegetes who knew Hebrew, including Andrew of St. Victor, Herbert of Bosham (d. 1190), Robert Grosseteste (ca. 1165-1253), Roger Bacon (ca. 1214-1292), and Guillaume de la Mare. Most literate medieval Christians, however, relied on Jerome for their secondhand acquaintance with Hebrew names and words (Reventlow 2009-10, 2:220). In public disputes, Christian scholars would try to persuade Jews of their christological interpretation of the Jewish scriptures, but Jews would insist in response that they had the proper understanding of their sacred texts (220).

Of special importance was Nicholas of Lyra (ca. 1270-1349), who, Henning Graf Reventlow notes, was "the first to introduce the results of Jewish exegesis in the form of Rashi's *peshat* interpretation into Christian commentaries on the Old Testament" (2009-10, 2:251-52). Nicholas was very familiar with the fourfold interpretation of scripture, but he criticizes the usual figurative or mystical style of interpreting the Bible: "Although they said many good things, they have nevertheless uncovered the literal sense too little and increased the mystical sense in a way that the literal sense, buried under so many mystical interpretations, is nearly smothered" (*Postilla Literalis,* 2nd prologue; quoted by Reventlow, 2:252). Nicholas worries that theological arguments based on senses other than the literal lead to "the fallacy of equivocation and the fallacy of amphiboly" (quoted by Synan 2010, 230). Drawing on the biblical interpretations of Rashi two centuries earlier, Nicholas of Lyra helped transform Christian understandings of the Bible in respectful dialogue with Jewish scholarship (Reventlow, 2:259). A Reformation-era rhyme stressed Nicholas of Lyra's major impact on Luther: "Si Lyra non lyrasset, Lutherus non saltasset" (Reventlow, 2:248); "Had Nicholas his lyre not played, Luther in no dance had swayed" (Synan, 230).

Not all were impressed with Nicholas's efforts, however. Paul of Burgos (Pablo de Santa Maria, 1351-1435), a former rabbi who became a Christian in 1390 and eventually became archbishop of Burgos, criticizes Nicholas for his limited knowledge of Hebrew and for his reliance on Rashi. Philip Krey comments, "Spanish biblical commentators, especially the Bishop of Burgos, rightly felt superior in their knowledge of Hebrew to their northern colleagues" (1996, 159). However, Paul of Burgos's knowledge of Hebrew and his Jewish background did not dispose him favorably to the Jewish community. As Lord Chancellor of Castile, Paul drew up legislation separating Jews from Christians and restricting Jewish commercial activity (159).

The Reformation

During the Reformation, Martin Luther (1483-1546) initially did not blame the Jews too severely for not being Christian, because he thought that the Catholic Church had so distorted the gospel that Jews were not unreasonable in rejecting the Catholic faith. However, in time he learned that Jews were no more eager to become Protestant Christians than they had been to become Catholic Christians, and he began writing against the Jews and Judaism. In these writings, Luther was drawing on medieval precedents. Kirsi Stjerna stresses the continuity between Luther and earlier Christians in the attitudes toward Jews: "Luther's demonization of the Jews reflects false or incomplete information, hearsay, and inherited anti-Jewish delusions, all of which have centuries-old roots in Christian imagination. The air he breathed since his childhood was poisoned with anti-Jewish laws, fears, jokes, and slander" (in Schramm and Stjerna 2012, 18).

In a sermon entitled "How Christians Should Regard Moses" (1525), Luther stated that God preached two sermons in the Law of Moses (Exodus 19–20) and the gospel of Christ at Pentecost (Acts 2:2-4). The Law of Moses offers promises of Christ but is only for the Jews and is no longer valid after the coming of Christ: "What God said to Moses by way of commandment is for the Jews only. But the gospel goes through the whole world in its entirety; it is offered to all creatures without exception" (Gritsch 2012, 67).

One of Luther's central theological contrasts is between Law and gospel. According to Luther, the theological use of the Law convicts of us sin and drives us to despair of our own works; thus it prepares us to hear the word of the gospel, the saving grace given freely by God in Jesus Christ apart from the Law. Luther comments on Romans 10:15: "For the law shows nothing but sin and makes [people] guilty and thus terrifies the conscience. But in this way the gospel proclaims the wished-for help to those in terror" (quoted by Reventlow 2009-10, 3:83). Luther's own interpretation of the Bible was subtle and complex; what he meant by the Law is not simply the Old Testament, for he found Christ hidden there as well. However, in later history, the Law was often identified with Judaism and was viewed negatively. Christianity was identified with grace and was seen as the antithesis of Judaism. As Christopher Probst has shown, the negative heritage of Luther's remarks lasted into the twentieth century.

While Martin Luther challenged and rejected the patristic and medieval tradition of interpreting the Bible allegorically, he nonetheless continued the christological reading of the Old Testament, finding Christ hidden in it. Eric Gritsch notes that in 1543, in "On the Last Words of Daniel," Luther bitterly opposes the rabbis' interpretation of the Jewish scriptures:

> May God grant that our theologians boldly apply themselves to the study of Hebrew and retrieve the Bible for us from those rascally thieves. And may they improve on my work. They must not become captive to the rabbis and their distorted grammar and false interpretation. Then we will again find and recognize our dear Lord and Savior clearly and distinctly in Scripture. (Luther, quoted by Gritsch 2012, 94)

In the same work, Luther interprets the promise to Abraham in Genesis 22:18 in an anti-Jewish manner: "However, they, these circumcised saints, want to see us Gentiles damned and claim they are the only seed of Abraham. But because they curse the Gentiles and want to be a seed through which all the Gentiles are cursed, it is manifest that they are not Abraham's but the devil's seed" (Gritsch, 94).

At the end of his life, Luther was extremely bitter against the Jews and wrote vehement attacks on them, calling for the destruction of synagogues. In "On the Jews and Their Lies" (1543), he sets forth a program of action against the Jews: "First, to *set fire to their synagogues or schools* and to bury and cover with dirt whatever will not burn, so that no man will ever again see a stone of center of them" (Gritsch, 86). Luther continued this program by citing the command to punish idolatry (Deut. 13:12-18) and applying it to the Jews: "Second, I advise that their houses also be razed and destroyed. For they pursue in them the same aims as in their synagogues" (86).

Schleiermacher

The development of historical criticism in the seventeenth, eighteenth, and nineteenth centuries rejected the allegorical interpretation of the Bible and challenged the tradition of finding New Testament figures and themes in texts of the First Testament. Scholars sought to understand the scriptures independently of dogmatic commitments, but historical criticism by itself did not resolve all the problems of anti-Jewish bias in Christian hermeneutics. Biblical criticism shaped a new context for Christian systematic theology, but it did not resolve the problem of anti-Jewish interpretations of the Bible.

Friedrich Schleiermacher acknowledged and lamented the long history of Christians reading their own thoughts and theologies into the Jewish scriptures. In light of historical criticism, Schleiermacher thought it was time to bring this tradition to a close. Schleiermacher understands Christian theology as grounded in the God-consciousness of Jesus, which finds expression in the New Testament witness and which continues through the activity of the Spirit in the Christian church; however, he separates this from Jesus' Jewish context: "Christianity cannot in any wise be regarded as a remodeling or a renewal and continuation of Judaism" (1976, 61). Schleiermacher sees the Judaism of his day as "being almost in process of extinction" (37).

Despite his acceptance of historical criticism, Schleiermacher nonetheless continues the stereotype of Jews as materialistic, describing Jewish monotheism as "everywhere tinctured with materialistic conceptions, whether cruder or finer" (1976, 387). He ignores the Hebrew Bible's portrayal of God's universal care for humanity, asserting instead that "Judaism, by its limitation of the love of Jehovah to the race of Abraham, betrays a lingering affinity with Fetishism" (37). Accepting historical criticism and rejecting the allegorical projections of earlier ages, Schleiermacher draws the radical conclusion that the Jewish scriptures in principle cannot express the God-consciousness of Jesus and thus are not part of the Christian Bible. He urges Christian theologians to study them as background for the Christian Bible but not to consider them part of the Christian Bible. Schleiermacher explains:

Hence the rule may be set up that almost everything else in the Old Testament is, for our Christian usage, but the husk or wrapping of its prophecy, and that whatever is most definitely Jewish has least value. So that we can find rendered with some exactness in Old Testament passages only those of our religious emotions which are of a somewhat general nature without anything very distinctively Christian. (1976, 62)

For Schleiermacher, Christian faith and theology do not have any unique, intrinsic relation to Judaism: "The truth rather is that the relations of Christianity to Judaism and Heathenism are the same, inasmuch as the transition from either of these to Christianity is a transition to another religion. . . . Now if Christianity has the same relation to Judaism as to Heathenism, it can no more be regarded as a continuation of the former than of the latter: if a man comes from either of them to Christianity, he becomes, as regards his religion, a new man" (1976, 60-61). P. E. Capetz notes the paradox: "Schleiermacher's methodological insistence upon the distinctiveness of each positive religion cleared the way for the possibility of an impartial historical treatment of Judaism in its own right. Nevertheless, his interpretation of Judaism betrays certain prejudices that reflect his own Christian starting point" (2009, 304).

Nineteenth-century Christian historical critics of the Bible often viewed Judaism in a negative fashion, seeing the Torah in a legalistic way and referring to Second Temple Judaism in a pejorative manner as *Spätjudentum* ("late Judaism"), a supposedly decadent religion on the brink of destruction. The influential scholar of ancient Israel, Julius Wellhausen (1844-1918), esteemed the biblical prophets as great individuals who "carried out their tasks without a previously given law" (Reventlow 2009-10, 4:320). Wellhausen praises what he called "The Prophetic Reformation"; for him, the prophets' "credo is not in any book. It is a barbarism, in dealing with such a phenomenon, to debase its physiognomy with the law" (Reventlow, 4:320). Wellhausen interprets Second Temple Judaism as a debased form of religion: "The cult is now alienated from the heart. . . . it is a dead work" (Reventlow, 4:321). He views the Law in a negative light and reports that he was delighted when he learned the historical theory that the biblical prophets were to be dated earlier than the Torah: "I was won over to it: I allowed myself to confess that Hebrew antiquity could be understood without the Book of the Torah" (Reventlow, 4:316). He was quite harsh in his judgment of Judaism after the exile: "The cultus was the pagan element in the religion of Yahweh. . . , a constant danger for both morality and monotheism" (Reventlow, 4:322). From Wellhausen's Protestant point of view, this legalistic form of "late" Judaism resembles the Catholicism to which it gave birth: "It is in its nature closely related to the early Catholic church, whose mother Judaism in fact was" (Reventlow, 4:321).

Another influential proponent of historical criticism, Adolf von Harnack (1851-1930) argued that it was a mistake for Christians to retain the Jewish Bible as part of the Christian Bible. He wanted to break with the tradition of treating the Old Testament as texts with canonical authority. He hoped that this would emphasize the centrality of the Gospel to Christian faith and prevent literalistic Biblicism. For Harnack, authentic Christianity was based only on the religion of Jesus himself, namely, the kingdom of God, the Fatherhood of God, the infinite value of the human soul, and the commandment of love. Toward the end of his life, he wrote *Marcion: The Gospel of the Alien God*, in which he praised Marcion for sharply distinguishing between Law and gospel and in some ways anticipating the Reformation. In *The Mission and Expansion of Christianity*, Harnack asserted that the early Gentile Christians appropriated the Jewish scriptures for themselves and rejected the Jewish people: "The daughter first robbed her mother, and then repudiated her!" (Harnack [1904] 1961, 69). But then he went on to justify the disenfranchisement: "By their rejection of Jesus, the Jewish people disowned their calling and dealt the deathblow to their existence; their place was taken by Christians as the new People, who appropriated the whole tradition of Judaism" (69). As Clark Williamson comments, "A critical-historical approach to Jesus is used to restate this ancient ideological claim" (1993, 182).

Karl Barth, who vigorously rejected Harnack's approach to Christian theology, nonetheless also discounted Jewish perspectives, insisting that "apart from Jesus Christ we can say nothing at all about God" (1957b, 45). Barth was personally courageous in denouncing the Nazi ideology, including anti-Semitism. Nevertheless, regarding the Jews, he wrote: "But the Church knows of man's misery only insofar as Israel too lives it—as a reflection of the divine judgment" (1957a, 206). Barth continues the tradition of blaming Jews for Jesus death: "As things stand, however, Israel as such and as a whole is not obedient but disobedient to its election. What happens is that Israel's promised Messiah comes and in accordance with His election is delivered up by Israel and is crucified for Israel" (1957a, 208). Barth interprets the fall of Jerusalem in 70 C.E. as confirming the conclusion of the history of Israel (1957a, 208). In the aftermath, Israel bears witness against its will: "The Jews of the ghetto give this demonstration involuntarily, joylessly and ingloriously, but they do give it. They have nothing to attest to the world but the shadow of the cross of Christ that falls upon them" (1957a, 209).

Christian biblical scholars often extricated Jesus from the history of his people. One of the most influential twentieth-century historical critical scholars of the Pentateuch, Martin Noth, expressed a widely influential judgment: "Jesus himself . . . no longer formed part of the history of Israel. In him the history of Israel had come, rather to its real end. What did belong to the history of Israel was the process of his rejection and condemnation by the Jerusalem religious community" (1967, 3). Such attitudes were widely influential through the early twentieth century.

The Impact of the Shoah

The Second World War and the atrocities of the Shoah dramatically changed the hermeneutical situation of Christian biblical interpreters. As Susannah

Heschel has documented, some Christian theologians supported the Nazi party and even argued that Jesus was actually an Aryan and was not Jewish at all. The Institute for the Study and Eradication of Jewish Influence on German Church Life, founded in 1939, sought to dejudaize Christianity altogether. One "German Christian" catechism issued in 1940 stated, "Was Christ a Jew? It is the greatest lie that the Jews have brought into the world, that Jesus is a Jew" (Heschel 2010, 127).

In 1948, just a few years after the end of the war and the Shoah, French Jewish historian Jules Isaac launched a full-scale assault on traditional Christian interpretations of the Bible, hoping that a more accurate study and careful reading of the Bible would support better Jewish–Christian relations. In *Jesus and Israel,* Isaac compares the texts of the New Testament to the later interpretations by Christian authors, arguing that Christians have interpreted Jesus and the New Testament in an anti-Jewish manner that is not supported by the scriptures themselves or by historical evidence. Isaac asserts in his Proposition 10:

> Nothing would be more futile than to try to separate from Judaism the Gospel that Jesus preached in the synagogues and in the Temple. The truth is that the Gospel and its entire tradition are deeply rooted in Jewish tradition and in the attempts at renovation and purification which had been manifested for almost two centuries in Palestine. (1971, vi, 74)

Isaac directly rebuts the claim of Adolf Harnack that Jesus' teaching has "only a loose" connection to Judaism" (quoted by Isaac 1971, 74). On the contrary, Isaac insists "that every root of Jesus' gospel is sunk deep in the soil of Jewish tradition, which it is specious to distinguish from 'the Judaism of his time', itself far more diversified in its aspirations than is generally accepted" (74). Isaac maintains that Jesus did not reject or curse the Jewish people, and he quoted Romans 11:29 as bearing witness that "the gifts . . . of God are irrevocable" (viii, 385). Isaac does sharply challenge the New Testament's presentation of the Jewish people's collective responsibility for the passion of Jesus, especially the infamous cry of the crowd in Matthew 27:25 (311-64). Isaac calls Christians to a more authentic understanding of Jesus as a Jew and of the New Testament, trusting that such a renewal of biblical interpretation concerning the past would improve Christian–Jewish relations in the future.

Many Christians took Isaac's challenge to heart. Gregory Baum challenged some of Isaac's particular interpretations. Years later, Baum looked back: "I remember that in the late 1950s, I was greatly disturbed by Jules Isaac's book, *Jésus et Israël,* published in 1948, which tried to demonstrate that contempt for Jews was already present in certain texts of the New Testament" (Baum 2005, 110). Baum learned much from Isaac concerning the anti-Jewish rhetoric in the Christian tradition, but Baum commented that Isaac "did not convince me that anti-Jewish sentiments were already expressed in the New Testament" (110). Biblical scholarship in recent decades has taken up the broad challenge posed by Isaac, interpreting Jesus as a faithful Jew and the New Testament as Jewish texts.

Even though the Nazi ideology and crimes were profoundly anti-Christian, many Christians came to recognize that centuries of Christian vilification of the Jews had tragically prepared the way for Nazi propaganda and atrocities. Christians came to see that the entire history of hostility toward Jews and Judaism is a fundamental contradiction of the teaching and practice of Jesus himself about not judging others (Matt. 7:3-4). Historically, Christians were often very quick to blame Jews for wrongs real or imagined, while ignoring their own far more grievous sins.

Much has changed in the relations between Christians and Jews in recent decades. For over half a century, there have been numerous efforts to overcome this often violent heritage. In recent decades Christians in dialogue with Jewish scholars have taken this challenge seriously and have sought to interpret both testaments of the Christian Bible in light of new historical studies and revised attitudes toward Jews and Judaism. Christians came to see the prophets' critiques of ancient Israel as one of the great contributions of the Jewish tradition to world religious history. Christians also came to see that these critiques target themselves at least as much as their Jewish neighbors. Christians realized that the Bible's message is not that Jews are uniquely perverse but rather that both Jews and Christians face serious challenges in seeking to live in covenant with the God of Abraham.

Given the many centuries of harshly anti-Jewish biblical interpretation, it is remarkable how radically Christians have changed the fundamental assumptions for interpreting the Bible in relation to the Jewish community. Before World War II, adversarial interpretations of Scripture continued to fuel harsh Christian views of Jews, and negative perceptions of Jews in turn reinforced hostile readings of biblical accounts. The past negative descriptions were interpreted as finding confirmation in the present.

In a dramatic reversal during a very short period of time, biblical scholars, theologians, and church leaders sought to put aside the traditional hermeneutics and adopted a profoundly different set of assumptions. There are at least three levels to this transformation: academic scholarship on the scriptures, theologies, and histories of Judaism and Christianity in relation to each other; the official statements of Christian churches and of interreligious organizations of Jews and Christians; and the attitudes of the broader Christian communities toward Jews. All three aspects are intimately interconnected.

In the wake of the Shoah, Christians began to hear the teaching of Jesus about being reconciled before presenting a gift at the altar (Matt. 5:22-23) in relation to their traditional attitudes to the Jewish people. Both of these principles challenge Christians to overcome the history of hostility toward Jews and Judaism. It is impossible to overstate the importance of this task for the Christian tradition.

In recent decades Jewish and Christian scholars have worked together to understand our scriptures and the history of our relationships in more accurate ways that open up innovative paths of interpreting both the Bible and the relationships of the later Jewish and Christian traditions. Changes in official ecclesiastical attitudes toward Jews have gone hand in hand with changes in biblical interpretation. These scholarly and ecclesial transformations have, in turn, both supported and been supported by the broader improvement of relations between Jews and Christians in all areas of life. In the aftermath of the horrors of the Shoah, many Christians recognized that the long Christian tradition of vilifying Jews needed to be changed. Christian biblical scholars became more conscious and critical of the biases that Christians had traditionally brought to their studies; at the same time church leaders began to call for revised assessments as well.

Second Vatican Council

Since World War II, there have been numerous Christian statements condemning anti-Semitism and seeking to improve Christian–Jewish relations (Sherman 2011). For Catholics, the most dramatic and influential of the official church statements was *Nostra Aetate* (NA), The Declaration on the Relationship of the Catholic Church to Non-Christian Religions, which was issued by Pope Paul VI and the Second Vatican Council in 1965. Vatican II radically revised centuries of Catholic teaching about the Jewish people and was very influential on other Christian churches as well. *Nostra Aetate* acknowledges that the Church receives the First Testament from the Jewish people and cites Ephesians 2:14-16 on the reconciliation that Christ has brought to Jews and Gentiles (NA §4; Tanner 1990, 2:970). The Council Fathers cite Paul's Epistle to the Romans, chapters 9-11, as teaching that God's gift and call to the Jewish people are irrevocable, *sine poenitentia*, without regret (Rom. 11:29; NA §4; Tanner, 2:970). This means that the covenant God made with ancient Israel has not been broken off and that Jews should not be viewed as accursed, for they are still God's beloved people. Pope John Paul II later stated publicly to the Jewish community in Mainz, Germany, that the covenant with Israel was "never revoked" (1980, §3, p. 179).

There were debates in the council deliberations over whether to say anything about Catholic hopes for the conversion of the Jewish people. The second draft of the declaration cited Romans 11:25 and stated that the Catholic Church "waits with unshaken faith and deep longing for the entry of that people into the fullness of the people of God established by Christ" (Connelly 2012, 104). As this draft became public, there was vigorous protest, and Rabbi Abraham Joshua Heschel stated that he was "ready to go to Auschwitz any time if faced with the alternative of conversion or death" (*Time*, September 11, 1964; Connelly, 104). A European Jewish leader, Ernst Ludwig Ehrlich, questioned the use of Romans 11:25, since Paul does not say anything about the "entry" of the Jewish people into "the fullness of the people of God established by Christ." Instead, Ehrlich observed, Paul wrote that "a hardening has come upon part of Israel until the full number of Gentiles has come in, and so all Israel will be saved" (Rom. 11:25 RSV). Ehrlich commented, "Paul is speaking in a clearly eschatological sense, because *plenitudo gentium* ["the full number"] is clearly the apocalyptic full number of the Gentiles . . . any notion of conversion is excluded entirely" (letter of September 15, 1964; Connelly, 107). Here a Jewish scholar was persuasively advising Catholic bishops on how to read the New Testament in relation to Jews. Ehrlich had a remarkable confidence that careful scrutiny of the New Testament itself would contribute to harmony between Jews and Christians: "In dealing with it over the years I have learned that the New Testament itself—when the text is properly interpreted—is the only chance, the only means of promoting understanding between Christians and Jews" (letter of September 15, 1964; Connelly, 108). The final text of *Nostra Aetate* drops the offending interpretation of Paul, turning instead to the prophet Zephaniah for an expression of a common hope: "Together with the prophets and the same apostle [Paul], the church awaits the day known only to God on which all peoples will call upon the Lord with one voice and 'will serve him with one arm' (Zeph 3:9)" (NA §4; Tanner 2:970).

The Second Vatican Council clearly rejects the traditional practice of collectively blaming Jews of all times and places for the death of Jesus. *Nostra Aetate* notes that only a small number of Jews of that time would have been involved in any way in Jesus' crucifixion; and the council asserts that later generations of Jews cannot in any way be blamed for the death of Jesus. The council forcefully condemns anti-Semitism from any source at any time (NA §4; Tanner 2:970-71). While the document does not explicitly mention earlier popes and councils, anyone who knows Catholic Church history knows that this condemnation encompasses a wide array of earlier Catholic teachings and practices. *Nostra Aetate* closes with condemnation of religious discrimination or harassment (NA §5; Tanner, 2:971). Two months later, Vatican II expanded on this principle and, for the first time in the history of the Catholic Church, fully endorsed the right of religious liberty in *Dignitatis Humanae,* the Declaration on Religious Freedom.

Jewish leaders recognized the dramatic change. Rabbi Gilbert S. Rosenthal, executive director of the National Council of Synagogues, described *Nostra Aetate* as "a Copernican revolution in Catholic thinking about the Jewish religion and people" (Connelly 2012, 110). Geoffrey Wigoder, editor-in-chief of *Encyclopedia Judaica,* praised Pope John XXIII and the Vatican Council for launching "a new era in the history of the church" (Connelly, 110).

Christian Zionism and Palestinian Christians

One of the greatest challenges to Christian biblical interpretation in relation to Jews and Judaism at the present time involves the unresolved situation among Jews, Christians, and Muslims in Israel/Palestine. Some Christian Zionists interpret the Bible to justify the Israeli Jewish conquest and displacement of Palestinians, arguing that the Palestinians have no right to the lands they have traditionally inhabited because in the Bible God granted these lands to the Jewish people. There is currently a vigorous debate over Christian Zionism, as some Christians interpret the Bible in ways that strongly support Zionism (see Spector). Gary M. Burge rebuts Christian Zionists and argues that for Christians the New Testament modifies the various discussions of land in the Old Testament: "Thus the most sacred of all places, the Temple, is found in Christ. And so he too offers the 'place' of residence for Christians who yearn for a 'better country.' This means that the New Testament is free to deflect interest away from the land *as land*" (Burge 2010, 129). Rejecting Christian Zionism, Burge warns: "When Christian theology serves at the behest of political or historical forces in any generation—be it ancient crusades, religiously fueled nationalism, or the call of Christian Zionists—it loses its supreme mission in the world" (131).

Palestinian Christians, including Arab citizens of Israel, have very different experiences of Jews than most European or North American Christians; many of the older generation still remember the massacres and forced displacements of Christians by Jewish fighters in 1948. When he was a young boy, Archbishop Elias Chacour, the Catholic bishop of the Galilee, was forcibly evicted from his home and sent with his family to live in another village. While playing there one day, he discovered the bodies of Christian villagers who had been massacred by Jewish fighters (1984, 44-45). Later, the leaders of his Christian village won a legal victory in the Supreme Court of Israel and were promised approval to return to their homes. However, his family went back to the site of their home, only to discover that their entire town was being destroyed by Israeli troops (1984, 71-81). In response to these catastrophes, Chacour meditated upon the Sermon on the Mount, especially Jesus' commands to be poor in spirit, to be peacemakers, to be pure of heart, to hunger and thirst for justice, and to love one's enemies. This became the foundation of his ministry as a priest, educator, and bishop working for reconciliation among Jews, Christians, and Muslims (2008, 112-16). Chacour agrees with Burge in rejecting Christian Zionism: "For me, who am not a Jew but a Christian, the land is not important. It is not something sacred. I do not believe in a 'Holy Land.' It is only the people who should become holy" (2008, 59).

Similarly, Palestinian Christian Naim Ateek remembers being expelled by Israeli forces from his town in 1948. As a theologian and church leader, he faces the problem of interpreting the Bible's conquest narratives in relation to the Palestinians' experience of displacement and conquest by Israeli Jews: "For most Palestinian Christians, as for many other Arab Christians, their view of the Bible, especially the Hebrew Scriptures, or Old Testament, has been adversely affected by the creation of the State of Israel. Many previously hidden problems suddenly surfaced" (1989, 77). Ateek ponders the problem of finding a reliable criterion for reading the Bible: "The criterion that Palestinians are looking for must be both biblically and theologically sound, lest it in turn become a mere instrument to oppose Jewish and Christian Zionists and support subjective Palestinian claims and prejudices. . . . The canon of this hermeneutic for the Palestinian Christian is nothing less than Jesus Christ himself" (79). Starting from the life, death, and resurrection of Jesus Christ, Ateek states that Palestinian Christians must read both Testaments critically: "The Bible for

Palestinian Christians, then, can be retained in its entirety, while its contents would be judged by this hermeneutic and scrutinized by the mind of Christ" (80).

In this light, Ateek considers the book of Joshua's command to destroy all the inhabitants of Jericho (chapter 6); questioning whether the command of mass destruction reflects God as revealed in Jesus Christ, he concludes: "In other words, such passages are revelatory of a stage of development of the human understanding of God that we must regard, in light of Christ's revelation, as inadequate and incomplete" (1989, 83). Ateek notes that Rabbi Moshe Segal compared Palestinians to the biblical Amalekites, whom Samuel commanded Saul to destroy in the name of God (1 Sam. 15:1-3). Ateek notes that many religious Zionists, both Jewish and Christian, have interpreted the contemporary Palestinians as the Canaanites who were in the promised land at the time of the exodus: "For to need an exodus, one must have a promised land. To choose the motif of conquest of the promised land is to invite the need for the oppression, assimilation, control, or dispossession of the indigenous population. That is why it is difficult, in a Palestinian theology of liberation, to find the whole of the Exodus event meaningful" (87). Ateek hopes: "Instead of the wars and bloodshed of the biblical account, it is my hope that Palestinians will return to *share* the land of Israel-Palestine" (87).

Despite the seemingly insuperable obstacles, both Chacour and Ateek hope that active nonviolent resistance can contribute to justice and peace among Jews, Christians, and Muslims in Israel-Palestine. Ateek comments, "I have always believed that the Church in Israel-Palestine can play a powerful role in promoting justice and peace through active nonviolent means" (1989, 135). He inscribes this hope in the trajectory of the strategy of Jesus Christ, as interpreted by Mahatma Gandhi (Ateek 2008, 179-83). He quotes Gandhi as a guide to following the path of Jesus Christ in relation to Israeli Jews: "Non-violent resistance implies the very opposite of weakness. . . . It requires strength, and there is nothing automatic or intuitive about the resoluteness required for using non-violent methods in political struggle and the quest for Truth" (quoted by Ateek 2008, 179-80).

Reading the Bible in Dialogue with Jews and Judaism

Because Judaism is so intimately related to Christianity, relations with Jews have a direct and strong impact on Christian theology. One of the most consistent Jewish responses to Christian claims about Jesus Christ is that the coming of the Messiah is inseparable from the Messianic Age, a time of peace and justice on earth. Since the hopes for peace and justice have obviously not been realized to date, many Jews have stated that they cannot accept that Jesus is the Messiah. Martin Buber explains, "The church rests on its faith that the Christ has come, and that this is the redemption which God has bestowed on mankind. We, Israel *are not able* to believe this" (quoted by Moltmann 1990, 28). Jürgen Moltmann has taken this response to heart, acknowledges its legitimacy, and incorporates it into his Christology, *The Way of Jesus Christ*. Moltmann acknowledges, "Even the raised Christ himself is 'not yet' the pantocrator. But he is already on the way to redeem the world" (32). Christians can acknowledge that the world remains broken and in many respects unredeemed.

Moltmann follows Paul in finding that Israel's rejection of the messianic claims for Jesus has had a positive result in the mission to the Gentiles, which was the matrix for the church's emergence from Judaism. Regarding Paul's expectations, Moltmann sees that Paul "does not expect of this Deliverer the Jews' conversion, and that they will arrive at Christian faith" (1990, 35). Thus, in contrast to Christologies that were triumphalistic, Moltmann proposes a more modest Christology for pilgrims, a Christology "of the way," following Jesus Christ "as on the road and walking with us" (33).

The guiding principle for postconciliar Catholic efforts to read the Bible with respect for the Jewish people and Judaism is taken from *Nostra Aetate* §4: "Since the spiritual patrimony common to Christians and Jews is thus so great, this sacred Synod wishes to foster and recommend mutual understanding and respect." In 1974, the Holy See issued *Guidelines and Suggestions for Implementing the Conciliar Declaration 'Nostra Aetate.'* About a decade later, in 1985, the Holy See issued *Notes on the Correct Way to Present the Jews and Judaism in Preaching and Catechesis of the Roman Catholic Church*. This document begins with the mandate from Pope John Paul II to Catholic bishops and catechists: "We should aim, in this field, that Catholic teaching at its different levels, in catechesis to children and young people, presents Jews and Judaism, not only in an honest and objective manner, free from prejudices and without any offences, but also with full awareness of the heritage common" to Jews and Christians. Following the call of Pope John Paul II, the document stresses: "Because of the unique relations that exist between Christianity and Judaism—'linked together at the very level of their identity' (John Paul II, March 6, 1982)—relations 'founded on the design of the God of the Covenant' (ibid.), the Jews and Judaism should not occupy an occasional and marginal place in catechesis; their presence there is essential and should be organically integrated."

As Rabbi Jonathan Sacks insists, each religious interpretive community chooses which texts to place in the foreground of its attention and practice. In most of the recent Christian hermeneutical proposals, there is a stark recognition of how deeply harmful traditional Christian exegesis of passages such as Matthew 27:25 has been. Historical criticism and contextualization are important but insufficient. The horizon of interpretation, including the entire network of interpretive presuppositions, began to shift.

According to the book of Genesis, after Isaac had already blessed Jacob, Esau came in search of blessing, asking: "Have you only one blessing? Bless me, me also, father!" (Gen. 27:38). But Isaac has no more blessing to give his elder son, but instead foretells conflict: "See, away from the fatness of the earth shall your home be, and away from the dew of heaven on high. By your sword you shall live, and you shall serve your brother; but when you break loose, you shall break his yoke from your neck" (Gen. 27:39-40). Hoping for a different answer, Mary Boys rephrases the poignant question posed to Isaac by Esau:

"*Has God Only One Blessing?*" Boys surveys the daunting challenges facing Christian interpreters of the Bible in relation to Jews and Judaism. She finds that a "plain reading" of some New Testament texts (Matthew 23 and John 9) yields a very negative portrait of the Pharisees as "blind guides" and "legalistic traditionalists"; these stereotypes cast the Pharisees as representatives and symbols of all that is wrong with Judaism (2000, 180, 182). As an alternative approach, she offers examples of an "informed and imaginative reading" that seeks more respectful harmonious relations. Integral to her approach is background information on Second Temple Judaism and the customs of rhetoric and polemics in the first century C.E., which regularly used harsh, scurrilous language to attack foes. However, she moves beyond historical criticism to take the New Testament portrait of the Pharisees as a mirror to religious leaders of other times and places, such as a contemporary local ministerial association in the United States: "*The Pharisees—if we will let them—play a central role in the drama of the Gospel by provoking us to question the sort of person our practice of religion has fashioned. . . .* On what basis do we judge others, and what do our judgments reveal about our image of God?" (2000, 188). Thus, reflecting on the negative images of the Pharisees in the New Testament becomes a stimulus to Christians to examine their consciences and reflect on the basis of their judgments of others.

Boys approaches the Bible as "neither a container of definitively fixed propositions nor a blueprint for contemporary church life" (2000, 191). She notes that biblical texts have been used to justify not only anti-Semitism but also slavery, holy wars, patriarchal structures, and homophobia. On numerous levels, many biblical teachings are problematic. Regarding relations with the Jewish people, Boys asserts: "*In light of all that Christianity has visited upon the Jewish people, a refusal to reinterpret our sacred scripture would be a sinful disregard of tradition*" (2000, 194). She turns to Sandra Schneiders (1999) and Paul Ricoeur for guidance, especially Ricoeur's distinction of the world behind the text, the world of the text, and the world before the text. Exploring the world behind the text involves the study of the original context through the tools of historical, literary, and ideological criticism. The world of the text explores the text itself as discourse, regardless of the intention of the original author or the first reception. In classic texts, including the scriptures, there is what Ricoeur calls a "surplus of meaning," similar to what Kant claimed for aesthetic ideas for which no concept is adequate. Classic texts reveal new potentialities in new situations and are contemporaneous to each context of readers and hearers.

Perhaps most important for interreligious discussions is what Ricoeur calls the world before the text, that is, the way of being in the world opened up by the text. Texts like the Bible invite readers to live in a new world of possibilities. The upshot for Boys is this: "*Texts can come to mean something different from what they originally meant or were understood to mean because of their surplus of meaning and character of effective history*" (2000, 196). She allows for the possibility of "rejection of biblical subject matter that is untrue or immoral" (197). While this may appear contrary to much of the received Christian tradition, we have seen that in very different ways and in different contexts, both

Origen and Augustine provided criteria for what meanings could be accepted from biblical texts. Boys concludes with a call to struggle with interpretation: "It is our sublime vocation at this juncture in our history to repudiate the distortions that have arisen from our 'plain readings' and to wrestle incessantly with our Scriptures so that we might see anew" (198).

Conclusion

For centuries Christians largely read the Bible in ways that were highly critical of Jews and of the entire Jewish tradition since the time of Jesus. Jewish interpretations of the Hebrew Bible were frequently dismissed as literal-minded and misguided. It is one of the most profound transformations of recent decades that Christians and Jews now collaborate in reading their scriptures together. Increasingly, Christians today have a far greater respect for the entire history of Jewish interpretations of the Bible. The earlier survey of New Testament scholarship gives a suggestion of the new horizon of interpretation. While there continue to be many difficult challenges, major shifts have begun to happen in Jewish–Christian dialogue over the last half-century. To be sure, crucial differences remain, with no likely prospect of complete agreement on many issues. But in many contexts, there is an atmosphere of respect and companionship that allows Christians to welcome Jews as partners and friends in discerning together the significance of their respective scriptures.

CHAPTER FOUR

Christian Interpretations of Scripture in Relation to Muslims and Islam

The ambivalent and troubled history of Muslim–Christian relations, ranging from violent conflict to cooperation, is reflected in Christian interpretations of scripture in relation to Muslims and Islam. While the repeated conflicts have often received the most attention, Richard Bulliet has noted that there were extensive areas of cooperation and shared concern and values, and he argues for consideration of an "Islamo-Christian Civilization." Throughout much of history, Christians usually interpreted the Bible in relation to Muslims and Islam in harshly negative ways. These interpretations played a major role in shaping European Christian awareness. Christians in many Muslim-majority nations face difficult challenges today, and there are numerous voices demonizing Islam and proclaiming that Islam is inherently violent. Nonetheless, especially in recent decades there have also been numerous respectful, cordial exchanges and efforts to improve relations between Muslims and Christians.

Christian interpretations of the Bible play an integral role in this tangled history. For centuries, Jews, Christians, and Muslims have debated over the significance of the heritage of Abraham and ancient Israel, with each tradition claiming to be its legitimate heir. Many major figures of the Christian Bible appear in the Qur'an and the Islamic tradition. The Qur'an teaches that God communicated revelations to the major figures of ancient Israel, including Jesus; but Islam understands these revelations in a very different way from Jews and Christians. Christians have frequently interpreted Muslims in light of biblical figures such as Ishmael, the Antichrist, and the Son of Destruction, usually very negatively. Hostile Christian apocalyptic interpretations of Islam began in the seventh century C.E. and have by no means ended. The Muslim proposal of *A Common Word between Us and You* looks to the biblical commands to love God and neighbor as the common ground among the Abrahamic religions. This initiative has called forth numerous Christian responses exploring commonly shared beliefs and values (Volf et al. 2009).

The Middle East prior to Islam

The earliest Christian interpretations of the Bible in relation to Muslims and Islam emerged from the complex context of the Middle East in antiquity.

Long before the appearance of Islam, Jewish, Christian, and other Hellenistic authors in the Mediterranean world interpreted Arabs in light of the Genesis narrative of Abraham, Sarah, Hagar, and Ishmael (Millar 1993, 23-45; Sarris 2011, 264). According to the book of Genesis, the angel of the Lord told Hagar to name her son Ishmael and foretold: "He shall be a wild ass of a man, with his hand against everyone, and everyone's hand against him, and he shall live at odds with all his kin" (Gen. 16:12). According to Eusebius of Caesarea, Molon, a first-century B.C.E. Greek historian, described Ishmael as going to Arabia, where he reportedly fathered twelve sons who became kings and who were allegedly the ancestors of the twelve kings of Arabia in Molon's day (Eusebius of Caesarea, *Preparatio evangelica* 9.19; Lamoreaux 1996, 10). In the first century C.E., the Jewish historian Josephus referred to Arabs as descendants of Ishmael (*Antiquities of the Jews* 1.12.2; Lamoreaux, 10-11).

Before the appearance of Islam, Christians sometimes called Arabs "Hagarites" because they were allegedly descended from Hagar; they also called them "Saracens," understanding this term to mean "empty of Sarah," because Sarah was responsible for Abraham's decision to drive Hagar and Ishmael out of their home into the desert (Lamoreaux 1996, 10). According to the Talmud, the only gift that Abraham gave to Ishmael was magic, and this was why the later Ishmaelites were alleged to practice magic (Lamoreaux, 11). The biblical image of Ishmael would have an enormous influence on Christian perceptions of Muslims, who were frequently called "Ishmaelites" or "Saracens." Early Christian interpretations of Arab Muslims were influenced by these earlier negative images of Arabs.

The bitter divisions among Christians over Christology also shaped the context for the first Christian perceptions of Muslims. Many Christians in Mesopotamia and the Sassanian Empire in ancient Persia belonged to the Church of the East, which had been established in the first or second century C.E. (Baumer 2006; Soro 2007). The Sassanian rulers, who were Zoroastrian, were chronically in conflict with the Roman Empire. After the time of Constantine, the leaders of the Sassanian Empire distrusted the Church of the East, suspecting its members of secret allegiance to the Christians who ruled the Roman Empire. In a climate of intense suspicion, in 426 the Church of the East declared itself independent of any outside church authorities.

Five years later, in 431, the Church of the East rejected the decision of the Council of Ephesus to acclaim Mary as the Mother of God (*theotokos*), believing that this term sounded too much like Greek mythology. The Church of the East supported the teaching of Nestorius that Mary should be called the Mother of Christ (*christotokos*). As a result, they were traditionally but inaccurately called Nestorians—Nestorius was patriarch of Constantinople and was not even a member of the Church of the East, let alone its founder. As we will see in later chapters, members of the Church of the East went to India, spread along the Silk Road across Central Asia, and entered seventh-century China, developing extensive experience in interreligious relations with Buddhists, Daoists, and Hindus.

The Church of the East lived in difficult circumstances for centuries, and often communication with Roman and Byzantine Christians was limited. Since the nineteenth century, this church has called itself the Assyrian Church of the East. In recent years there have been ecumenical dialogues between this church and the Roman Catholic Church, leading to the clarification that the Church of the East did not ever intend to deny the divinity of Jesus Christ. In 1994, Pope John Paul II and Mar Dinkha IV, the Catholicos of the Assyrian Church of the East, signed a major ecumenical agreement resolving the issue of Christology ("The Common Christological Declaration between the Catholic Church and the Assyrian Church of the East").

There were divisions among other Christian communities as well. The Roman Catholic and Byzantine Orthodox communities accepted the decision of the Council of Chalcedon in 451 that Jesus Christ has two natures, united in one person or hypostasis. Many of the Byzantine emperors sought to impose this belief on other Christians within their realm. The Oriental Orthodox Churches, including Coptic Orthodox, Armenian Orthodox, and Syrian Orthodox Christians, refused to accept the language of the Council of Chalcedon and affirmed that Jesus Christ has only one nature, which is divine. Even though the Oriental Orthodox Churches have traditionally been called "Monophysites," they do not accept this term and prefer to be called "Miaphysites." Oriental Orthodox Christians stress the distinction in Greek between *monos* and *mia*; *monos* means "one" in an exclusive sense that would exclude Jesus' humanity; *mia* means "one," but in an inclusive sense that allows for acknowledging Jesus' full humanity even though this is not a separate nature. Recent ecumenical agreements between the Roman Catholic Church and the Oriental Orthodox Churches have jointly acknowledged the legitimacy of both Chalcedonian and Miaphysite language (Lefebure 1999).

During the lifetime of Muhammad, the Byzantine emperor Heraclius sought to resolve the christological dispute by proposing the Monothelite claim that Jesus had only one will, but this failed to resolve the issue. The debates continued to rage in the seventh century; the Byzantine Orthodox and Latin Churches eventually rejected Monothelitism at the Third Council of Constantinople in 680/681. These intra-Christian conflicts shaped the context of the first Christian interpretations of Muslims and Islam.

The christological debates furnished Christians with some of the most influential categories for interpreting Islam. Traditionally, most Christians did not see Islam as a distinct religion but rather as the last and most dangerous of the christological heresies. Frequently, Christians interpreted Muslims as Arians or as Nestorians because they honor Jesus as a prophet but deny the divinity of Jesus.

The context of the first Muslim–Christian encounters was also shaped by the early-seventh-century battles between the Christian Byzantine Empire and the Zoroastrian Sassanian Empire. The Sassanian forces captured Jerusalem in 614, conquered much of Anatolia and even threatened the imperial city of Constantinople in 626. In response, Emperor Heraclius led the Byzantine forces to victory over the Sassanians at the battle of Nineveh in 627 and reconquered Jerusalem in 629. This war left both parties exhausted and depleted, paving the way for the early Arab Muslim victories over both.

Early Christian Perspectives on Muslims and Muhammad

According to the Islamic tradition, Muslim–Christian relations began in friendship. When Muhammad was facing opposition in Makka, he reportedly sent some Muslims to the protection of an African Christian king in a land called Axum, usually known as Abyssinia—present-day Ethiopia and Eritrea. When the Makkans asked the king to send the refugees back, the king questioned the Muslims. They told him about their conversion from idolatry to monotheism, and they presented what would later become Sura 19 of the Qur'an, a passage that describes the miraculous virginal conception and birth of Jesus as a prophet. The Christian king allegedly wept for joy, welcomed them as refugees, and gave them safety (Goddard 2000, 20-21).

After the death of Muhammad in 632 c.e., there began a long period of military confrontation between Muslims and Christians, and Arab Muslim-led armies won a number of early victories against the forces of the Christian Byzantine Empire. Early sources indicate that the invading Arab armies included a mixed population, with non-Muslims and Muslims fighting together (Sarris 2011, 268; Hoyland 2006, 409). In December 634, the Arab Muslim army encamped between Jerusalem and Bethlehem, preventing Christians from journeying from Jerusalem to Bethlehem for the usual Christmas Eve celebrations. In the following decades and centuries, there were many battles between Muslims and Christians, often with Muslims gaining the victory. Christian views on the Arab Muslim conquests were sharply divided, with some Christians viewing the Arab Muslims favorably and others with great hostility.

For Christians of the Church of the East, the Arab Muslim conquests brought relief from conflicts with the Byzantine Orthodox Christians, who had not allowed the Church of the East to establish monasteries in Byzantine-ruled territories. Iso'yaw III, the Catholicos of the Church of the East in the 650s, writes quite positively about the Muslim victories and describes the conditions of Arab Muslim rule, which included respect for Christianity and permission for the opening of monasteries:

> These Arabs, whom God has now given sovereignty over the world, are disposed towards us as you know. They are not opposed to Christianity. Indeed, they respect our religion and honor the priests and the saints of our Lord and they give aid to the churches and monasteries. (quoted by Lamoreaux 1996, 13)

Oriental Orthodox Christians, who had suffered persecution from the Byzantine Christian rulers, also express a positive regard for the Arab Muslims. In 661, the Armenian Orthodox bishop Sebeos describes Muhammad as learned in the Mosaic Law and as having taught Arabs to know the God of Abraham; the result was that "[a]bandoning their vain cults, they turned to the living God who had appeared to their father Abraham" (Sebeos 42, 135; 1999, 1:96). Bishop Sebeos expected the Arabs to take possession of the lands that God had promised to Abraham.

Similarly, John of Nikiu, a Coptic Orthodox bishop and chronicler in Egypt, believed that God, "the guardian of justice," permitted the Arab Muslims to defeat the Byzantine Orthodox Christians who "had dealt treacherously against Him" (*Chronicle* 186; quoted by Lamoreaux, 13). Later, the Oriental Orthodox historian Severus interpreted the Arab Muslim victories as God's just punishment on the Byzantine Christians for their acceptance of the christological decisions of the Council of Chalcedon (Severus ibn al-Muqaffa, 492-93; quoted by Lamoreaux, 14). For Christians in the Church of the East and the Oriental Orthodox Churches, Muhammad and the Arab Muslims appeared in a favorable light as worshipers of the God of Abraham and bringers of divine vindication from Byzantine imperial oppression.

The perspective of the Melkite or Byzantine Orthodox Christians was quite different; for them, the Muslim conquests were an unmitigated disaster. Maximus the Confessor wrote to Peter the Illustrious from Alexandria between 634 and 640, describing the Arab Muslims as "a barbarous nation of the desert overrunning another land as if it were their own!" (quoted by Lamoreaux, 14). Applying the familiar pattern of the Deuteronomic historians of the Bible, Maximus trusted that if Christians repented for their sins, they would be restored to God's favor and win victory over the Arab Muslims (Lamoreaux, 15).

Confronted with the Muslim army camped between Bethlehem and Jerusalem during the Christmas season of 634, Patriarch Sophronius of Jerusalem applied the perspective of the prophets of ancient Israel to his community's experience, interpreting this calamity as God's punishment for the sins of Christians: "Because of countless sins and very serious faults, we have become unworthy of the sight of these things [the Holy Places of Bethlehem]" (F. E. Peters 1985, 175). Like Maximus, Sophronius draws on the tradition of Deuteronomy and the biblical prophets, urging his Christian congregation to repent so that God would once again grant them victory:

> I call on and I command and I beg you for the love of Christ the Lord, in so far as it is in our power, let us correct ourselves, let us shine forth with repentance, let us be purified with conversion and let us curb our performance of acts which are hateful to God. If we constrain ourselves, as friendly and beloved of God, we would laugh at the fall of our Saracen adversaries and we would view their not distant death and we would see their final destruction. (F. E. Peters 1985, 175)

After Muslims had entered Jerusalem, Patriarch Sophronius reportedly drew on biblical apocalyptic language to interpret the construction of the al-Aqsa mosque. According to Theophanes, a ninth-century Byzantine historian,

Sophronius interpreted the al-Aqsa mosque as the Abomination of Desolation described in the book of Daniel, but it is unclear how accurate Theophanes' sources were (McGinn 1994, 305 n. 40). This interpretation was a harbinger of a much broader pattern of apocalyptic reflection that shaped Christian perceptions of Muslims. Maximus and Sophronius do not appear to have viewed Islam as a new religion, and Sophronius refers to the "Saracens" as "godless and impious" (Lamoreaux, 15). Their biblically informed model of interpreting Muslim victories as punishment for Christian sins would be followed countless times in different later contexts, for example, by medieval Syriac and Armenian Christians under Mongol rule (Bundy 1996) or by the thirteenth-century Flemish poet Jacob van Maerlant (ca. 1230-1288; Claassens 1996, 211).

Meanwhile, in England, Theodore, the archbishop of Canterbury, interpreted the Muslims' warfare in light of biblical comments on the Ishmaelites. Theodore was originally from Tarsus, but he left that region because of the coming of the Muslims, traveling to France and eventually to England, where he served as archbishop of Canterbury between 668 and 690. In his biblical interpretation, he explains to his Anglo-Saxon audience: "The race of Ishmael was that of the Saracens, a race which is never at peace with anyone but is always at war with someone" (Bischoff and Lapidge 1994, 325; quoted by Sarris 2011, 378).

For a millennium, Islam was the most successful and dangerous competitor that Christianity had to face. Much of the heartland of early Christianity, the sites of many early church councils, and some of the oldest sees, including Alexandria, Antioch, and Constantinople, are today in lands that are predominantly Muslim. This challenge left medieval Christians profoundly uneasy concerning Islam. Applying the theology of history of Deuteronomy and the historical books of the Bible, Christians could argue that the subordinate situation of the Jews demonstrated God's wrath at them for their rejection of Jesus; Islam, however, was from the beginning immensely successful in the military and political field. In large measure, the initial threat was political and military, and thus the political and military dimensions of Islam were often most prominent to Christians at the beginning of the relationship. However, as the early Middle Ages developed, Muslim cultural and intellectual life far surpassed developments in Western Europe. In this period, Islam had more vibrant cities, wealthier courts, and better scientists and doctors.

The great medieval historian R.W. Southern asserted, "The existence of Islam was the most far-reaching problem in medieval Christendom. It was a problem at every level of experience" (1962, 3). Southern noted that the major options for relationship were: "Crusade, conversion, coexistence, and commercial interchange"; but the theological challenge was that Islam "called persistently for some answer to the mystery of its existence: what was its providential role in history"? (3). Some of the most influential responses to this question came from new interpretations of the apocalyptic heritage.

Kenneth Baxter Wolf notes that the *mentalité* of medieval Christians regarding Muslims and Islam was profoundly shaped by the monastic-based curriculum of education, with its strong focus on the Bible and the patristic heritage:

> The scriptural and patristic focus of this curriculum, combined with a highly cultivated appreciation of the role of divine providence in history, determined that early medieval observers of something new like Islam would describe it in terms of age-old categories and patterns found in the Bible and the writings of the church fathers. (1996, 86)

This meant that Islam was understood in the categories already developed to interpret earlier threats to Christian life and practice. One available category was Christian heresy; and to a large degree, medieval Christians did not perceive Islam as a new religion but rather as a variation on earlier Christian heresies already familiar. Another category, rooted in the Bible, was apocalyptic eschatology.

Apocalyptic Interpretations of Islam

Since the fourth century, Byzantine Orthodox Christians had largely followed the lead of Eusebius of Caesarea in viewing the Christian Roman Empire as a manifestation of God's providential plan for history. The swift Arab Muslim military victories came as a major shock to Byzantine Christians; the rising power of Muslim rulers and armies posed a sharp theological challenge to Eusebius's confident vision. Soon many Christians turned to apocalyptic eschatology inspired by the Bible to make sense of these events. Bernard McGinn comments on the role of apocalyptic eschatology in making sense of unexpected historical developments:

> One of the characteristics of apocalyptic eschatology is its drive to find meaning in current events by seeing them in light of the scenario of the end. Such *a posteriori,* or after-the-fact, uses of apocalypticism are often reactions to major historical changes (like the conversion of the Empire or the rise of Islam) that do not fit into the received view of providential history. By making a place for such events in the story of the end, the final point that gives all history meaning, apocalyptic eschatology incorporates the unexpected into the divinely foreordained and gives it permanent significance. (1994, 88)

One of the earliest interpretations of Muhammad in apocalyptic imagery comes from the *Doctrina Jacobi* (*Doctrine of Jacob*), written about 637, which tells of Jacob, a convert from Judaism who is reportedly preaching Christian faith to Jews in North Africa. In dialogue with a Jew named Justus, Jacob argues that the final judgment is close at hand, since Jesus the Messiah has already come and now the Antichrist has walked the earth. In response, Justus refers to a message he had received from his brother Abraham in Caesarea about a false prophet who had appeared among the Saracens. When Abraham had asked an elderly rabbi about the false prophet, the rabbi reportedly responded, "He is false, for surely the prophets do not come with sword and chariot. . . . But go, Abraham, and enquire about the prophet that has appeared" (Sarris 2011, 260). Abraham investigated "and learned from those that had met him, that you find nothing true in the so-called prophet, save shedding the blood of men; for he says he holds the keys of paradise, which is untrue" (Sarris, 260-61). As the conversation continues, Jacob persuades Justus that Muhammad is in fact Hermolaus Satan, the horn of the beast predicted by Daniel (7:23-25), and that Jesus Christ is indeed the true Messiah. As a result, Justus becomes a Christian (Lamoreaux, 16). The *Doctrine of Jacob* interprets Muhammad as the false prophet of the end-time who has brought about the end of the Roman Empire and as an apocalyptic figure predicted by Daniel in the image of the beast's horn.

Not long afterward, during the middle or late seventh century, an anonymous writer known as Pseudo-Methodius produced an *Apocalypse* whose interpretation of Muslims would shape Christian attitudes for a millennium and more (*Apocalypse of Pseudo-Methodius* 222-42; Martinez 1985, 58-246). The author wrote in Syriac using the pseudonym of the revered fourth-century martyr Methodius, the bishop of Olympus in Lycia who was killed in the Roman persecutions in 312. *The Apocalypse of Pseudo-Methodius* recounts an angel's supposed revelation to Methodius on Mount Singara in present-day northwest Iraq. The work views the Arab Muslim triumphs as part of the ongoing drama of the four kingdoms described by the book of Daniel. Pseudo-Methodius sees the "Ishmaelites," that is, the Arab Muslims, as preparing the way for the Son of Perdition (2 Thess. 2:3); and he identifies the "Children of Ishmael" with "the people whom Daniel (11:5) calls 'the arm of the South,'" that is, the king of the south who Daniel predicts will destroy the empire of the Persians (*Apocalypse* 10.6; Martinez, 230). Pseudo-Methodius interprets the victory of the Muslim army against Byzantine forces at the River Yarmouk in 636 as the fulfillment of the prophecy of Ezekiel 39:17-18, which invites the wild animals and birds to come and eat the flesh of fattened men and drink the blood of warriors in an apocalyptic feast (*Apocalypse* 11.1-2; Martinez, 230).

Continuing the style of interpretation of the biblical prophets, Pseudo-Methodius sees the Muslims' victories not as due to their righteousness or to God's favor for them but rather as God's punishment on the sinfulness of Christians. Pseudo-Methodius quotes Moses' warning to the Israelites in Deuteronomy as applicable to the situation of the Muslims. Moses pointedly tells the Israelites that God is bringing them to the promised land not because of their virtue but rather because of the sinfulness of the inhabitants of the land (Deut. 9:4-7). Pseudo-Methodius applies this model to the Islamic victories: "Similarly with these children of Ishmael: it was not because God loves them that he allowed them to enter the kingdom of the Christians, but because of the wickedness and sin which is performed at the hands of the Christians, the like of which has not been performed in any of the former generations" (*Apocalypse* 11.5; Martinez, 231).

Pseudo-Methodius interprets the Son of Destruction in 2 Thessalonians 2:3 in the context of the Muslim victories: "This is the chastisement of which the Apostle spoke: 'The chastisement must come first, only then will that Man of Sin, the Son of Destruction, be revealed'" (*Apocalypse* 11.17; Martinez, 233; see also Alexander 1985, 20-21). Pseudo-Methodius understands Jesus' parable of the wheat and the tares (Matt. 13:24-30) to mean that the sufferings of Christians under Muslim rule must increase so that the faithful may be tested and known (*Apocalypse* 13.4; Martinez, 236). He recalls Jesus' teaching in the Sermon on the Mount: "Blessed are you when people revile and persecute you, saying all sorts of bad things about you falsely for my Name's sake: rejoice then and exult, for your reward is great in heaven" (Matt. 5:11-12; *Apocalypse* 13.5; Martinez, 237). He also holds out the hope of Jesus' promise: "He who endures to the end shall have life" (Matt. 10:22; 24:13; *Apocalypse* 13.5; Alexander, 48; Martinez, 237).

After this suffering, Pseudo-Methodius prophesies that a future Byzantine emperor will fight and defeat the Muslims: "the king of the Greeks shall go out against them in great wrath," bringing destruction to the Ishmaelites and peace to Christians, a peace unprecedented in the history of the world (*Apocalypse* 13.11; Martinez, 237). There will, however, be more suffering when the king of the Greeks dies and the Son of Destruction appears and works the signs of deception foretold by Jesus (Matt. 24:24). The Son of Destruction will then take his seat in Jerusalem until the return of Jesus Christ. "But at the Advent of our Lord from heaven he will be delivered over to 'the Gehenna of Fire' (Matt. 5:22) and to 'outer darkness', where he will be amidst 'weeping and gnashing of teeth'" (Matt. 8:12; *Apocalypse* 14.13; Martinez, 242).

Pseudo-Methodius interprets Muhammad as a forerunner of the Antichrist and the Son of Destruction; he holds out the expectation of the coming king of the Greeks, the Last Emperor, that is, the final Byzantine Christian emperor, as hope for faithful Christians in difficult times. Pseudo-Methodius believes that the ultimate victory of Christ and his final emperor is assured, and thus he urges Christians to resist the Muslims and continue to struggle against them through all hardships. Inspired by confidence in Christ's final triumph over all enemies, Pseudo-Methodius opposes any form of collaboration or acceptance of Muslim rule (McGinn 1979a, 70).

The *Apocalypse of Pseudo-Methodius* was translated into Greek and circulated widely for centuries, becoming the third most important apocalyptic text for medieval Christians, after the biblical books of Daniel and Revelation (on the relation between the Syriac original and the Greek translation, see Alexander 1985, 31-60). This text was still being reprinted and distributed a millennium later in 1683, when the Ottoman army was besieging Vienna (McGinn 1979a, 72). The style of biblical interpretation modeled by Pseudo-Methodius is a classic example of the hermeneutics of hostility; tragically, it was widely influential in shaping Christian perceptions of Muslims for a millennium and more.

Medieval Christians repeatedly interpreted Muhammad either as the Antichrist or as a forerunner of the Antichrist (McGinn 1994, 85-86; N. Daniel 2000). Christians in Spain calculated the death of Muhammad to have occurred in the year 666 of the Spanish Christian calendar; since 666 is the number of the beast in Revelation 13:8, many believed that Muhammad was the Antichrist (Goddard 2000, 83). In this climate, Eulogius and Paul Alvarus interpreted the books of Daniel and Revelation as applying to their situation. According to them, the mythological beast symbolized the coming of Islam, which attacked the empires of the Greeks, Franks, and Goths and spoke against the Most High (Wolf 1996, 97-99; Goddard, 82-83). Alvarus understood the eleventh horn of the fourth beast in Daniel 7:23-25 as predicting Muhammad (Wolf, 98). Eulogius and Alvarus interpreted the prophecy of Jesus in Mark 13 regarding the coming desolation of Jerusalem as referring to the Islamic conquest of the city. The book of Revelation's prophecy of the beast persecuting the people of God (chapter 13) was seen as referring to Cordoba (Goddard, 83).

A long tradition in Latin Christianity related the Antichrist to the Son of Destruction (or Perdition) of 2 Thessalonians (Hughes 2005) and associated both with Muslims. Medieval Christians frequently believed the members of "the synagogue of Satan" in the book of Revelation (2:9; 3:9) to be the Muslims (N. Daniel 2000, 133-34). In the twelfth century, Joachim of Fiore understands Muslims to be the last of seven kingdoms that are predicted by the images of the four beasts in Daniel 7 and the seven heads of the beast of the sea in Revelation 13 (Burr 1996, 133). Joachim interprets the beast rising from the abyss in Revelation 17:8 to refer to Islam rising again after temporary defeats and thereby scandalizing Christians (Burr, 134). In calling for a new Crusade in 1213, Pope Innocent III condemns Muhammad as the Son of Perdition (2 Thess. 2:3), expecting him to have a reign of 666 years, almost all of which has already passed (McGinn 1994, 150).

In the later thirteenth century, Peter Olivi continued the apocalyptic tradition of interpreting Muslims by weaving them into his interpretation of Daniel and Revelation. He expects two Antichrists to come, first a mystical Antichrist and then another, "the great Antichrist"; he believes that either or both might be pseudo-popes (Burr 1996, 138). Olivi understands the seven heads of the beast (Rev. 13:1) to refer to seven centuries from the beginning of Islam to the arrival of the Antichrist. He understands the wounded head (Rev. 13:3) to foretell the death and then the recovery of Islam; from this he predicts the future conversion of many Muslims to Christianity, followed by a revival of Islamic strength (Burr, 137). Olivi interprets the seventh head of the beast in Revelation 13 to refer to the "Saracens," and he understands the beast from the land (Rev 13:11) to refer to Christians who apostatize to Islam during the time of the Antichrist (Burr, 136-37). He expects the Antichrist to come in the near future, speculating that the number of the beast 666 could refer to the years between 635 C.E., when Muslims defeated the Sassanians, and the coming year 1300; or the number could refer to the period from 648, when Muslims conquered Africa, to 1323, which would be 1,290 years after the death of Christ

(Daniel 12:11 predicts 1,290 years from the end of sacrifices to the coming of the "detestable thing"; Burr, 137).

Later Franciscan apocalyptists Alexander Minorita (d. 1271), Pierre Auriol (1280-1322), and Nicholas of Lyra (1270-1349) continue to speculate on the place of Muhammad and Muslims in the predictions of Daniel and Revelation. They all interpret the beast on the land (Rev. 13:11) to refer to Muhammad and offer various speculations on the number 666 in relation to Islamic history (Burr 1996, 139-40; Krey 1996, 154). However, they differ in their assessments of history. Alexander and Pierre are more triumphalist regarding Crusader victories against Muslims, while Nicholas revives Augustine's skepticism regarding human achievements and predictions of future events. Where Alexander and Pierre confidently look forward to the defeat of Islam, Nicholas laments that its power is increasing (Krey, 154-57). Nicholas also rejects the widespread expectation that Jews and Muslims would convert to Christianity. Philip Krey comments: "Lyra chose realism and practicality over apocalyptic hopes. To the continuing late-medieval academic discussion over the role of Islam in the Apocalypse, Lyra proposes that historical facts take precedence over ideology and wishful thinking. Nicholas also relativizes and debunks the nature of the crusading propaganda he has inherited" (157). Nicholas is skeptical regarding the effectiveness of Crusades, and he refused to predict the fall of Islam or the coming of the Antichrist. The loss of Acre and the increasing power of the Mamelukes defied any notion of divine providence. For Nicholas, the persistence and strength of Islam remained an unresolved challenge.

However, writing in Spain about a century later, Paul of Burgos (a.k.a. Pablo de Santa Maria, 1351-1435), a former rabbi who converted in 1390 and eventually became archbishop of Burgos, chides Nicholas for his doubts regarding Islam and seeks to explain the riddle of its strength by stressing the positive aspects of Islam. Paul expresses his views on Islam by adding notes to Nicholas of Lyra's commentary on the Bible (*Additions to the Postillae of Nicholas of Lyra on the Bible*); he added notes to the commentary on Revelation 13 after a major Christian victory against the Moors in southern Spain in July 1431 (Krey 1996, 161).

Paul of Burgos in Spain is much more intimately familiar with Islam than Nicholas was in distant Paris, and Paul knows of Islamic tolerance of Christian life and practice. He refuses to identify Muslims with the Antichrist, preferring to use the language of an anti-apostle and an anti-prophet; and he refuses to call Muslims idolaters, seeing their worship of God as one reason God has tolerated them for so long. Krey describes Paul's evaluation of Islam: "Although Islam could be found in the images of Revelation 13, it was not like other pagan religions: the Saracens were not idolatrous; they did not force Christians to apostatize but only to pay taxes. There were many Christians in Islamic territories, and Islam considered Jesus to be the most excellent of all creatures" (Krey 1996, 155). Nonetheless, Paul of Burgos is fiercely critical of Islam and embraces the crusading spirit, with particular reference to fighting the Moors in Spain (Krey, 161).

Henry of Cossey interprets the white horse in Revelation 6:8 as referring to Muslim hypocrisy (Burr 1996, 143). Henry follows Joachim of Fiore in identifying Islam with the last of the four beasts in Daniel 7, the last major threat to Christianity (Burr, 144). Henry notes Innocent III's belief that 666 refers to the number of years that Islam will endure, but he acknowledges that that time has already expired, explaining the number instead as referring to the name of the Antichrist (Burr, 145).

Late medieval interpreters pondered why Islam had lasted so long with so much success. They responded by incorporating Muslims into a variety of apocalyptic scenarios. David Burr comments on the anxieties of late medieval Franciscans regarding Muslims: "As exegetes saw the crusader kingdoms disappear and the Mongols converting to Islam, they could hardly help thinking that the head of the beast, once nearly slain, had somehow been healed and menaced them more than ever" (1996, 147). Apocalyptic literature inspired Christians to fight against their Muslim adversaries for centuries, offering hope of eschatological vindication even in the most hopeless of earthly situations.

Theological Disputations: Islam as a Christian Heresy

Alongside the apocalyptic literature, there also appear theological works that respond to the Islamic challenge with doctrinal arguments, usually in polemical style (Bertaina). Christian authors such as John of Damascus (ca. 675-749), Theodore Abu Qurrah (ca. 750-825), Patriarch Timothy I (ca. 727-823), Nicetas of Byzantium (early to late ninth century?) write fictional dialogues between a Christian and "a Saracen," in which the Christian poses difficult questions to which the Muslim cannot effectively reply. Daniel Sahas describes the rhetorical strategy of using the Bible in these dialogues: "The Christian treats the Muslim as a Christian and uses his own sources, especially the Bible, as well as his Christian thinking and arguments, to judge Islam. This approach places the Muslim seemingly in a nondiscriminatory, but nevertheless in a disadvantageous position" (Sahas 1990, 63; see also Hanson 1996, 59).

One of the earliest of these writers, Anastasius of Sinai (d. ca. 700), relates Islamic teachings to Jewish and Samaritan teachings and to earlier Christian heresies. He interprets the Arab Muslims' victories as punishment for Byzantine emperor Constans II sending Pope Martin I into exile over christological controversies ("Sermo III"; Lamoreaux 1996, 20).

For European Christians, John of Damascus was the most influential of the early Christian apologists regarding Muslims and Islam. John came from a family of civil servants, and his grandfather, Mansur ibn Sarjun, reportedly served both the Byzantine Christian emperor Heraclius and also the Umayyad Muslim rulers in Damascus. His biographer, John of Jerusalem, tells us that John of Damascus also served the administration of the caliph in Damascus; but neither he nor the Muslim sources ever mention such service, and this claim has been questioned. According to a later tradition, John entered the monastery of St. Sabas (Mar Saba), was ordained there in 735, and lived there until his death in about 749 or 750 (Louth, 5-14).

Whatever the details of his early career, John demonstrates an intimate familiarity with Islamic perspectives, which he rebuts with bitter polemics. He wrote the first Summa of Christian theology, *The Fount of Knowledge* (John of Damascus 3-406). After a philosophical introduction, *Dialectica*, he reviews the various aberrations from the true faith in *On Heresies in Epitome*. The final section is *An Exact Exposition of the Orthodox Faith*. Toward the end of *On Heresies*, John discusses "the superstition of the Ishmaelites" (#101; p. 153) and describes it in insulting terms as a Christian heresy. Drawing on the earlier tradition regarding Arabs, John refers to Muslims as "Saracens," accepting the etymology "destitute of Sarah" (*Sarras kenoi* in Greek), "because of what Agar said to the angel: 'Sara hath sent me away destitute (Gen. 16:8)," that is, driven out by Sarah from Abraham's home (#101; p. 153). He also calls them "Agarenes" because they are descended from Agar (Hagar). John ridicules Islam, charging that Muhammad fabricated stories of revelation to justify his sexual appetites and that Muhammad invented the teachings of the Qur'an based on instruction from an Arian monk (later named Sergius in Byzantine and Western legend, Sargis-Bahira in Syriac, and Bahira in Arabic) (John of Damascus #101; p. 153; N. Daniel 2000, 15).

John of Damascus set a major precedent by not acknowledging Islam as a new religion but rather writing against "the heresy of the Ishmaelites" and never using the term "Islam." This would dominate European Christian terminology for centuries. Islam's view of Jesus Christ as merely a prophet and its denial of the Trinity were seen as proofs of this perspective, and Islam was often seen as a variant of the Arian or Nestorian christological heresies. Given that Muhammad and other Muslims directly denied the divinity of Jesus Christ, John saw them as forerunners of the Antichrist (#101; p. 153). John insisted that there was no testimony in favor of the Qur'an and that no prophets had foretold the coming of Muhammad (#101; pp. 154-55). He asked pointedly why Muhammad had no one to bear witness to him (#101; pp. 154-55).

John notes that Muslims accuse Christians of idolatry for venerating the cross; he turns the charge around, accusing them of idolatry for venerating the Kaaba, which he identifies as the head of a statue of Aphrodite (#101; pp. 156-57). John notes that Muslims accuse Christians of associationism for believing in the Trinity of God, the Word, and the Spirit (#101; p. 155). He observes pointedly that Muslims themselves refer to Jesus as the Word of God and the Spirit of God and charges that they do not understand what they are saying, for their own language affirms the divinity of Jesus. He charges that Muslims are guilty of mutilating God by denying the divinity of the Word and the Spirit (#101; p. 156). John also claims that the Qur'an was delivered to Muhammad in his sleep and thus was not reliable. He criticizes the Muslim practices of polygamy and divorce (#101; p. 157). John Renard notes that John of Damascus is accurate in his description of Islamic teachings and cites him as the classical example of "the polemical model" of Christian interpretations of Islam (2011, xvii).

Muhammad himself was repeatedly vilified, often being portrayed as an epileptic who invented stories of an angel to excuse his fits. He was also accused of lascivious practices and hypocrisy (N. Daniel 2000, 100-130). The allegedly immoral character of Muhammad's life was taken to be disproof of his claims to be a prophet. Christians also asked polemically what future events Muhammad had prophesied and what miracles he had performed, charging that he lacked the traditional credentials of a true prophet (Pelikan 1977, 238). The Qur'an was generally seen as a collection of biblical stories poorly reported and misunderstood and was viewed as an object of ridicule.

In the ninth century, Nicetas of Byzantium argues that the God of Islam is actually a devil. Nicetas's argument that the "God of Muhammad" was in fact the devil had a major influence and finds an echo in the medieval Byzantine ritual of condemnation, which was to be professed by those converting from Islam to Christianity: "And before all, I anathematize the God of Muhammad about whom he [Muhammad] says, 'He is God alone, God made of solid hammer-beaten metal; he begets not and is not begotten, nor is there like unto Him any one" (Hanson 1996, 55). This is likely a repudiation of Sura 112 of the Qur'an, which professes the divine unity (*Tawhid*). Craig Hanson explains that the Arabic word *samad* (Sura 112.2) "means 'solid, massive,' or more figuratively, 'permanent, everlasting, eternal'" (62); while John of Damascus and Theodore Abu Qurra understood the correct meaning of the Arabic word, a long line of Byzantine polemicists beginning with Nicetas of Byzantium translated the term into Greek as meaning "made of solid hammer-beaten metal," thereby casting the God of Muhammad as an idol (Hanson, 62-64). This mistranslation evokes the polemic of Second Isaiah against the images of the gods of Babylon, who could not hear or speak.

Emperor Manuel I Comnenus, however, rejected this translation and sought to drop the anathema from the Byzantine ritual, sparking an intense controversy. Manuel was in effect going back to the earlier Byzantine tradition of viewing Muhammad as a Christian heretic and of seeing the God of Muhammad as the one true God (Hanson 1996, 74). Manuel was concerned to convert Muslims to Christianity and feared that using a distorted caricature of Islamic faith could hinder this process. After much discussion, Manuel prevailed, and the mistranslation was dropped from the rite. Manuel died a few months after this decision, and later sources are silent on this matter; thus, we do not know the history or the effectiveness of the implementation of the decision (Hanson, 75).

The question whether Muslims worship the same God as Christians was debated among Christians in Spain in the ninth century. In deliberate provocations to the Islamic rulers, Christians in Cordoba began insulting Muhammad and professing faith in the divinity of Jesus Christ, which resulted in their martyrdom. Other Cordoban Christians objected to the martyrs' behavior and asked how their actions could be legitimate when they had "suffered at the hands of men [i.e., Muslims] who venerated both God and a law" (Eulogius, *Liber apologeticus martyrum* 19; quoted by Wolf 1996, 96). However, Eulogius sharply rejected the Cordoban Christians' claim that Muslims worship the same

God as Christians on the basis of a different law. Eulogius quoted Paul's rebuke to the Galatians: "But even if we or an angel from heaven should proclaim to you a gospel contrary to what we proclaimed to you, let that one be accursed!" (Gal. 1:8). On the basis of this verse, Eulogius denied that there could be any later legitimate law before God (Wolf, 96-97). Eulogius attacked Muhammad as an Antichrist like Arius because he denied the divinity of Christ (Wolf, 98).

In 1142, Peter the Venerable (1092-1156), abbot of the influential Benedictine monastery at Cluny in France, traveled to Muslim areas of Spain and commissioned the first translation of the Qur'an into Latin, laying the groundwork for more serious consideration of Islam by Western Christians. Robert of Ketton translated the Qur'an into Latin as *Lex Mahumet pseudoprophete* ("The Law of Muhammad the Pseudo-prophet") and worked to spread reliable knowledge of Islam. These efforts improved the quality of knowledge of Islam among Latin Christians, but they also suffered from numerous distortions, and Robert's translation was widely criticized. Peter the Venerable viewed Islam as a Christian heresy and wrote *Summa totius haeresis Saracenorum* ("Compendium of the Entirety of the Saracen Heresy") and also a handbook, *Liber contra sectam sive haeresim Saracenorum* ("Book against the Sect or Heresy of the Saracens").

The thirteenth-century Flemish poet Jacob van Maerlant, who was strongly influenced by Vincent of Beauvais, repeats the charge that Muhammad was an epileptic who invented the story of meeting the angel Gabriel to explain his fits and who learned a distorted version of Christian teaching from Sergius, a Nestorian monk. According to Maerlant, the Qur'an was composed by Muhammad under the influence of Sergius to present a more lenient form of the Law, which both Jews and Christians had allegedly found too burdensome (Claassens 1996, 220-21). He also charges that Muhammad's Law was written under the influence of the devil, lacking reason or grace (Claassens, 226).

Thomas Aquinas may have written the *Summa contra Gentiles* as an aid for Christian missionaries addressing Muslims in the Iberian Peninsula and beyond. Aquinas was familiar with Islamic philosophical thought, especially Ibn Rushd and Ibn Sina; and David Burrell has shown that Aquinas's philosophical interpretation of monotheism was deeply influenced by Islamic thinkers (1992). However, Aquinas repeated the familiar charge that Muhammad "seduced the people by promises of carnal pleasure to which the concupiscence of the flesh goads us" (*Summa contra Gentiles* 1.6; quoted by Waltz 2013, 112). John Renard laments, "Here it is most uncharacteristic of Thomas that he relies on hearsay or unreliable tertiary sources in his characterization, not of Islamic thought, but of the venality of Muhammad and the gullibility of his followers" (2011, xxi). He suggests that Thomas probably did not know any Muslims personally, and he speculates that Thomas may have known John of Damascus's writings on Islam and certainly was familiar with Peter the Venerable's *Summa of the Entirety of the Saracen Heresy.* Renard cites Thomas Aquinas as the classic representative of the "scholastic model" of Christian encounter with Islam.

Regarding the interpretation of the Bible, Thomas Aquinas believed he had nothing to learn from Muslims. The Angelic Doctor views Muhammad as distorting the biblical teachings, charging:

Nor do divine pronouncements on the part of preceding prophets offer him [Muhammad] any witness. On the contrary, he perverts almost all the testimonies of the Old and New Testaments by making them into fabrications of his own, as can be seen by anyone who examines his law. It was, therefore, a shrewd decision on his part to forbid his followers to read the Old and New Testaments, lest these books convict him of falsity. It is thus clear that those who place any faith in his words believe foolishly. (*Summa contra Gentiles* 1.6; quoted by Waltz 2013, 113)

Sacred Warriors, Sacred Combat

Christians and Muslims repeatedly fought military contests across the centuries, and thus it is not surprising that much of Christian interpretation of the Bible in relation to Muslims and Islam involves the imagery of sacred combat and holy war. During the long struggle in the Iberian Peninsula, James the Apostle, the son of Zebedee, became the heavenly patron of Christians in battle against Muslims. Jesus had nicknamed James and his brother John *Boanerges* ("sons of thunder," Mark 3:17), apparently because the two brothers wanted Jesus to call down thunder on those Samaritans who rejected him (Luke 9:54). Even though Jesus sharply rebuked his fiery disciple for his temper (Luke 9:55), medieval Christians honored James for his ferocity, and he became the patron of Spain. According to legend, he miraculously intervened in the battle of Clavijo in 844, when Ramiro I of Asturias was leading Christians in battle against Muslims led by the Emir of Cordoba. James's heavenly assistance in battle earned him the new sobriquet "Matamoros," the Moor-slayer who kills the enemies of Christ. The church built in his honor at Compostela in northwestern Spain, where his remains were allegedly discovered, has long been one of the most important pilgrimage places of Europe (Dunn and Davidson 1996; Garcia Turza 2000).

Medieval Christians frequently imagined Jesus as a warrior in conflict with his adversaries and interpreted his harsh words as justification for their own attacks on opponents. The Christian imagination transformed Prince of Peace into the Heroic Warrior of Sacred Combat. Christians believed that their wars were, after all, waged in order to establish a just peace. An early English poem, "The Dream of the Rood," calls Jesus "the Warrior . . . the Mighty King, Lord of Heavens" and "the Wielder of Triumphs" (1:23, 24). Charlemagne appeared as the ideal Christian warrior who asked the pope to pray that he might defeat his enemies by "the arms of Faith" (Tyerman 2006, 36). Ideals of chivalry combined monastic-style devotion to Christ with the warrior's courage in fighting for justice (Baker 2003, 158-90). These images shaped the climate in which the First Crusade was proclaimed.

John Meyendorff summarizes the reasons for a constant state of holy war from the perspective of Byzantine Christians:

There was an abyss between the two religions which no amount of polemics, no dialectical argument, no effort at diplomacy, was able to bridge. Insurmountable on the spiritual and the theological level, this opposition from the very beginning also took the shape of a gigantic struggle for world supremacy, because both religions claimed to have a universal mission, and both empires world supremacy. . . . This made mutual understanding difficult and led both sides to consider that holy war was, after all, the normal state of relations between the two Empires. (Meyendorff 1964, 129, quoted by Hanson 1996, 56-57)

In the eleventh century and throughout the Middle Ages, Christians regularly interpreted passages from the Bible without regard for their original historical context. Christopher Tyerman describes the usual practice of biblical interpretation during the eleventh century: "As it had developed by the beginning of its second millennium in western Christendom, Christianity was only indirectly a scriptural faith. The foundation texts of the Old and New Testaments were mediated even to the educated through the prism of commentaries by the so-called Church Fathers" (2006, 29). Individual sayings were often taken out of their original context and applied to situations undreamed of by the biblical authors.

At the center of the imagery of the First Crusade was Jesus' command to take up one's cross and follow him (Matt. 16:24). In the Gospel of Matthew, this command comes after Jesus' teaching in the Sermon on the Mount concerning love of enemy and nonviolent responses to evil. In the late eleventh century, however, the original context was neglected, and taking up the cross was interpreted as violent combat on behalf of Christ. Tyerman comments: "The holy war [against Muslims] was perceived and possibly designed to revolve around Matthew 16:24" (2006, 32). For centuries the successive Crusades took shape as concrete ways to accept this challenge.

Crusading Christians found new meaning in the prophecy of the angel in Genesis 16:12 that Ishmael would have "his hand against everyone and everyone's hand against him; and he shall live at odds with all his kin." This prediction came to have greater significance and importance as Christians formed the notion of a "divided world," with the new concept of *christianitas* as the good side and the "Ishmaelites" as the evil side (Claassens 1996, 212).

Medieval Christians repeatedly interpreted their earthly enemies, especially Muslims, as the accomplices of the Son of Destruction of 2 Thessalonians and the Antichrist of 1 John. The sacred combat of the book of Revelation was of particular importance in this process. The bloody images of battle in the book of Revelation shape the accounts of the sack of Jerusalem by the First Crusade in 1099. Raymond of Aguilers described the scene on the Temple Mount after the Crusaders' victory: "It is sufficient to relate that in the Temple of Solomon and the portico crusaders rode in blood to the knees and bridles of their horses" (Tyerman 2006, 31). Tyerman notes the biblical reference: "Raymond was quoting Revelation 14:20: 'And the winepress was trodden without the city, and blood came out of the winepress, even unto the horse bridles.' It is hard to exaggerate the dependence of Raymond's contemporaries on the Scripture for imagery and language" (31).

Brett Edward Whalen notes that when medieval Christians were triumphant, as in the capture of Jerusalem by the First Crusade in 1099, they could apply the biblical theology of holy war directly and see their victories as guided by God's providence. When, however, they suffered reversals, they followed the model of Deuteronomy and ancient Israelite prophets in interpreting their defeats as God's punishment of them for their sins (2009, 56-70).

At the end of the Fourth Lateran Council in 1215, Pope Innocent III issued a bull proclaiming another Crusade, *Ad liberandum terram sanctam* (Lomax 1996, 176). In the years that followed, however, Emperor Frederick II did not follow the pope's leadership and established an Islamic community in Lucera in central Italy with full religious freedom; later, in 1228-29, Frederick would peacefully take back control of the Holy Land. As John Philip Lomax explains, "Rather than engage the Muslims at the periphery, Frederick nurtured them at the center; rather than force his Saracens to choose between death and conversion, he employed them in his wars against Christian powers, including the papacy's most reliable client, the Lombard League" (177).

Pope Gregory IX sent Dominican friars to preach to the Muslims, and he ordered Frederick II to help Christianize the Muslim community in Lucera, invoking the example of the prophet Jonah, who had terrorized the people of Nineveh, leading to their repentance. In *Post vicarium Iesu Christi*, Gregory urged Frederick to use the "material sword," instructing him to "drag this people, who are openly deceived by the error of perdition, to the font of regeneration and renewal by means of terror, because then their servitude will be more fruitful, since the one God shall have come to you and to them" (Lomax 1996, 182). Thus, the example of the prophet Jonah came to serve as a biblical precedent for the "means of terror." Nothing seems to have come of the effort, and no missionaries are reported to have visited the area (Lomax, 184; Kedar 1984, 145). Later popes fulminated against succeeding emperors over the existence of this Muslim enclave so close to Rome. The community was finally destroyed in 1300.

In later centuries, a hermeneutic of hostility continued to dominate Christian interpretations of the Bible in relation to Muslims. Protestants continued the medieval Catholic association of Muslims with the Antichrist. Martin Luther associated Muhammad and Muslims with the Antichrist, whom he identified more properly as the pope; and later Lutherans would develop a theology of the dual Antichrist of pope and Turk (McGinn 1994, 206). He also identified the Ottoman Turks with the Devil incarnate or as minions of the Devil (Francisco 2013, 132). He did admire certain aspects of Turkish culture; but because Muslims reject the Trinity, Luther turned around the charge of idolatry against Muslims, charging that they "invent a god such as they wish to have, not as God has revealed Himself" (Francisco, 141). Luther did not have a detailed personal knowledge of Muslims or Islamic theology but followed the main lines of the medieval Christian critique (Francisco, 129). After years of trying, he finally obtained a copy of the Qur'an in 1542. On reading it, Luther decided that Islam presented a religion of works righteousness similar to Roman Catholicism (Francisco, 144).

Medieval Christians were aware of the teachings of Jesus regarding love of enemies, forgiveness, and nonviolent response to evil. Medieval Christians honored the pacific ideals of Jesus as noble principles; but they generally applied them to private, personal relations while looking to the theology of war in the battles of the Hebrew Bible and the book of Revelation for guidance in their public affairs (Tyerman 2006, 30). As we will see, it was a Hindu, Mahatma Gandhi, who would later provide the first widely influential example of applying Jesus' nonviolent teachings to situations of political and social conflict.

Conversation and *Convivencia*

Despite the vilification, violence, and repeated military campaigns, in many regions during the Middle Ages Christians and Muslims did live peacefully together at least during certain periods. In these situations there were respectful exchanges. In or around 781, there were peaceful theological discussions between Patriarch Timothy I of the Church of the East and the caliph Mahdi (Moffett 1998, 351). Each partner maintained his own beliefs. Patriarch Timothy looked to aspects of the biblical heritage that Christians share with Muslims as he generously praised Muhammad for teaching monotheism and for following in the path of the biblical prophets. Even though the debate was held on Muslim territory, there was no clear winner and no threat of violence.

In 1076, Pope Gregory VII wrote to Al-Nasir, the Muslim ruler of Bijaya, in present-day Algeria:

> Almighty God, who wishes that all should be saved and none lost, approves nothing in us so much as that after loving him one should love his fellow man, and that one should not do to others, what one does not want done to oneself. You and we owe this charity to ourselves especially because we believe in and confess one God, admittedly in a different way, and daily praise and venerate him, the Creator of the world and ruler of this world. (Quoted by John Paul II 1991, 66)

In a situation of potential conflict, Pope Gregory invoked Jesus' teaching of universal love and of treating others as we wish to be treated as the norms for interaction with Muslims. He placed the differences between Christians and Muslims in the context of God's universal salvific will (1 Tim. 2:4). This letter was cited by the Second Vatican Council (*Nostra Aetate* §2) and by Pope John Paul II (1991).

There were positive relations in some settings. In about 1175, Emperor Frederic Barbarossa sent Burchard of Strasbourg as his envoy to Saladin. Burchard wrote an account of his journey, the *Itinerarium*, in which he describes harmonious relations between "Saracens" and Christians. He describes Alexandria, Egypt: "In Alexandria, everyone freely follows his religion. In this city there are many Christian churches" (Tolan 2008, 106). In Cairo, he writes, "Saracens, Jews and Christians live; each nation follows its own law and there are many Christian churches in this city" (Tolan, 106). Burchard notes that Saracens and Christians alike venerate the shrine of Mary at Matariyya near Cairo, where Mary reportedly washed the diapers of Jesus during the flight to Egypt. He also describes a Marian shrine at Saydnaya near Damascus as a place where Muslims and Christians alike come to pray: "During the feast of the Assumption of the Virgin and during the feast of her birth, all the Saracens of this province come to this place, together with the Christians, to pray. And the Saracens offer their ceremonies with great devotion" (Tolan, 108-9). Burchard expresses none of the usual Christian invective toward Muslims and Islam. Instead, John Tolan notes, Burchard "affirms that Saracens, Christians and even Jews are united in their devotion to Mary. She grants miracles to all her faithful, apparently showing no preference for the Christians" (Tolan, 109).

R. W. Southern described the thirteenth century as "the century of reason and hope" in Muslim–Christian relations (1962, 34-66). At least in certain places and at certain times, such as Sicily under Frederick II and Toledo before and after the Reconquista, Christians, Muslims, and Jews gathered together to share their wisdom, exchange translations of ancient Greek texts, and make possible the spread of knowledge across religious boundaries. The rebirth of Western medieval scholarship in the twelfth and thirteen centuries was made possible by the open dialogue between Christians and Muslims in Spain and the Middle East.

The contrast between hermeneutics of hostility and of generosity can be seen in the attitudes of Bernard of Clairvaux and Francis of Assisi toward Muslims. Both Bernard and Francis were deeply rooted in the scriptures, shaping their lives and thought in the biblical witness. But in regard to the proper relationship to Muslims, they drew opposite conclusions. Bernard preached the Second Crusade, developing a theology of sacred violence that informed the military religious orders of the age and shaped Christian warfare for centuries. In his work *In Praise of the New Knighthood: A Treatise on the Knights Templar and the Holy Places of Jerusalem,* Bernard combines elements of Catholic monastic life with dedication to fighting Muslims in the name of God. Bernard's preaching of the Second Crusade at Vezelay had an immense influence both on his contemporaries and on later generations (Tyerman 2006, 278-79). Thomas Merton comments on Bernard preaching the Crusade: "Here the sleeping power of Bernard's warlike atavism wakes and fights its way to the front of his life like some smiling Romanesque monster pushing through the leafage of a pillar's capital in the cloisters of Cluny" (Merton 1954, 40).

Even though Francis of Assisi did not write academic tomes, he was one of the most influential interpreters of the Bible in the history of Christianity. As a young man, he was a soldier involved in combat; but after a reported vision from God at Spoleto, he left the military life to serve God, the Master, rather than one of God's servants. Steven McMichael comments, "The dream of being a glorious knight on a Crusade was replaced by a higher purpose" (2012, 129). In renouncing his inheritance from his earthly father in front of the bishop and people of Assisi, Francis was also rejecting the career of warfare.

Thereafter, there is no evidence that Francis ever again approved of violence; instead he sought reconciliation not only with humans but with all creation. McMichael places Francis's visit to the sultan in this context: "In 1219, Francis extended his experience of reconciliation beyond the Christian world to the Muslim world" (2012, 130). At a time when Christian Crusaders and Muslim warriors were fiercely battling each other, Francis renounced the path of warfare, sought an opportunity to speak with Muslims peacefully, and in the autumn of 1219 journeyed to Damietta, Egypt, to meet with Sultan al-Malik al-Kamil and explain the message of peace of Jesus to him. The sultan reportedly welcomed him and listened to Francis with respect, apparently viewing him as like a Sufi holy man. While the sultan did not convert to Christianity, he appreciated the courage of Francis and sent him home in honor with a safety guard. Jacques de Vitry, writing in 1220, gives us the earliest account of this encounter:

> The head of these brothers, who also founded the order, came into our camp [at Damietta, in Egypt]. He was so inflamed with zeal for the faith that he did not fear to cross the lines to the army of our enemy. For several days he preached the Word of God to the Saracens and made a little progress. The sultan, the ruler of Egypt, privately asked him to pray to the Lord for him, so that he might be inspired by God to adhere to that religion which most pleased God. (Armstrong et al. 1999, 1:581; quoted by McMichael 2012, 127)

There has been much debate and speculation over reconstructing Francis's motivation, his actual contact with the sultan, and the effects. Though much remains unknown, McMichael argues that "Francis most probably disapproved of the Crusades but used the occasion to present his case for Christian truth before Sultan al-Kamal at Damietta" (1228). We do not know the actual content of Francis's discussion with the sultan; we can surmise that Francis would have viewed the Muslims as being in need of salvation through Jesus Christ and would have shared his faith with them. Central to the Rule of Francis is the spirit of the Sermon on the Mount. Francis learned from Jesus not to respond to evil with evil but to love even those who are perceived as enemies. The Rule directs the friars to greet all they meet with "Peace to this house" or "The Lord give you peace" (McMichael 2012, 133).

The Rule for the Third Order, written in 1221, instructs followers of Francis not to take up arms against anyone: "It extends a non-violent policy to others outside the First Order of Friars" (McMichael 2012, 133). It seems likely that Francis brought the spirit of the Sermon on the Mount to his encounter with the sultan. Chapter 22 of the Rule for the Third Order was probably written shortly before or after Francis's meeting with the sultan; it expresses his spirit, based on the Sermon on the Mount:

All my brothers: Let us pay attention to what the Lord says: *Love your enemies* and *do good to those who hate you,* for our Lord Jesus Christ, Whose footprints we must follow, called His betrayer a friend and willingly offered Himself to his executioners. Our friends, therefore, are all those who unjustly inflict upon us distress and anguish, shame and injury, sorrow and punishment, martyrdom and death. We must love them greatly, for we shall possess eternal life because of what they bring us. (McMichael 2012, 134)

McMichael speculates: "If Francis wrote this after visiting the sultan, he would have been referring to his Muslim hosts as his enemies-turned-friends" (134). Francis's rule for the friars instructs them on how to behave among the Saracens:

As for the brothers who go, they can live spiritually among the Saracens and non-believers in two ways. One way is not to engage in arguments or disputes but to be subject *to every human creature for God's sake* [1 Peter 2:13] and to acknowledge that they are Christians. The other way is to announce the Word of God, when they see that it pleases the Lord, in order that [nonbelievers] may believe in the all-powerful God, Father, and Son, and Holy Spirit, the Creator of all, the Son the Redeemer and Saviour, and be baptized and become Christians because *no one can enter the Kingdom of God without being reborn of water and the Holy Spirit* [John 3:5]. (McMichael, 134-35)

It is significant that centuries later, during the tensions of the Cold War, Pope John Paul II invited leaders of the world's religious communities to come to Assisi in 1986 to pray for world peace.

In contrast to the dominant medieval view of Islam, Andrea da Barberino (1371-1431), a Florentine, followed the example of Giovanni Villani in viewing Islam not as a Christian heretical sect but as a religion alongside of Judaism, paganism, and Christianity, though in his description of Islam he conflates Muslim and pagan practices (Allaire 1996, 247-48, 263 n. 24). In his prose romance *Guerrino il Meschino*, Andrea presents a travel narrative that draws on multiple sources; its young protagonist, though descended from Charlemagne, is sold as a slave in infancy and goes through many challenges and adventures as he journeys through the world and fights many battles, all the while seeking to know his own identity and origins. While Andrea repeats much of the negative imagery of Islam that was familiar in medieval culture, he also expresses respect for Muslims. Gloria Allaire comments:

If *Guerrino* at times roundly condemns the Islamic religion, at others he participates fully in Islamic culture, even to the extent of fighting to defend Mecca from its attackers. . . . Although the hero defiantly rejects the Saracens' religion, he never allows these feelings to eclipse his awareness of their common humanity. . . . In *Guerrino*, despite the lingering presence of conventional antipathies, a new spirit emerges that does indeed make possible revisionary literary depictions of Muslims based on tolerance and understanding. (1996, 260)

Juan de Segovia (ca. 1400-1458), professor of theology at the University of Salamanca, proposed respectful dialogue with Muslims. He criticized Robert of Ketton's translation of the Qur'an for inaccuracies, and he sponsored a new translation of the Qur'an into Spanish and Latin, trusting that in an open, intellectual exchange Christianity would emerge the victor. In the aftermath of a Catholic victory in 1431, Juan organized dialogues with a Muslim soldier and ambassador.

Raymond Llull (1232-1316) dedicated much of his life to efforts to convert Muslims. He sought to reason respectfully with them on the basis of the divine attributes, arguing that God must necessarily be triune. For the most part, Llull's arguments do not involve the citation of scripture but rather are arguments for attributes of God that Muslims would be expected to accept. On this basis Llull tries to demonstrate the Trinity and the possibility of the incarnation of God in Jesus Christ. In *The Book of the Gentiles and the Three Wise Men*, Llull constructs a dialogue among a Gentile, a Jew, a Christian, and a Saracen, which is noteworthy for its respectful, cordial tone. The Gentile seeks wisdom from the representatives of the three traditions, and each in turn presents the case for his religion to the Gentile inquirer. At the conclusion of the conversation, the Gentile understands and is moved by each of the three presentations. The work ends with a leave-taking that is a model of a hermeneutics of respect and generosity. The Gentile departs the company; and the Jew, the Christian, and the Muslim journey together to the city gates, where they first had met

and there they took leave of one another most amiably and politely, and each asked forgiveness of the other for any disrespectful word he might have spoken against his religion. Each forgave the other, and when they were about to part, one wise man said: "Do you think we have nothing to gain from what happened to us in the forest? Would you like to meet once a day, and . . . have our discussions last until all three of us have only one faith, one religion, and until we can find some way to honor and serve one another, so that we can be in agreement? For war, turmoil, ill will, injury, and shame prevent men from agreeing on one belief." (Llull, 172)

Recent Interpretations

Islam as Jewish Christianity
Adolf von Harnack argues that Islam should be understood as a continuation of the Jewish Christian trajectory:

Islam is a transformation of Jewish Christianity, which was in turn a transformed version of Judaism, that took place on Arabian soil at the hands of a great prophet. . . . [B]ecause of its strict emphasis on the oneness of God and its rejection of image worship, and, generally, because of its simplicity, which let spiritual religion once again shine through, Islam had a decided advantage over Christianity. . . . Along with Islam's liberating reduction of monotheism to a few crucial factors not a few Christians were willing to accept the new prophet, especially since they were allowed to go on venerating Abraham, Moses, and Christ." (quoted by Küng 1986, 124)

This program harmonized well with Harnack's own agenda to free the gospel of Jesus from the alleged Hellenization of church dogma.

In 1918, the German Protestant exegete Adolf Schlatter developed Harnack's observation and noted the complex relationships among Gentile and Jewish Christians and Muslims. He observes that Jewish Christians west of the Jordan River died out after a certain point; but further to the east, Jewish Christians continued to survive, often in rather isolated circumstances, in Nabatea, on the edge of the Syrian wilderness and toward Arabia. Schlatter writes:

> None of the leaders of the imperial Church ever dreamed that a day would come when this group of Christians, whom they so despised, would once again shake the world and shatter the ecclesiastical system they had built up. That day came when Mohammed took over the legacy of the Jewish Christians, their consciousness of God, their eschatological prophecies of the coming Judgment, their customs and legends, and, as the one sent by God, set up a new apostolate. (quoted by Küng 1986, 123)

Jewish scholar Hans-Joachim Schoeps continues the trajectory, drawing the conclusion:

> Though it may not be possible to establish exact proof of the connection, the indirect dependence of Mohammed on sectarian Jewish Christianity is beyond any doubt. This leaves us with a paradox of truly world-historical dimensions: the fact that while Jewish Christianity in the Church came to grief, it was preserved in Islam and, with regard to some of its driving impulses at least, it has lasted till our own time. (quoted by Küng 1986, 124)

Louis Massignon: Sacred Hospitality

Louis Massignon (1883-1962) studied Arabic and Islam as a young agnostic scholar. In 1904, he went to Algeria, where he encountered Muslims and Islam and became aware of Charles de Foucauld (1858-1916), who had earlier left the life of a soldier and was living as a Catholic hermit. In 1907, Massignon came across a statement by Attar Fariduddin (1140-1220?) concerning the martyred

Sufi mystic Husayn Ibn Mansur al-Hallaj (858-922): "Two moments of adoration suffice in love, but the preliminary ablution must be made in blood" (quoted by Gude 1996, 23). The line stayed with him and would resonate through his life. Massignon had a profound experience of Islamic hospitality from the Alussy family in Baghdad. Later he had a dramatic experience of danger during an anti-Turkish uprising in 1908, which led to a severe personal crisis, a failed suicide attempt, and his first prayer to God, made in Arabic. During the crisis he experienced a mysterious presence, which he later called "the visitation of the Stranger" (Gude, 43) and which he compared to Abraham's experience of the three angels at Mamre (Genesis 18). The example of Hallaj, the experience of Islamic hospitality, and the personal crisis transformed his life and prepared his entry into the Catholic Church in 1908. Toward the end of his life, in 1961, he looked back: "This notion of sacred hospitality that I have deepened over many years, since 1908, when Foucauld supported me like an older brother, seems to me essential in the search for Truth among men, in our journeying and work here below, up until the very threshold of the beyond" (quoted by Gude, 86).

Massignon placed the biblical virtue of hospitality at the center of his approach to Islam, becoming a pioneer in developing a hermeneutics of generosity toward Muslims and Islam. Massignon immersed himself in the study of Hallaj and Sufi Islam for decades, and his multi-volume study of Hallaj had a dramatic influence in sparking interest in Sufism and Islamic mysticism in the West. In light of his study of the similarities between the sacrifices of Jesus Christ and of Hallaj, Massignon developed an understanding of *Badaliyya* (mystical substitution of one person for some else's salvation). With Mary Kahil, he journeyed to Egypt and prayed in the remains of the same church in Damietta where Francis of Assisi had reportedly met Sultan al-Malik al-Kamil in 1219. The two made a vow of *Badaliyya*, offering their lives in service to Muslims without seeking to convert them, and they established a prayer group in Cairo in 1934. He sought the approval of Pope Pius XI and received a papal blessing for his commitment. Massignon describes the encounter:

> He [Pope Piux XI] blessed the oblation of my life and death for my Muslim brothers and sisters. . . . He stood up and blessed my particular "way" and all my collaborators. He teased me, saying that by dint of loving them, I had become a "Catholic Muslim" in order that Muslims might be loved, on account of me, in the Church. (Letter of July 24, 1934; in Salenson 2012, 36 n. 12)

In 1947, Massignon and Kahil received official church approval for the statutes of the *Badaliyya* Prayer Association. Massignon had a significant influence on Giambattista Montini, who became Pope Paul VI in 1963, less than a year after Massignon's death. Even though Massignon died in October 1962, the same month that the Second Vatican Council opened, his influence on it was strong.

In 1921, two Muslims who were seeking to safeguard the endangered Islamic caliphate informed Massignon about the example of Mahatma

Gandhi's nonviolent campaign of *satyagraha* ("truth-force" or "the grasping of truth") in India; in the following years this would become increasingly a dominant ideal shaping Massignon's life. Massignon met Gandhi in Paris in 1931 and was deeply impressed; he later tried to apply Gandhi's *satyagraha* to the Israeli–Palestinian conflict and to the issues and crises of the French empire in the Islamic world. From 1953 until the end of his life in 1962, Massignon tried to practice together the ideals *Badaliyya* and *satyagraha* through his participation in protests against French atrocities in Algeria. Massignon reflects on the interreligious context of his discovery of *satyagraha*:

> It was through Muslims that I knew Gandhi and I understood the ideals of Gandhi, the ideal of *satyagraha*, the pursuit of truth by steadfastness in will, by *vrata*, by oath. I also learned . . . that *satyagraha* was a sacred thing for the Muslims also. I realized immediately there was something in Gandhi that was valuable. For perhaps the first time in the world, there was a man influencing people of other religions and with great social results. (quoted by Gude 1996, 128)

In the lives and deaths of Jesus, Hallaj, and Gandhi, Massignon found a shared and inspiring model of nonviolent witnessing to the truth even at the cost of one's life. Massignon looked to Abraham as a model of hospitality for Jews, Christians, and Muslims and deepened his understanding of this ideal in light of Gandhi's concern for Muslims. In situations of conflict, Massignon extended a welcome to the stranger and sought a basis for solidarity across religious and cultural differences. Confronted by the suffering caused by the fighting between Arabs and Israelis, Massignon invokes the example of Gandhi as an example of how to live out Abrahamic hospitality:

> The one to whom I owe the most in this regard is Gandhi, whom I saw twice. He taught me to listen to the cries of the excluded, the pariahs, and the displaced persons. . . . [W]e must offer ourselves to God in substitution for what they lack, because it is God who attracts us to Him by our common destitution; to them we provide the alms of hospitality which Abraham, the first displaced person, gave to God. (quoted by Gude 1996, 175)

Massignon meditates on Abraham's prayer to God for Ishmael, whom he sees as the ancestor of the Arabs. Abraham prays: "O that Ishmael might live in your sight!" (Gen. 17:18). In contrast to most earlier Christian interpreters, Massignon stresses that God responded positively to Abraham's prayer and thus Ishmael received God's blessing: "God said, . . . 'As for Ishmael, I have heard you; I will bless him and make him fruitful and exceedingly numerous; he shall be the father of twelve princes, and I will make him a great nation'" (Gen. 17:19, 20). Massignon notes that Ishmael's exile came after this blessing, and he compares Ishmael's being banished at the urging of Sarah (Gen. 21:9-21) to Muhammad's later forced migration from Makka, the *Hijra* (1997, 65).

In an abrupt reversal of earlier Christian tradition, Massignon interprets Muhammad not as the Antichrist but rather as a prophet, the announcer of the judgment that will come upon all creation, and he views Islam as a mysterious divine response to Abraham's prayer regarding Ishmael and the Arabs (1997, 141). For Massignon, Abraham represents a model of natural religion that centers on mysticism and that demands sacrifice; Muhammad is a negative prophet who calls Christians away from moral failings and back to the truth of the religion of Abraham (Griffith 1999, 70-71). Massignon prods Christians to reflect on Islam as a healthy challenge to the unfaithfulness of Christians, and he poses the provocative question of whether Islam would have appeared if Christians had truly lived out their calling (1997, 141-42).

After Massignon's death, Pope Paul VI and the Second Vatican Council promulgated *Lumen Gentium* and *Nostra Aetate,* both of which speak respectfully of Muslims. Mary Louis Gude comments on the impact of Massignon's contribution to these events: "More than any other single person, Massignon was responsible for modifying the [Catholic] Church's stance toward Islam, a change he did not live to see" (1996, xi).

Thomas Merton

One of the many Christians whom Massignon influenced was Thomas Merton (Griffith 1999, 53). Merton was especially impressed by the role that Hallaj had played in Massignon's own conversion; Sidney Griffith comments that, for both Massignon and Merton,

> their own access to God ran through the hearts of other people. . . .
> In addition to their faith in Jesus Christ, their encounters with other
> people who had met God were also of great moment. And nowhere
> was this more the case than in their encounters with people of other
> religions. For both of them, other religions were other people, and not
> just sets of doctrines. (Griffith 1999, 69)

Merton was very moved by the phrase that Massignon drew from his study of Sufism: *le point vierge.* Merton found that this Sufi-inspired image resonated deeply with Catholic monastic life:

> Again, that expression, *le point vierge* (I cannot translate it) comes
> in here. At the center of our being is a point of nothingness which
> is untouched by sin and by illusion, a point of pure truth, a point or
> spark which belongs entirely to God, which is never at our disposal,
> from which God disposes of our lives, which is inaccessible to the fan-
> tasies of our mind or the brutalities of our own will. This little point
> of nothingness and of *absolute poverty* is the pure glory of God in us.
> (Merton 1966, 142)

Merton interprets the Sufi experience of *fana* ("annihilation") in light of the challenge of Jesus to lose oneself for the sake of the gospel:

The real purpose of this whole Sufi life is a kind of extinction of the self, and that is interesting. Of course they emphasize this much more than we do, but nevertheless it is important for us too because we come here to, in a certain sense, lose ourselves, and to find ourselves by losing ourselves. . . . According to the Gospel concept, "He that would lose his life for My sake shall find it." It's this ultimate losing and ultimate finding. (quoted by Dieker 1999, 154)

In contrast to those who make a sharp opposition between alleged Sufi "pantheism" and biblical faith, Merton finds instead an analogy, noting that Sufis teach that God is the only Reality and that everything else "is only a sham and any other thing is only a lie. And this runs through the Bible. And basically, this is why the great sin, the sin of all sins, is idolatry" (quoted by Dieker 1999, 161). Merton found his own spiritual life enriched by his contact with the Sufi tradition.

Kenneth Cragg

Kenneth Cragg (1913-2012), a distinguished Anglican bishop with long experience in the Middle East, was another major figure seeking to improve understanding between Christians and Muslims. From 1939 to 1947 he ministered in Beirut, Lebanon, learning Arabic and becoming intimately familiar with Muslims and Islam. Like Massignon, he experienced Islam as issuing a call and a challenge to Christians; his classic work bears the title, *The Call of the Minaret*. John Renard cites Cragg as an eminent example of "the dialogical model" of Christian engagement with Islam (Renard 2011, xxv).

Cragg acknowledges the difficult obstacles to Muslim–Christian understanding, lamenting the Qur'an's omission of many elements of the New Testament witness to Jesus Christ:

Consider the Quranic Jesus alongside the New Testament. How sadly attenuated is this Christian prophet as Islam knows him! Where are the stirring words, the deep insights, the gracious deeds, the compelling qualities of him who was called the Master? . . . There is in the Qur'an neither Galilee nor Gethsemane; neither Nazareth nor Olivet. . . . Is the Sermon on the Mount never to be heard in the Muslim world? (Cragg 2000, 235)

Cragg blames Christians for failing to witness adequately to Jesus Christ (2000, 235-37), but he confesses that the appearance of Islam remains to him "a painful puzzle" (238). He further blames the Crusaders for distorting the meaning of Christian faith, as well as the modern Western powers who dominated the Islamic world (239-41). Cragg presents the Bible, trusting in its "inherent worth" (257).

To investigate the affinities between the Qur'an and the Bible, Cragg explores the theme of *Magnificat,* which appears not only in Mary's hymn of praise in the Gospel of Luke but also in Psalms 34:3 and 40:16 and in other biblical passages: "such joyous and perpetual celebration of the greatness of God (in that sense 'making' him great) belongs squarely with the Qur'an of Islam, in its own idiom" (1986, 29-30). Cragg finds the same theme in the call issued in Qur'an 17:111: "make him greatly great." Muslims obey this command in the liturgical acclamation: "*Allahu akbar*," which Cragg sees as "the clue to all Islamic theology" (1986, 30).

Cragg juxtaposes Mary the mother of Jesus and Muhammad, comparing their respective presentations of God's mercy as "theologies of *Magnificat*." Both Mary and Muhammad express a sense of the grandeur and the mercy of God. Cragg quotes the statement of Mary: "His mercy is on them that fear him" (Luke 1:50). He compares this to the themes of *Rahmah* ("mercy") and *taqwa* ("fear"), which he finds "at the heart of the human annunciation in the Qur'an" (1986, 37). Cragg, following Fazlur Rahman, understands "fear" in Islam as "a conscience which guards the self from willfulness and self-wronging. It may be seen as analogous, to a degree, with the Christian sense of the Greek noun *sophrosune*, the 'wisdom' that guards and saves the self from *superbia* and all that follows from inflated notions of oneself" (Cragg 1986, 38). Cragg proposes a convergence of theologies in the priority of mercy in both traditions: "It is here that a common theology of *Magnificat*, if all too seldom recognized for what it is, is most surely recognizable between Muslims and Christians" (38-39).

Cragg also compares the hymn of Christ's self-emptying in Philippians 2:6-8 with Qur'an 4:172: "The Messiah would never shrink from being servant of God." Where Philippians asserts that Christ emptied himself and became a servant, the Qur'an implies that a servant would not claim to be a son. Cragg suggests that even in rejecting Christian claims for Jesus Christ, "Islam has Christian criteria, just as there are, one might truly say, Islamic reasons for continuing Christian!" (Cragg 1977, 2-3; Renard 2011, xxvi). Cragg further notes that both the Bible and Islam affirm God's sovereignty, but in both traditions God allows creatures to refuse God's Lordship.

Vatican II

For Catholics, the Second Vatican Council marks the decisive turning point in attitudes toward followers of other religious paths, including Muslims. Aware of the long history of hostility between Catholics and Muslims, the council invites Catholics to attitudes of cooperation and reconciliation with those who practice Islam, looking for shared values and concerns as a basis for mutual respect and collaboration. The council places aspects of the biblical heritage shared by Muslims and Catholics in the foreground of attention. After referring positively to the Jewish people, as ever dear to God, *Lumen Gentium* (The Dogmatic Constitution on the Church [LG]), issued in 1964, declared: "The plan of salvation also embraces those who acknowledge the Creator, and among these the Muslims are first; they profess to hold the faith of Abraham and along with us they worship the one merciful God who will judge humanity on the last day" (LG §16; Tanner 1990, 2:861). *Lumen Gentium* quietly drops the hermeneutic of hostility and adopts a hermeneutic of respect. Instead of associating Muslims with the Antichrist and the Son of Destruction who are moving toward eternal damnation, the council instead dramatically includes Muslims in the salvific plan of God, interpreting them as worshipers of the one God in continuity with the faith of Abraham and as anticipating the final judgment.

One year later, the council issued *Nostra Aetate* (The Declaration on the Church's Relation to non-Christian Religions [NA]), which develops further the perspective of *Lumen Gentium,* again rejecting the hermeneutic of hostility of the earlier tradition and adopting instead a hermeneutic of generosity:

> The church also looks upon Muslims with respect. They worship the one God living and subsistent, merciful and almighty, creator of heaven and earth, who has spoken to humanity and to whose decrees, even the hidden ones, they seek to submit themselves whole-heartedly, just as Abraham, to whom the Islamic faith readily relates itself, submitted to God. They venerate Jesus as a prophet, even though they do not acknowledge him as God, and they honour his virgin mother Mary and even sometimes devoutly call upon her. Furthermore they await the day of judgment when God will requite all people brought back to life. Hence they have regard for the moral life and worship God especially in prayer, almsgiving and fasting. Although considerable dissensions and enmities between Christians and Muslims may have arisen in the course of the centuries, this synod urges all parties that, forgetting past things, they train themselves towards sincere mutual understanding and together maintain and promote social justice and moral values as well as peace and freedom for all people. (NA §3; Tanner 1990, 2:969-70)

The council makes no direct mention of Islam, the Qur'an, or Muhammad. Nonetheless, Vatican II proposes a new framework for reading the Bible in relation to Muslims, emphasizing aspects of the biblical heritage that Catholics share with Muslims, such as worship of the one God, veneration for Abraham, Jesus, and Mary, the expectation of a final resurrection and judgment, as well as the virtues of prayer, fasting, and almsgiving, which are central to the practice of Islam. In what may seem a surprising move, the council also proposes that Catholics and Muslims pursue reconciliation through the act of forgetting so that they can together collaborate in realizing values that are important to both traditions.

Hans Küng

Hans Küng has devoted considerable attention to Islam as part of his effort to contribute to world peace through interreligious understanding and dialogue. Küng argues that "the New Testament doesn't bid us reject in advance Muhammad's claim to be a prophet *after* Jesus and in basic agreement with him" (1986, 28). He continues the reflections of Adolf von Harnack and Hans-Joachim Schoeps on Islam as closely related to Jewish Christianity, noting that there is little contradiction between Islam and this trajectory of early Christianity. As a Catholic, Küng accepts the councils of Nicaea and Chalcedon, which pose starker doctrinal differences from Islam; but he also acknowledges the legitimacy of pursuing the trajectory of early Jewish-Christian reflections in relation to Muslims. Because Küng begins his discussion of Islam from Christian norms and standards, John Renard cites him as an example of "the Christian-inclusivist model" (2011, xxiii). Renard notes that Küng assumes that the Renaissance and Enlightenment developments in Western thought are universally valid for any reasonable approach to religion (Renard 2011, xxiv). From the perspective of Catholic theology, Küng considers what may be acknowledged regarding the Qur'an and Muhammad; he poses the question: "Might it now therefore be purely dogmatic prejudice which recognizes Amos and Hosea, Isaiah and Jeremiah as prophets, but not Muhammad?" (2013, 245).

Rejecting the harsh condemnations of Muhammad in the earlier tradition, Küng calls for Christians to go through a "correction of viewpoint," acknowledging that Muhammad was accepted as a prophet, that Islam raised the Arabs' religion "to a completely new level, that of a monotheistic high religion," and that Muslims have received from the Qur'an "an endless amount of inspiration, courage and strength for a new religious start" (2013, 245-46). Küng cites *Nostra Aetate's* acknowledgment that Muslims pray to God "who has spoken to mankind," as opening the door to recognition of Muhammad as a prophet of God (246).

Küng ponders whether Christians can acknowledge that the Qur'an is the Word of God. Building on the tradition of viewing Islam as a development of Jewish Christianity, Küng proposes that this poses a question for Christians today: "To Muhammad, Jesus' greatness was due to the fact that in him and through him as the servant of God, God himself had worked. Thus Muhammad's 'Christology' was not too far removed from that of the Judaeo-Christian church" (2013, 253). While Küng accepts the legitimacy of the Christology of the Councils of Nicaea and Chalcedon, he opens the door for accepting other formulations as well: "I have every right to draw attention to that original and thus thoroughly legitimate Christological option which, though pushed aside and concealed, originated by the scattered Judaeo-Christian church communities from east of the Jordan to Arabia, thus to be finally passed on to Muhammad" (2013, 253).

Küng maintains that the New Testament references to "son of God" need not present a barrier to Muslims because they refer to "an appointment to a position of justice and power in the Hebrew Old Testament sense. This is not a physical divine sonship of the kind that occurs in the Greek myths, which is often supposed and rightly rejected by Jews and Muslims, but an election and authentication of Jesus by God, completely in keeping with the Hebrew Bible" (2007, 493). Küng understands Jesus being "begotten" in the New Testament as "being 'appointed' as representative and 'son'" (493). In this sense of the term, Küng hopes that Muslims could accept it.

Küng seeks to move beyond the alternative of choosing either Jesus or Muhammad to a synthesis that can embrace both figures. Küng expresses his personal version of accepting Jesus and Muhammad: "As a Christian I can be sure that, as long as I have chosen this Jesus as the Christ for my life and death,

I have also chosen his follower Muhammad, inasmuch as he appealed to the one and same God and to Jesus" (2013, 254). He does not want to deny differences but hopes to "put them in a different light"; that is, "Christians should no longer see the Qur'anic understanding of Jesus as Muslim heresy but as a Christology with a primitive Christian colouring on Arabian soil" (2007, 501).

Efforts toward Reconciliation

The Second Vatican Council briefly noted the history of hostility between the two traditions and then challenged Catholics and Muslims alike to forget past conflicts. Memories of violence risk calling forth more violence in retaliation, locking believers into an unending cycle of blaming and scapegoating. Memories of past suffering can establish an identity based on victimization and can imprison both parties in mutual hostility. Indeed, this pattern can constitute the core of a hermeneutics of hostility.

During the 1990s, as Yugoslavia broke up into new units, there were bitter, violent conflicts between Christians and Muslims. In the wake of these difficulties, the Croatian Protestant theologian Miroslav Volf, who was very familiar with the acrimonious history of interreligious relations in the Balkans, reflected on the dilemma of memory: "In my memory of the other's transgression the other is locked in unredemption and we are bound together in a relationship of nonreconciliation. The memory of the wrong suffered is also a source of my own nonredemption. . . . A remembered wound is an experienced wound" (1996, 133). As a way to move beyond this dilemma, Volf notes the promise of God through Jeremiah: "I will forgive their iniquity and remember their sin no more" (Jer. 31:34) (136). For Volf, this is an eschatological hope that challenges history.

Volf also reflects on the importance of affirming that Muslims and Christians worship the same God:

> For Muslims and Christians each to worship a different God would mean that one group is made up of idolaters while the other worships the true God, and that the two groups have a very different (though not necessarily *completely* incompatible) set of ultimate values. An extreme version of this position on the Christian side is a radical contrast between the "moon god" of Muslims and Yahweh of Jews and Christians. If, on the other hand, my argument is right and Christians and Muslims have a common God, they will have a larger set of overlapping ultimate values, which will provide them with a common moral framework in which to debate their differences other than feeling that they have to resort to violence. (2011, 259-60)

Addressing the symposium entitled "Holiness in Christianity and in Islam" in Rome in 1985, Pope John Paul II compares the understanding of the holiness of God in the Bible and in the Qur'an (1999, 59-60). He quotes the Qur'an favorably: "He is God, beside whom there is no other, the Sovereign, the holy, the (source of) Peace" (Qur'an 59:23). Then he notes the similarity to the prophet Hosea: "I am God, not man; I am the Holy One in your midst and have no wish to destroy" (Hos. 11:9). Pope John Paul II also cites the challenge of Jesus: "Be holy, even as your heavenly Father is holy" (Matt. 5:48) (1999, 60). The pope also notes that the Qur'an calls Muslims "to uprightness [*al-salah*], to conscientious devotion [*al-taqwa*], to goodness [*al-husn*], and to virtue [*al-birr*]" (Qur'an 2:177). John Paul compares these virtues to St. Paul's call to love others and lead a blameless life before God: "May the Lord be generous in increasing your love and make you love one another and the whole human race as much as we love you. And may he so confirm your hearts in holiness that you may be blameless in the sight of our God and Father when our Lord Jesus Christ comes with all his saints" (1 Thess. 3:12-13) (1999, 60). In sharp contrast to Pope Innocent III and popes of earlier centuries, at the end of Ramadan in 1991, Pope John Paul II expressed the hope that Muslims and Christians together can enjoy the presence and mercy of God: "May the Most High God fill us all with his merciful love and peace!" (1991, 66)

John Paul II reflected eloquently on the challenge of forgiveness. On May 6, 2001, he became the first pope ever recorded to visit a mosque—the Umayyad Mosque in Damascus, which was built on an earlier Byzantine Christian church honoring the grave of St. John the Baptist. John Paul II urges:

> It is my ardent hope that Muslim and Christian religious leaders and teachers will present our two great religious communities as communities in respectful dialogue, never more as communities in conflict. It is crucial for the young to be taught the ways of respect and understanding, so that they will not be led to misuse religion itself to promote or justify hatred and violence. . . . In Syria, Christians and Muslims have lived side by side for centuries, and a rich dialogue of life has gone on unceasingly. . . . For all the times that Muslims and Christians have offended one another, we need to seek forgiveness from the Almighty and offer each other forgiveness. (2001)

In line with Pope John Paul II's perspective, Archbishop Michael Fitzgerald and John Borelli reflect on forgiveness in Christianity and Islam and a point of contact and dialogue (Fitzgerald and Borelli 2006, 212-19). In a similar vein, Thomas Michel examines "the ethics of pardon and peace" in the thought of John Paul II and Bediuzzaman Said Nursi. Michel notes John Paul II's insight that justice by itself does not lead to reconciliation, and Michel compares the command of Jesus to love one's enemies and pray for one's persecutors (Matt. 5:43-44) to the holy Qur'an: "But it is better to forgive" (42:40) (Michel 2010, 110). For Fitzgerald, Borelli, and Michel, the common value placed on forgiveness and pardon unites Muslims and Christians in relating to God and to each other, moving beyond the history of hostility.

Spiritual Values

A hermeneutic of respect and generosity can look beyond the tragic conflicts that have divided Muslims and Christians and seek out common spiritual values. Greek Orthodox Bishop Kallistos Ware notes the importance of the "deep heart" mentioned in Psalm 63:7 [64:6], for reflecting on Muslim–Christian relations. Ware relates the deep heart in Greek Orthodox spirituality to what Thomas Merton referred to as *le point vierge*, the term that we have seen Merton learned from Sufi sources through the scholarship of Louis Massignon (Ware 2002, 2-23). Both Ware and Merton find considerable convergence between the spiritual path of Sufi Muslims and the hesychast tradition of Byzantine spirituality, which cultivates remembrance of God and stillness of the heart (Thurston 1999, 40-50). As we have seen, Merton compared the Sufi experience of extinction to the teaching of Jesus about losing one's life for his sake and finding it again. Merton also finds a deep similarity between St. Benedict's practice of cultivating awareness and the Sufi "awareness that one is totally penetrated by God's knowledge of us" (quoted by Dieker 1999, 160).

In conversation with Sufi Muslims, Bishop Ware notes that the tenth-century Sufi saint and martyr Hallaj had said, "Our hearts are a virgin that God's truth alone opens" (Ware 2002, 3). Ware claims that Hallaj's notion of the heart "is exactly what is signified by the 'deep heart' in the neptic theology of the Orthodox Church" (3). For Ware, "neptic theology" (from *nepsis*, "sobriety, vigilance") "includes the realms of both 'ascetical theology' and 'mystical theology,' as these are understood in the Roman Catholic tradition" (3-4, n. 6). Ware argues that there is a profound agreement among St. Mark the Monk, Hallaj, and Merton concerning this deep, inner heart that "belongs only to God. It is pre-eminently the place of Divine immanence, the locus of God's indwelling" (4).

Both Sufism and Christianity ponder the meaning of spiritual death. Christian mysticism involves initiation into the death of Jesus Christ so as to share in his resurrection. Annemarie Schimmel comments that, in Sufism, "the goal of the mystic attained, sometimes, through constant meditation is *fana*, annihilation, and subsequent perseverance in God. This final experience is always regarded as a free act of divine grace, which might enrapture man and take him out of himself, often in an experience described as ecstatic" (1975, 178). This description cannot be identified with the Christian initiation into the death of Jesus Christ, but it suggests analogies to be explored.

Maria Jaoudi reflects on the traditional stages of purification, transformation, and union with God in Christian spirituality in relation to the Sufi path, finding analogies at each stage. In both traditions she finds "a gradual recognition of one's own sense of worth . . . because of having allowed God to truly enter the heart" (1993, 3). The eighth-century Sufi mystic Rabi'a al-Adaqiyya experienced God as "the Friend who lives in my house/Is the lover of my heart"; Jaoudi compares this to Jesus in the Gospel of John promising to abide in his friends (John 15:4-11). Rabi'a is a model for Muslims "of the selfless lover who ceaselessly seeks God first, and thereby avoids any of temptation's pitfalls"; Jaoudi views Rabi'a as "she who lived only for God, the second Mary" (1993, 18).

John Renard also calls attention to elements that the Christian and Islamic ethical and spiritual traditions share, pointing out that Christianity and Islam both "cherish the hope that the aspirations of a sincere heart cannot be for naught" (2011, 220). Both traditions believe that God inspires the initial quest for God.

Christian de Chergé: Mercy in the Bible and the Qur'an

In many situations today, Christians live in fear and insecurity in Muslim-majority lands, where there have been violent attacks on Christian communities. One of the most powerful interpretations of the Bible in relation to Muslims comes from the pen of Dom Christian de Chergé, prior of the Trappist monastery at Atlas in Algeria (Kiser 2002). The story of Dom Christian and his confreres was powerfully presented in the movie *Of Gods and Men.* From 1959 to 1961, while he was a seminarian, de Chergé had served in the French Specialized Administrative Sections in Algeria, where he came to know a village policeman named Mohammed. One day during a skirmish, Mohammed saved de Chergé's life. The following day, Mohammed was murdered. Mohammed's gift of himself, which for de Chergé recalled Jesus Christ's own gift of his life, resonated deeply inside him: "In the blood of this friend, I came to know that my call to follow Christ would have to be lived out, sooner or later, in the very country in which I received the token of the greatest love of all" (Salenson 2012, 24).

In the aftermath, like Massignon, de Chergé felt a lifelong call to develop positive relations with Muslims. From Mohammed, de Chergé learned the meaning of the eucharistic gift of self. Many years later, in a homily on Holy Thursday, 1995, de Chergé reflected on the gift he had received in terms that applied to Jesus Christ, but that could also be understood to refer to the village policeman who had given his life for him: "He loved me to the end, to the end of me, to the end of him. . . . He loved me as I do not know how to love: this simplicity, this self-forgetting, this humble service without self-gratification, without any self-regard" (Salenson 2012, 26).

As a monk in Algeria, de Chergé pondered the meaning of mercy in the Bible and the Qur'an, where he discovered 339 instances of the root *rhm,* "mercy." He found in God's mercy the common word binding Muslims and Christians together, since the vocation of both communities is to "reflect on the merciful presence of their Creator" (Salenson 2012, 44). This set forth for him the path of interreligious relations: "The world would be less of a desert if we could recognize for ourselves a common vocation: to multiply the fountains of mercy along the way. And how can this vocation be in doubt if we let the All-Merciful call us together to a single table, the table of sinners?" (45)

De Chergé meditated on the Qur'an in Arabic, reflecting on it in the monastic practice of *lectio divina,* contemplative reading, which opened up to him its closeness to the Bible. He commented that *lectio divina* with the Qur'an "has allowed me, as the Christian that I am, to have an authentic spiritual experience in and through what others have received as properly their own for the sake of cultivating within them a taste for God: the call to prayer, the spontaneous prayerful utterance, the act of sharing" (Salenson 2012, 65). He discovered that, for both Muslims and Christians, scripture offers food for the journey: "The Word of God is present to Christians and Muslims as a viaticum, provisions for the crossing of the desert" (71). He compared the opening of the Rule of St. Benedict, "Listen my son," to the opening of the Quran: "Recite!" (71)

De Chergé reflected on the challenge of relating to Muslims and Islam in light of the Christian understanding of communion as a union of differences, wondering whether the differences can have the sense of a communion. He notes that Jesus reached out to those who were different, inviting them to union with him and with God the Father (John 14:2; 17:21). At the center of the Gospel, he finds a welcoming of difference and a challenge to be open to the movement of the Holy Spirit among those who are dissimilar. Dom Bernardo Olivera, abbot general of the Trappist Order, recalls that three weeks before Christian was kidnapped he preached a retreat, recommending to his hearers: "'Thou shalt not kill': not kill yourself, not kill time (which belongs to God), not kill trust, not kill death itself (by trivializing it), not kill the country, the other person or the Church. There are five pillars of peace: patience, poverty, presence, prayer and pardon" (Olivera 1997, 6).

After Dom Christian and his confreres knew that their lives were in danger during the period of turmoil in Algeria, he wrote a final testament, which he sent to his brother in France to be opened in the event of his death. It was opened on Pentecost Sunday, May 26, 1996. In it Dom Christian faces an "A-Dieu," a possible farewell in the event of his becoming a victim of terrorism. He addresses his community and church and family, recalling that "the One Master of all life was not a stranger to this brutal departure" (Olivera 1997, 127). The mercy of God shapes his perspective to the end. De Chergé states that if he is to undergo a violent death, he hopes "to have a moment of spiritual clarity which would allow me to beg forgiveness of God and of my fellow human beings, and at the same time forgive with all my heart the one who will strike me down" (Olivera, 127). He closes the testament by addressing his prospective killer alluding to the repentant thief who finds forgiveness on the cross (Luke 23:42-43).

> And also you, my last-minute friend,
> Who will not have known what you were doing:
> Yes, I want this THANK YOU and this "A-DIEU"
> To be for you, too,
> because in God's face I see yours.
> May we meet again as happy thieves
> In Paradise, if it please God, the Father of us both.
> Amen! In Sh'Allah! (Olivera 1997, 129)

Conclusion

Christian relations with Muslims have long been contentious, and much of the history of Christian biblical interpretation from the seventh century to the present reflects and expresses the animosity between the two traditions. While conflicts continue in many regions, there are nonetheless important efforts to read the Bible in light of a respectful attitude toward Muslims and Islam.

CHAPTER FIVE

Christian Interpretations of Scripture in Relation to Hindus and Hinduism

Christians have been in contact with Hindus from at least the second century C.E., and Christians have been in India continuously from the time of the early church. However, for most of this time Hindus were not nearly as prominent as Jews or Muslims in shaping European Christian self-understanding. For the most part, European Christians focused on the history of Christianity in the Mediterranean basin and Europe, neglecting the developments in Asia and sub-Sahara Africa. In recent decades, Western Christians have begun to develop greater awareness that from the beginning Christianity has had a broader history, and historians today are exploring the experience of Christianity across the globe in greater detail. Given the relative absence of Hindus from the awareness of earlier generations of Christians, it is striking that in the twentieth century, it was a Hindu, Mahatma Gandhi, who arguably transformed Christian understandings of the scriptures more profoundly than any other non-Christian.

The meaning of the term "Hindu" is ambiguous. The traditions we know as "Hinduism" developed from the early religious heritage of South Asia and are intimately related to the Buddhist, Jain, and Sikh traditions. "Hindu" was originally not a religious designation but rather a geographical term referring to the Indus River. Indians traditionally refer to their religion as *Sanatana Dharma,* which has been translated as "the Eternal Truth" or "Eternal Law." The British employed "Hinduism" as a name for a family of differing religious traditions on a subcontinent, and thus the name includes a wide variety of forms of religious faith and practice. There is no central Hindu organization or creed, and almost any generalization about Hinduism can be contradicted. While the use of the word "Hindu" by British colonialists may render it problematic, contemporary Hindus accept it as a term of self-designation (Sharma 2005).

There have often been questions of the boundaries of Hinduism, especially in relation to the Buddhist tradition. The Buddhist and Hindu traditions arise from the religious heritage of ancient India and have long intertwined. Siddhartha Gautama grew up in a milieu that later generations would call "Hindu," but he would not have used that term. His search and breakthrough challenged and reformed that tradition. For several centuries, Hindus and Buddhists in

India debated with each other, fought with each other, and imitated each other, and so their early histories were intimately intertwined. Today many Hindus see Buddhism as a variation within Hinduism, but Buddhists generally do not accept this assessment. The Japanese Zen Buddhist Masao Abe once asked the Hindu scholar Arvind Sharma how Hindus view Buddhists. Sharma was surprised by the question. When Sharma was young, his favorite Hindu deity had been the Buddha; and so he was at a loss over how to respond to Abe: "It took me some time even to comprehend the question, for modern Hindus barely differentiate between the two. Certainly I was not brought up to do so" (Sharma 1998, 330). Abe himself sharply distinguished the Buddhist understanding of *shunyata* (emptiness) from the role of *Brahman* in Hindu thought (1995b, 33). One can frame the relationship between the Hindu and Buddhist traditions so that the differences appear to be either minimal or quite important. Today they are usually but not always distinguished as separate religious traditions, and I will follow the usual practice in distinguishing them.

Early Christians in India

From antiquity to the present, Christian relationships with Hindus have been complex and often conflicted. For more than a millennium of Christian history in India, we do not know very much about how Christians interpreted the Bible in relation to Hindus and the Hindu tradition. Nonetheless, the fragmentary records suggest some aspects of Christian–Hindu relations, including both adaptation and resistance. These fragmentary glimpses allow us to surmise something of how Christians would have understood the Bible in relation to their Hindu neighbors.

We do not know exactly when Christians first came to India. One early Christian tradition claims that St. Thomas the apostle landed at Cranganore on the southwest coast of India sometime around 52 C.E. in what today is the state of Kerala (Frykenberg 2000, 148-52). It is impossible to verify the tradition; many scholars are skeptical, though some scholars, both Christian and secular, are inclined to acknowledge its plausibility. There was regular trade between India and the Roman Empire, and a Roman trading station was built south of Chennai/Madras sometime before 50 C.E. Shortly before this, the Romans had learned from the Arabs the art of sailing with the monsoon winds, and so they could sail with favorable winds across the open sea and no longer had to follow the shore. The ancient geographer Strabo, writing in 19 C.E., tells us there were 120 ships a year sailing from Roman-ruled Egypt to India (*Geographica* 2.5.12; Kuriakose 1982, 1). Another tradition tells that the apostle Thomas came to India by a land route from the north (Kurikilamkatt 2005; Frykenberg 2000, 148), but there is no way to verify this report.

Many shrines in southern India bear witness to Thomas the apostle, including seven churches he allegedly founded, as well as the shrine on the mount in Mylapore, now part of Chennai/Madras, where he was reportedly martyred after a dispute with Brahmins in 72 C.E. Two different traditions concerning his death both place him in deadly conflict with Hindu adversaries. According to one tradition, as Thomas was walking one day, he encountered Brahmins in procession preparing for a blood sacrifice to the goddess Kali. When Thomas refused to participate in the ritual, the Hindu crowd allegedly became so furious that people attacked him with a three-pronged lance and killed him. As he lay dying, Thomas purportedly sang a hymn that is still sung by Thomas Christians in his honor on his feast day (Frykenberg 2000, 149; 2010, 99-100).

Another tradition attributes Thomas's martyrdom to his ascetic preaching. According to the apocryphal *Acts of Thomas*, the apostle preached a rigorous ascetic message against marriage. The queen and other leading women accepted Thomas's strictures and shunned the marriage beds of their husbands. The king was outraged, accused Thomas of bewitching the women, and ordered his death. As Thomas was being put to death, he reportedly repeated the words he says to the risen Lord Jesus in the Gospel of John, "My Lord and my God" (John 20:28; *Acts of Thomas* 13.167; Moffett 1998, 28-29). While it is doubtful that either tradition is historically reliable, both narratives testify to a later impression that Christians in India from the beginning had been in deadly conflict with some Hindus.

From ancient times there have been Thomas Christians in Kerala in southwest India, but we do not know much about their early history, including how they related to Hindus or how they interpreted the Bible in an Indian context. Other traditions relate that there were early Christians in the northwestern part of India (Kurikilamkatt 2005), but again these reports are impossible to verify.

In his *History of the Church,* Eusebius of Caesarea tells us that the apostle Bartholomew went to India, where he preached and "left behind Matthew's account in the actual Aramaic characters, and it was preserved till the time of Pantaenus's mission [late second century]" (5.10; Eusebius 1981, 214). Jerome also mentions the apostle Bartholomew going to India and preaching "to the Brahmans" (*Epistola LXX ad Magnum oratorem urbis Romae*; Moffett 1998, 38).

Both Jerome and Eusebius also report that Indians came to Alexandria, Egypt, in the late second century, where they were impressed by the learning of Pantaenus, a noted Christian scholar and the teacher of Clement of Alexandria and Origen. According to Jerome, the Indian visitors asked Bishop Demetrius of Alexandria to send Pantaenus to India for discussions with their philosophers, and Demetrius did so (Jerome, *Liber de viris illustribus*; Moffett 1998, 37). This suggests an atmosphere of cordial intellectual discussion. Eusebius of Caesarea mentions that Pantaenus "was one of the most eminent teachers of his day, being an ornament of the philosophic system known as stoicism. He is said to have shown such warm-hearted enthusiasm for the divine word that he was appointed to preach the gospel of Christ to the peoples of the East, and travelled as far as India" (5.10; Eusebius 1981, 213). It is difficult to know what lies behind the reports of Jerome and Eusebius. While some historians have dismissed their reliability, Samuel Hugh Moffett notes that Clement and Origen write knowingly of India, and Pantaenus could have been the source of their information (1998, 38).

Whatever the truth may be of the first Christian arrivals in India, we know virtually nothing about the earliest history of Christian interpretations of scripture in relation to the religious traditions of India. Nonetheless, the conflicting reports of the martyrdom of the apostle Thomas and of the cordial interest of Indian philosophers in Christian thought are harbingers of two sides of Hindu–Christian relations that extend through later centuries down to the present. In some contexts Christians in India have been in bitter conflict with Hindus, suggesting interpretations of scripture that directly challenge aspects of Hindu belief and practice, as represented by Thomas's refusal to participate in the sacrifice to Kali; in other contexts Christians have been in harmonious relations with Hindus, suggesting interpretations of scripture that allow for mutual acceptance and respect.

About 300 C.E., the Church of the East in ancient Mesopotamia and Persia organized itself under a patriarch known as the "Catholicos" and began reaching out across southern and central Asia. According to the *Chronicle of Seert* of the Church of the East, Bishop David of Basra journeyed to India about 300 C.E., "where he converted a multitude of people" (Moffett 1998, 100). About 345, a delegation of the Church of the East led by a merchant, Thomas of Cana, reportedly arrived in the south of India, where they met Thomas Christians who were disorganized and divided among themselves. Thomas of Cana reportedly secured recognition of the church with high-caste status from the local king in Malabar (northern part of Kerala). Again, it is difficult to know how reliable this tradition is.

By the sixth century there are more reliable reports of Indian Christians as a tiny minority community which is in communion with the Church of the East in Persia but which claims its own, independent apostolic foundation from Thomas the apostle. After the Muslim conquest of the Sassanian Empire in present-day Iraq and Iran, communication between the patriarch of the Church of the East and Indian Christians appears to be minimal and at times broke off. Patriarch Yeshuyab III (650-660) in the seventh century reportedly complained that episcopal succession in India had been broken off (Moffett 1998, 270). After the seventh century, the church in India appears to be independent of the Church of the East. We do not know much about Christian relations with Hindus at this stage. The first Indian Christian records are on copper plates from Kerala, probably dating to about 850. One copper plate records a grant of land to Christians; another copper plate records that an Indian king granted honors and commercial rights to Ravi-Korran, who was the head of a community that appears to have been Christian (Kuriakose 1982, 10-12).

There are sporadic notices of Thomas Christians during the Middle Ages; they appear to have held high-caste status, though the basis for this is not known (Rajkumar 2010, 26). However, since there is no continuous narrative history extant, we do not know how Indian Christians related to Hindus or how they interpreted the scriptures in relation to Hindus in this period. In the thirteenth century, Catholic missionaries reached the south of India, possibly passing through on their way to China. In 1291, John of Monte Corvino, a

Franciscan priest, visited the tomb of St. Thomas near Chennai and reported that Christians were much persecuted at that time (Dawson 1955, 222-32).

It appears that, after the Muslims had conquered much of India, Christians were displaced by Muslims from work as traders and moved into agriculture instead. Because they had high-caste status, they did not plow but used low-caste Indians as serfs. Anand Amaladass comments: "For several centuries before the arrival of the Portuguese St. Thomas Christians did not baptize those of low castes lest they lose their social position" (1990, 19). Ian Gillman and Hans-Joachim Klimkeit suggest that Indian Christians adopted Hindu customs, such as the fire of Agni, and interpreted them in Christian terms, such as Christ the light of the world (Gillman and Klimkeit 1999, 178-79). K. P. Kesava Menon speculates that, by the fifteenth century, Thomas Christians were "Hindu in culture, Christian in religion and oriental in worship" (quoted by Moffett 1998, 501). The few reports we have prior to 1500 alternate between harmonious relations with Hindu rulers, including recognition of Christians in high-caste status, and conflict, including accounts of persecution. The issues of inculturation, caste status, and discrimination have continued to challenge the Christian communities in India to the present day.

European Catholics

The situation of Christians in India changed dramatically after the arrival of Portuguese Catholics in 1498. The Portuguese came in search of trade relations, hoping to take away the profitable spice trade from the Venetians and Genovese. In 1506, the Portuguese opened a Catholic school in Cochin, which educated high-caste and low-caste boys together; this reportedly angered the local Hindus (Moffett 2005, 9). The Thomas Christians accused the Portuguese of using coercion to try to convert Hindus, but there is debate over how reliable these accusations are. The issue of how to respond to the traditional social and economic distinctions of caste would be a repeated source of tension and debate for Christians in India.

When Jesuit missioners arrived in India in the middle of the sixteenth century, they first reached out to the communities of the lower castes. Francis Xavier, the most famous Jesuit missioner to India, worked among poor, lower-caste fishing communities and converted a significant number of them to the Catholic faith (Schurhammer 1977). Francis Xavier and his colleagues encountered strong opposition from the Brahmin caste, who apparently despised Catholics because of their customs of eating meat, drinking wine, and mixing with all classes of society without discrimination. Jesuit leaders such as Alessandro Valignano and Andreas Fernandes interpreted Hindu deities as idols created by demons (Pomplun 2010, 232 n. 22).

A generation after Francis Xavier, another Jesuit missioner, Roberto de Nobili (1577-1656) made a significant and controversial attempt to understand respectfully the Brahmin intellectual tradition and to reinterpret Christianity in light of Brahmin perspectives. De Nobili came from an aristocratic Italian family and was the nephew of a cardinal; thus he was familiar with the social distinctions of class hierarchy. When he arrived in India in 1605, he worked first with the poor, Christian fisherfolk who had been evangelized by Francis Xavier. The following year he was transferred to the independent Indian empire of Vijayanagar, which included Madurai in Tamil territory in the far south. De Nobili studied classical Tamil and Sanskrit and lived according to Brahmin customs, not eating meat, not touching or baptizing non-Brahmins, and discussing philosophy and theology with Brahmins. He dressed as a Hindu renunciant, describing himself as "a Brahmin sannyasi" (Correia-Afonso 1997, 139). He cited the apostle Paul for a biblical precedent: "I have become all things to all people, that I might by all means save some" (1 Cor. 9:22). De Nobili adapted Paul's principle to the Indian context: "I too will make myself Indian in order to save the Indians" (Moffett 2005, 21). De Nobili reinterpreted the Sanskrit term for moral order, *dharma*, and incorporated it into Christian theology (Arokiasamy 1986).

Anand Amaladass and Francis X. Clooney note that de Nobili's early Catholic education had already established his central theological categories before he came to India. This perspective assessed other religions in light of the analysis and critique of idols in the Wisdom of Solomon 13-15, a text that influenced Augustine and Thomas Aquinas (Amaladass and Clooney 2000, 16). The Wisdom of Solomon judiciously commented on the idolaters of the Hellenistic world: "Yet these people are little to be blamed, for perhaps they go astray while seeking God and desiring to find him. For while they live among his works, they keep searching, and they trust in what they see, because the things that are seen are beautiful" (13:6-7). Anand Amaladass stresses the similarity between the Wisdom of Solomon 13:6 and de Nobili's gentle assessment of Hindu worship of the Indian deities: "Maybe we are too harsh with these people. After all, they may have really wanted to find God, but they could not" (Amaladass and Clooney 2000, 36). In light of this biblical precedent, de Nobili accepted whatever he could in the Hindu tradition, while rejecting anything he perceived to be immoral or idolatrous.

The biblical and early Christian wisdom traditions did not make a systematic distinction between the natural and the supernatural. In the biblical tradition *ḥokmâ*, the wisdom of God, extends throughout all of creation and is the way humans experience the gift of life from God (Prov. 8:35). Early scholastic philosophy and theology transformed the heritage of the biblical wisdom tradition by making a systematic distinction between the natural order of creation and the supernatural order of revelation and redemption. Thomas Aquinas used this distinction to clarify many questions of Christian doctrine. De Nobili inherited the distinction from Thomas Aquinas, which allowed him respectfully to engage Hindu philosophy and culture as containing the natural wisdom that is open to all through the order of creation, apart from any question of supernatural divine revelation. Thus, as Amaladass and Clooney propose, de Nobili preached "wisdom to the wise"; that is, he understood himself to be bringing the supernatural, revealed wisdom of Jesus Christ to complement the natural wisdom already known to the Hindu philosophers. In this approach, de Nobili's dialogue with Hinduism mostly uses philosophical argumentation rather than direct reference to scripture (de Nobili). He was quite open to adapting elements of Hindu practice and giving them a new meaning in Christianity. Ines Zupanov comments: "All signs and actions designating a religion other than Christianity became, in Nobili's view, transformable into signifiers of the 'true religion.' In the last instance, this meant that the name was the problem and not the essence" (1999, 100).

De Nobili's approach found a favorable reception among a number of upper-caste Hindus. Between 1607 and 1611, de Nobili converted 108 high-caste Hindus, a class that had earlier been completely resistant to Catholic overtures. Because de Nobili allowed Hindus to keep customs that he viewed as cultural, other missioners accused him of turning Hindu and of perverting the Catholic faith. In 1623, Pope Gregory XV exonerated him of all charges but also warned him and the other Jesuits to avoid any appearance of superstition and idolatry (Moffett 2005, 22). De Nobili later modified his approach to the lower castes, allowing high-caste and low-caste Christians to worship together in the same church at the same time. This was a change from earlier Syrian Christian practice in India. Amaladass notes that after de Nobili, "There was no followup, although this was not de Nobili's fault, since other factors impeded the continuation of his approach. . . . In any case, no tradition embodying de Nobili's methods flourished in the later history of the Catholic missions in India" (Amaladass and Clooney 2000, 40).

After de Nobili, there continued to be controversy over how Catholics should treat the distinctions of caste (Zupanov 1999; Rajkumar 2010). Catholic missionaries developed a two-pronged approach, with some missionaries being assigned to minister to the Brahmin caste exclusively and others having responsibility for the lower castes or pariahs. Eventually, in 1734, Pope Clement XII condemned the Malabar Rites, which included the accommodations to Hindu culture, including caste. In particular, the pope directed that all priests had the obligation to bring the sacraments publicly to all persons, including those of a lower or backward caste, in their homes. This pastoral practice violated the rules of caste distinctions and thus rendered further ministry to the Brahmin caste impossible. After this, there were few conversions from the Brahmin caste. Nonetheless, a few years later in 1741, Pope Benedict XIV allowed a case for beatification to move forward that involved a missioner who had been involved in the Malabar Rites. When the Society of Jesus was suppressed in 1773, the question of dual-track missionaries for various castes became moot. Roman Catholics and Thomas Christians generally viewed the caste system as a matter of social classification and accommodated to it (Rajkumar 2010, 26-27).

British and American Protestant Missionaries

In 1600, Queen Elizabeth I of England granted a charter to "certain adventurers for the trade of the East Indies." This venture became the English East India

Company. As time went on, English and French companies set up trading settlements along both coasts of India, from which they progressively expanded their operations and came into conflict with each other. In 1757, the English won a decisive battle against the French at Plassey, which gave them control of Bengal and forced the French to withdraw. As a result, at the time the Society of Jesus was suppressed in 1773, the British were coming to control more and more of India. As the British were in the process of coming to dominate India, Protestant missioners arrived, and Hindu–Christian relations entered a new stage.

In contrast to Thomas Christians and Roman Catholics who had often sought to accommodate Christian life to the caste system, Protestant missioners launched a fierce critique of many Hindu practices, including the caste system and sati, the immolation of widows (Rajkumar 2010, 28). Protestants were not, however, successful in eliminating caste discrimination in their communities (Rajkumar, 30). Protestants often condemned Hinduism as idolatrous and barbarous, citing the biblical condemnations of false gods. Scottish missionary John Anderson saw himself in a holy war against the idolatrous "Heathendom" of the Hindus; he condemned the accommodating government of the East India Company as "Hindoo" and "Idolatrous" (Frykenberg 2010, 282). Some Protestants charged that Hindus engaged in "devil worship" (Frykenberg 2010, 287).

In 1813, American Protestant missionaries began arriving in India; like their British counterparts, they condemned the Hindu deities as idols. They brought word of the idolatry back to the United States. In November 1816, one of the first American missionaries to India, Samuel Nott, delivered his "Sermon on the Idolatry of the Hindoos" in Franklin, Connecticut, an address that received wide attention in America (Pathak 1967, 79-80). American missionaries drew the sharpest contrast between the immoral Krishna, who was a cunning thief, and Jesus Christ (81). They portrayed Hinduism in the worst possible light, emphasizing sati (the immolation of widows), female infanticide, and the caste system, and stressing the urgent need for Christianity. American missionary John C. Lowrie commented, "The gods and goddesses are the examplars of every vice and crime" (quoted by Pathak, 80). He concluded with a dramatic plea: "No people more greatly needed the enlightening, purifying and saving influence of the religion of the Bible than the Hindoos" (quoted by Pathak, 80).

Hindu Responses to Christianity

The nineteenth century saw a major rethinking of Hinduism in India in the context of the Protestant critiques. In time, Hindu reflections on Jesus would have a deep impact on Christians, not only in India but around the world. While a few Indians converted to Christianity, most Indians remained traditionally Hindu. A number of Hindus venerated Jesus and incorporated Christian values into the practice of Hinduism, which then had an influence on Christians. One influential Hindu response to Jesus and Christianity came from Ram Mohan

Roy (1772-1833). Born into a Brahmin family that had traditionally served the Muslim rulers of India, he was a polyglot who was very interested in religious questions from the time he was young. Ram Mohan Roy was one of the most learned and progressive Hindus of his time. He focused on the Hindu scriptures that were supportive of ethical monotheism and reinterpreted them, offering Hindus a way to reform their tradition on Hindu grounds and to maintain their self-respect in the face of the severe critiques by Protestant missioners.

In 1828, Ram Mohan Roy founded a religious society called Brahmo Samaj ("Society of the Worshippers of God"), which had a tremendous impact on shaping modern Hinduism. He studied Christianity carefully and esteemed the teachings of Jesus and the humanitarian message of Christianity, but he did not believe in the Christian Trinity or other Christian doctrines. He presented to Indians his personal selection of the moral teachings of Jesus, omitting the miracles and doctrines: *The Precepts of Jesus, the Guide to Peace and Happiness.* A vehement controversy ensued, with evangelical theologian Joshua Marshman fiercely criticizing Ram Mohan Roy's selection of only Jesus' moral teachings. Marshman insisted on the importance of Jesus' miracles and of Christian doctrine, especially the atoning sacrifice of Jesus Christ for sins, without which, he insisted, moral actions are insufficient for salvation. Ram Mohan Roy astutely responded by quoting Jesus' summary of the entire law in the twofold command to love God and neighbor (Crawford 1988, 18-30). Ram Mohan Roy's historical and literary approach to the Christian Bible as a nondogmatic sourcebook of wisdom set an important example for later Hindu perceptions of Jesus, including Mohandas Gandhi.

A number of other Hindus also honored Jesus Christ and incorporated veneration of him into their Hindu practice. Inspired by the example of Ram Mohan Roy, Keshub Chandra Sen (1838-1884) worked vigorously for social reforms within Hinduism while appreciating the resources of the Christian Bible as well. His Hindu rival Dayananda Sarasvati even chided him for being more familiar with the Bible than with the Hindu scriptures. Like Ram Mohan Roy, Keshub Chandra Sen was strongly attracted to Jesus. In a famous speech in Calcutta in 1866, he praised Jesus' teaching of universal harmony, while criticizing the "muscular Christianity" of the Christian missionaries in India. He charges that the Christian missionaries despised the Indians and betrayed Christ; he mockingly chastises Christians for not realizing that Jesus Christ himself had been a victim of Roman imperialism, not a perpetrator of it (Kopf 1988, 111). Making a strong contrast between the genuine Christ and the preaching of the missionaries, Sen contends, "It is my firm conviction that his [Jesus'] teachings find a response in the universal consciousness of humanity, and are no more European than Asiatic, and that in His ethics there is neither Greek nor Jew, uncircumcised nor circumcised, barbarian, Scythian, bound or free" (Sen 1879, 27; quoted by Kopf 1988, 112). Sen embraces Jesus as an Asian teacher of transcendent moral truths, and he proclaims himself an apostle of Jesus and a servant of Paul. Some thought he was quite close to converting to Christianity. While Unitarian Christians embraced him as one of their number, he presented himself as a Hindu apostle of Jesus, claiming to have eaten and absorbed the ideas and character of Jesus into his own life. He challenged Indians to follow the example of service and self-sacrifice of Jesus.

In 1879, Keshub Chandra Sen tried to synthesize various ideas from different world religions into the New Dispensation. He brought the Brahmo Samaj movement to the height of its influence and prestige but also damaged it fatally by dividing it into factions. Sen reflected on the Godhead in terms of *Sat-Chit-Ananda* ("Being-Consciousness-Bliss") (Rajkumar 2010, 32; Lipner 1999, 191 n. 17). These reflections strongly influenced some Christian theologians, especially Brahmabandhab Upadhyay, who developed a Christocentric trinitarian theology based on Sat-Chit-Ananda and presented Jesus Christ as the fulfillment of traditional Hindu longing (Rajkumar 2010, 33).

The Hindu mystic, Sri Ramakrishna (1836-1886), had a series of ecstatic experiences of God, seeing God in variety of manifestations, as the Divine Mother, as Sita, as Rama, as Krishna, as Jesus, and as Muhammad. He had no formal education in Sanskrit or English. He went to a branch of the Ganges River when he was sixteen, and there he practiced a variety of spiritual disciplines in an influential search for God. With Keshub Chandra Sen and Ramakrishna, the boundary between Hinduism and Christianity becomes porous, and Jesus becomes a significant figure in some forms of Hindu devotion and practice. Swami Vivekananda continued the mission of Ramakrishna, bringing this tradition of Hinduism to the World Parliament of Religions in Chicago in 1893, where he won widespread acclaim for his presentation of Hinduism as accepting all religions. Vivekananda combined the mystical approach of Ramakrishna with openness to other religions and a concern for social transformation.

Brahmabandhab Upadhyay: A "Hindu Catholic"

These developments in nineteenth-century neo-Hindu thought influenced a number of Indian Christians. Brahmabandhab Upadhyay (1861-1907) was born into a Bengali Brahmin family and was originally named Bhavani Charan Banerjea. Keshub Chandra Sen inspired him to take an interest in Jesus Christ, which eventually led to his conversion to the Catholic faith. He adopted the named "Brahmabandhab" ("friend of Brahman") as an analogy to the Greek name Theophilus ("friend of God"). As a Catholic, he continued his interest in Hindu thought.

Upadhyay was concerned that the Catholic Church in India presented a Western form of Christianity, which posed unnecessary obstacles because it was so alien to Indian ways of thought. To remedy this problem, he proposed a rethinking of Catholic theology in dialogue with the images and concepts of Vedantic philosophy. He compares this project to Thomas Aquinas's purification and transformation of Aristotelian philosophy into an intellectual platform for Catholic theology. He proposes to replace the Aristotelian-Thomistic philosophical framework of Catholic theology with a Vedantic-based approach, which he called "Hindu philosophy" (Lipner 1999, 186-87).

While he acknowledges that Vedantic thought contains errors, he judges it on the whole to be superior to Aristotelianism. Rejecting Vivekananda's pantheistic interpretation of Vedanta as a distortion, Upadhyay turns instead to theistic forms of classical Hinduism, seeking to establish correspondences between Vedantic ideas and Thomas Aquinas. He judges Vedic theism to be a natural knowledge of God that is fundamentally sound, even though it is not perfect. As such, it can serve as a natural "platform" for expressing the supernatural faith in Jesus Christ (Lipner 1999, 178). He distinguishes the cultural and the religious elements in Hinduism: "We are Hindus so far as our physical and mental constitution is concerned, but in regard to our immortal souls we are Catholic. We are Hindu Catholics. . . . The test of being a Hindu cannot therefore lie in religious opinions" (quoted by Boyd 1969, 68).

This approach allowed Upadhyay to construct a friendly conversation between the Hindu and Christian scriptures. Upadhyay interprets the Rig Veda in a theistic manner that stresses its similarities to Christian faith, as teaching

> the idea of a Supreme Being, who knows all things, who is a personal God, who is father, friend, nay even brother to his worshippers, who rewards the virtuous, punishes the wicked, who controls the destinies of man, who teaches the Rishis [ancient seers], who watches over the welfare of his creatures temporal as well as spiritual. (Lipner 1999, 178-79)

While he acknowledges that there is polytheism in the Vedas, he nonetheless stresses the emergence of pure theism in this tradition: "Hindu scriptures abound with Theistic conceptions though they are encrusted with the hard layers of pantheism and idolatry" (Lipner 1999, 180). The prologue of John says that the Word of God enlightens all people (John 1:1-5); Upadhyay interprets this statement as applying to the hymns of ancient India (Lipner, 182). He juxtaposes the question of the Sanskrit hymn *"Ka"* ("Who?") with biblical answers. The ancient Hindu hymn ends each verse with the question: "Who is that *deva* [deity] whom we should worship with oblation?" Upadhyay responds that "Ka" refers to the Word of God: "Is he the same of whom David sang: 'The Lord said to me, "Thou art my son, this day have I begotten Thee?"' [Psalm 2:7]. . . . Is he the same who was in the beginning with God, by whom all things were made, and without whom was made nothing that was made? [John 1:1-3]" (Lipner, 181, 182). Thus, for Upadhyay, the theistic themes of the Hindu scriptures harmonize with the Christian Bible. He cites the Isa and Kena Upanishads and the Bhagavad Gita as teaching "an ineffable, omnipresent, omniscient, imperishable, provident, sovereign, spiritual, personal Supreme Being" (Lipner, 185).

Upadhyay develops Keshub Chandra Sen's interpretation of the Trinity as *Sat-Chit-Ananda*. As *Sat*, God is necessary being, immutable and infinite, existing in and for itself. According to Upadhyay, *Sat* is *Om*, the mystic sound, and also *Parabrahman* (literally, "supreme Brahman," i.e., absolute Being) in Vedanta, as well as God (Being itself) as understood in the Thomistic tradition (Lipner 1999, 192).

In a questionable etymology, Upadhyay interprets *Cit* as "increasing," "growing," "becoming more" (Lipner 1999, 192). He understands self-consciousness or self-awareness to imply being self-reproductive, and Upadhyay comments that for *Parabrahman*, "to be is to know. It is written in the Upanishads that he grows by brooding (*tapas*) and his brooding is knowledge" (Lipner, 193). Finding an immanent relationship in both Hindu and Christian notions of God, Upadhyay relates the Hindu *Parabrahman* to the Christian Logos proceeding from God the Father. He argues, "To be is to act and to be related, internally and externally" (Lipner, 193). Finally, Upadhyay relates *ananda* ("bliss") to the Christian belief in the Holy Spirit. He comments that the "Infinite . . . naturally and necessarily takes delight in the objective self projected by thought" (Lipner, 194). Upadhyay believes that Catholic theology "completes" the natural wisdom of Advaita (Lipner, 196).

Upadhyay composed a hymn in praise of the Trinity that draws on biblical and Hindu language together:

> I bow to Him who is Being, Consciousness and Bliss.
> I bow to Him whom worldly minds loathe, whom pure minds yearn for,
>   the Supreme Abode.
> He is the Supreme, the Ancient of Days, the Transcendent,
> Indivisible Plenitude, Immanent yet above all things,
> Three-fold relation, pure, unrelated,
>   knowledge beyond knowledge. (Boyd 1969, 70)

Upadhyay compared Shankara's notion of the world as *maya*, usually translated as "illusion," to Aquinas's notion of the world as contingent being, which is not fully real in itself. Upadhyay draws on the language of Vedanta and interprets it in line with Aquinas's understanding of God as necessary Being and the world as having no being in itself (Boyd 1974, 26-27).

Julius Lipner notes that Upadhyay's dialogue with Hinduism was exclusively with the Sanskrit, Brahmin tradition: "On the Hindu side, Upadhyay's dialogic poles were exclusively and unabashedly Sanskritic" (1999, 204). This leaves open the question of dealing with the many castes and communities who experience the Brahmin, Sanskrit tradition as a source of and justification for oppressive social, political, and economic structures.

Mahatma Gandhi

For recent Christian interpretations of the Bible, by far the most influential Hindu is Mohandas Gandhi (1869-1948). Gandhi resembles Keshub Chandra Sen in his nondogmatic appreciation of the ethical teachings of Jesus and in his critique of established Christianity; he also acknowledges his debt to the heritage of Vivekananda. Few non-Christians have ever had as great an influence on how Christians understand the teaching of Jesus, especially regarding nonviolence.

While the early church fathers generally assumed that Jesus' teaching on nonviolence in the Sermon on the Mount applied to all Christians (Kissinger 1975), later generations of Christians generally applied Jesus' teaching of nonviolence to an elite few or saw it as a utopian ideal not suitable for practical questions of social ethics. Francis of Assisi modeled his life on the Sermon on the Mount (Pelikan 2001, 48); but most Christians did not see his example as realistic for shaping society. Erasmus did see the Sermon on the Mount as intended for all Christians, but he interpreted the seemingly impossible commands as hyperbolic rhetoric (Betz 1995, 47).

Martin Luther interpreted the Sermon on the Mount as addressing all Christians, but only in their personal relations and not in political or governmental matters. Regarding the beatitude "Blessed are the peacemakers," Luther explains that it "does not prohibit the waging of war, for Christ has no intention here of taking anything away from the government and its official authority, but is only teaching individuals who want to lead a Christian life" (Luther [ca. 1530] 1956, 5:8; quoted by Pelikan 2001, 129). According to Luther, all the teachings of the entire Sermon on the Mount "have nothing to do with secular affairs or the imperial government"; instead they are intended "in relation to spiritual life and spiritual affairs, not outwardly, physically, or publically before the world, but in your heart and in the presence of God" (Luther [ca. 1530] 1956, 5:27-30; Pelikan 2001, 129).

John Howard Yoder and Terrence Rynne survey a number of ways in which Christians traditionally rejected the applicability or relevance of Jesus' teaching for the practical task of changing society (Yoder 1994; Rynne 2008, 98-100). Some, following Albert Schweitzer, viewed Jesus' nonviolent ethic as intended as an "interim ethic" for the short period before the end of the world; some thought Jesus' teaching applied directly only to a simple rural context, not to the sophisticated world of urban life; some distinguished Jesus' spiritual teaching from social and political questions; some relativized all human ethics in relation to worship of God; some understood justification to be a forensic act of God alone and did not see Jesus as giving precepts for social action (Rynne, 98-100). One of the greatest ironies of the history of Christianity is that it took a Hindu to demonstrate in practice that the nonviolent teachings of Jesus to love your enemies, to turn the other cheek, to go the extra mile, and to do good to those who persecute you (Matt. 5:39-44) are not simply counsels of perfection for monks or for private, spiritual relationships but can lead to effective social-political transformation in situations of conflict.

Gandhi was raised in a devout Vaishnavite family in Gujarat in the northwest of India. The family had a number of friends who were Jains; and in general the Jain influence in this part of India was very strong, including the high value placed on *ahimsa,* nonviolence to all creatures. Gandhi's mother fasted frequently and also taught him the example of *ahimsa.* When he was young, he had relatively little exposure to Western secular influence.

Gandhi went to England to study law, and theosophists there introduced him to the Bhagavad Gita in Sir Edwin Arnold's translation, as well as Arnold's presentation of Shakyamuni Buddha in *The Light of Asia.* About the same time Gandhi also discovered Jesus' Sermon on the Mount, and it pierced his heart. He later recalled that "the Sermon on the Mount . . . went straight to my heart. I compared it with the [Bhagavad] *Gita. . . .* My young mind tried to unify the teaching of the *Gita,* the *Light of Asia* and the Sermon on the Mount" (Gandhi

1983, 60). Gandhi later commented that in the Sermon on the Mount "Jesus put in picturesque and telling manner the great doctrine of non-violent non-cooperation" (2001, 375).

Gandhi often attended Christian church services in England to hear sermons by the best preachers of the day. He read and corresponded with Leo Tolstoy and was profoundly impressed by his vision of a moral, nondogmatic Christianity centering on nonviolent love of all creatures (Andrews 2003, 134-39). Gandhi was sharply critical of Western Christianity, telling Indian Christians: "I consider Western Christianity in its practical working a negation of Christ's Christianity" (Rao 1990, 29). In particular, he charges that Christians misunderstood Jesus' central teaching: "the ministry of Jesus lasted for only three brief years. His teaching was misunderstood even during his own time and today Christianity is a denial of his central teaching: 'Love your enemy'" (Prabhu and Rao 1967, 181).

Gandhi saw himself not as an innovator but as following the path of Jesus Christ and Shakyamuni Buddha: "Christ died on the Cross with a crown of thorns on his head defying the might of a whole empire. And if I raise resistance of a nonviolent character, I simply and humbly follow in the footsteps of the great teachers [the Buddha and the Christ]" (Gandhi 1991, 28). During World War I, he thought that European Christians had not understood Jesus and that Asians may have to help them see him more clearly:

> I know I am now treading upon thin ice; but I do not apologize in closing this part of my subject by saying that the frightful outrage that is just now going on in Europe perhaps shows that the message of Jesus of Nazareth, the Son of Peace, has been little understood in Europe, and that light may have to be thrown upon it from the East. (Andrews 2003, 79)

When Gandhi traveled to Rome in 1931, he was inspired by the vision of Jesus being crucified: "I saw there at once that nations, like individuals, could only be made through the agony of the Cross and in no other way. Joy comes not out of infliction of pain on others, but out of pain voluntarily borne by oneself" (1991, 29). Gandhi's experience of Jesus affected Christians most powerfully, especially Gandhi's conviction that the core of Jesus' teaching was non-violent resistance to evil and that this could be a practical strategy for social and political transformation.

Gandhi advises his followers to learn from Jesus' wisdom as applying to all: "By all means drink deep of the fountains that are given to you in the Sermon on the Mount. But then you will have to take sack-cloths and ashes. The teachings of the Sermon were meant for each and every one of us" (quoted by Rao 1988, 148). As he formulated his philosophy of *satyagraha* ("truth-force" or "the grasping of truth"), he came to see Jesus as "the Prince of satyagrahis":

> It was the New Testament which really awakened me to the value of passive resistance. When I read in the Sermon on the Mount such

passages as "Resist not him that is evil: he who smiteth thee on thy right cheek turn to him the other also, and love your enemies, pray for them that persecute you, that ye may be the sons of your father which is in heaven", I was overjoyed. (Quoted by Rao 1988, 149)

Gandhi believed that satyagraha was implementing Jesus' teaching: "Though I cannot claim to be a Christian in the sectarian sense of the term, the example of Jesus's suffering is a factor in the composition of my undying faith in non-violence which rules all my actions—worldly or temporal" (quoted by Rao 1988, 149-50). Gandhi combines the teachings of Jesus with the Hindu and Jain virtue of *ahimsa.* He believes that the use of violence degrades both the perpetrator and the victim, but Jesus offers a nonviolent way to resist evil while loving the evildoer. In his reflection on the struggle in South Africa, Gandhi used the term *dharmayuddha* ("righteous war") to complement satyagraha: "It is not so much the holy war as the war for holiness" (quoted by Rao 1988, 150). Gandhi saw himself as striving to realize Jesus' teaching about the kingdom of heaven: "I am striving for the kingdom of heaven which is spiritual deliverance. For me the road to salvation lies through incessant toil in the service of my country and humanity" (quoted by Rao 1988, 148).

As is well known, Gandhi led a long and ultimately successful nonviolent protest of civil disobedience against the British, leading to their withdrawal in 1947 (Lelyveld 2011; Adams 2011). His example had a tremendous impact on Christians around the world. Gandhi's friend, C. F. Andrews, an English Christian, notes the paradox that those who challenged Christians most strongly on social questions were not other Christians but either atheists like Karl Marx or members of another religion like Mohandas Karamchand Gandhi. Andrews comments that Gandhi "pointed us so nearly towards a truly Christian solution and . . . carried it out so far in action as to make it appear practicable" (quoted by Rynne 2008, 86). Through Gandhi, Andrews came to understand Jesus' opposition to racial and religious exclusiveness and Jesus' Sermon on the Mount (Andrews 2003; Rynne 2008, 89).

In a similar vein, E. Stanley Jones, a Methodist missionary who knew Gandhi well, comments:

> Never in human history has so much light been shed on the Cross as has been shed through this one man, and that man not even called Christian. Had not our Christianity been so vitiated and overlain by our identification with unchristian attitudes and policies in public and private life, we would have seen at once the kinship between Gandhi's method and the Cross. Non-Christians saw it instinctively. (*Gandhi: An Interpretation*, 105; quoted by Rao 1988, 150)

Jones later reflected on how Gandhi had converted him to nonviolent non-cooperation and a more authentic practice of Christianity: "Here a Hindu was converting me to my own faith!" (1968, 172-73). In his 1925 book *The Christ of the Indian Road*, Jones reinterprets Jesus' statement "I am the Way, the Truth, and the Life" in relation to the traditional ways of action, knowledge, and devotion: "Turning to the Hindus he [Jesus] says, 'I am the Way'—the Karma Marga, a method of acting; 'I am the Truth'—the Gyana Marga—the method of knowing; 'I am the Life'—the Bhakti Marga—the method of emotion, for Life is emotion" (1925, 188). In dialogue with Gandhi and other Hindu leaders, Jones presents Jesus as "the supreme mystic" to "India, the land of mysticism," stressing the concrete appeal of Jesus' actions (1925, 191).

During World War II, a number of European Christians looked to Gandhi's example for inspiration and guidance in difficult situations. André Trocmé, a leader in nonviolent resistance to the Nazis in France, expresses the experience of many Christians:

> The coming of Mahatma Gandhi, whose life and teaching surprisingly resemble those of Jesus, revived the whole issue of nonviolence just when majority theology thought it had already answered the question negatively. . . . Gandhi showed that the Sermon on the Mount can be politically effective. (Trocmé 2004, 153, 156; see also Rynne 2008, 1)

Martin Niemoeller, an outspoken German Lutheran critic of the Nazis, reinforces this perspective:

> When the Christian church and Christian world did not do anything effective about peacemaking, God found a prophet of non-violence in Mahatma Gandhi. . . . In our days Gandhi has shown this [no hope in retaliation] to a great part of the world, and I wish that Christians would not be the last group of men and women to learn the lesson that God is teaching us through this prophet. (Niemoeller 2000, 62-63; see also Rynne 2008, 169)

Reinhold Niebuhr, one of the most influential North American Christian theologians of the twentieth century, watched carefully what Gandhi was doing in India in the 1920s and 1930s. He critiqued Gandhi for not acknowledging that satyagraha involved using forms of violence such as economic pain. Nonetheless, Niebuhr thought Gandhi's approach could be helpfully applied to the situation of African Americans. In 1932, Niebuhr related Gandhi's practice to the African American context and set forth the agenda that Martin Luther King Jr. would later take up. Using the terminology of his day, Niebuhr describes what he called "peculiar spiritual gifts of the Negro," proposing that a prospective leader "would need only to fuse the aggressiveness of the new and young Negro with the patience and forbearance of the old Negro, to rob the former of its vindictiveness and the latter of its lethargy" (1960, 254).

A few years after Niebuhr wrote those lines, the noted African American Christian leader Howard Thurman led a delegation visiting Mahatma Gandhi and found much inspiration (Thurman 1979, 131-35). Gandhi told Thurman that the greatest enemy of Jesus Christ in India was Christianity as practiced and as associated with colonialism. Another major African American leader,

Benjamin E. Mays, visited India in 1936 and had extensive conversations with Gandhi; he later taught Martin Luther King Jr. and became president of Morehouse College.

The young Martin Luther King Jr. studied both Reinhold Niebuhr and Gandhi carefully and traveled to India in 1959. King later told E. Stanley Jones: "It was your book *Mahatma Gandhi, An Interpretation* that gave me my first inkling of non-violent non-cooperation. Here, I said to myself, is the method we can use to gain the freedom of the American Negro" (Jones 1968, 178). King comments on the impact Gandhi had on him:

> Gandhi was probably the first person in history to lift the love ethic of Jesus above mere interaction between individuals to a powerful and effective force on a large scale. Love for Gandhi was a potent instrument for social and collective transformation. It was in this Gandhian emphasis on love and nonviolence that I discovered the method of social reform. (M. L. King 1958, 97-98)

King later commented that Gandhi taught him for the first time that "the Christian doctrine of love, operating through the Gandhian method of nonviolence, is one of the most potent weapons available to an oppressed people in their struggle for freedom" (Ansbro 2000, 7). King did not accept Gandhi uncritically and did differ with Gandhi on some points (Ansbro, 134, 140). Nonetheless, King's widow, Coretta Scott King, recalls her husband saying repeatedly: "Christ gave us the goals, and Mahatma Gandhi provided the tactics" (C. S. King 2010, ix).

Numerous Christians around the world accepted Gandhi's lead in interpreting the teaching of Jesus on nonviolence. Thomas Merton took Gandhi's perspectives into the heart of his own worldview, commenting, "Here is a statement of Gandhi that sums up clearly and concisely the whole doctrine of nonviolence: 'The way of peace is the way of truth'" (Merton 1966, 71). John Howard Yoder, a Mennonite theologian, embraced the nonviolent ethic of Gandhi, and in light of it strongly critiqued the "Christian Realism" of Reinhold Niebuhr (Rynne 2008, 105-10; Yoder 1983, 115, 356). Catholics James Douglass and Bernard Häring embraced Gandhi's ethic of nonviolence (Rynne, 114-25). Douglass claims that "the relationship of the Hindu Gandhi to the person of Christ can be described as the most living belief in the Incarnation given in our time, and that in full recognition of the fact that Gandhi did not confess Jesus as the only Son of God" (1970, 55).

Anglican bishop Desmond Tutu applied Gandhi's principles to the struggle against apartheid in South Africa, and Catholics did likewise in the Philippines in struggling against Ferdinand Marcos. In light of Gandhi's example, Protestant biblical scholar Walter Wink developed a thoroughgoing interpretation of Jesus' "Third Way," neither accepting injustice nor resorting to violence but nonviolently resisting (1992; 2003, 43, 51, 105). Catholic theologians John Chattanatt and John Moniz studied the relation between Gandhi and Christian liberation theology's option for the poor.

Abhishiktananda

A short time after Gandhi was assassinated, a French Benedictine monk, Henri Le Saux (1910-1973), arrived in India, intending to bring the gospel of Jesus Christ to Hindus. Together with another French priest, Jules Monchanin (1895-1957), Le Saux hoped to establish a new form of Catholic monastic life in India; in India he encountered Hindu forms of practice that led to personal experiences of nonduality and liberation that resulted in different ways of understanding the Christian scriptures. In the Last Supper discourse of the Gospel of John, Jesus prays to the Father that his followers "may be one, as we are one" (John 17:11). As a result, Christians have always sought the goal of becoming one with God, and the exact meaning of oneness has long been the focus of Christian reflection and prayer, especially in the Gospel of John and the mystical tradition. In the life of Henri Le Saux and his colleagues, the ancient Hindu tradition of nonduality (*advaita*) and the Christian mystical tradition of seeking oneness with God flow together. In particular, the encounter with Sri Ramana Maharshi changed forever Le Saux's understanding of oneness and his manner of interpreting the Bible. For both figures, nonduality was an experience they lived more than a theory they developed.

Sri Ramana Maharshi (1879-1950) was a renowned Hindu spiritual leader who had a strong experience of nondual Being when he was seventeen (Maharshi 1988, xiii-xiv). Even though not engaged in any exceptional religious quest at the time, the young Maharshi went through a profound religious transformation that shaped his entire life. At the beginning of this experience, the thought abruptly came to the youth that he must die. He lay down and felt the sensation of life leave his limbs. His senses closed down, and his mind stopped its normal movements. In a flash he experienced: "I AM." Beyond all sensations, beyond all divisions, beyond the prospect of death, Maharshi experienced the nondual unity of which the ancient Upanishads speak (Abhishiktananda 1979, 17). He realized that beyond the body's sense impressions, beyond his changing consciousness, at the center of his being was the mystery of reality itself, unchanging, undying, and eternal. At the time, the young Ramana was not familiar with the Upanishads; it was only years later that he discovered the Upanishadic precedent: "Only many years later, when he happened to read some Vedantin books, did he recognize that his own experience was the same as that which the rishis [seers] of old had known and handed on in the Upanishads" (Abhishiktananda 1979, 17).

As a result of this experience, Ramana left his usual daily routine and spent the remainder of his life living at the foot of Mount Arunachala, one of the most sacred mountains of India. This mountain is revered as the god Shiva. The mountain of Shiva had called Ramana Maharshi. When people came to Maharshi seeking his wisdom, he would invariably ask questions in return: "Who are you?" "Who poses the question?" "Who fears death?" He challenged his disciples to look beyond the impermanent ego, which dies at each moment, to the true Self beyond all change, beyond life and death.

Toward the end of Maharshi's life, Le Saux, came to visit him. Though filled with hopeful expectations, at first Le Saux was dismayed by what he viewed as a "cultic" atmosphere and the excessive respect showed to Maharshi by his attendants. However, Ethel, an English woman, sharply challenged him:

> "You have come here with far too much 'baggage,'" she said. "'You want to know, you want to understand. You are insisting that what is intended for you should necessarily come to you by the path which *you* have determined. Instead you should make yourself empty; simply be receptive: make your meditation one of pure expectation." (Abhishiktananda 1979, 8)

Le Saux was suffering from a fever at the time, and he later posed the question to himself: "Did I really try to make myself empty on the lines suggested by Ethel? Or rather, was it the fever itself that got the better of all my efforts to meditate and reason?" (Abhishiktananda 1979, 8). Within a short period of time, he had an experience that changed his life: "Even before my mind was able to recognize the fact, and still less to express it, the invisible halo of this Sage had been perceived by something in me deeper than any words. Unknown harmonies awoke in my heart" (8). However, he soon experienced a clash between the new experience and his earlier religious categories: "My dreams also included attempts—always in vain—to incorporate in my previous mental structures without shattering them, these powerful new experiences which my contact with the Maharshi had brought to birth; new as they were, their hold on me was already too strong for it ever to be possible for me to disown them" (9).

Le Saux came to understand this event as an Upanishadic experience of nonduality similar to that of the young Maharshi. In the aftermath, he adopted the lifestyle of a Hindu *sannyasi* and the name of Abhishiktananda, which means "Bliss of the Anointed One, the Lord" (Du Boulay 1998, 83). He experienced religious truth in both the Catholic and the advaitic traditions even though he knew that on an intellectual level there was a conflict between Christian articulations of the Trinity and the advaitic tradition of Hinduism. He wrote in his diary on September 27, 1953: "From now on I have tasted too much of *advaita* to be able to recover the 'Gregorian' peace of a Christian monk. Long ago I tasted too much of that 'Gregorian peace' not to be anguished in the midst of my *advaita*" (Abhishiktananda 1998, 74). He spent years agonizing over the conflict he experienced between his trinitarian faith as a Catholic monastic, and the Hindu Upanishadic experience (Abhishiktananda 1965). He continued to celebrate the Catholic Eucharist and Liturgy of the Hours, and he also engaged in Hindu forms of meditation.

During the time of the Second Vatican Council, Abhishiktananda attended a meeting in Nagpur, where he proposed the practice of reading both Christian and Hindu scriptures: "We shall read the Bible in the morning and the Upanishads in the evening, seeking to hear in them what God has to say to us at the present time in each one's situation. If only the Church could at last understand the summons which the Spirit sends her through India!" (Stuart 1995, 157). Anticipating possible controversy, he encouraged a colleague: "Like you I feel a little nervous. Let us be good *advaitis,* and not mind what people may think of us, but go straight on our way seeing only the 'atman' in everything, and being so void of everything inside that the Spirit may use us at his own free will" (Stuart, 158).

Abhishiktananda describes his experience of reading the Gospel of John in light of his Upanishadic experience of nonduality:

> John revealed to us in his turn the mystery which the rishis [the seers who received the Hindu Vedas] had dimly perceived, seen now in all its splendor and depth, the splendor and depth of the Word and of the Spirit. . . . It was as though we had returned from the Upanishads to the Bible with eyes miraculously unsealed, eyes accustomed to the depths, capable of a wholly new penetration into the mystery of the Lord. (Quoted in Amaladoss 1992, 69)

In light of his advaitic experience Abhishiktananda came to see the Gospel of John in a new way, believing that the "incredible experience of being (the 'I am' of John 8) . . . is at once the axis and the summit of Hindu mysticism" (Stuart 1995, 118). He interpreted Jesus' experience in relation to the Upanishads: "What I discover above all in Christ is his 'I AM.' . . . Christ's experience in the Jordan—son/Abba—is a wonderful Semitic equivalent of '*Tat tvam asi'/'aham brahmasm*' ['That art thou/I am Brahman'] (Amaladoss 2011, 55). Michael Amaladoss explains, "For Swamiji [Abhishiktananda], the ultimate reality and experience is 'I AM.' It is not the 'i' becoming the 'I,' but the 'i' disappearing in the 'I.' It is not the conclusion of an argument or reflection, but an awakening" (2011, 57). In light of this experience, Abhishiktananda expressed his hope: "And the completion in Christ of the mystical intuition of *advaita* is the fundamental ontological condition for the building up (not in statistics, not in masonry, but in reality) of the Church in India" (Stuart 1995, 123). Abhishiktananda believed that such experiences were available to all, including non-Christians:

> It would be quite wrong to suppose that such graces are reserved only for the chosen few. . . . Moreover, such graces are not infrequently bestowed on those who have never even heard mention of Christ's revelation. This is an undeniable fact, despite the astonishment felt by many Christians when they come to realize it—just as Paul was amazed to discover that Gentiles too were called to have faith in Christ. (Abhishiktananda 1993, 55)

In his experience of both the Hindu and Christian traditions of nonduality, Abhishiktananda referred to his "uncomfortable situation of belonging to both sides" of the Hindu–Christian relationship (Bäumer 2011, 3). Later in his life, he felt a sense of peace, but he could not express the resolution of his struggle in a conceptual manner. He came to believe that the advaitic experience was universal and was at the center of Christian experience: "The mystery of the

Heart of Christ is present in the mystery of every human heart. . . . And in the end it is this mystery—at once of oneself and of each person, of Christ and of God—that alone counts. The Awakening of the Resurrection is the awakening to this mystery!" (Stuart 1995, 277). His editor, Murray Rogers, visited him about a year before his death and later described him at this time:

> Indeed Swamiji felt more keenly than I had ever known before the pull toward the awakening to Self, the moment when all that can be said or known is "I AM," the "Ah!" of the Kena Upanishad. Already every notional idea, every -ology related to history or thought was beginning to disintegrate. There was nothing left, for what was left was everything, the revelation that we are "sons of God." "The blazing fire of this experience," he once wrote, "leaves nothing behind; the awakening is a total explosion." One goes, and one IS. (Stuart 1995, 280)

Bede Griffiths

A few years after Abhishiktananda's arrival in India, another European Benedictine monk, Bede Griffiths (1906-1993), came to India, also seeking a new form of monastic life. Like his friend C. S. Lewis, Griffiths had come from a secular agnostic background in which a rationalist understanding of science radically separated the mind from the physical world. After converting to the Christian faith and entering the Catholic Church, Griffiths entered the Benedictine community. After living as a monk in England for many years, he traveled to India, where he succeeded Abhishiktananda as director of Shantivanam. In India, he came to view the Vedas, the Upanishads, and the Bhagavad Gita as cosmic revelation and integrated them into his understanding of Christianity. For Griffiths, the experience of Hinduism opened him to what he called "the other half of my soul."

Griffiths interprets the Christian Bible in dialogue with the Hindu and Buddhist scriptures, as well as with a holistic interpretation of modern science. He notes that in the Vedas of the Hindu tradition the universe consists of three worlds, the physical, the psychological (or psychic), and the spiritual, which are integrated into a unified whole (Griffiths 1990, 78). On the physical level, Agni, the god of fire, is the fire used to burn sacrificial offerings; but Agni has another meaning as well, "a psychological aspect, being the fire of life and the fire of the mind. Agni is said to know everything" (59). Finally, there is the spiritual aspect of fire; both the physical and psychological levels are seen "as manifestations of the one supreme Spirit, which is manifesting at all levels of the universe" (59). In the Vedic tradition, fire is the origin of the universe, existing spiritually in heaven, physically in the material world, and psychologically in the human world in between (60). The fire sacrifice, which is central to Vedic ritual, is a way of "returning all things to their source": "In the Vedic view, if we live constantly returning things to their source, then we are living in the harmony of the universe, the rhythm, *rita,* of the universe. Conversely, if we do not turn the wheel of the law, if we appropriate things to ourselves, then we are committing sin" (61).

Griffiths finds analogies to the Vedic perspective in the Bible and in religions around the world, as well as in modern science. Griffiths believes that ancient peoples in general were aware not only of the physical world but also of a psychic world populated by spirits and powers, including their ancestors and other human beings. These cultures developed gradually toward monotheism: "In the course of time these spirits and powers were conceived to be manifestations of one supreme Spirit and Power" (1990, 78). In the Bible, he notes that the Hebrew word for God, *'elōhîm*, is a plural form: "This clearly points to a time when many gods were recognized. It can even be used of a ghost, as when the witch of Endor called up the ghost of Samuel and said, 'I see Elohim coming up out of the earth' (1 Sam 28:13)" (79). He speculates: "The word Elohim must at one time have signified the whole world of the sacred, the psychic world" (79). El could appear in various forms on different occasions, such as in Jacob's vision of the angels ascending to heaven at Bethel ("the house of El," Gen. 28:16-19) or as the man with whom Jacob later wrestles (Gen. 32:30). Griffiths compares the henotheism of the early biblical writings, where El appears in different forms, to the image of the *deva* (deity) in early Vedic religion (79). He believes that both early Israel and early India moved in similar fashion from faith in multiple divine beings to affirming one transcendent reality. In ancient Israel, the other gods came to be regarded as "demons," "that is, as powers opposed to the one God like the *asuras* in Hindu tradition" (80).

Similarly, according to Griffiths, YHWH developed from being a thunder god at Mount Sinai to being the Lord of the "hosts of heaven," and to being recognized as the Cosmic Lord. Griffiths notes that the Bible interprets the name YHWH as "I am," that is, as absolute Being (Exod. 3:14), and he compares this to the Upanishads: "This is the same insight which is found in the *Katha Upanishad,* where it is said: 'How shall we speak of him except by saying, "He is" (*asi*)?'" (1990, 80). Griffiths interprets the independent developments in ancient Israel and India in relation to each other: "Thus one can trace the slow stages by which the idea of God evolved in Israel as in the *Vedas,* the *Upanishads* and the *Bhagavad Gita.* Each appears as a unique revelation by which the true nature of absolute Truth and Reality came to be known" (80-81).

In many biblical passages, Griffiths finds a deep sense of solidarity uniting humans with God and the earth: "The main theme of the Bible is the restoration of humanity and, through humanity, of the whole creation to its original harmony" (1990, 83). However, he warns of the dangers of religiously motivated violence that also appear in the Bible: "The Psalmist never ceases to proclaim his hatred for his enemies and to ask God to destroy them. When personal or racial enemies are seen as enemies of God there is no limit to the violence and hatred which they evoke" (87). He laments the tragic history of consequences of this biblical heritage in later wars of religion, but he stresses there are also biblical resources for resisting this legacy: "This is the dark side of the Semitic religions which has so disfigured their history. . . . Yes, when we have said this, we must always remember that there is another side to the religion of Israel. Together with its exclusive character, which rejected all other religions, there was also a complementary trend" (87-88).

Citing Isaiah's prophecy of a new heaven and a new earth (65:17-18), Griffiths hopes: "We are destined to pass beyond our present level of consciousness, where we see everything in terms of dualities, of subject and object, time and space, heaven and earth, and to enter into the unifying consciousness beyond the dualities of the mind" (1990, 89). Griffiths sees the challenge of the present time as a passage from the historical divisions that have caused so much violence to a nondual consciousness in which various religious traditions are harmonized: "Our present mode of consciousness is dualistic, but as the mystics of all religions have discerned, the ultimate reality is non-dual" (106).

Central to this realization is Griffiths's interpretation of Jesus Christ as the Cosmic Person in the New Testament in relation to the Cosmic Person (*Purusha Sukta*) in the Vedas: "Christ is not only the man who comes at the end, but the man who was in the beginning" (1990, 123). Jesus' significance embraces all of human history and the entire cosmos: "The Son comes forth eternally from the Father as his Self-manifestation, his Self-expression, and manifests God in the whole creation, drawing everything in time and space into the fullness of the divine being" (127).

Griffiths compares this cosmic interpretation of Jesus Christ to the Primordial Person in Hinduism. In the Rig Veda, the hymn of creation, Purusha Sukta, describes Purusha ("man"), the Primeval Person: "This purusha is all that has been and all that will be, the Lord of Immortality" (Rig Veda 10:90; Griffiths 1990, 128). Purusha manifests in the entire universe but also transcends it; as Purusha is sacrificed, the world comes into being, including the four *varnas* or classes of humans, which would be the basis for the caste system. Griffiths compares the cosmic sacrifice of purusha to the book of Revelation's description of "the lamb who was slain before the foundation of the world" (Rev. 13:8; Griffiths 1990, 129).

Griffiths quotes the *Brihadaranyaka Upanishad*: 'In the beginning this was the Atman in the form of Purusha" (1.4.1; Griffiths 1990, 129). He comments: "This means that this whole creation was originally the *atman*, the Spirit, in the form of the cosmic Person" (1990, 129). The cosmic Person integrates both the conscious and the unconscious in the universe, gathering all into a unity. This figure develops further in the later *Svetasvatara Upanishad*: "Those who know beyond this world the high Brahman, the vast (the *brihad*), hidden in the bodies of all creatures and alone enveloping everything, as the Lord, they become immortal" (3:7; Griffiths 1990, 130). Griffiths comments: "The 'supreme Brahman' is the name for absolute reality and this text is saying that this absolute or ultimate reality is in the midst of everything and envelops everything and that he is the Lord. He is not only the impersonal *brahman* but also the personal God" (1990, 130). The Upanishad closes by inviting: "Let us know that the highest Lord of Lords, that highest God of Gods, the ruler of rulers, the highest above, the Lord of the world, the adorable" (6:7; Griffiths 1990, 131). Griffiths sees this affirmation as very close to the pure monotheism of Second Isaiah and to the cosmic Christ of the New Testament. He also reads the revelation of Krishna to Arjuna in the Bhagavad Gita as a development of this trajectory of the Cosmic Person. Krishna proclaims: "I am the origin of all. From me the all proceeds" (Bhagavad Gita 10:8; Griffiths 1990, 132).

Griffiths draws the intuitions of the Hindu scriptures deeply into his interpretation of the Bible, proposing a cosmic vision to inspire a unified, integrated human community. He does, however, acknowledge contrasts between the traditions: "The Hindu in his deepest experience of *advaita* knows God in an identity of being. 'I am Brahman,' 'Thou art that.' The Christian experiences God in a communion of being, a relationship of love, in which there is none the less perfect unity of being" (1990, 220). This contrast has implications for social life: "The Christian mystical experience is always in terms of community. The Hindu experience is essentially individual and has no positive relationship to the community whereas the Christian experience, although certainly personal and individual, is always also implicitly or explicitly a community experience" (221).

Despite all the points of convergence, Griffiths acknowledges that there remains a major difference: "But in the normal [Hindu] understanding, as seen in the advaitic school, the individual self is identified with the supreme Self. . . . By contrast, in the Christian understanding the human spirit is never identified with the spirit of God. . . . We enter into the dynamic of the trinitarian experience" (1990, 222-23).

Griffiths relates the Christian experience to the Jewish background: "In the Hindu experience the immanence of God is dominant and there is more concern with realizing God as within one and oneself as within God, whereas for the Christian, coming out of the Hebrew background, God is always transcendent and one never identifies oneself with God" (1990, 224). In contrast to Hindu advaitic experience, Griffiths turns to Paul's image of Christians as members of the body of Christ and to Augustine's vision of a communion of persons in love, transformed by God's grace (225). Griffiths interprets the differences as appropriate to our present level of consciousness:

> We have constantly to learn to see beyond the passing forms of this world to the eternal reality which is always there. It means passing from our present mode of consciousness, which is conditioned by time and space, into the deeper level of consciousness which transcends the dualities external and internal, subject and object, conscious and unconscious, and becomes one with the non-dual Reality, the Brahman, the Atman, the Tao, the Void, the Word, the Truth, whatever name we give to that which cannot be named. It is this alone that gives reality to our lives and a meaning to human existence. (1990, 226)

Sara Grant

Sara Grant (1922-2000), was a Scot trained in Western classics at Oxford who came to India in 1956 and who integrated the experience of advaita (nonduality) into her faith and practice as a Catholic sister. Her encounter with the Hindu tradition of nonduality brought her this realization: "After living in India for some time I realized that I had been a non-dualist from birth" (2002, 5). From the time she was young, Grant recalled:

> It was only gradually that I became aware of a sense of somehow living in two dimensions of consciousness, that of the visible world of everyday life, and that of another, mysterious world, least inadequately described as the sense of a presence which was also an absence, a rather crude way of expressing the transcendence-in-immanence which characterizes the non-dualist position as distinct from that of the absolute monist. (2002, 7)

In India she explored the advaitic tradition of Shankara and was inspired and challenged by Abhishiktananda. Richard R.V. De Smet proposed that she compare the notions of relation in Shankara and Thomas Aquinas (Grant 2002, 32). She studied Shankara's original texts with care and came to believe that many of the traditional interpretations of his thought were mistaken. She concludes that Shankara "agrees with St. Thomas Aquinas in regarding the relation between creation and the ultimate Source of all being as a *non-reciprocal dependence relation*" (2002, 40). She compares Shankara's perspective to that of the fourteenth-century Christian text *The Scale of Perfection*: "He is thy Being, but thou art not his Being" (2002, 42). She argues that Shankara would have accepted Aquinas's theology of creation and also insists that Shankara, like Pseudo-Dionysius the Areopagite, "not only *learns* but *experiences* divine things" (2002, 43).

In light of these discoveries, Grant proposes to theologize from an "alternative experience." As an adult living Catholic religious life in India, she invokes the apostle Paul's statement: "I live now no longer I but Christ in me" (Gal. 2:20). In light of her experience of advaita, she finds that there is "a profound metaphysical impulse for a depth of union which transcends all subject–object dichotomy, and yet is emphatically not pantheistic: "The supreme Mystery is experienced as the Self of one's own self ('I live now no longer I . . .')" (2002, 5).

Grant found words for her own experience in the writings of the late medieval Hindu saint Sadashiva, who prayed: "I can find no corner within my heart where I may take my stand to worship him, *for every 'I' which I attempt to utter, his 'I' is already glowing*" (Grant 2002, 6). In language that resonates across traditions, Grant comments that

> non-dualism is not merely a matter of intellectual conviction: it consists also in an existential experience, confirming intellectual conviction of the absolute transcendence-in-immanence of the ultimate Mystery in relation to all that exists or occurs at the relatively ephemeral level of "ordinary" life, a kind of wordless and conceptless adherence to the truth of one's own being which, however, obscure and painful, is also strangely liberating. (2002, 21)

Grant believes that most people receive glimpses of "awareness of another dimension of being, of the Eternal in the fleeting Now of time. . . . To be pursued by this awareness with the relentless persistence of the Eumenides is the crucifying and liberating lot of the typical *jnani* or non-dualist" (2002, 3). She laments that much of the Catholic tradition in the modern period had developed a distrust and fear of mysticism. Grant believes it is vitally important for Christians to retrieve and nurture an awareness of this depth-dimension of life, and she thinks contact with the advaitic tradition of India can help in this endeavor. She hopes for a deeper Christian experience of the words of the gospel through engagement with advaita.

Many European and American Christians found inspiration in the examples of Abhishiktananda, Bede Griffiths, and Sara Grant. For many, the encounter with forms of Hindu spirituality provided an opportunity to renew their lives as Christians, as Abhishiktananda had hoped: "I believe that it is necessary to go to the Hindu sources in order to be able to draw more deeply on our own Christian sources" (Blée 2011, 65). However, many Indian Christians who came from lower-caste, Dalit, or tribal backgrounds were not enthusiastic about this path because this approach engaged the elite Brahmin tradition from which their communities had long been excluded. Some Indian Christians were suspicious of the way that Abhishiktananda and Griffiths adapted Hindu symbols and perspectives into Christian life and practice. Toward the end of his life, some Hindus vigorously criticized Griffiths for his use of Hindu customs. Moreover, some Indian Christians preferred their traditional expressions, albeit derived from the West, as way of asserting their minority Christian identity (Blée, 64). Nonetheless, Raimon Panikkar, who was a close friend and associate of Abhishiktananda, continued to reflect on the implications of this trajectory. This form of engagement with the tradition of advaita challenges Christians to reflect on the mystical implications of the Bible.

The Second Vatican Council, Indian Christian Theology, and Inculturation

The statement of the Second Vatican Council in *Nostra Aetate* regarding Hindus is very brief:

> Thus in Hinduism the divine mystery is explored with an inexhaustible wealth of myths and penetrating philosophical investigations, and liberation is sought from the distresses of our state either through various forms of ascetical life or deep meditation or taking refuge in God with loving confidence. (*Nostra Aetate* §2; Tanner 1990, 2:969)

This statement notes various aspects of Hindu life and practice without making any particular assessment of any of them. What is most noteworthy is that just a few sentences later, the same document expresses the respect of the Catholic Church for whatever is true and holy in this tradition as in others. No ecumenical council in the history of the Catholic Church had issued such a statement about the Hindu tradition. The council both affirmed the existing

Catholic efforts to improve relations with Hindus and encouraged further ini-
tiatives. The council did not make any comment on the situation of the Dalits
("untouchables") and *adivasis* (tribals) in India.

Many Christians in India have related the Bible to the Hindu tradition's
wealth of concrete images, narratives, and poems of divine–human encounters. George M. Soares-Prabhu relates the Gospels to India's heritage by stressing the dialogical character of Jesus' teaching: "The parables of Jesus are dialogical. They do not convey information, offer prescriptions, or give lessons to a
passive and receptive listener. Instead by telling a 'shocking' story, they provoke
and tease the listener into a radically new insight into his own situation" (2003,
35-36). Soares-Prabhu laments that Jesus' teaching was later abused by Christians "as a means of repressive socialization; for history shows clearly enough
how frequently the Gospels have been invoked to legitimize feudal oppression,
colonial exploitation, anti-Semitism, and religious persecution of every kind"
(35). In contrast to this history of hostility, Soares-Prabhu insists that freedom
"*was* a value for Jesus—precisely because his teaching was not so much the
imparting of 'sound doctrine' as the communication of a message of love. But
there can be no love without freedom—that is why there is always a dialogical
element in the teaching of Jesus" (35). He sees Jesus' teaching as "non-elit-
ist, transforming, prophetic, dialogical, and critical"; and he cites the apostle
Paul as grounding this principle: "Christ has set us free in order that we might
remain free" (Gal. 5:1; Soares-Prabhu 2003, 37).

On this basis, Soares-Prabhu reads the teachings of Jesus creatively in relation to Hindu tradition, seeking insights from non-Christians. He compares
outsiders to the Roman centurion whom Jesus praises (Matt. 8:5-13). He finds
much illumination in Jesus' teachings from Mahatma Gandhi and also from
Bab Amte, who was inspired by the Gospels to improve the lives of lepers in
India (2003, 85). He sees Nachiketas in the Katha Upanishad, who visited Yama
(Death) in search of an answer to the riddle of death, as a "precursor" of Jesus
(2003, 85).

Informing Soares-Prabhu's approach is the principle that "such dialogue,
and the Third World Christology it nourishes will focus on the 'mystery' of
Jesus, not on the 'mechanisms' that have been put forward to explain this mystery" (2003, 85). The mystery is the person of Jesus and the events of his life,
death, and resurrection; the mechanisms are "the models that have been proposed to explain the mystery" (85): "Mysteries mediate significance; mechanisms offer explanations" (86). Soares-Prabhu stresses the primacy of experience over the mechanisms of metaphysical categories: "The experience is
an immediate contact with the reality of experience, so that the distinction
between the experiencing subject and the object experienced disappears. It
needs no demonstration, no argument, no explanation. The explanation is not
the mechanism" (87).

We have seen that Roberto de Nobili and Brahmabandhab Upadhyay
interpreted Hinduism as containing a natural wisdom but not a supernatural
gift from God. Mariasusai Dhavamony accepts the position of Karl Rahner that
there is no purely natural order; we live always in a supernatural order affected

by God's grace. This approach is grounded biblically in a wisdom Christology based on Colossians 1, according to which Christ reconciles all things in heaven and on earth. This profoundly modifies de Nobili's and Upadhyay's Thomistic-based assumption that there is a strict distinction between natural and supernatural orders in human experience. This approach builds on the statement of Vatican II and offers a basis for a hermeneutics of respect and generosity in reflecting on the varieties of Hindu perspectives. Following Rahner, Dhavamony bases his approach to Hinduism

> on the theological principle that all people are one in community of their origin and destiny, and that there is only one human order which is supernatural, because the whole universe has been created through and for Jesus Christ (Colossians 1:16). This means that Christianity has to respect and uphold the nobility and unity of human nature. Whatever is true and good in Hinduism is to be recognized as such and given due importance and whole-hearted acceptance. (2002, 19)

M. Thomas Thangaraj draws on the Saiva Siddhanta tradition of southern India to present Jesus as "the Crucified Guru." He compares the Hindu term "guru," especially in the Saivite tradition, to *didaskolos* ("teacher") in the New Testament and to Clement of Alexandria's interpretation of Jesus as a teacher (Thangaraj 1994, 126-27). He notes that a Saivite guru is inseparable from the disciples (*sisya*), and he suggests that this is appropriate for interpreting Jesus: "Our Christological project has been organized around the guru-sisya relation, rather than simply the individual guru. Therefore the profound significance of Jesus of Nazareth lies precisely in his ability to engender a community of disciples" (Thangaraj, 131).

Geoffrey Parrinder considers the relation between Jesus Christ as the incarnation of God and Hindu avatars. He explains: "An Avatar is a descent, a 'down-coming' (*ava-tara*), partly in the spatial sense of a deity descending from heaven. But the word is used generally of any distinguished person as a disclosure of the divine, and of any new and unusual appearance" (1964, 66). While noting the uniqueness of the Christian doctrine of the incarnation, Parrinder notes that Christians drew on Greek and non-Jewish ideas to interpret it and suggests: "Yet there are more parallels with Hindusim than are often thought" (66).

In contrast to Abhishiktananda's approach to Hinduism through advaitic experience, R. C. Zaehner believed that the avataras of Hindu tradition offer the most promising basis for a dialogue with Catholic faith: "The Bhagavad Gita, not the Vedanta, is the starting-point from which any fruitful converse between Eastern immanentism and Western transcendentalism can begin. It is the eastern end of the great religious bridge, the building of which should be our ideal; the western end is Catholic Christianity—and both ends are built on the foundation of God made man" (1970, 150). Zaehner acknowledges that the starting points are quite different: "In Christianity it is the transcendent Lord of history who becomes man, in the Bhagavad-Gita it is the immanent principle of the universe" (150). Zaehner hopes that this bridge can provide a platform for religious unity: "It is the laying of the foundations of the bridge that may come to unite and bring into concord the apparently irreconcilable poles of total immanence and total transcendence, however discordant these may appear to be" (150). Zaehner stresses the difference in the Christian valuation of matter: "Much more dangerous is the mysticism of pure spirit, for it makes nonsense of the Incarnation . . . to equate Indian with Christian mysticism, as many neo-Vedantins and neo-Buddhists so often do, is to deny the central theme of Christianity itself, God's concern with matter, with the world, and with men" (361).

Christians have read the Bible in relation to the Hindu tradition's wealth of concrete images and narratives of God, especially in the literature concerning Krishna, Ram, Shiva, and Devi. As we have seen, some Christians have approached Jesus as Guru, as Satyagrahi, and as Avatar. Some have presented him also as a Dancer. Michael Amaladoss notes that David dances before the ark of the covenant (2 Sam. 6:5) and that the Psalms and the Song of Songs invite dancing, and he explains: "Dance is an expression of joy and freedom. . . . Dance is purposeless action" (2006, 149). Dance offers an image of God's love: "God has no needs . . . God is dancing and inviting humans and the cosmos to dance along"; this image resonates deeply in India because "God's actions are often called *lila* or play in Indian tradition. It may seem meaningless or purposeless. It has no purpose outside itself. It is its own purpose" (Amaladoss 2006, 149). In India, Shiva is portrayed dancing as Nataraja, the Lord of the Dance, whose movements are the cosmos; Sara Grant reinterprets the title "Lord of the Dance" as a name for Jesus (1987, 195).

Dalit Theology: Social Justice and the Caste System

While many Christians in India have drawn creatively on the resources of the Brahmin Hindu tradition in interpreting the Bible, Christian communities also face the difficult challenge of social justice in a society traditionally shaped by the caste system. In this respect, Mahatma Gandhi's practice of Satyagraha did not satisfy all those seeking to reform Indian society. Gandhi wanted to call the "untouchables" by the name "Harijan" ("children of God") and sought to improve their situation within a reformed caste system. But many found his approach to be condescending. Gandhi even compared the Harijan to a cow— worthy of respect in Hindu tradition but lacking intelligence and therefore incapable of understanding religious teachings (Fernando and Gispert-Sauch 2004, 197).

The great leader of this community, B. R. Ambedkar (1891-1956), strenuously rejected the name "Harijan," preferring the term "Dalit" ("crushed"); he publicly criticized Gandhi for continuing to accept the caste system, charging that Gandhi's "defence of the caste system is the most insensible piece of rhetoric one can think of. Examine Mr Gandhi's arguments in support of caste and it will be found that everyone of them is specious if not puerile" (Ambedkar 2002, 161). Ambedkar eventually left the Hindu tradition, became a Buddhist, and proposed a Dalit interpretation of the Buddha's message (2011). Ambedkar's example has had a powerful influence on Christian Dalits (Fernando and Massey 2007, 6); for example, G. Cosmon Arokiaraj quotes a Dalit song: "You say Gandhi but we say our leader's name Ambedkar" (2007, 34).

Most Christians in India today come from the marginalized communities commonly known as "Dalits" ("suppressed" or "crushed," that is, those formerly known as the "untouchables" or "Pariahs") and "adivasis" ("from the origins" or "aboriginal," that is, the indigenous, tribal peoples of India). Some estimate that 65 to 70 percent of Indian Christians come from a Dalit background, and another 15 to 20 percent from an adivasi (tribal) context (Robinson and Kujur 2010, 5). The government of India uses the term "scheduled castes" for Dalits and "scheduled tribes" for adivasis. The adivasis are the indigenous peoples of India who were never integrated into any of the classical societies. They lived on the margins, often in remote hills or jungles; in many cases regular contact with the mainstream society of India is relatively recent. Like the Dalits, they suffer from historical discrimination, poverty, and lack of opportunities. Leonard Fernando and G. Gispert-Sauch comment on the decisions of Dalits and adivasis to become Christian: "We have also seen the importance of the desire of the discriminated people for a new social order, a legitimate aspiration. . . . It is not strange that some Dalits and tribals should choose change of religion as the road to a fuller human life" (2004, 192).

Some Hindus want to consider Dalits and adivasis as Hindus and bitterly protest their conversions to Christianity, claiming that Christian missionaries are exploiting the vulnerability of these populations and luring them into the Christian churches (Fernando and Gispert-Sauch 2004, 192-99). The government of Madhya Pradesh established a commission to investigate Christians; it concluded that Indian Christians are "anti-national" and reflect "a foreign hand," that is, American influence (Frykenberg 2000, 189). Frykenberg describes the situation: "Hindu nationalists continue to view Indian Christians as belonging to a foreign power. . . . Christian church buildings are now regularly destroyed in various parts of the continent, usually on the pretext that they were built under colonial rule and that they stand upon the foundations of some former temple" (2000, 189). In numerous places, notably in the Kandhamal district of the state of Orissa, there have been violent attacks by Hindu extremists against Christians. Churches have been burned, Christian women have been raped, and Christians have been beaten and murdered (Baumann 2010). Some nationalist Hindus have claimed that the underlying cause of such actions lies in forced conversions. However, many from these communities deny that they ever were Hindu, and Christians deny the accusations of forced or manipulated conversion. Chad M. Baumann observes that there is a sharp divide within the Hindu community and that some Hindu leaders deliberately fostered hostility:

> On one side [are] those whose Hinduism is tolerant, friendly and hospitable to strangers and minorities; on the other side stand those whose Hinduism is intolerant, suspicious and aggressively chauvinistic. . . . I argue that the Orissa violence was exacerbated by the involve-

ment of those who intentionally politicized and communalized local tensions, in part by portraying communal identities at both the local and national level as if they were singular, rigid and mutually exclusive. (2010, 264)

Some of the most creative interpretations of the Bible have come from the context of the struggle of Dalits and adivasis for equality and justice. To date, there are numerous works of biblical interpretation from a Dalit perspective; there is less scholarship from the adivasi Christian community. Leonard Fernando notes the powerful stimulus that Ambedkar and other Dalit leaders gave to Christian Dalits: "The Dalits and those on their side began to read the Bible and look at Jesus from the perspective of the oppressed. They began to own Jesus as *the* Dalit. They experience in Yahweh the God who has intervened in history on behalf of the oppressed. This is the source of their hope" (Fernando 2007, 6). Maria Arul Raja stresses that the implications of such biblical interpretations are not restricted to the Dalits: "It has to be borne in mind that the fruits of this dialogue are not to be reaped only by Dalits. Any Dalit initiative to break the shackles of caste slavery is bound to redeem also the humanity of those who seek to perpetuate the same system of hierarchy" (quoted by Massey 2007, 19).

Christian Dalit biblical interpretation moves between the Dalit context and the biblical text, for example, relating the shepherds in the Bible (e.g., the infancy narrative of Luke 2:8-20) to Dalit experience. In many Indian contexts, the shepherds today are Dalits, who, like the shepherds in biblical times, live outside the towns (Luke 2:8) and are often seen as "abhorrent" (Gen. 46:34) (Massey 2007, 14). James Massey notes that despite the low estimate of this occupation by ancient society, major biblical figures, including the patriarchs, Moses, and David, are shepherds. The biblical descriptions of shepherds as despised but nonetheless as playing important roles is important for the experience of Dalits today (2007, 14).

Monodeep Daniel develops this project in relation to the problem of dry latrines in India today; even though some government officials have denied the existence of dry latrines, in many areas Dalits work as scavengers transporting the night soil by hand, soiling themselves in the process, and thus confirming their status as "untouchable" in the broader society (M. Daniel 2007, 28-29). Daniel notes that the biblical Philistines tried to block the wells of Isaac with rubbish (Gen. 26:12-25) and speculates that this would have rendered the nomadic shepherds "as ritually unclean and consequently untouchables" (29). He believes that this action would make sense as part of a strategy to dispossess the shepherds, end their nomadic wandering, and potentially reduce them to slavery (29). The shepherds, however, resist assimilation and domination and continue to increase in wealth. Daniel compares the expulsion of Isaac to the subjection of indigenous peoples in India during the time of the Aryan invasions (30). However, Daniel stresses, Isaac and the other shepherds "re-opened the blocked sources of water. Retrospectively it is this act of re-opening our sources of life in which we have failed. We need to underscore the act of digging new wells, besides reopening the old ones, in this narrative" (31). This sets a program for Dalits today. From ancient times to the defeat of B. R. Ambedkar in 1950, Daniel laments, "We seem to have accepted the loss of our power, dignity and wealth as our social condition with complacency" (M. Daniel 2007, 31). The Genesis narrative offers motivation and a precedent to "re-open our old wells and dig new sources" (31). In opposition to the self-complacency that Daniel finds among too many Dalit leaders, the biblical narratives and images become a potent source of critique of the caste system and related ideas, rejecting the "rake and rubbish of casteist ideas, false notions of karma, rebirth and so on. In the light of this Dalit condition this text of the Bible directs and challenges to dig new sources of life" (32).

E. C. John also expresses sharply the contradiction between the Bible and the caste system: "Obviously, the caste system contradicts the biblical understanding of humankind" (2007, 40). He also notes that the biblical genealogies list ordinary people by their names: "they are bearers of God's image. Therefore they have dignity and names. Names also mean identity, honour and history" (40). John reads the biblical prophets' concern for the poor as addressing the situation Dalits and other subaltern peoples of India (42). He also compares the laments of the psalms, Habakkuk, Jeremiah, and Job to the situation of the Dalit Christians (44). John then formulates a pointed challenge to Indian Christians: "We have to confess that we have nurtured a mindset whether 'upper caste' or 'lower caste' or 'outcaste', that has valued the caste distinctions above the new being in Christ" (49). He closes with the stark challenge: "The Christian Dalits in rural India are the poorest of the poor in our country. Political equality remains only a dream" (49).

A number of Christian theologians have used the experience of the Dalits to interpret the meaning of God, the Suffering Servant of Isaiah, and Jesus Christ (Amaladoss 1997, 28-29). In this vision, God enters the world in Jesus as a Dalit. Jesus as a Dalit has nowhere to lay his head (Matt. 8:20), and he eats and drinks with the outcastes, the Dalits, of his society, the publicans, tax collectors, and sinners (Mark 2:15-16). When Jesus reads from the book of Isaiah in the synagogue in Nazareth, he proclaims a Jubilee Year (Luke 4:16-29) and thereby promises liberation for Dalits. At the end of his life, Jesus dies rejected and forsaken as a Dalit (Amaladoss 1997, 29).

A wide variety of Asian theologians have placed liberation or freedom at the center of their programs in recent decades. For Indian Christians, the age-old question of caste is still an issue of controversy. Some Dalits have become Christian seeking equality and freedom, and find in the exodus a hopeful paradigm for their experience: "For the Christian Dalits, the move to Christianity from Hinduism is a liberating exodus experience. This experience guarantees an exodus hope for full liberation" (Amaladoss 1997, 28).

While many Indian theologians, including Felix Wilfred, have developed an inspiring Christian Dalit theology, these hopes have not been completely fulfilled in the Christian churches of India today. In many communities in India, Christians from an upper-caste background dominate the lower or scheduled castes. Amaladoss laments: "Religious communities are meant to be counter-cultural. Unfortunately, they are as caste-ridden as the wider church" (1997, 30). Peniel Rajkumar bitterly notes the irony in the Christian experience in India:

> On the one hand we have the growing academic influence of Christian Dalit theology as a form of contextual theology, whereas on the other we have the glaring discrimination of Dalits within Christianity as well as the continued passivity of the Church to engage in issues of Dalit liberation. This incompatibility in my opinion is symptomatic of the practical inefficacy of Dalit theology. Dalit theology does not seem to have significantly influenced the social practice of the Indian Church. (2010, 1)

This issue remains unresolved.

Adivasi Experience

In addition to the Dalit communities, there are also the indigenous peoples of the Indian subcontinent. These tribal or *adivasi* communities did not form part of traditional Hindu caste society; they were historically on the margins of the dominant Indian cultures. Even when the adivasi traditions use Hindu terms, the meaning and context are generally quite different from the Brahmin tradition. Some Hindus call them *vanavasis* ("forest dwellers"), but adivasis generally reject this as a pejorative term. Often these are among the poorest communities on the Indian subcontinent. To date, there has not been extensive biblical interpretation or theological discussion coming from adivasis themselves. Francis Minj claims that his adivasi interpretation of Jesus Christ "is the first Christian theology developed explicitly *from an Adivasi* perspective, *for Adivasis,* and written to nourish the Christian faith of the local *Adivasi* church" (Minj 2011, 187).

The biblical condemnations of idolatry furnished the basis for previous assessments of adivasi religious traditions; earlier Christian missionaries interpreted the traditional adivasi religion as "primitive, satanic, uncivilized" and viewed it as a form of "devil worship" (Minj 2011, 188). Minj laments that when contemporary Indian Christians seek to indigenize Christianity, they often use Hindu concepts and symbols; but this alienates adivasi Christians even more (189). Minj complains that even though the Catholic Church in principle accepts the resources of different cultures to interpret Catholic faith, "there is no carefully thought out, convincingly argued, and well discerned interpretation of Jesus Christ through Adivasi cultural concepts and idioms" (189).

To remedy this problem, Minj reads the Bible from the perspective of adivasi Christians, beginning with the prologue of John (1:1-14). He proposes a new term of his own creation, *"Paramadivasi,"* as the center of an adivasi approach to Jesus Christ. *Param* means "supreme"; *adi* means "primordial"; and *vasi* means "dweller" (2011, 189). He explains that "the prefix *param* radically transforms the socio-anthropological category *adivasi,* transporting it to the realm of both human and divine" (189). Drawing on the biblical notion of the Word of God extending throughout all creation, Minj argues "that the term *Adivasi* signifying original dweller can be legitimately applied to Jesus Christ in whom God reveals himself (Heb. 1:1)" (189). The image of *Paramadivasi,* which is grounded also in Christ as the "firstborn of all creation" (Col. 1:15), provides "an experiential basis for *Adivasi* theological reflection on Jesus" (190).

Drawing on imagery familiar to adivasi Christians, Minj proceeds to inter- pret Jesus as Ancestor, Messiah/Liberator, High Priest, and Healer/Exorcist. Jesus challenges adivasi culture in various respects. In traditional adivasi soci- ety, someone who suffered a violent death could not become an ancestor, that is, someone with supernatural status who can protect the family on earth and assist in relating to God. Minj notes that the violent death of Jesus overturns this prior assumption: "Through his violent death Jesus challenges *Adivasi* cul- tural taboos. His murder would disqualify his ancestorship, but he defies the *Adivasi* taboos of denying ancestorship to those who die violently" (2011, 191). Adivasis traditionally did not have kings or any central ruler. Today they are threatened by outside forces, and the biblical images of Jesus as Messiah and Liberator offer hope: "Unlike the [outside] powers that work tirelessly for their own power, Jesus becomes the voice of the voiceless and inserts himself among the *Adivasis* because he knows them well (John 10:27). He regards the poor and exploited masses as his own" (Minj 2011, 194). Traditional adivasi myths present the horse as a symbol of "hostility, power, anti-life, and disharmony." As Liberator, Jesus Christ appears to the adivasis as the horse tamer who "trans- forms the horse into a new symbol of life, of obedience to God, and of one who lives in harmony with his creation. Jesus liberates humanity from the slavery of horse-like greed, pride, jealousy, and the tendency to destroy life in all its forms" (Minj 2011, 195).

The traditional *pahan* ("priest") in adivasi society offers sacrifices of food or animals in order to praise and thank God and avoid evil. Minj reinterprets and applies this image: "Jesus as priest, mediator, and victim enriches and revo- lutionizes the *Adivasi* understanding of the priestly task" by adding dimensions of service (2011, 197). Historically, adivasis experienced Christian missionar- ies as the first outsiders to care for them and to help them against the colo- nial authorities. This was a powerful expression of the concern of God in Jesus Christ for them. The priestly mission of Jesus Christ includes concern for the poor and marginalized, transforming the priesthood away from being "merely ritualistic" (Luke 4:18; Minj 2011, 198). Jesus' question to Peter, "Do you love me?" (John 21:15-19) grounds a new form of priesthood as service (198).

Adivasi culture is filled with belief in spirits, some of which can cause harm. Persons who are considered to be *deonras* ("exorcists") are both revered and feared because their powers over the spirit world can be exercised for good or harm. Earlier Christian missionaries condemned the *deonras* and forbade contact with them, but Minj finds Jesus performing the role of a *deonra*. In the Gospels Jesus repeatedly heals people, sometimes by "touching the 'untouch- ables'" such as lepers, blind persons, dead persons (Mark 1:31, 41; 5:38-41;

7:33-35; 8:22-25; 10:3, 6); the image of Jesus as healer and exorcist resonates powerfully in adivasi society (Minj 2011, 199). Minj notes the historical background in adivasi experience:

> Indian civilization is built on the sweat and blood of untouchables, the *dalits,* and *Adivasis,* who nonetheless remain untouchables, taken advantage of by the ruling classes. . . . For centuries the *Adivasis* have been treated like "quarantined animals." When the *Adivasis* encountered the missionaries they accepted Jesus as their healer, exorcist, and the new *deonra.* (2011, 199)

Conclusion

Just as India and the Hindu tradition are extremely varied, so relations with Hindus have influenced Christian interpretations of the Bible in various ways. A traditional hermeneutic of hostility can condemn Hindu images as so many idols and graven images. On the other hand, Christian sannyasis have explored the meaning of nonduality in relation to advaita and found new ways to read the biblical traditions. Mahatma Gandhi powerfully illumined how the nonviolent teachings of Jesus could be effective tools of social transformation. Dalit and adivasi interpreters of the Bible relate the biblical message of social justice to India.

CHAPTER SIX

Christian Interpretations of Scripture in Relation to Buddhists and Buddhism

Christians have been aware of Buddhists since about the year 200 C.E., but for most of Christian history Buddhists have not played a major role in the awareness of European Christians. Nonetheless, some of the most innovative presentations of Christian faith have come in relation to the Buddhist tradition, including in relation to Buddhism and Daoism in seventh- and eighth-century China. Christian interpretations of scripture in relation to the Buddhist tradition have ranged widely from bitter hostility to positive appreciation and even to the incorporation of Buddhist perspectives into Christian biblical hermeneutics. Since Buddhism is a non-theistic tradition, many fundamental assumptions of the two traditions are different. Shakyamuni Buddha did not take a position on metaphysical questions that he deemed unimportant for release from suffering. There have been various ways of interpreting and engaging these differences.

Early Contacts

The first Christian notice of Buddhists comes from Clement of Alexandria, who comments on Buddhists in about the year 200 C.E.: "Among the Indians some follow the instructions of the Buddha, whom they have honored as a God because of his unusual holiness" (*Stromateis* 1.71.6; trans. Ferguson, 76). Not long after the time of Clement, the first desert fathers and mothers left Alexandria to live in the desert. While some have speculated that Buddhist monasticism may have been an influence on the formation of Christian monasticism in Egypt in the third and fourth centuries, there is no firm evidence of direct influence.

The first Christians to have extensive contacts with Buddhists were from the Church of the East, which developed quite early in Mesopotamia and Persia. The Church of the East, which spread across much of Central, South, and East Asia in the first millennium, has often been called "Nestorian" because of later controversies, but the name is misleading. Nestorius, who served as patriarch of Constantinople in the fifth century C.E., was not even a member of the

Church of the East, let alone the founder of it. The Church of the East, which had existed long before the time of Nestorius, honored Nestorius's teaching in the controversies of the fifth century c.e., though it did not accept the Catholic and Byzantine Orthodox interpretations of him; modern scholarship has also challenged traditional understandings of Nestorius, leading to important ecumenical agreements (Stirnemann and Wilflinger 1994, 1996, 1998). From the sixteenth century to the present, the patriarchs of the Church of the East have asked other Christians not to call them "Nestorians" (Davids 1994, 134), but nonetheless the practice persists (Moffett 1998; Tang). Since the nineteenth century, members of this tradition have called themselves the Assyrian Church of the East (Soro 2007).

First Christians in China
During the first millennium c.e., the Church of the East enjoyed a phenomenal growth across much of Asia. In the first millennium, Central Asia was a diverse meeting place for the cultures and religions of Greece, Persia, India, and China. As members of the Church of the East traveled from present-day Iraq and Iran along the Silk Road through Central Asia, they encountered Buddhists along the way. We do not know exactly when Christians first came to China. There is a legend that the apostle Thomas twice preached in China, but there is no reliable historical evidence to support it. A large iron cross has been discovered in China that is dated to the Three States Period of China (228-251 c.e.), and there are various indications that Christians in the fifth and sixth century were in touch with the Chinese, but there are no reliable written records of Christians in China before the Tang Dynasty (Tang 2004, 78).

A more trustworthy report of Christians in China comes from a stone stele or tablet erected in 781 c.e. in Chang'an (present-day Xian) during the reign of Emperor Dezong (r. 780-805). The tablet recounts that in 635 c.e. Aluoben (Alopen), a monk and probably a bishop of the Church of the East, arrived at the border of China and was warmly welcomed and escorted with honors to the imperial court in Chang'an. The welcome seems to have been organized beforehand, which suggests that other Christians prepared the way for him. The stele was later forgotten and lay hidden in the earth until 1623 or 1624, when a farmer plowing a field accidentally uncovered it. The language on the upper part is Chinese, and the bottom is Syriac, one of the languages used by the Church of the East. The tablet contains a cross of the Church of the East on a lotus blossom, with clouds and a pearl, combining Christian, Daoist, and Buddhist symbols. Jing Jing, a scholar of the Church of the East who was also known as Adam, composed the text inscribed on the tablet, which proclaims the basis for the harmonious dialogue:

> The Way [Dao] does not have a common name and the sacred does not have a common form. Proclaim the teachings everywhere for the salvation of the people. Aluoben, the man of great virtue from the Da Qin Empire, came from a far land and arrived at the capital to present the teachings and images of his religion. His message is mysterious

and wonderful beyond our understanding. . . . The message is lucid and clear; the teachings will benefit all; and they shall be practiced throughout the land. (Palmer et al. 2001, 42)

The text of the stele offers an overview of central Christian beliefs, including creation, the fall of humans, the incarnation, redemption, baptism, and the ascension of Jesus into heaven (Tang 2004, 112-13; Palmer et al. 2001, 224-32). In 638 C.E., the Chinese emperor Taizong, the second emperor of the Tang Dynasty (r. 627-649 C.E.), met with Aluoben in his private chambers, which were normally forbidden to foreigners. The emperor approved of Aluoben's message and built a new Christian monastery within sight of the most prestigious Daoist monastery of the age. During the reigns of Taizong and his successor Gaozong (r. 650-683 C.E.), Christian monasteries were established in hundreds of towns in every province of China. Later emperors alternated between supporting and persecuting Christians. Christians flourished under Emperors Daizong (r. 762-780) and Dezong, but they were persecuted under Empress Wu Zetian (r. 698-712) and also during the severe general persecution of foreign religions by Emperor Wuzong in 845.

During the reigns when the Church of the East enjoyed imperial favor, there appears to have been intense dialogue among Daoists, Buddhists, and Christians. During the late eighth and early ninth centuries, when Prajna, a scholar of Indian origin, and other Buddhists in China, were translating Buddhist texts from Sanskrit and other Indian languages into Chinese, Jing Jing offered them assistance in one of the great translation projects of world history (Tang 2004, 111, 133, 143).

The Chinese called Christianity "The Religion of Light" or "The Luminous Religion." In addition to the stone tablet, the Church of the East produced a number of other Christian texts for a Chinese audience influenced by Buddhism and Daoism.[1] These remarkable texts draw on Buddhist and Daoist language and imagery to convey the person and message of Jesus. They constitute the earliest surviving Christian interpretations of scripture in relation to Buddhists and Daoists.

Aluoben either wrote or was intimately involved in the production of two texts: *Book of Jesus, the Messiah* and *On the One God.* Aluoben may well have presented the *Book of Jesus, the Messiah* to Emperor Taizong when Aluoben met him in his private apartments (Tang 2004, 107). This work introduces the one God, as distinct from idols, and calls for reverence to God, the emperor, and parents. It also sets forth ethics based on the Ten Commandments and the golden rule of Jesus. The text discusses John the Baptist and the birth, baptism,

---

1. These texts, written between the seventh and the tenth centuries C.E., were discovered in the late nineteenth century in a cave at Dunhuang (Palmer et al. 2001, 50; Tang 2004, 86-87). Some scholars have referred to these texts as the "Jesus Sutras," from the Buddhist word for scripture, "sutra"; but Li Tang argues that the use of the term "sutra" is misleading and prefers to call them "books" (2004, 105 n. 9).

suffering, and death of Jesus. The document breaks off abruptly before discussing the resurrection of Jesus. The conclusion is lost.

The *Book of Jesus, the Messiah* uses the term "Buddhas" for heavenly beings, possibly intending angels (Tang 2004, 150 n. 42). It uses the word *Fo*, which Chinese Buddhists used to refer to the Buddha: "When a human being is in crisis, he always calls the name of Fo" (Tang, 146). Sometimes it is unclear whether the author is using "Fo" to refer to the God of Christianity: "Who will pay a debt of gratitude to the grace of Fo and take it into account?" (Tang, 146). It also invokes the "law of Fo," apparently meaning the law of the God of Christianity (Tang, 150). The text uses the word "Dao" in a manner parallel to Logos or the Way: "Then one can get the Dao of Heaven" (Tang, 147).

In telling the story of Jesus, this text draws on Buddhist imagery: "The Messiah was orbited by the Buddhas and arhats [disciples of the Buddha who have attained saint-like status]. Looking down he saw the suffering of all that is born, and so he began to teach" (Palmer et al. 2001, 159). Interpreting the compassion of the Messiah for a Chinese context, this presentation would resonate with the images of Shakyamuni Buddha in the Lotus Sutra and Guan Yin, the bodhisattva of compassion, a very influential figure in Chinese Buddhism. The sutra tells the story of the birth of Jesus, calling the Holy Spirit "the Cool Breeze":

> So God caused the Cool Breeze to come upon a chosen young woman called Mo Yan [Mary], who had no husband, and she became pregnant. The whole world saw this, and understood what God had wrought. The power of God is such that it can create a bodily spirit and lead to the clear, pure path of compassion. Mo Yan gave birth to a boy and called him Ye Su [Jesus], who is the Messiah and whose father is the Cool Breeze. (Palmer et al. 2001, 166)

With regard to the multitude of Chinese deities, the *Book of Jesus, the Messiah* is very similar to Isaiah 40-55, the Wisdom of Solomon 13, and Acts 17 in viewing images of other gods as idols fashioned in ignorance:

> The heavenly Lord worked laboriously to create all beings. All beings were not far from the knowledge of Fo. They made human figures to be devoted to (worship). . . . Ignorant beings used clay and wood to make camels, cows and horses. . . . They made these figures with faces, but they could not give them life. Human beings should measure their wisdom if they have it. (Tang 2004, 148)

The companion text, *On the One God*, was composed in 641 C.E. and is very similar to the *Book of Jesus, the Messiah* in calligraphy, writing materials, and paper. This text includes a section of parables presenting the oneness, mystery, and power of God. It also includes a number of homilies based on Jesus' teaching in the Sermon on the Mount. This text uses the term "emptiness," which is central to many forms of Mahayana Buddhism that flourished in China: "The most holy one of great wisdom is equal to emptiness. He cannot be grasped. Only this One-God is everywhere" (Tang 2004, 159). This is an extremely evocative claim that could be understood in different ways. In Buddhism there is no belief in God as creator, and thus *On the One God* transforms the meaning of emptiness by interpreting Buddhist language in a Christian creation-based theology. It is not completely clear how this text intends the equation of "the most holy one of great wisdom" and "emptiness," but it uses the important Buddhist term as complementary to Christian faith. The relation between the God of Jesus Christ and Buddhist understandings of emptiness has been a topic of intense discussion in recent decades.

On the One God also draws on the Buddhist analysis of the five *skandhas*, the five elements that make up human experience, but it uses them in a non-Buddhist manner as the elements comprising soul or spirit: "Soul and Spirit were made of five components" (Tang 2004, 162). Buddhists traditionally do not acknowledge any permanent soul. *On the One God* suggests that some traditional Chinese spirits are devils: "Do not kneel down and worship devils" (165). The conclusion is a robust assertion of monotheism: "Serve only the One-God, the heavenly Lord. Worship the One-God. Seek the One-God" (166). Here again, Buddhist language is being used in a very different context, since Buddhists do not acknowledge any permanent soul or creating God. Here also, as we will see, the issues involving the relation of the Bible to the Buddhist teachings on no-self and the unconditioned have been the focus of recent scholarly discussion.

Over a century after Aluoben, Jing Jing composed what is perhaps the most innovative and interesting text of this entire corpus, *The Book on Mysterious Peace and Joy*. This work presents the teaching of Jesus as a series of negations in a style that would be familiar to some forms of Mahayana Buddhism. The Prajnaparamita (Transcendental Wisdom) Sutras of Mahayana Buddhism rigorously negate all claims, even the Four Noble Truths of Shakyamuni Buddha himself. The Heart Sutra proclaims, "There is no suffering, no origination [of suffering], no stopping [of suffering], no path. There is no cognition, no attainment and no non-attainment" (Conze 1988, 111). Japanese Buddhist scholar Gadjin Nagao explains that because humans begin in profound, beginningless ignorance, the first stage of the Mahayana path involves rigorous negation of all assertions. Clinging to the insight gained in this stage, however, can lead to spiritual pride; thus Mahayana Buddhists negate the negation, reengaging the world with compassion on the path of the Bodhisattva (Nagao 1991, 198-206). The end result of the negations is positive.

Using analogous language, *The Book on Mysterious Peace and Joy* encapsulates Jesus' teaching in the negative principles, "no desire, no doing, no fame (virtue) and no demonstration" (Tang 2004, 117). While this rhetorical style may sound surprising to many Christians, the effect of these negations, as in Mahayana Buddhism, is positive: "If one has no desire, no doing, then one can remain clean and pure" (189). Jesus instructs his hearers: "Therefore, I say: no desire, no action, no merits and no demonstration. There are four such principles. One should not boast off. . . . Be gentle, humble, empty, and patient" (191).

Like both the biblical wisdom tradition and the teachings of Shakyamuni Buddha, *The Book on Mysterious Peace and Joy* stresses the transience of all things and the inevitability of separation from loved ones. In this theme the biblical wisdom tradition, Christian wisdom, and Buddhism all converge.

The Book on Mysterious Peace and Joy presents a number of teachings that are common to biblical wisdom literature and to Buddhism. It warns that those who are insolent and self-seeking in the end harm themselves, as do those who engage in excessive drinking and licentious behavior. Practicing religion for impure motives leads to illusion and harm. Pretending to practice religion for the sake of praise from others is self-deception. In adopting a Mahayana style of interpretation, *The Book on Mysterious Peace and Joy* poses another question that still challenges contemporary reflection: Is it appropriate for a Christian to use a Buddhist hermeneutic to interpret the Bible?

Jing Jing also wrote *Gloria in Excelsis Deo*, a text that praises the Triune God of Christianity by using the style of classical Chinese poetry. It gives praise to God the Father, the Son, and the Pure Wind (the Holy Spirit), who gives rain to withered plants. A related text, *Honored Persons and Sacred Books*, is similar to Jing Jing's texts but probably comes from a later period. Li Tang notes that "it omits the word 'great' when referring to the Tang Emperor," which means it comes from a later time, probably between 906, the end of the Tang Dynasty, and 1036, when the cave of manuscripts at Dunhuang was sealed (Tang 2004, 116).

Daoists, Buddhists, and Christians flourished together during the reigns of favorable emperors for a couple centuries. Until the ninth century in China, the church may not have been considered an independent religion but rather a Buddhist sect (Baumer 2006, 193). In 845 the Chinese emperor launched a persecution of foreign religions, including both Buddhism and Christianity. Buddhist and Christian monasteries were closed. Monastics were forced to return to the world, marry, raise families, and engage in regular employment.

The later history of the Church of the East in China is checkered. About the year 980, there was reportedly only a single Christian remaining (Moule 1977, 76), but there are reports of Christians of the Church of the East again being in China in the twelfth century. The Mongol Yuan Dynasty (1271-1368) favored Christians and established many churches. Thus, when the Franciscan missionaries arrived in the late thirteenth century, they found so-called "Nestorians" in favor at the imperial Chinese court. After the Yuan period, the Church of the East declined in China. We do not know exactly why the Church of the East did not continue in China, but Francis C. M. Wei speculates that the reason was loss of identity:

> The first attempt to Christianize China thus came to an end apparently because the Nestorians went too far in compromising with Buddhism, an older religion in the country. Christianity paid a heavy price for losing its identity. It had no contribution to make to the religious life of the Chinese, at least from the point of view of the Chinese who could not distinguish it from another religion. (1947, 11)

Christian Views of Buddhists in Early Modernity

Beginning in the fifteenth and sixteenth centuries, European Christian missionaries increasingly came into contact with Buddhists across Asia. Many Christian missionaries during this period viewed Buddhist images as the idols condemned in the Bible and sharply rejected Buddhist practices. In many places, the hermeneutics of hostility was so strong that no serious dialogue between Buddhist and Christians was possible. In the seventeenth century, Jesuit Athanasius Kircher described the Dalai Lama of the Tibetans as "their false Deity," and he called the Tibetan Buddhists' veneration of him "rather mad and brain-sick idolatry" (Pomplun 2010, 79). As Christians discovered resemblances between Christian beliefs and practices and other religions, many interpreted the similarities in a hostile manner as "demonic plagiarism." Others, however, proposed more generous theological options: the similarities could be seen (1) as based on God's direct inspiration, (2) as remnants of the primordial revelation given to Adam and Eve and handed down through the various religious traditions around the world, and (3) as expressions of the universal and natural human desire for God (78-79).

Like Roberto de Nobili in India, Matteo Ricci (1552-1610) and his Jesuit colleagues and successors in China were respectful of the religious traditions they encountered. Seeking to interpret the Christian faith in terms accessible to the Chinese, Ricci originally dressed as a Buddhist and studied Buddhism as the key to presenting the Gospel to the Chinese. However, as he came to know China better, he decided that Buddhism was a minor religion in China, and he devoted his mature attention to interpreting Christianity in relation to the Confucian tradition.

Another Jesuit, Alexandre de Rhodes (1593-1660), was the leading early Catholic missioner in Vietnam. As he became acquainted with the Vietnamese customs, he came to believe that the deities that they venerated were idols; but he also believed that the Vietnamese in some way adored the "unknown God" whom Paul had proclaimed to the Athenians at the Areopagus (Acts 17:23; Phan 2005, 50). Like de Nobili in India and Ricci in China, de Rhodes carefully studied the language, religion, and culture of the people to whom he proclaimed the gospel. He respected everything in Vietnamese culture that he saw as compatible with the teaching of Jesus Christ, often giving a Christian interpretation to established customs. Like Ricci, he highly respected Confucius's teachings, finding nothing in them contrary to Christian faith (Phan 2005, 89-90). He was more critical of Daoism because of its alleged superstition, sorcery, and witchcraft. In the case of dubious practices that could be superstitious, de Rhodes sought to purify them and accept them in a Christian manner. He also opposed the use of Christian practices that would cause conflict by distinguishing Vietnamese Christians too strongly from other Vietnamese (Phan 2005, 81).

De Rhodes viewed Buddhism as a "superstition" imported from China (Phan 2005, 83). While he respected the devotion of ordinary Buddhists, he strongly rejected Buddhist monasticism and sometimes publicly debated with Buddhist monks. De Rhodes opposed what he thought Shakyamuni Buddha taught in two regards. He thought that the Buddha taught his lay followers an "external way," which involved the worship of idols and belief in rebirth. He further thought that the Buddha taught his monastic followers a somewhat different, atheistic, "internal way," which denied the existence of a creating and providential God. De Rhodes interpreted the Buddhist terms "nirvana" and "shunyata" to mean nothingness; he lamented that the Buddha teaches that "nothingness is the origin of all things, and that at death all things return to nothingness as to their ultimate end" (84). In response to this dual threat, de Rhodes proposed arguments in favor of theism (against atheism) and monotheism (against idols). In adapting Catholic practice to the Vietnamese context, de Rhodes rejected statues of the Buddha, Confucius, and deities as the idols condemned in the Bible; however, he forbade Christians to destroy the statues (73-74).

Elsewhere, relations were often acrimonious. In Sri Lanka, Christian missionaries regarded Buddhism as "the citadel of Satan" and accordingly did their best to undermine the tradition (De Silva 1976, 39). Portuguese Catholics stole a relic of the tooth of the Buddha, took it to Goa, and claimed that they destroyed it (Lai and von Brück 2001, 39-42). Buddhists responded that the Catholics had not obtained the real relic. The Portuguese Catholic mission schools forced children to use Christian names, and the Portuguese rulers forced families to take Portuguese family names, abandoning their own family and clan tradition. This was deeply resented. Later, during British rule in the nineteenth century, many Sri Lankan Buddhist leaders initially held Jesus and his teachings in high regard and even invited Christians to come to their temples to speak. However, the continuing disdain of most Christian missionaries for Buddhist practices prompted polemical responses in return and a fresh examination of Buddhist sources (Lai and von Brück, 42-47).

In the seventeenth century, Jesuit missioner Francisco Godinho praised the Tibetan Buddhists for worshiping the one God: "The peoples of the great Tibet are not idolaters, since we have found that they acknowledge the adorable Unity and Trinity of the true God" (Pomplun 2010, 82). From 1715 to 1721, another Jesuit, Ippolito Desideri (1684-1733), explored Tibet's religious and cultural heritage. He expresses a variety of assessments of Tibetan Buddhism; in some writings he accepts the theory of demonic plagiarism, but elsewhere he is more generous. He reflects on the Three Jewels of Buddhism, the Buddha, the Dharma (Buddha's teaching), and the Sangha (monastic community); and he suggests that they are similar to the Trinity and wonders if they may be "an obscure symbol" reflecting a primordial revelation from God (89).

At the beginning of his stay, Desideri believed that the Tibetans had some knowledge of the One God and even a sense of the Trinity (Pomplun 2010, 74-75). He initially compared the Tibetan mantra *om ah hum* to the triune God: "the word *om* signified knowledge or an arm, that is, power; *ah* is the word, and *hum* is the heart, or love, and that these three words mean God" (75).

Desideri later changed his mind about this assessment. After studying the great commentaries on the Mahayana scriptures by Nagarjuna and Candrakirti, he realized that Tibetan Buddhists do not believe in God or divine providence (Pomplun 2010, 92-93). He attributed this error to the work of the devil: "It is almost as if the Devil has hidden behind a skillfully embroidered curtain of gold, whose beauty and luster had bedazzled his spectators, and thereby blinded their minds with an artificial and beggarly light" (93). However, he distinguishes Buddhists from Epicurean atheists, who believe there is no reward for good or punishment for evil after death. He stresses that Buddhists possess a refuge that has many of the attributes of the God of Christianity: "goodness, peace, omniscience, omnipotence, and infinite compassion. He also noted that Tibetans recognize that no one is really able to do good or avoid evil without the assistance of this very object of refuge" (95). This approach opened for Desideri the possibility of recognizing an implicit faith in God, in spite of the explicit denial of God's existence.

Desideri pondered the paradox that even though Tibetan Buddhists differed profoundly from Catholics on what dogmas are to be believed, they nonetheless largely agreed on what precepts and directions should be followed in life (Pomplun 2010, 96). He warns missionaries to expect a hostile reception. Desideri notes that at the Areopagus Paul sought common ground with the Athenians (Acts 17:22-34), but he emphasizes that Paul was mocked and dragged before the crowd and accused of preaching new deities, and he warns missionaries that they should expect to suffer for their message (Desideri 2010, 559).

Even though Desideri is aware of multiple points of contact, nonetheless, his theology of missions is founded on an interpretation of the Bible in hostile opposition to Buddhists and Buddhism. He sees Buddhism as a foe to be defeated: "What is the dispatching of missionaries to infidel kingdoms for the purpose of their conversion other than an open war against error and superstition?" (2010, 571). Thus, Desideri proposes studying Buddhist doctrine in order to triumph over Buddhists. Desideri notes that Indians are very learned and clever, with elaborate logical arguments. To overcome them, he warns missionaries that their own learning is not enough; and so they must use weapons taken from "infidelity itself," that is, the philosophy and theology of the other tradition. Desideri cites biblical examples to encourage the study of Buddhism, but in a very hostile framework. For example, Desideri urges missionaries to imitate the example of Judith; she used not only her beauty, skill, and wiles, but in the end she took the dagger of Holofernes from its sheath in order to kill him (Jdt. 13:6-8; Desideri, 563). Desideri recalls the victory of David over Goliath, in which David used the sword of the giant to slay him (1 Sam. 17:51; Desideri, 563, 569). For Desideri, the philosophical and theological learning of the missionary is like the weapons that Judith and David used to slay their enemies: "If you wish to extinguish infidelity, if you wish to cut off its stubborn head so that it can never return to live in the hearts of converts, you must do this only with the arms and the swords that you will take from infidelity itself" (Desideri, 563).

He finds another example in Daniel opposing Babylonian idols and surviving the lions' den (Daniel 14; Desideri 2010, 564-65). Desideri looks to the victory of Judas Maccabeus, who triumphed over the cities of Bozrah and Carnaim because he called every man to fight (1 Macc. 5:38), as a model for Catholics engaged in struggle against religious foes (Desideri, 571-72). Desideri recalls that the Philistines' idol Dagon was destroyed after the Philistines brought the Israelites' ark of the covenant close to it, interpreting this as a sign that the false doctrines of superstitious religions cannot survive when they "are faced with and confronted by the precepts of natural religion and the instincts that the Author of nature has placed in every person" (1 Sam. 5:1-5; Desideri, 564-65).

Protestant missionaries in China in the nineteenth century generally viewed Buddhism as a form of idolatry. Eric Reinders comments: "Most Protestant categorizations of the religions of the world were ultimately quite simple: there was the true religion, and then there was idolatry. The term *idolatry* could be applied to any and all non-Protestants, including Chinese Buddhists, Catholics, and the prophets of Baal" (2004, 8). Protestants cited the polemic of Psalm 115 against idols, as well as similar biblical texts, as the basis for rejecting Chinese Buddhist images. The Protestant critique of Chinese Buddhism built on and reinforced the traditional critique and rejection of Catholicism:

> Because early images of China had been monopolized by Jesuits, the debunking of idealized images of China was at the same time a critique of Catholicism. . . . By demonstrating idolatry, absurdity, and clerical parasitism in Chinese religion, anti-Catholics simultaneously imputed those qualities to Rome. In anti-Catholic works, the "Papists" were compared to Chinese idolaters; and in English works on China, Chinese religion was consistently viewed as identical to Catholicism. (Reinders 2004, 25)

In many countries today memories of the hostile attitudes of earlier Christian missionaries continue to shape Buddhist attitudes toward Christians. As a result, many Asian Buddhists are suspicious of Christian motives in seeking to establish better relations.

Efforts toward Better Relations

In the twentieth century there were numerous efforts by Christians to improve relations with Buddhists and to appreciate the values of Buddhist perspectives and practices. For the first time in the history of ecumenical councils, *Nostra Aetate* publicly expresses the respect of the Catholic Church for Buddhists and Buddhism. In contrast to the often harsh judgments of earlier centuries, the Second Vatican Council expresses a greater openness to appreciate the values of Buddhism: "In Buddhism, according to its various forms, the radical inadequacy of this changeable world is acknowledged and a way is taught whereby those with a devout and trustful spirit may be able to reach either a state of perfect freedom or, relying on their own efforts or on help from a higher source, the highest illumination" (*Nostra Aetate* 2; Tanner 1990, 2:969). The reference to "relying on their own efforts or on help from a higher source" likely refers to the Mahayana Buddhist discussions of "Self-Power and "Other-Power." As in the case of the Council's reference to Hinduism, this statement is very brief and makes no pretense of being a complete description. What is most significant is the expression of respect that follows the short description. *Nostra Aetate* states that the Catholic Church is open to discovering and appreciating truth and holiness in the path of the Buddha and his followers. In recent decades many Catholics and Protestants as well have explored the Buddhist tradition with respect and appreciation.

Lynn de Silva: Dialogue with Theravada Buddhists in Sri Lanka

In Sri Lanka, the acrimony between Christian missionaries and local Buddhists was especially strong, and thus the challenge of overcoming the hostility of the colonial era has been particularly acute. Lynn de Silva (1919-1982), a Methodist theologian and biblical scholar, comments on the distrust of Buddhists toward Christian overtures in Sri Lanka: "Even dialogue between the two religions is suspect, regarded by some as a tactical move, a smoke screen, to break down the mental resistance of the Buddhists and to lure the unwary among them into the Christian fold" (1976, 39). Despite the difficulties, de Silva has offered some of the most creative interpretations of the Bible in Sri Lanka. De Silva was a leader in translating the First Testament of the Bible into Sinhalese for the *New Sinhala Bible.*

In his essay "Christian Reflection in a Buddhist Context," de Silva reflects on the similarities between Shakyamuni Buddha's analysis of the three marks (*Tilakkhana*) of existence, that is, the impermanence (*anicca*), the unsatisfactoriness or existential anxiety (*dukkha*) of life, and no-self (*anatta*), on the one hand, and the Bible's view of the human predicament on the other (de Silva 1980, 97). He observes that Psalm 90 presents an understanding of "no-self," in the sense that humans are turned back into the dust whence they came. This psalm teaches impermanence, since life is "like a dream, like the grass that withers." Finally, since our short time in this world is marked by "toil, trouble, and anxiety," he concludes that the Bible also teaches that "Life is *dukkha*" (99). Turning to the New Testament, de Silva finds that Romans 8:18-25 teaches the same marks of existence: all creation is "subject to vanity," that is, subject to corruption and thus impermanent; creation is "groaning in travail" and thus in *dukkha*; and finally, "The creature is subject to corruption (*phthora*)"—that is, humans have no substantial self (*anatta*). De Silva suggests that this teaching, which he calls the "bedrock of Buddhism" is also found in Christian mysticism, but Christians have often forgotten this. Thus, he proposes that assimilating Buddhist perspectives can help Christians retrieve their own tradition.

De Silva compares the Buddhist view of the humans as name (*nama*) and form (*rupa*) to the biblical view of humans as a psycho-physical unity of *psychē* (translated as "soul") and *sarx* (flesh), with *nama* and *psychē* naming "the psychical aspect of man, which represents more or less those processes that come within the field of psychology," and *rupa* and *sarx* representing the physical processes studied by biology (1980, 100).

De Silva notes the major difference between the two traditions in that the

Bible always assumes faith in God who creates, while Shakyamuni Buddha does not mention God. De Silva speculates: "Perhaps the Buddha declined to say anything about God, for to assume that there is such a reality which gives a sense of security could be an obstacle for one to realize and understand the fact of non-egoity or self-emptiness" (1980, 100). Creation out of nothing means that creatures were nothing before God's Word created them and that they vanish into nothingness at God's Word. Thus, de Silva proposes, the nothingness of creation according to the doctrine of creation *ex nihilo* is similar to the Buddhist teachings of impermanence and no-self. He quotes Karl Barth: "Man without God is not; he is neither being nor existence" (de Silva 1980, 101).

The other aspect of the doctrine of creation is the absolute lordship of God, which de Silva compares to the Unconditioned (*Asamkhata*) in Buddhism. De Silva claims that the Christian awareness of no-self requires an absolute, unconditioned Reality for there to be hope. He then compares this to the teaching of the Buddha in the scripture *Khuddaka Nikaya:* "Monks, there is a not-born, a not-become, a not-made, a not-compounded. If that unborn, not-become, not-made, not-compounded were not, there would be apparent no escape from this here that is born, become, made, compounded" (1980, 101).

De Silva compares the statement of the Buddha to the Johannine Jesus' claim, "Before Abraham was I am" (John 8:58), finding this to be "unborn, unbecome, not-made, and unconditioned" (1980, 101-2). De Silva interprets the *kenōsis* of Christ in Philippians 2:7-11 not in reference to his divinity but rather in terms of the Buddhist marks of existence, (*Tilakkahana*), that is, "as the negation of the self in which the divinity of love is disclosed. In his self-emptying there is nothing of self to be seen—no notion of I, me, mine—but only the ultimate, unconditional love of God" (102). Using the language of Paul Tillich, de Silva sees Christ as having "negated himself without losing himself" (102) and sees this dynamic as close to the Buddhist teaching of emptiness: "This is the principle of *kenosis,* which has deep affinities with the Buddhist doctrine of *shunyata* (the doctrine of the void)" (102). De Silva closes his essay by suggesting an analogy between God and *Nibbana* as names for transcendence, "an ultimate reality towards which one inclines" (104). Not all scholars would agree on this last point. In the Lankavatara Sutra, Shakyamuni Buddha strenuously rejects such an interpretation of Nirvana (Lankavatara, section 74; pp. 209-13). De Silva repeatedly proposes similarities without giving comparable attention to the significant differences between the traditions. The result may appear somewhat one-sided.

De Silva also authored a larger study comparing the meaning of "the self" in the Bible to Buddhist perspectives on *anatta* ("no-self"). Stressing that the Bible does not share the Greek belief in the immortality of the soul (1979, 75-77), de Silva combines Buddhist perspectives with the biblical understanding of *pneuma* ("spirit"): "The nature of man can thus be described as *anatta-pneuma. Anatta* indicates man's organic nature; the fact that within the psycho-physical organism there is no permanent immortal entity and that, as such, man is subject to *dukkha* and *anicca*. . . . *Anatta-pneuma* signifies the self-empty but spirit-full life" (89).

De Silva hopes that by bringing together the Buddhist teaching of *anatta* and the Christian understanding of *pneuma*, new dimensions can be opened up, with each tradition complementing and enriching the other. First, the Buddhist understanding of no-self can help purify Christian theology of incorrect popular notions of innate immortality; on the other hand, the Christian notion of spirit can clarify for Buddhists that their own analysis is not to be restricted merely to the psychosomatic. Second, de Silva hopes that the Buddhist notion of no-self, by stressing nonattachment, can purify Christian notions of love from subtle self-striving. Christian love, on the other hand, can prevent Buddhist ethics from becoming individualist to the point of isolation and social irrelevance. Finally, de Silva comments, "*Anatta* implies the realization of emptiness; the fully realized man is totally emptied of self. That realization is *Nirvana*" (1979, 102-03). But he adds that Buddhism "stresses that this does not mean annihilation" (103).

To understand this classic paradox of Buddhist thought, de Silva proposes interpreting *pneuma* as the "capacity for transcending oneself, of going out of oneself and beyond oneself, of losing oneself in communion with Reality" (1979, 103).

> *Pneuma* signifies communion. . . . *Anatta* serves to stress the non-egocentric aspect and *Pneuma* the relational aspect of personhood. *Anatta-Pneuma* therefore signifies what might be called non-egocentric-relationality, or egoless mutuality. Thus, the *anatta-pneuma* formula captures in a nutshell, as it were, the essence of the nature of man. (1979, 103)

De Silva combines both Buddhist and Christian notions in his vision of human fulfillment: "In the idea of the Kingdom of God, I suggest, we have an answer to the Buddhist quest for self-negation as well as for a form of self-fulfilment, without one contradicting the other" (1979, 130).

Even though de Silva draws on Buddhist notions, the language of his eschatological vision is heavily Christian: "Love is neither union nor absorption, but communion. In communion, love integrates being with being and being with Being. There is a perfect integration of the self with the eternal in which individuality disappears. Here is the Hindu quest for union or absorption and the Buddhist quest for self-negation" (1979, 135). While many scholars might question the degree of similarity that de Silva finds between the two traditions, he has proposed a very careful and thoughtful reflection.

Aloysius Pieris: An Asian Theology of Liberation
Aloysius Pieris is a Jesuit priest who was the first non-Buddhist in history to receive a doctorate in Buddhist studies from the University of Sri Lanka. Pieris proposes an Asian theology of liberation, interpreting the Bible in relation to Buddhist values regarding issues of poverty and social justice and seeking to

cooperate with Buddhists in addressing concrete economic and social problems, including the situation of women. Like liberation theologians elsewhere, Pieris views the Bible and all issues from the perspective of the poor and the oppressed; for Pieris, "a liberation theology stimulates commitments to Jesus who is God-become-our-neighbor" (1988a: 13). In Sri Lanka, as in the rest of Asia, this requires considering the many religions in relation to the many poor, resulting in a distinctively Asian approach to liberation theology. Pieris insists that neither issue can be considered in isolation: "The *theological* attempts to encounter Asian religions with no radical concern for Asia's poor and the *ideological* programs that presume to eradicate Asia's poverty with naïve disregard for its religiousness, have both proved to be misdirected zeal" (69).

Pieris assumes that each religion springs from a central experience, and he proposes a dialogue between the core experience of Christianity, *agapē* ("redemptive love")," and the core experience of Buddhism, which he calls by the Greek word *gnōsis,* interpreted as "liberative knowledge" (1988b, 111). To express the core experience of each religion, Pieris looks to the visual representations of two trees—of knowledge and of love: Gautama the Indian mystic sits beneath the "tree of knowledge," while Jesus the Hebrew prophet hangs from the "tree of love" "in a gesture of painful protest" (111). Pieris understands each core experience to be complementary to the other and believes that all genuine religious practice must unite the gnostic and the agapeic elements.

For Pieris, the greatest obstacle to dialogue lies not in these experiences themselves but rather in "the failure on the part of Buddhists and Christians to acknowledge the reciprocity of these two idioms" (1988b, 111). While acknowledging "gnostic aberrations" in the history of Christianity, Pieris retrieves the authentic Christian gnosis of Clement of Alexandria and Thomas Aquinas; and he challenges Buddhist leaders to embrace the practice of *bhakti,* the devotional tradition of South Asia:

> There is a *Christian gnosis* that is necessarily agapeic; and there is also a *Buddhist agape* that remains Gnostic. In other words, deep within each one of us there is a Buddhist and a Christian engaged in a profound encounter that each tradition—Buddhist and Christian—has registered in the doctrinal articulation of each religion's core experience. What seems impossible—the interpenetration of the two irreducibly distinct idioms—has already taken place both within Christianity and within Buddhism. (1988b, 113)

Grounding Christianity's agapeic gnosis in the Bible, Pieris suggests that biblical "knowing" is related to "truth"; the Hebrew word *'emet* "weighs more toward 'truthfulness' rather than simply 'truth.' . . . it means fidelity or *'being true to'* each other. . . . to *know* God amounts to a faithful adherence to the covenant obligation to *love*" (1988b, 114). Pieris suggests that the Christian Neoplatonists developed this perspective in ways that come very close to Buddhist perspectives, "living close to the border between Buddhism and Christianity and hence speaking a language that makes sense to Buddhists" (116).

Pieris suggests that Christian gnosis, especially in Neoplatonic interpretations, uses both personalist and impersonalist language because both forms are inadequate; thus ultimate reality is both fullness (*plērōma*) and emptiness (*kenōsis*). "Thus, the Neoplatonist's 'contentless knowing' or 'knowing as such' is also what a Buddhist sees in impersonalist terms as the final purpose of all love. It is a knowing that does not admit a knower or a known" (1988b, 118). Pieris relates Buddhist "no soul" theory to the Christian experience of creatureliness, as the "'dust-ness' of one's origin and destiny (Gen. 3:19)—and to the Christian this is the practical fruit of the gnostic path of the Buddha" (118). Pieris concludes that "the core experience of Christianity is not agape pure and simple but agape in dialogue with gnosis; conversely, the core experience of Buddhism is not mere gnosis, but a gnosis intrinsically in dialogue with agape" (119).

Pieris suggests a series of inexact similarities between Buddhism and Christianity in three dimensions of mystery: source, medium, and path. The ultimate source of salvation, which Christians name *theos* or God the Father, has no exact counterpart in Buddhism; Nirvana is the ultimate metacosmic destiny for Buddhists. Despite the profound differences this implies, Pieris finds convergence in that both traditions believe "(1) that a positive human endeavor (an *ascesis*) is a necessary condition for the arrival of final liberation, and yet (2) this final liberation (the absolute future or the further shore) is never really the automatic end-product of human causation" (1988b, 132).

Regarding the medium of salvation, Pieris finds a stronger similarity between *dharma* and *logos*. In each tradition "the inaccessible 'beyond' (source) becomes one's salvific 'within' (force), and the incomprehensible comes within the grasp of human insight. This is possible only because the Absolute contains within its own bosom a *mediatory* and *revelatory self-expression*, an *accessible dimension*: the *dharma/logos*" (1988b, 132).

Finally, in each tradition there is a path (*hodos/marga*) grounded in the goal. Christians find the capacity to respond in the force of the Holy Spirit within the person. Buddhist teachings of "no soul" and "no God" deny any permanent substance. Nonetheless, Pieris suggests, "The idea of a *given* human potentiality for the transcendent is the most significant presupposition in Buddhist soteriology, though it is never explicitly analyzed" (1988b, 133).

Pieris proposes a liberation Christology focusing on the form of Jesus on the cross symbolic of a twofold struggle: "(1) Jesus' *renunciation* of biological, emotional, and physical ties that bound him to the 'world' (Jesus' *struggle to be poor*), and (2) his open *denunciation* of mammon, which organizes itself into principalities and powers by dividing humankind into the class of Dives and the class of Lazarus (Jesus' *struggle for the poor*)" (1988b, 134). The first struggle corresponds to the image of "the Buddha seated under the *tree of gnosis*" (134). The second demands structural change in relationships, which led to Jesus' death on "the *tree of agape*" (134). Pieris suggests that Christians can join Buddhists on the one path of liberation as co-pilgrims, recounting their respective scriptures, "retelling the story of Jesus and Gautama in a core-to-core dialogue that makes their hearts burn (Luke 24:32) and it is only at the end of the path, as at Emmaus, that the path itself will be recognized by name if a 'name' would then be necessary" (135).

As an example of a retelling of a biblical story, Pieris offers a scriptural meditation on "Asia's Search for Christ," based on Matthew's account of the Magi coming to the Christ-child as the basis for an Asian theology of religions. The first act of the drama is the search, inspired by the appearance of the light of the star in the East. Pieris notes that "Christ's coming is revealed in the East even before Jerusalem hears about it" (1988a, 127). The Magi accept the light as a *"sacramental pointer,"* but they want to find its source, which requires a long, difficult journey through deserts to a city on a mountain.

The second act brings disillusionment in Jerusalem, as Matthew presents the ironic contrast of the "seriousness of the Asian sages with the complacency of God's priests in Jerusalem" (1988a, 127). Even as the Asian sages have seen the light of the star, "Jerusalem is in the dark with regard to the birth of Christ" (127). Thus, the Eastern sages bring the good news to Jerusalem, prompting the priests to read their own scriptures afresh (Matt. 2:2-6). Pieris stresses that the question of the Asian sages is "Where is he?" rather than who or what he is. They seek not an explanation but the experience of doing him homage. Herod, meanwhile, along with "the whole of Jerusalem" is reportedly upset by the good news of the birth of Christ. The Asian seekers depart alone to find him, as the interpreters of the Jewish tradition remain behind.

In the third act, the Asians' quest leads them to "a *laborer's hut!* They discover that the light shining in the East radiates from a *rural house! . . .* Asian wisdom crouches in humility before a villager's son" (1988a, 128). They return home without going through Jerusalem. Pieris draws the pointed conclusion that providence "has them bypass Jerusalem, the institutional center of God's people. Its leadership was not available for the Asians in their search for Christ, and, therefore, it is not indispensable for proclaiming him in Asia (2:12)" (128). In this last comment, Pieris, as a Catholic, is likely thinking about the European-based institutional authorities of the Roman Catholic Church. While his retelling is evocative and suggestive, one might raise concern about its possible anti-Jewish overtones, seeming to identify the Jews with Herod, who was an Idumaean and was unpopular with most Jews of his time. Nonetheless, Pieris's interpretations of the Christian scriptures in light of his extensive experience of Buddhism are among the most powerful and persuasive in recent literature.

Christian Attitudes toward Buddhists in China

In China, a number of Protestant missionaries went through a deep change in attitude toward Buddhism and Chinese religions in the early twentieth century, moving away from the usual fierce condemnation to a warmer appreciation. In 1918, Frank J. Rawlinson published an article by a Protestant missionary in *The Recorder* that expressed a very positive evaluation of Buddhism for its "remarkably high conception of the divine" and its examples of "love . . . and compassion and self-sacrifice" (Lian 1997, 70). Rawlinson himself in time came to a greater understanding and appreciation of Buddhist practices and perspectives (Lian, 86). In 1924, another Protestant missionary, Dwight Goddard, published

"Where Christ Meets Buddha" in *The Forum,* assimilating Buddhist and Christian ideals: "Buddhist ideals of purity, goodness, moral beauty, mercy, kindness, love, faith, trust, are identical with Christian ideals. . . . In both there is the recognition of a divine element in human nature that is the ground of, and which ultimately will be united in, the Divine" (Lian, 183). Goddard thought that Buddhism was superior to Christianity because it acknowledges many Buddhas rather than only one Son of God and thus is not exclusivist, like the form of Christianity that Goddard knew. He hoped for a common Christian–Buddhist monastic foundation for interreligious understanding. The missionaries' change in attitudes in turn influenced Protestant views in the United States, fostering more open views of other religions and sparking a lively debate. As Lian Xi explains, the Christian missionaries who came to China to convert others were themselves converted, in the sense of finding their theological views profoundly changed (Lian, 207).

Timothy Richard (1845-1919), a Welsh Baptist missioner, vigorously emphasized the similarity between Mahayana Buddhism and Christianity. In 1910 he published *The New Testament of Higher Buddhism,* presenting an English translation of the Mahayana Buddhist treatise *The Awakening of Faith* and texts that he called *The Essence of the Lotus Scripture,* which he believed to be part of the Lotus Sutra. In lengthy introductions Richard compares these texts very positively to the Christian faith. He seeks to demonstrate that *The Essence of the Lotus Scripture* proposes "the same teaching as in the Gospel of St. John in regard to Life, Light, and Love, a teaching which forms a wonderful bridge crossing the chasm between Eastern and Western religion and civilization" (2). Richard praises the development of early Buddhism from "Atheism into Theism; and secondly, the development of that Theism into a Monotheistic Trinity in Unity" (Richard 1910, 12; Lai 2009, 27). Richard exclaims: "This great religion is so marvelously like Christianity in its central teaching that it might well be called Pre-Nestorian Christianity" (1910, 12). He compares the vision of heaven in the book of Revelation to the Pure Land of Amitabha Buddha (1910, 13-14) and the infinite love and compassion of Bodhisattva Guan Yin to the tenderness of God in Jesus' parable of the Prodigal Son (1910, 135).

Reflecting on the Bodhisattva of compassion, Guan Yin, Richard comments, "Both the Christians and the Buddhists regard their chief object of worship as Divine and full of compassion for human suffering"; in support of this claim, he cites the hymn of Christ's self-emptying (Philippians 2), Jesus' prayer asking forgiveness for his executioners (Luke 23), as well as Jesus' promise to prepare a place for his followers in heaven (John 14:1-3). He suggests, "When devout Buddhists read these sentiments, they find much that commends itself to them as of exceptionally high merit" (1910, 23). Similarly, Richard claims that when Christians read of the compassionate vows of Amitabha Buddha and of the Buddhist Great Physician, they will be also moved (22-25). His conclusion is a ringing call for an interreligious hermeneutic of respect and generosity: "Thus both Christians and Buddhists, by dwelling on their respective ideals rather than on their respective imperfections, will find themselves inspired to co-operate and exert themselves more than ever before for the salvation of their fellowmen and to study each other's most sacred books" (25).

In his introduction to *The Awakening of Faith*, Richard explains his assumption that Mahayana Buddhism and Christianity are fundamentally complementary: "It is also getting clearer each year that different truths, wherever found, cannot be antagonistic. They do not neutralize, but complement each other; they do not destroy but fulfill one another" (1910, 49). Richard hoped to shape a single, worldwide faith that would draw on the best of various religious traditions, especially Mahayana Buddhism and Christianity (Lai 2009, 31).

Norwegian Lutheran missioner Karl Ludwig Reichelt (1877-1952), one of the most influential missioners in China in the early twentieth century, recognized the resurgence of Chinese Buddhism and sought to preach the gospel more effectively by adapting Buddhist images and terms. He adopted a Buddhist vegetarian diet and used bells, incense, and candles in his worship services. He recommended that Christians wear Buddhist dress, and he adapted the Buddhist ritual of taking refuge in the Buddha, the Dharma, and the Sangha for Christian use (Lai 2000, 146-47). Reichelt intended what he called the "Buddhistization" of Christianity to be a matter of external changes that would aid in converting Chinese. Reichelt, though a Lutheran, founded a Christian monastery, Ching Feng Shan ("Mountain of Luminous Wind/Spirit"), near Nanjing. After a while, he foresaw the importance of Hong Kong for the future of China, and so in 1930 he decided to move his center for Buddhist–Christian dialogue, Tao Fong Shan, from Nanjing to Sha Tin in Hong Kong. Reichelt's efforts were controversial, with some Christian intellectuals supporting him and others fiercely criticizing him. In an effort at indigenization during the 1920s, some Christian churches in Shanghai burned incense and lit candles during worship.

Wang Zhixin (1881-1968) noted that, since the Han Dynasty, Buddhism had adopted the resources of Chinese thought and culture; thus it was no longer seen as foreign. Wang thought Christianity should follow the example of Buddhism and immerse itself in Chinese thought and culture and become an indigenous Chinese religion (Lai 2000, 148). Wang did not think this could be a matter of externals alone, like "painting Buddhist makeup on a Western Christ" (Lai 2000, 149).

Others proposed a very different diagnosis and prescription. In the 1940s, Francis C. M. Wei (1888-1976) noted that Christianity had been in China for a thousand years since the Tang Dynasty without much success; he thought the failure of the so-called "Nestorian" Christian efforts came from what Lai Pan-chiu describes as "over-reliance on Buddhism. This resulted in its inability to distinguish itself from other Chinese religions and hence led to the loss of its independent identity" (Lai 2000, 150). Wei believed that this was the reason that Emperor Wu viewed Christianity as a sect of Buddhism and included it in the persecution of 845 C.E. Thus, Wei sharply rejected the efforts of Reichelt and others to make Christianity appear more like Buddhism. Wei noted that it had taken centuries for Buddhism to become indigenized and accepted, and he expected Christianity to take a long time as well. Wei wanted to build a Christian pilgrimage center in addition to the churches, social service centers and educational centers (Lai 2000, 152). Just as Chinese pilgrims made journeys to Buddhist and Daoist pilgrimage sites, so Wei hoped that a new Christian pilgrimage center in the mountains would attract many. He proposed that the center would serve also as a cemetery where Christians could honor their ancestors, an educational center with a school, a library, and a museum, and a holy place for retreat.

C. S. Song

C. S. Song, a Presbyterian theologian from Taiwan who has long taught in the United States, criticizes other Asian Christian theologians for neglecting the Old Testament, which he describes as "essentially an oriental book," that presents "thought-forms, social structure and psychology of the people . . . so much akin to" East Asians (1960, 12-14). Focusing on practical responses to suffering in the two traditions, Song likens Shakyamuni Buddha's critique of the caste system to Jesus' critique of his own religious tradition to make it more inclusive and compassionate (Fleming 2002, 195). He compares Shakyamuni Buddha's expression of the golden rule to the teaching of Jesus:

> All people tremble at the rod. All people fear death.
> Putting oneself in the place of others, kill not, nor cause to kill.
> All people tremble at the rod, unto all people life is dear;
> Doing as one would be done by, kill not nor cause to kill.
>   (Dhammapada 10.129-30; Song 1994, 219)

Song comments, "We Christians will be surprised how close these thoughts are to Jesus' version of the Golden Rule when we know that 'showing mercy' in the Sermon on the Mount is translated from the Hebrew word *chesedh* (mercy) meaning 'the ability to get right inside the other person's skin'" (1994, 219).

Song turns to the Pure Land Tradition of Buddhism, proposing that the teaching of Amitabha's compassion "bears some *substantial* resemblance to the Christian experience of God's love and grace" (1991, 90). He also compares the experiences of Shinran and Paul and Martin Luther, arguing that behind these experiences there is a "basic, primal, and primordial sensibility that underlies human religious consciousness" (1999, 248-49, 254). The result is that Song moves quite rapidly from a comparison between Shin Buddhism and Protestant Christianity to the claim of a universal religious experience. Kenneth Fleming comments, "The dialogue with Pure Land Buddhism, then, serves as a means to emphasise a primal divine presence of grace and love operating within all peoples" (2002, 194). This is a point at which Jewish–Christian dialogue becomes important for Asian Christian theology; if, as recent biblical scholarship suggests, Paul's experience is not simply to be identified with Luther's, then Song's comparison is less persuasive.

Nonetheless, Song does not want to identify the experiences of the Buddha and the Christ: "The Buddha, for example—is not Jesus Christ. For that matter neither is Jesus Christ a Bodhisattva. . . . But the ultimate difference from the Christian point of view comes from our faith in Jesus Christ as the direct and complete embodiment of God's saving love" (1991, 133). While refusing to identify Nirvana with the God of Jesus Christ, Song nonetheless finds compassion in Buddhism to be a reflection of the love of the one God of Jesus Christ and poses the provocative question, "But the restoration of health, harmony, and peace *here and now* for life afflicted with pain and suffering—this is essentially what nirvana is all about. May this not be the way that God has chosen to bring salvation to the masses in Asia for whom to live is to suffer?" (1982, 168).

Kosuke Koyama

Japanese theologian Kosuke Koyama (1929-2009) grew up in a Christian family in Tokyo and was baptized during World War II. He studied Christian theology in both Japan and the United States and then worked as a missionary in northern Thailand for the United Church of Japan. He later served as dean of the South East Asia Graduate School of Theology in Singapore and then taught at the University of Otago in Dunedin, New Zealand, and later at Union Theological Seminary in New York City. He comments on his extensive journeys in interreligious relations:

> Over the years I have been touched by the truth of other religious traditions. As far as I am concerned, this is what religious experience means. Notice that it is not that I touched them; they touched me. I cannot quite explain why and how they have touched me. What I do know is that each experience of being touched has brought a sense of simplification that makes my soul more spacious, and therefore also more free. (1996, 173)

Koyama sees this primarily in the area of concern for his welfare and that of humanity. He believes that Christianity is going through a second major encounter with other religions. The first was with the Mediterranean world of Christianity's birth; now it is with Asia's religious traditions. After living among Buddhists in Thailand and seeing their concern for others, he rejected Karl Barth's charge that other religions are all human grasping: "Is feeding the hungry, clothing the naked, visiting prisoners in the name of the Buddha an act of no value in the light of the name of Jesus Christ? Impossible!" (Koyama 1974, 35).

Koyama firmly rejects an exclusivist interpretation of biblical texts like Acts 4:10 or Elijah's attack on the prophets (1 Kgs. 18:20-40), arguing that these passages need to be enveloped by the biblical teaching of God's universal love. To shape the context for interpreting the biblical texts of hostility, he places in the foreground Paul's command to think about "whatever is true, whatever is honorable, whatever is just, whatever is pure, whatever is pleasing, whatever is commendable" (Phil. 4:8); he also appeals to the exclamation of Paul and Barnabas that God "has not left himself without a witness in doing good" (Acts 14:16-17). In the name of the gospel, Koyama rejects all comparative judgments among religions: "Superiority is a cultural, not theological, concept. To say that

Christianity is superior to Buddhism, or vice-versa, is empty talk. The Gospel is not to be called superior. It calls us to bear 'good fruits' (Mt 7:17)" (1997, 58).

Above all, Koyama embraces Shakyamuni Buddha's teaching that greed is the root of suffering and that overcoming it is the key to salvation. Taking this as the heart of the Buddha's insight, Koyama relates this wisdom to the apostle Paul: "I agree deeply with the Buddha that the world is ablaze with human greed. That image exposes the sickness of our society. I bring this teaching to Jesus Christ as I kneel before him (Phil. 2:10-11)" (1996, 177). Koyama finds the same fundamental teaching expressed in different ways in the Buddha's dharma and the gospel of Jesus Christ: "The relationship between Buddhism and Christianity is not that of 'true religion' and 'false religion.' It is to do with two different yet intertwined understandings of the history of human greed. God 'did not leave himself without witness' (Acts 14:17)" (1984, 128).

The Buddha's teaching on greed, resonating with the teaching of Jesus, provides Koyama with the basis for a complete social ethic, as he reads the two teachers in relation to each other: "My Master said, I remember, seek the kingdom of God and all shall be added. He did not say to seek all these things and the kingdom shall be mine" (1979, 15). Koyama finds in the Buddha's teaching on greed a criterion for assessing Christian history, including the Crusades, the British Empire's sense of the "White Man's Burden," and America's "Manifest Destiny." Seen in this light, the much-vaunted Western linear vision of history appears as purposefulness in the service of greed: "The study of Buddhism has made me aware of a subtle inner connection between purposefulness and greediness. I am not saying that purposefulness always means greediness, but I am suggesting that purposefulness can be an expression of our greediness. Is there not a subtle linkage between purposefulness and imperialism?" (1984, 219-20).

Despite the profound similarities, Koyama is very aware of the differences between the two traditions. He notes that the mind of God in Christianity is very different from nirvana, and he believes that the sacrifice of Jesus contains a depth of compassion not found in the Buddha (Fleming 2002, 125). Koyama assumes that Buddha's insight into greed and the Buddhist tradition's practical compassion for others are the result of God's grace, but he admits, "I cannot define where they stand in relation to Jesus Christ" (1976, 66). Koyama recommends that Christians follow Jesus on the path of self-emptying and self-denial in order to learn more deeply about God's love in relation to Buddhists and Buddhism. At the end of the day, Koyama believes that God is more concerned about Buddhists than about Buddhism and that God is drawing Buddhists and followers of all religions to Godself (Fleming 2002, 127).

Koyama reflects on the contrast between Buddhist perspectives on karma and biblical views of God in relation to history. He notes that *karman* means "deeds" in Sanskrit and refers to the implacable law: "Human deeds are believed to generate an invisible force which creates a reaction or retribution" (1984, 222). Karman "works impersonally, precisely and objectively. Paul's words, 'whatever a man sows, that he will also reap' (Gal. 6:7) have a sound of the doctrine of karman" (222). He contrasts the teaching of karma to the prophet

Jeremiah, who pleads with God: "The important difference, however, is that Jeremiah can plead his case before God, but it would be nonsensical to do so before the karman. Karman remains to be karman by not being influenced by any human pleading. On the contrary God can change his mind" (227). Koyama believes that the Buddha's teachings of Conditional Arising and the Four Noble Truths are more fundamental than the working of karma: "I am tempted to say that in the gospel of the Buddha the karman is seen in the light of the shattering of the kingpost of greed rather than the other way round" (226).

Facing the painful experience of Japan's defeat in World War II, Koyama interprets the catastrophe in a threefold manner, combining the law of karma, the prophecy of Jeremiah, and the Buddha's teaching that greed leads to destruction:

> At last Japan's karman caught up with her. . . . Secondly, it can be interpreted in the manner of Jeremiah: 'All its cities were laid in ruins before the Lord, before his fierce anger' (4:26). . . . And thirdly, Japan was destroyed because she had not destroyed the kingpost of their greed. Her greed ruined her. . . . I can accept the Buddha's view, which is that it is greed that destroyed Japan. (1984, 229)

Kenneth Fleming comments, "There is an interplay of Buddhist and Christian views. Buddhist teachings are seen to deepen the biblical view, but it is the biblical that provides the framework for the overall understanding. Moving beyond this particular reflection, for Koyama it is Christ's suffering love that provides ultimate meaning and depth to this framework" (Fleming 2002, 128). Koyama notes the sharp difference between "the cool operation of karman" and the "agitated mind of God" who cares about history. To illustrate the contrast, Koyama cites Isaiah 48:9: "For my name's sake I defer my anger." He also notes Paul's comments on the foolishness of God being wiser than humans (1 Cor. 1:25) and the foolish wisdom of the cross (1 Cor. 1:18). "The word of the cross points to God's agitated emotions because of God's love towards us. The word of the cross heals our history by giving it hope and life" (1984, 241). While instructed by the Buddha's teaching on greed, Koyama is more deeply formed by the biblical challenge "to imitate the *pathos* (passion) and *ethos* (ethical involvement) of God whose attention is directed to our history" (1984, 231).

Thomas Merton

Thomas Merton (1915-1968) engaged in a dialogue with the influential interpreter of Zen Buddhism D. T. Suzuki, which led Merton to read the Bible in relation to Zen. At the end of his life, he traveled to India and Thailand and met a number of Buddhists, including the XIVth Dalai Lama. Merton learned from Suzuki that Zen casts away the judging mind. Merton is aware that "Zen is deliberately cryptic and disconcerting" (1968, 34) and that it is difficult to compare Zen and Christianity as if they were realities one could place side by side: "This would almost be like trying to compare mathematics and tennis" (33). Nonetheless, Merton finds areas of resonance, even a "Zen dimension" in the New Testament; he comments that Zen "does not erect its judgment into a structure to be defended against all comers. Here we can fruitfully reflect on the deep meaning of Jesus' saying: 'Judge not, and you will not be judged.' Beyond its moral implications, familiar to all, there is a Zen dimension to this word of the Gospel. Only when this Zen dimension is grasped will the moral bearing of it be fully clear!" (6-7).

Merton interprets the scene of Moses at the burning bush in Exodus in relation to words of the Prajnaparamita Sutra: "Form is emptiness, emptiness itself is form; form does not differ from emptiness (the Void), emptiness does not differ from form; whatever is form, that is emptiness, whatever is emptiness, that is form" (1968, 7). Merton comments on the similarity to what Moses hears from the burning bush: "'I am what I am.' These words go beyond position and negation, in fact no one quite knows what the Hebrew means" (7). Merton draws the insight: "In other words, we begin to divine that Zen is not only beyond the formulations of Buddhism but it is also in a certain way 'beyond' (and even pointed to by) the revealed message of Christianity" (8).

For Merton, Zen points to what the New Testament describes as the liberty of the children of God: "Not that they are theologically one and the same, but they have at any rate the same kind of limitlessness, the same lack of inhibition, the same psychic fullness of creativity, which mark the fully integrated maturity of the 'enlightened self'" (1968, 8). The *kenōsis* (self-emptying) of Christ "can be understood and has been understood in a very Zen-like sense as far as psychology and experience are concerned" (8). Acknowledging the "vast doctrinal differences" that divide Buddhists and Christians, Merton maintains that they nonetheless have "this psychic 'limitlessness' in common. And they tend to describe it in much the same language" (8).

Merton believes that Buddhist meditation, including Zen, is not a theory to be explained but a quest to be aware and mindful. Zen is an experience beyond conceptual formulations: "Zen is saying, as Wittgenstein said, 'Don't think: Look!'" (1968, 49). While Christians have often focused on doctrines, Merton finds at the heart of Catholic life "a *living experience* of unity in Christ which far transcends all conceptual formulations. . . . 'What we have seen and have heard we announce to you, in order that you also may have fellowship with us and that our fellowship may be with the Father and with His Son Jesus Christ'" (1 John 1:3; Merton 1968, 39-40). There is some possibility of comparing the experience of Christians and Buddhists. However, Merton notes that "the personal experience of the mystic remains inaccessible to us and can only be evaluated indirectly through texts and other testimonials" (43-44). The result is that we can never know if Christians and Buddhists experience "the same thing." Nonetheless, Merton trusts, "there are nevertheless certain analogies and correspondences which are evident even now, and which may perhaps point out the way to a better mutual understanding. Let us not rashly take them as 'proofs' but only as significant clues" (44).

Merton suggests that there are analogies between Zen experience, the experiences of ancient Israelite prophets, and the experience of the Holy Spirit in the New Testament. He notes that the apostle Paul distinguishes between "a rational, dialectical wisdom, and another which is at once a matter of paradox and of experience, and goes beyond the reach of reason" (1 Cor. 1:17; Merton 1968, 55). Paul says that "we must have the mind of Christ" (1 Cor. 2:16), and Buddhists speak of "having the Buddha mind." Merton does not identify Christian experience with Zen, but he conjectures that "there must surely be some possibility of finding an analogy somewhere between Buddhist and Christian experience," and he trusts that on the Christian side, the area to explore will be "theology as experienced in Christian contemplation" (57-58).

Merton suggests that the Bible and Buddhism both agree in seeing humans as not in right relationships to the world or to things in it because they have "a mysterious tendency to *falsify* that relation, and to spend a great deal of energy in justifying the false view" (1968, 82). Merton compares *avidya* ("ignorance") in Buddhism with what Christians mean by original sin, "a disposition to treat the ego as an absolute and central reality and to refer all things to it as objects of desire or of repulsion" (1968: 82). The consequences of the biblical story of the Fall correspond to Buddhist descriptions of life as *dukkha* ("suffering") as basic forms of inauthenticity. Paul expresses the Christian understanding of this dilemma and its resolution in the grace given in Christ Jesus (Rom. 7:21-25), and Merton compares Paul's perspective on sin and grace to the Four Noble Truths of Buddhism. He compares the charity and compassion in the two traditions: "Christian charity seeks to realize oneness with the other 'in Christ.' Buddhist compassion seeks to heal the brokenness of division and illusion and to find wholeness not in an abstract metaphysical 'one' or even a pantheist immanentism but in *Nirvana*—the void which is Absolute Reality and Absolute Love" (1968: 86). Merton trusted that familiarity with Buddhist and Hindu perspectives and practices could enrich Catholic monastic life (1973, 313). In the last talk he delivered just before his death in Bangkok, Merton expressed his confidence that contact with Buddhism and Hinduism could open Christians to the potential of their own tradition (1973, 343).

Bernard Faure has severely criticized D. T. Suzuki's interpretation of Zen. In light of this critique, John P. Keenan has cast doubt on the helpfulness of Suzuki's exchange with Merton, calling Merton's understanding of Buddhism "imperfect and incomplete" (Keenan 2007, 123). Nonetheless, Judith Simmer-Brown comments that "it is clear that Merton had done his homework [regarding Buddhism] as best he could" (52). Even though Merton's contribution to understanding Buddhism was limited by the stance of his primary dialogue partner and the resources available to him, he had a major impact.

On his trip to Asia in 1968, Merton met the young Dalai Lama, and the two had a number of conversations (Merton 1973, 100-102, 112-13, 124-25). The Dalai Lama later recalled: "This was the first time that I had been struck by such a feeling of spirituality in anyone who professed Christianity. Since then, I have come across others with similar qualities, but it was Merton who introduced me to the real meaning of the word 'Christian'" (Dalai Lama 1991, 189). The relationship between these two figures was cut short by the sudden death of Merton in 1968, but Monastic Interreligious Dialogue later continued the conversation with the Dalai Lama at the First Gethsemani Encounter in 1996, at Merton's monastery (Mitchell and Wiseman 1999). Malcolm David Eckel suggests that while Merton was in India he experienced dialogue not as an external performance of a play with actors in movement, nor even as a drama that he could actively shape: "There seems to have been a moment in Thomas Merton's exploration of Buddhism in India when he went even a step further and realized that he was the play. The dialogue was no longer something outside himself, but a struggle that was part of his own nature" (1987, 60).

Kenōsis and Shunyata: Masao Abe and Christian Interlocutors

A number of Japanese Buddhists have interpreted the Christian scriptures in relation to Mahayana Buddhism, thereby prompting Christians to respond and consider the Bible in light of Buddhist perspectives. The philosopher Kitaro Nishida (1870-1945) launched this movement in 1911 by publishing *An Inquiry into the Good,* which sought to express the core of Zen experience in Western philosophical terms. In the following decades, Nishida pursued this project in various ways, relating Zen Buddhism to Christian mystics such as Nicholas of Cusa and Meister Eckhart. Later Hajime Tanabe, Keiji Nishitani, and Yoshinori Takeuchi all reflected on Christian themes in light of Buddhist perspectives. They came to be known as the "Kyoto School." D. T. Suzuki was a friend and colleague of Nishida but is not usually considered a part of the Kyoto School.

Masao Abe (1915-2006), a Japanese Zen Buddhist philosopher, continued the work of the Kyoto School. Abe suggests that Jews, Christians, and Buddhists need to learn from one another's traditions to meet the challenges of contemporary thought and society, and he welcomed critical feedback (Mitchell 1998a). He proposes a Mahayana Buddhist interpretation of Jesus Christ and the Trinity in terms of *shunyata,* and he also rethinks the Mahayana tradition's understanding of *shunyata* in light of his encounter with Christianity. Abe applies the Mahayana Buddhist logic of negation to interpret the christological hymn in Philippians 2:5-8:

> Son of God is not the Son of God (for he is essentially and fundamentally self-emptying): precisely because he *is not* the Son of God he *is* truly the Son of God (for he originally and always works as Christ, the Messiah, in his salvational function of self-emptying. (Abe 1990a, 11)

Abe insists on interpreting theological and religious language existentially:

> All discussion of Christ as the Son of God will be religiously meaningless if engaged in apart from the problem of human ego, our own existential problem of the self. The notion of Christ's kenosis or his self-emptying can be properly understood only through the realization of our own sinfulness and our own existential self-denying. (1990a, 11)

A number of Christian theologians have responded to the Kyoto School in general (Buri 1997; Waldenfels 1980; Mitchell 1991, 1998a) and to Masao Abe in particular (Cobb and Ives 1990; Ives 1995; Corless and Knitter 1990).

Christian reactions to Abe have been mixed. Hans Küng is quite critical of Abe's interpretation of *kenōsis* in the New Testament. Where Abe proposes to see God as emptying, Küng insists that the New Testament uses the term *theos* to refer to God the Father, not to Jesus Christ: "Consequently, nowhere is there mentioned an incarnation or a renunciation (kenosis) of God Himself; the Philippian hymn only speaks of a kenosis of Jesus Christ, the Son of God" (Küng 1990, 33). Abe in response quotes Karl Rahner, who affirmed the *kenōsis* of God. Küng accuses Rahner of being "unbiblical (in fact monophysitic or Hegelian)" and poses the challenge: "Such a Christology cannot explain who brought this supposedly dead God back to life" (1990, 34). Küng charges that Abe necessarily neglects the resurrection in the hymn in Philippians "in order to be able to abide by his interpretation: the renunciation of God Himself in Buddhist shunyata. A very basic question arises here: the question of the effective hermeneutic for this inter-religious dialogue" (1990, 34).

Wolfhart Pannenberg proposes a very similar criticism of Abe: "But it is quite another thing to speak of a self-emptying activity on the part of the Father himself. With regard to this second idea, there is not the slightest evidence in Paul's letter to the Philippians, nor in any other place in the New Testament. Nowhere is it said that the Father emptied himself, and in no way is it a logical implication of the self-emptying action of the Son" (1995, 248).

Other Christians, however, responded to Abe with greater appreciation and with a more nuanced understanding of the different meanings of *kenōsis*. Allowing a legitimate use of the term *kenōsis* for the eternal trinitarian relations, Donald Mitchell praises Abe: "I greatly appreciate Abe's study of the Christian notion of kenosis. It does seem to me that the kenotic love seen in Christ is revelatory of the kenosis of God-Love in creation" (1991, 61). Mitchell explains that "the main point of his analysis of the kenosis of Christ on the cross is to show that it is revelatory of the innermost nature of God. Here, I agree with Abe. In the kenosis of Christ, God communicates himself" (65). Nonetheless, Mitchell believes that Abe misses another dimension of Christian faith by reducing *kenōsis* to creation: "Abe ignores the trinitarian spiritual experience of Christian mystics. . . . To reduce the dynamic of the kenotic interrelatedness within the divine and between the divine and creation to a mere identity between the creative kenosis of God and its creation is to lose the richness of the Christian vision of the mystery of God" (62). Mitchell insists on the distinction between the *kenōsis* of creation and inner-trinitarian *kenōsis*:

> While God creates "according to" his nature, the kenosis between the divine persons is just different in kind from the kenosis between the Creator and creation. And since God is *uniquely* incarnate in Christ, the kenosis of God in Christ is also different in kind from the kenosis of God in the rest of creation. To fail to make this distinction leads Abe to say that God is just as dependent on creation as creation is on God. (1998b, 134)

Mitchell reflects that Abe had been transformed in his encounter with Christianity, but "he had remained a Zen Buddhist, always interpreting the experience of God with a Buddhist nondualistic logic. On the other hand, I had been greatly changed by my encounter with Abe and Buddhism in my own understanding of the kenotic nature and action of God. But I remained a Christian interpreting the experience of God with a Christian trinitarian logic" (1998b, 136).

Ever-curious, Abe continued to ask Christian theologians whether they could acknowledge God as emptying. Realizing that Christian theologians disagreed with each other over this question, Abe wished to meet Joseph Cardinal Ratzinger (the future Pope Benedict XVI) in the Vatican to clarify matters and obtain an authoritative answer. In 1993, Abe, accompanied by Donald Mitchell, went to Rome and met with two collaborators of Cardinal Ratzinger in the Congregation for the Doctrine of the Faith, Jacques Servais and Piero Coda. Donald Mitchell recalls that in the interview Servais told Abe that

> the Christian view is that divine kenosis is absolute love, not just the boundless openness of the unlimited. . . . And while admitting both similarities and differences between Christian and Buddhist notions of ultimate reality, both Servais and Coda affirmed Abe's view that because Christ is the self-utterance of God, his kenosis reveals a fundamental kenosis, an *ur-kenosis,* that is of the essence of Godself. (Mitchell 1998b: 138)

Mitchell adds, "For this and other reasons, Abe told me that he found these Vatican theologians to be much more 'liberal' than most of the theologians he had encountered in the United States" (1998b, 138-39).

John Keenan

John Keenan has developed a distinctive approach to biblical interpretation based on the hermeneutics of Mahayana Buddhism. Keenan employs the Mahayana Buddhist perspectives of dependent co-arising and emptiness to express the meaning of the Christian scriptures without being imprisoned in a particular metaphysics. Keenan worries that traditional Western metaphysics has not been helpful in communicating the central Christian experience and comments: "Only when the experience of wisdom has uncovered the heart of the matter can interpretation truly express the intent and meaning of the scriptures" (1989, 164). To uncover the central meaning of the Bible, he proposes a series of analogies between biblical texts and Mahayana Buddhist perspectives, hoping that Buddhist categories can present biblical insights and values more effectively.

In particular, Keenan reads the Bible through the lens of two sets of central Mahayana notions, (1) emptiness and dependent arising and (2) ultimate truth and conventional truth:

Emptiness and dependent arising are offered as two different ways to describe the same thing—the essence-free being of all things, which arise in mutual dependence. These are two different ways to account for the phenomena of this world, and they are inextricably linked one to the other. By contrast, the two truths are *never* to be equated or identified with the other. The silent truth of ultimate meaning and the verbal truth of worldly convention are completely and utterly separate and different from one another. There can be no link between them. (Keenan, with Copp, Davis, Smith 2009, 64-65)

In Mahayana thought, the teaching of emptiness accompanies that of dependent co-arising; all things arise from all other things, as Keenan explains: "Nothing exists independently, but the world with all its variety does exist in a mutual conditioning and support" (1995, 28). Dependent co-arising is in sharp contrast to traditional Christian faith in creation, since in most interpretations, the Mahayana teachings of emptiness and dependent arising do not allow for any transcendent God who creates the universe. Thus, Keenan is proposing a radical transposition.

Qoheleth in the book of Ecclesiastes proclaims, "Vanity of vanities, says the Teacher, vanity of vanities! All is vanity" (1:2). The Hebrew word *hebel*, which is usually translated as "vanity," literally means "breath" or "vapor" and thus has connotations of being transient, ephemeral, and insubstantial. Keenan comments that in the Japanese translation, Qoheleth proclaims the "emptiness" (*shunyata,* Japanese *ku*) of all things. However, Keenan sees the emptiness of Qoheleth as "desolate and pessimistic," in contrast to the Mahayana notion of emptiness that "functions as a liberator from illusions. It is meant to counter the security of self-centered knowledge by undermining the belief that human ideas and images represent the very essences of things" (1995, 25). "Emptiness is a Mahayana commentary on the basic doctrine of no-self (*anatman*), i.e., no self apart from and independent of the contextual conditioning of all being" (1995, 26).

In the New Testament, Keenan finds a subversive movement shaping the teaching of Jesus himself, and he appeals to biblical scholar John Meier's interpretation of the historical Jesus: "As John Meier remarks, '. . . the historical Jesus subverts not just some ideologies but all ideologies'" (Keenan 1995, 16). Keenan finds an analogy between Meier's view of Jesus and the hermeneutics of the great philosopher Nagarjuna, who overturned every ideology but nonetheless valued conventional truth in its proper place: "Rather, the issue for Nagarjuna, as for all Mahayana thinkers, is how linguistic worldly convention 'manifests' an ultimate, from which it is forever completely other. All strategies, even the deconstructive logic of emptiness, remain conventional, without ever invading a realm of signified ultimate meaning" (9).

In approaching the Gospel of Mark, Keenan removes it from its original Jewish Hellenistic context: "The *Sitz im Leben* for Mark is not a fixed context to be discovered by careful reconstruction, but an ongoing history in the life of the Christian communities which have, at least in part, read themselves through this gospel" (1995, 17). Keenan finds an affinity between Mark's "rhetoric of indirection and irony" and the dialectical rhetoric of Nagarjuna (4).

> The present adoption of Mahayana philosophy as a reading grid for Mark can perhaps recommend itself in that it stresses both the emptying of all preconceived notions of just how to proceed, as well as the reclamation of such notions in terms of their dependently co-arisen and conventional validity, for insight into emptiness entails insight into the dependent co-arising of all things. . . . Such a reading is deconstructive in the extreme, tearing down any fixed textual stability, maintaining that truth is empty of any fixed essence and in the final analysis beyond the grasp of discriminative thinking. (1995, 5)

Keenan sees Mark as presenting Jesus without special status: "Jesus does not come with any divine pedigree or guarantee. Rather, by introducing Jesus as an earthly son of man, Mark empties the term of imagined content" (1995, 88). According to Keenan, the Markan Jesus has no clear teaching of his own: "If Mark is recommending Jesus' new teaching over the old teachings of the Torah, he has done a singularly inept job of presenting just what is specifically new in those teachings. Nowhere does he outline Jesus' ideological position" (94). The upshot is a sharp critique of all traditions: "Jesus empties not only the tradition of the elders, but also the Mosaic law of any final, fixed validity. . . . It is not a question of which traditions can at times be ignored, but of the validity of tradition itself, in all its forms" (96). Using the same methodology, Keenan interprets the Epistle of James and the Gospel of John in light of Mahayana perspectives.

After proposing a deconstructive hermeneutics to interpret the Bible in a manner free from metaphysical doctrines, Keenan defends apologetics in a pluralist world, seeking to avoid both arrogance and relativism: "This challenge is new in that it demands that we eschew both culturally arrogant claims for an all-engulfing single truth and the just as culturally arrogant claims of a vague and porous pluralism" (Keenan, with Copp, Davis, Smith 2009, 40).

Keenan claims that the distinction between the two truths offers a way to affirm contrasting perspectives: "The two truths offer us a paradigm for recognizing that conventional truths—the truths of Christianity, Buddhism, Islam, Judaism—can be meaningful and valid without needing to claim that their revelations are absolute or final" (Keenan, with Copp, Davis, Smith 2009, 65-66). The price that Keenan demands, however, is high:

> We must abandon the notion of any final goal or destination as the end point of the path. In synergistic tension, we seek and pray as practitioners of a middle path that threads its way through the complex interactions between faith and culture. . . . In other words: Out with metaphysics and overviews! In with human belief, thinking, and acting! (Keenan, with Copp, Davis, Smith 2009, 67)

The final criterion for Keenan is not metaphysical, symbolic, or universal but pragmatic: "Rather, an absolute life-affirmation is validated through its ability to transform the individual within a particular cultural milieu, and the cultural milieu within that individual" (Keenan, with Copp, Davis, Smith 2009, 110). Keenan's proposal is one of the most thoughtful in the current discussion. Critics may wonder, however, whether the Mahayana assumptions and categories dominate his interpretation too much, to the detriment of the original Jewish and Hellenistic contexts of the New Testament. Defenders of metaphysics like Alfred North Whitehead would question the coherence of Keenan's call to throw out "metaphysics and overviews" while endorsing "belief, thinking, and acting." Whitehead comments: "This notion of . . . history devoid of any reliance on metaphysical principles and cosmological generalizations, is a figment of the imagination. The belief in it can only occur to minds steeped in provinciality" ([1933] 1967, 4).

The Bible and Zen Practice: J. K. Kadowaki and Robert Kennedy

Masao Abe, like many practitioners of Zen, warns his Christian interlocutors that one can understand Buddhist terms like *shunyata* only through the practice of meditation. A number of Christians have practiced Zen and other forms of Buddhist meditation and have interpreted the Bible in light of their experiences (Kadowaki 2002; Graham 1994; Lee and Hand 1990; Clifford 1994; Habito 1989, 1993; Johnston 2002; Kennedy 1996, 2000). Because many Mahayana Buddhists, including many practitioners of Zen, interpret all their teachings as skillful means designed to heal suffering rather than as dogmatic affirmations, Christians can enter deeply into Buddhist practice, accepting its wisdom as complementary to Christian faith without worrying about conflicts in cosmology. Many who have done so have found that Buddhist meditation practice has opened up new and powerful ways of understanding the Bible.

J. K. Kadowaki was raised in Japan as a Buddhist, decided to become a Catholic Christian, and was baptized during his third year of college. Three years after graduating from college, he entered the Society of Jesus, eventually being ordained a priest. Knowing both traditions well, Kadowaki recognized, "In fact, Zen koans and Christian Scripture are so utterly different that there does not seem to be the remotest possibility of finding fundamental similarities between them" (2002, vi). After further practice of Zen, however, he "discovered that even though they differ greatly in externals, in their essentials there is a surprising resemblance between koans and Scripture" (vi). Not only did Zen practice contribute stillness to his mind, it opened up the significance of scriptural passages that previously had not made sense to him: "As this experience was repeated time and again, I began to see that koans and the Bible have something in common" (vi). "The reading of koans and Scripture with the whole 'body,' not just with the head, is the main point of this book" (vii). Kadowaki calls this "body-reading" (*shikidoku*), adapting a term from the medieval Buddhist leader Nichiren (vii).

Kadowaki offers an example of this approach by reflecting on the teaching of Jesus: "It is easier for a camel to go through the eye of a needle than for a rich man to enter the kingdom of heaven" (Mark 10:25) (2002, 54). Noting the contradiction in the imagery, Kadowaki comments, "It is an existential question directed to each one of us, and in it is hidden a blade to gouge out our attachments" (54). Kadowaki juxtaposes Jesus' saying to the traditional first koan given to a beginner in Zen: "*Mu!*" or "The sound of one hand clapping." No normal thinking can resolve either problem. The Mu koan comes from a brief narrative in which a student asks a noted monk whether a dog has Buddha-nature. The expected answer is yes, since in Mahayana Buddhism all beings have Buddha-nature. However, the monk responds, "Mu!", which ordinarily is translated, "No!" The student must then ponder this response and present his understanding to the Zen teacher. In wrestling with each koan, the Zen student must go through a transformation and "that method is to get rid of his own thinking and attain the same consciousness" as the master who devised the koan. In the case of "*Mu*" this means seeing with the eye of Master Joshu and the other Zen masters (55).

Kadowaki compares Zen experience to being able to enter into another person's viewpoint and see matters from another perspective. One abandons one's own ego to adopt a different angle of vision. Kadowaki notes the context of Jesus' saying in the Gospel of Mark, where Jesus challenges the wealthy young man to leave his possessions and follow Jesus. Zen, like Jesus, demands abandoning all attachments. A person bound by attachments cannot solve a koan. "But when such a person is stripped of attachment and becomes a free body through the practice of Zen, he can solve it easily" (2002, 58). Kadowaki compares the seeming harshness of Jesus toward his disciples to the attitude of a Zen master to the beginning student: in both cases what seems harsh is actually loving kindness. The obstacle is ultimately not intellectual but attachment: "The reason they failed to understand was not because they were illiterate or stupid, but because they still had faults and attachments in their hearts" (59).

Kadowaki finds a similar dynamic in the relation between Jesus or a Zen master and their respective disciples, conjecturing that "the reason Jesus said those words looking them in the face was to kill their hidden attachments and make them alive with the divine life. This can truly be called 'a thrust home.' In other words, Jesus is not teaching doctrine, but is forcing the disciples to make an existential conversion. . . . With these words he wanted to kill the disciples and bring them back to life" (2002, 61). Zen students face similar obstacles: "In most cases, when cross-examined by the master and confronted with a difficult problem, a Zen disciple is also perplexed and sometimes even struck dumb with astonishment. But he must remain undaunted by this and work to get rid of all egoism in order to deepen his enlightenment" (62).

Kadowaki compares a number of paradoxical sayings of the New Testament to the dynamics of Zen. Paul writes, "For as by a man came death, by a man has come also the resurrection of the dead. For as in Adam all die, so also in Christ shall all be made alive (1 Cor. 15:21-22)" (2002, 63). Similarly puzzling are Jesus' statements about the grain of wheat having to fall to the earth and die in order to bear fruit (John 12:24) and about Jesus drawing all people to himself when he is lifted up (John 12:32). Kadowaki compares the paradoxical logic of these statements to the dialectic of the part and the whole in Zen. "As I came to deliberate on various Zen koans, I was surprised and delighted to discover that one of the central themes of the Zen experience was a dynamic grasp of the contradictory dialectic of the part and the whole, and the whole and the part" (65).

Discussing a puzzling koan about all things coming back to the one and the one coming back to all things, Kadowaki reflects that Zen experience "teaches us that the dynamic dialectical relationship between the part and the whole cannot be grasped by rational speculation. Instead we must abandon our egos and unite with God who is the Source of all creation. If we are able to become one with God through complete abandonment of self, it will be easy to see that all being is one in God" (2002, 69). Kadowaki suggests a similarity in the implications of both the koan and Paul's teachings for how we live:

> What I learned from "The one comes back to all things" is that one must not rest on one's laurels in the *satori* of blind equality, but break free of it and come out into the real world of differentiation, making everything come alive by bringing out its full potential. In the same way, in the Christian experience one must not be completely immersed in the contemplative life of union with God but find God in all things of the real world and carefully make the most effective use of each one. (2002, 71)

Kadowaki went to Germany to study the thought of Meister Eckhart. Then Professor Joseph Ratzinger invited him to speak to a seminar of his doctoral students on "Zen and Christianity." After an extended and animated discussion, Kadowaki later remembered, "Professor Ratzinger said, 'How interesting it would be if we could compare the ideas of Zen with those of the bible. If that could be done, it would be a great event, not only for the dialogue between Zen and Christianity, but also in respect to the ideological exchange between East and West'" (Kadowaki 2002, v).

Another Jesuit pioneer in exploring Zen practice in the mid-twentieth century was a German, Hugo Enomiya-Lassalle, who came to Japan in 1929 and survived the nuclear attack on Hiroshima in 1945, though he suffered from the effects of radiation (1988, 149-50). Seeking to understand Japanese culture better, he did intensive Zen practice in Japan during and after World War II under Harada Daiun Sogaku Roshi. Eventually, he was recognized by his Buddhist teachers, particularly Yamada Koun Roshi, as able to teach Zen. Lassalle invoked 1 Thessalonians 5:21 as the criterion for Christian practice of Zen: "Indeed, we shall not hesitate to learn as much as we can from other religions. As Saint Paul said, 'Prove all things; hold fast that which is good'" (83).

American Jesuit Robert Kennedy also engaged in Zen practice in Japan and was eventually recognized as a roshi. Kennedy reflects on Jesus' statement on the cross in light of Zen: "My God, why have you deserted me?" (Mark 15:34). Kennedy suggests that this can be read as an invitation to the arduous, mystical journey of "not knowing" in prayer. For those on this path, Kennedy suggests that "Zen meditation can be a great help. For the very purpose of Zen meditation is for us to see into the emptiness of our concepts and emotions as well as into the emptiness of a culture that carries or expresses our faith" (2000, 30). Claiming that this awareness is also found in early Christian mystics, Kennedy suggests that the contribution of Zen is to help "move us from a notional understanding of the truth to a vital experience of it in our lives today" (31).

Kennedy notes that Zen is not analysis or theory of prayer but rather a plunge into "the contemplative act in which there is no subject or object" (1996, 37). He recalls that his teacher Yamada Roshi "gave us a Christian Japanese translation of Paul's letter to the Philippians. The phrase 'Jesus emptied himself' reads 'Jesus became *mu.*' The roshi urged us to become not good Buddhists but good Christians, to become *mu* in imitation of Christ" (Kennedy 1996, 37). For Kennedy, Zen helps Christians understand the meaning of the resurrection: "Very importantly, Zen reminds us that in our Christian tradition the risen Christ does not stand apart from us, objective to us, in heaven, even though many of our prayers use this form of imagery" (37). Kennedy comments that "Zen reminds us that Christian contemplation is not a looking at Christ, or a following of Christ, but a transformation into Christ" (37). Kennedy describes his own experience:

> The questions posed by the Zen master led me to discover that the Zen method and discipline help us to negate our superficial ego and find our true self—the hidden and mysterious person in whom we subsist before the eyes of God. And finding our true selves before the eyes of God, we will discover in the end, with Augustine, that in reality there is only one Christ loving himself. (1996, 37)

Kadowaki, Enomiya-Lassalle, Kennedy, and many other Christian practitioners of Zen have discovered that Zen opened up new dimensions in their experience of Christian faith and practice.

Conclusion

As in the case of other religious traditions, Christian interpretations of scripture in relation to the Buddhist tradition have ranged widely, from outright hostility to appreciation and to the acceptance of Buddhist perspectives into Christian hermeneutics. It is a great paradox that even though Buddhists and Christians differ profoundly on fundamental questions of cosmology and anthropology, nevertheless from various perspectives, participants in dialogue have repeatedly discovered resonances that have transformed and enriched their lives.

CHAPTER SEVEN

Conversion: Transformations in Interpreting Scripture in Light of Interreligious Understanding

In the preceding chapters, we have seen transformations in how Christians have interpreted the Bible in relation to the Jewish, Muslim, Hindu, and Buddhist traditions. In each case, there is a history of Christians employing a hermeneutics of hostility that views the other religion and its followers harshly in light of biblical themes. In many different contexts, a hostile hermeneutical circle increased tensions in relationships by interpreting followers of other religions as idolaters or as being in league with the devil, the Son of Destruction, and the Antichrist. Tensions in interreligious relationships in turn reinforced the hostile interpretation of biblical imagery. The negative cycle of mutual reinforcement between hostile relationships and negative scriptural interpretations continued for centuries. As a result, Christianity has had a tragic and violent relationship to all of the world's religious traditions, and this is particularly true of those religions with whom it is most closely bound in history and belief: Judaism and Islam.

The three Abrahamic religions share many important beliefs and values, but for centuries Christians have repeatedly vilified and demonized Jews and Muslims in light of biblical interpretations. When Christians came into contact with followers of other religions around the world, including Buddhists and Hindus, all too often they repeated the age-old patterns of intolerance, defamation, and violence, interpreting the Bible in hostile ways in relation to new interreligious contexts. The development of historical criticism made new resources available for understanding biblical texts in their original contexts but did not by itself overcome the pattern of a hermeneutics of hostility. For many years, leading practitioners of historical criticism viewed what they called "late Judaism" in very negative ways and tended to separate Jesus from the Jewish people.

Increasingly, Christians have come to see that these age-old attitudes and actions are profoundly contrary to the spirit and teaching of Jesus himself and have undertaken a critical reexamination of the received understanding of scripture and tradition. In each of these interreligious relationships, there have also been important changes in recent decades, as Christians have sought more respectful, generous interpretations of scripture in relation to other religious traditions. In a more benign hermeneutical circle, the search for improved interreligious relationships shapes fresh interpretations of the Bible that emphasize commonly shared values and concerns.

For Christians as for other religious traditions in which scriptures play a major role, a change from one mode of interpreting scripture to another is among the most important developments. For both individuals and communities, such a fundamental transformation is one of the strangest processes in life. Beforehand, there is a more or less stable paradigm, a view of the world with a set of perceptions, interpretations, judgments, and decisions based on certain data viewed in a certain way. At some point, new data and new interpretations pose questions that cannot be answered within the existing framework. A hermeneutics of hostility toward other religious traditions can appeal to numerous biblical texts and a long line of traditional authoritative interpreters in the Christian tradition. Even though the precise methods of biblical interpretation vary, early church fathers, medieval theologians, and Protestant Reformers converge in their negative interpretations of the Bible in relation to other religions.

Praying to God for forgiveness for historic sins against the Jewish people, Pope John XXIII abruptly reversed the traditional application of the curse of Cain to Jewish–Catholic relations. Where Augustine and Pope Innocent III had applied the curse of Cain to the entire Jewish people for their alleged responsibility for the death of Jesus Christ, John XXIII applied it to Catholics, and asked God's forgiveness:

> We are conscious today that many, many centuries of blindness have cloaked our eyes so that we can no longer see the beauty of Thy chosen people nor recognize in their faces the features of our privileged brethren. We realize that the mark of Cain stands upon our foreheads. Across the centuries our brother Abel has lain in the blood which we drew, or shed tears we caused by forgetting Thy love. Forgive us for the curse we falsely attached to their name as Jews. Forgive us for crucifying Thee a second time in their flesh. For we know not what we did. . . . (quoted by *Catholic Herald*, May 14, 1965; Lapide 1967, 318)

We saw at the outset that in 1964 Pope Paul VI called for *metanoia*: "Herein lies the secret of the Church's renewal, its *metanoia*, to use the Greek term, its practice of perfection" (*Ecclesiam Suam* §51). *Metanoia*, literally "afterthought: change of mind on reflection, repentance," is a "thinking after," that is, thinking differently, a change of mind and heart, a new way of seeing the world. *Metanoia* in interreligious relationships is one way of responding to the programmatic challenge of Jesus in the Gospel of Mark: "The time is fulfilled, and the kingdom of God has come near; repent (*metanoeite*), and believe in the good news" (Mark 1:15).

In his 1994 Apostolic Letter *Tertio Millennio Adveniente: Apostolic Letter on Preparation for the Jubilee of the Year 2000,* Pope John Paul II addressed this issue by calling Catholics to go through a purification of memory in relation to the injuries inflicted by Catholics on other religious communities. This involves acknowledging the wrongs inflicted in the name of Christ and asking God's forgiveness:

> Hence it is appropriate that, as the Second Millennium of Christianity draws to a close, the Church should become more fully conscious of the sinfulness of her children, recalling all those times in history when they departed from the spirit of Christ and his Gospel and, instead of offering to the world the witness of a life inspired by the values of faith, indulged in ways of thinking and acting which were truly *forms of counter-witness and scandal.* . . . She cannot cross the threshold of the new millennium without encouraging her children to purify themselves, through repentance, of past errors and instances of infidelity, inconsistency, and slowness to act. (*Tertio Millennio Adveniente* §33)

John Paul II uses the word *poenitentiam* ("repentance") to name an ongoing challenge, stating that "the Church does not tire of doing penance" (§33). In 1998, the Holy See's Commission for Religious Relations with the Jews issued *We Remember: A Reflection on the Shoah,* which expresses the need for a profound conversion of attitudes, using the Hebrew term for repentance, *teshuvah*:

> At the end of this millennium the Catholic Church desires to express her deep sorrow for the failures of her sons and daughters in every age. This is an act of repentance (*teshuvah*), since as members of the Church we are linked to the sins as well as the merits of all her children. . . . We wish to turn awareness of past sins into a firm resolve to build a new future in which there will be no more anti-Judaism among Christians or anti-Christian sentiment among Jews but rather a shared mutual respect as befits those who adore the One Creator and Lord and have a common father in faith, Abraham.

In 2000, Pope John Paul journeyed to Jerusalem, prayed at the Western Wall, and inserted a prayer asking God's forgiveness for the horrible crimes that Christians have committed against the Jewish people. These transformations in relation to earlier Catholic positions regarding other religious traditions constitute nothing less than a conversion of attitudes, teachings, and actions. Regarding the closely related issue of religious freedom, Gregory Baum has written of "The Conversion to Human Rights" in his survey of official Catholic teaching on human rights from Pope Gregory XVI in the 1830s to the present (2005, 14-34). Baum argues that these changes constitute "Discontinuous Development" (29).

The challenge of repentance and conversion flows from the prophetic heritage, demanding that we acknowledge our sins and become involved in shaping a better world. Conversion need not mean a move from one religious tradition to another. As we have seen, E. Stanley Jones experienced a conversion in his encounter with Gandhi, but it was a conversion to his own religion: "Here a Hindu was converting me to my own faith!" (Jones 1968, 172-73). In an article published in 1919, "Converting the Missionary," Earl H. Cressy wrote about the paradoxical turn of events in the experience of many a Christian missionary to China: "He had come to the Far East with a message that he was on fire to give, but in the process of transmission the East had spoken its message to him. He had gone out to change the East and was returning, himself a changed man" (quoted in Lian 1997, 207).

Conversion involves acknowledgment of responsibility, turning away from sin, repentance, making amends when possible, and forgiveness of sins. In the Catholic tradition, the term *conversio* can also refer to the ongoing life of prayer and growth in grace. The Rule of Saint Benedict describes the first stage of the life of prayer as a conversion, which Pierre de Béthune presents as "a reorientation of one's own life toward God. It is a step one has to take again and again during one's spiritual life—and even at the beginning of each individual prayer. . . . The point of conversion is to break from a certain way of life and a certain logic" (1998, 83). De Béthune notes that conversion leads to following Christ more deeply in meditation and communion and climaxes in the joy of the Holy Spirit, which brings freedom. Conversion leads to healing in relationships and a new sense of community.

The movement of conversion in the Catholic and Eastern Christian traditions leads ultimately to *theosis*, divinization, becoming one with God. In becoming one with God, we are called to become one with other humans, as in the prayer of Jesus at the Last Supper in John 17:20-26. Here from differing perspectives various traditions speak of nonduality in relation to the ultimate. There are multiple ways in which such a transformation can be analyzed. Hans Küng draws on the philosophy of science of Thomas Kuhn to describe paradigm change in theology (Küng and Tracy 1989). René Girard describes the surrogate victim mechanism as losing its effectiveness when it is brought into the open by the revelatory power of the gospel message. One of the most thoughtful analyses of conversion as a dynamic, ongoing process is that of Bernard Lonergan.

Bernard Lonergan

Bernard Lonergan's analysis of conversion can shed light on the shift from a hermeneutics of hostility to a hermeneutics of respect and generosity. In interreligious discussions the word "conversion" often refers to a change from one religious tradition to another (Nock 1998). In many settings past and present, this has been an issue of intense interreligious controversy, sometimes involving violence. However, as used by Bernard Lonergan, conversion does not refer primarily to a change from one religious affiliation to another. Rather, the term refers to a major change in intellectual, moral, and religious orientation, which need not involve a move from one religious tradition to another.

For Lonergan, conversion involves changes in experience, understanding, judgment, and decision regarding the true, the good, and the holy, bringing new awareness, interpretations, decisions, and commitments. In interreligious discussions, all participants can seek conversion in the sense of coming to a deeper knowledge and commitment to the true, the good, and the holy, without this necessarily involving a change from one tradition to another. Christian interpretations of the Bible, whether conducted consciously in relation to other religious traditions or not, can seek conversion in this sense.

Lonergan wrote his major philosophical work, *Insight: A Study of Understanding,* to invite readers to move through a process of intellectual conversion by appropriating their rational self-consciousness. By thematizing the process of understanding and knowing, Lonergan invites his readers to reflect critically on their own experience and assumptions and to overcome the danger of systemic bias. In the years that followed, he reflected more explicitly on the concept of conversion in the multiple levels of intellectual, moral, and religious transformation. While Lonergan did not engage extensively in interreligious discussions, nonetheless, Vernon Gregson (1985) and William Johnston (2000, 211-15) have explored the implications of Lonergan's method for interreligious relations.

Insight: Levels of Consciousness

The aim of Lonergan's book *Insight* is, as its name suggests, "to convey an insight into insight" (1997 [1957], 4). To suggest a sense of what he means by insight, Lonergan evokes the perfect detective story in which the reader has all the clues necessary to solve the crime but fails to do so, not for lack of information but for lack of a distinct "activity of organizing intelligence that places the full set of clues in a unique explanatory perspective" (3). Like the British philosopher R. G. Collingwood, Lonergan liked to imagine the historian as a detective on the scene of a crime, seeking the insight that will make sense of the data. "By insight, then, is meant, not an act of attention or advertence or memory but the supervening act of understanding" (3). Lonergan's goal in studying how we come to insight is "to seek a common ground on which men of intelligence might meet" (7). Two detectives can look at the same evidence and formulate different theories of what happened; thus insights can clash with each other because they construe the data in very different ways.

Insights occur in the natural sciences, in philosophy, in common sense, in religion, and in any pursuit of understanding. Lonergan's goal in *Insight* is not directly to conduct any of these various pursuits but to reflect on what is happening in all of them. The goal of any discipline is to facilitate the regular recurrence of insights, and so this reflection is useful for method in any discipline. Lonergan hopes to assist his readers in "effecting a personal appropriation of the concrete, dynamic structure immanent and recurrently operative in his own cognitional activities" (1997, 11). Lonergan expects that this will occur through a fourfold process of (1) heightening awareness of the way we experience, understand, judge, and decide, and then (2) understanding these processes and making (3) judgments and (4) decisions appropriate to the dynamic movement of human consciousness. Lonergan presents *Insight* to his readers as "an invitation to a personal, decisive act—the appropriation of one's own rational self-consciousness" (13).

Lonergan distinguishes four levels of consciousness: experience, understanding, judgment, and decision (1967, 221-39), and he proposes a transcendental precept for each level. On the level of experience, we encounter the data of sense and of consciousness: the experiences of "colors, shapes, sounds, odors, tastes," as well as the conscious "acts of seeing, hearing, tasting, smelling, touching, perceiving, imagining, inquiring, understanding, formulating, reflecting, judging, and so forth" (1997, 299). Lonergan insists that this raw experience is not knowledge but only the basis for further investigation that may eventually lead to knowledge. Lonergan warns that human knowledge is not like taking a look because it requires the further processes of understanding and judging. For the experiential level of consciousness, Lonergan proposes the transcendental precept: Be aware! The challenge here is not to exclude unwanted data.

The second level moves beyond the raw data of experience to formulate hypotheses, conjectures, and theories, which may or may not be accurate. Understanding addresses the question, "What is it?" (1997, 298). This is the level of understanding which in classical Western philosophy involves the question of essence. Interpretation takes place on this level, and there are dangers of bias from unconscious motivation or of individual or group egoism (1979, 153-73). The transcendental precept for understanding is: Be intelligent! Lonergan again insists that understanding is not yet knowledge; it is the formulation of a hypothesis; but there can be various hypotheses based on the same data. Lonergan argues that knowledge only comes with the next level of consciousness, which is judgment,

The third level of consciousness makes a judgment about the hypotheses and theories formulated by the understanding. A judgment answers the question, "Is it so?" by affirming either yes or no (1997, 296-303). Here the transcendental precept is: Be reasonable! In situations where there is sufficient evidence, one can make a virtually unconditioned judgment, that is, a judgment for which there are no more relevant questions.

Method in Theology

Lonergan's *Insight* focuses mainly on the aforementioned three levels of consciousness. Later, in *Method in Theology,* he explored more fully the fourth level of decision, which involves acting in accordance with the judgments we have made. Here the transcendental precept is: Be responsible! ([1972] 1979, 231). At times, when considering religious experience, he also names a fifth level of religious consciousness, which consists of being in love in an unrestricted manner and which corresponds to what Paul described as the love of God flooding our hearts through the Holy Spirit (Rom. 5:5; Lonergan [1972] 1979, 105). Here the final transcendental precept is: Be in love! Lonergan believes that classical Christian theology described this level of consciousness in the language of grace (1979, 120).

Lonergan assumes that there is a drive to know deep within us. When individuals and communities follow the transcendental precepts, there is a self-correcting process of learning channeled by focused questions; when the process works properly, life flourishes through the intake of information, recurring insights and responsible judgments. The dynamic process of the human mind constantly attends to new data, questions the significance of new experiences, formulates hypotheses, tests the evidence for these theories, makes judgments when appropriate, and then decides to live in accordance with reasonable judgments. Uniting the entire process is the dynamic self-transcendence of the human person toward God, whose love envelopes, supports, and challenges humans at every moment.

While Lonergan is aware that his analysis of these levels of consciousness is historically and culturally conditioned by Western philosophy and culture, he believes that the underlying operations are universal: persons in all cultures and religions experience, understand, judge, and decide. Humans experience a restless desire to know. Thus, anyone who would challenge his proposal would have to appeal to different experience and formulate a better understanding leading to a different judgment and then to better decisions. However different the descriptions of human consciousness may be, Lonergan trusts that the operations themselves are universal and thus provide a forum for interreligious and intercultural discussion (1979, 18-19).

Lonergan unfolds his work on three levels: (1) a study of human understanding; (2) an unfolding of the philosophical implications of understanding (cognitional theory leads to epistemology, which in turn leads to metaphysics); and (3) a campaign against the flight from understanding. Lonergan hopes that philosophy can play a therapeutic role in life. If we understand correctly, we will be cured of certain illusions: "Thus, insight into insight brings to light the cumulative process of progress. . . . It follows that if insight occurs, it keeps recurring. . . . Similarly insight into oversight reveals the cumulative process of decline" (1997, 8).

Lonergan is well aware that human life does not always flourish and that his hope for the efficacy of insight may well sound utopian. All too much of human existence takes the form of a flight from insight to bias, leading to unnecessary suffering, sometimes on an incalculable scale. Lonergan analyzes individual and group bias, warning: "Besides the love of light, there can be a love of darkness. If prepossessions and prejudices notoriously vitiate theoretical investigations, much more easily can elementary passions bias understanding in practical and personal matters. Nor has such a bias merely some single and isolated effect" (1997, 214). Lonergan names the unconscious process of systemic bias and oversight "scotosis," and he calls the resulting blindness "scotoma" (215). Lonergan explains that scotosis "arises, not in conscious acts, but in the censorship that governs the emergence of psychic contents. Nonetheless, the whole process is not hidden from us, for the merely spontaneous exclusion of unwanted insights is not equal to the total range of eventualities. Contrary insights do emerge" (215). Both as individuals and as groups, we avoid insights that threaten our fragile constructions and call us to change; we repress our awareness to avoid painful acceptance of responsibility. Lonergan comments: "The refusal of insight is a fact that accounts for individual and group egoism, for the psychoneuroses, and for the ruin of nations and civilizations" (259).

Lonergan sees bias as "a block or distortion of intellectual development," which can occur in unconscious motivation and in both individual and group egoism and in the warping of common sense so that it considers itself omni-competent (1979, 231). Communities and societies can shield themselves from awareness of their faults: "Once a process of dissolution has begun, it is screened by self-deception and it is perpetuated by consistency. . . . Increasing dissolution will then be matched by increasing division, incomprehension, sus-picion, distrust, hostility, hatred, violence" (244). Fortunately, the love of dark-ness and the resulting blindness are never totally successful. Lonergan believes that repression is always uneasy because it is an aberration of the fundamental drive of the human mind. Lonergan hopes that insight can arrest and reverse the disease of oversight and the flight from insight. However, to be freed from the disease of scotoma, humans must go through an intellectual conversion, which Lonergan describes as a radical clarification gained through the appro-priation of one's rational self-consciousness (1979, 238; 1967, 221-39).

In *Method in Theology,* Lonergan expands his discussion of consciousness to include feelings as intentional responses that shape and motivate acts of knowing and deciding. Because some feelings are disagreeable, we often seek to protect ourselves from suffering by excluding them from consciousness. The feeling that something is agreeable or disagreeable is not a reliable criterion for whether it is good, since the good may feel disagreeable (1979, 31). Values call us beyond the demand for immediate satisfaction and beyond our individual and group biases; thus they are crucial for moral and religious conversion. As a response to values, a feeling "both carries us towards self-transcendence and selects an object for the sake of whom or of which we transcend ourselves" (31). "Religious values, finally, are at the heart of the meaning and value of man's living and man's world" (32).

Lonergan finds a self-transcending movement from one level to the next: "The transcendental notions, that is, our questions for intelligence, for reflec-tion, and for deliberation, constitute our capacity for self-transcendence" (1979, 105). For Lonergan, the end of the whole process is the final impera-tive: Be in love without restriction. He comments, "As the question of God is implicit in all our questioning, so being in love with God is the basic fulfillment of our conscious intentionality" (105). For Christians, this means accepting the love of God flooding the human heart. Lonergan describes this as the heart of religious conversion (107).

But the process can go awry. Lonergan warns of the aberration of feelings such as "ressentiment," as analyzed by Friedrich Nietzsche and Max Scheler. Following Scheler, Lonergan sees "ressentiment" as

> a re-feeling of a specific clash with someone else's value-qualities. The someone else is one's superior physically or intellectually or morally or spiritually. The re-feeling is not active or aggressive but extends over

time, even a life-time. It is a feeling of hostility, anger, indignation that is neither repudiated nor directly expressed. (1979, 33)

Lonergan warns that this can warp our entire scale of values; he counsels, "More generally, it is better to take full cognizance of one's feelings, however deplorable they may be, than to brush them aside, overrule them, ignore them" (1979, 33). The resolution of the dilemma of warped values comes through moral conversion, which requires self-transcendence: "Moral conversion changes the criterion of one's decisions and choices from satisfactions to values. . . . Moral conversion consists in opting for the truly good, even for value against satisfaction when value and satisfaction conflict" (240).

Despite the danger of scotosis, Lonergan trusts the movement of self-transcendence toward values: "The transcendental notions are the dynamism of conscious intentionality. They promote the subject from lower to higher levels of consciousness, from the experiential to the intellectual, from the intellectual to the rational, from the rational to the existential" (1979, 34-35). The transcendental notions provide goals and criteria for assessing oneself and one's community. Lonergan summarizes the healthy movement of consciousness:

Self-transcendence is the achievement of conscious intentionality, and as the latter has many parts and a long development, so too has the former. There is a first step in attending to the data of sense and of consciousness. Next, inquiry and understanding yield an apprehension of a hypothetical world mediated by meaning. Thirdly, reflection and judgment reach an absolute; through them we acknowledge what really is so, what is independent of us and our thinking. Fourthly, by deliberation, evaluation, decision, action, we can know and do, not just what pleases us, but what truly is good, worth while." (1979, 35)

For Lonergan, the dynamic, self-correcting process of self-transcendence culminates in the religious experience of being in love with God without restriction: "Being in love with God, as experienced, is being in love in an unrestricted fashion. All love is self-surrender, but being in love with God is being in love without limits or qualifications or conditions or reservations" (1979, 106). Religious conversion is a response to the gift of grace: "It is total and permanent self-surrender without conditions, qualifications, reservations. But it is such a surrender, not as an act, but as a dynamic state that is prior to and principle of subsequent acts" (240). Some have seen this self-transcending process as moving to mystical experience. William Johnston recalls: "When I met Lonergan in Boston, I told him that his understanding of religious conversion leading to being in love is in fact a way to mysticism. He was delighted and smiled, saying, 'Yes, that's it!'" (Johnston 2006, 147).

Lonergan found this experience expressed in numerous biblical texts, especially in Paul's description of the love of God flooding our hearts through the Holy Spirit (Rom. 5:5), his confidence that nothing can separate us from the love of God (Rom. 8:35, 38-39), his description of the effects of the fruits of the Spirit (Gal. 5:22), and his hymn to love in 1 Corinthians 13. Lonergan also cites the gift of the Spirit blowing where it wills (John 3:8) and the affirmation that God is love (1 John 4:8).

The process of being in love without restriction is not to be taken for granted, however, for it involves a continual reversal of self-centeredness and demands what Lonergan calls religious conversion:

> It is the type of consciousness that deliberates, makes judgments of value, decides, acts responsibly and freely. But it is this consciousness as brought to a fulfillment, as having undergone a conversion, as possessing a basis that may be broadened and deepened and heightened and enriched but not superseded, as ready to deliberate and judge and decide and act with the easy freedom of those that do all good because they are in love. So the gift of God's love occupies the ground and root of the fourth and highest level of man's intentional consciousness. (1979, 107)

This conversion is made manifest in a changed way of life: "Religious experience spontaneously manifests itself in changed attitudes, in that harvest of the Spirit that is love, joy, peace, kindness, goodness, fidelity, gentleness, and self-control" (1979, 108). This is never earned but comes as a result of God's love flooding the heart, which is grace. This gift, however, is never secure: "Of itself, self-transcendence involves tension between the self as transcending and the self as transcended. So human authenticity is never some pure and serene and secure possession. It is ever a withdrawal from unauthenticity, and every successful withdrawal only brings to light the need for still further withdrawals" (110). There is no final resting place: "Besides conversions there are breakdowns. What has been built up so slowly and so laboriously by the individual, the society, the culture, can collapse" (243). There is always need for an ongoing process of self-critique and reform: "Genuine religion is discovered and realized by redemption from the many traps of religious aberration. So we are bid to watch and pray, to make our way in fear and trembling" (1979, 110; see also 1985, 113-65).

Lonergan recognizes the historicity and relativity of cultures. Where classical Christian theology had long assumed the normativity of Western culture and its philosophy, Lonergan proposes an empirical notion of culture as "the set of meanings and values that informs a way of life" (1979, xi; see also 1974a, 1-10). Lonergan describes the resulting transformation in the approach to theology: "When the classicist notion of culture prevails, theology is conceived as a permanent achievement, and then one discourses on its nature. When culture is conceived empirically, theology is known to be an ongoing process, and then one writes on its method" (1979, xi). Lonergan claims that his generalized empirical method of critical realism offers a way to abandon the classical notion of culture, that is, the hubris of belief in one normative culture reigning over history, and to acknowledge an empirical notion of culture according to which no one culture is normative, but there are normative demands implicit in human knowing that can be discovered.

Lonergan and Interreligious Relations

While Lonergan did not engage in extensive interreligious discussions, his thought has many ramifications for these relationships. His comments on other religious traditions were tentative. Vernon Gregson comments, "He is primarily a theological methodologist in his own work in this area, not a historian of religions or even a systematic theologian" (1985, 71). Regarding criteria for assessing religious claims, Gregson applies Lonergan's principles to interreligious reflection: "There are no criteria which can rightfully be imposed; there are only the criteria which emerge in a subject striving for self-transcendence" (71). Lonergan rejects the quest for allegedly objective criteria apart from personal transformation through conversion. Lonergan's approach has implications for interpreting the Bible in relation to other religious traditions. To the degree that interpreters read the Bible within a horizon of bias and hostility, all judgments and decisions will be systemically warped. To overcome the bias and hostility, a purification of categories is required. Lonergan comments:

> The purification of the categories—the elimination of the unauthentic—is proposed by the functional specialty, dialectic, and it is effected in the measure that theologians attain authenticity through religious, moral, and intellectual conversion. Nor may one expect the discovery of some "objective" criterion or test or control. For that meaning of the "objective" is mere delusion. Genuine objectivity is the fruit of authentic subjectivity. (1979, 292)

Regarding the interpretation of the Bible in interreligious relationships, Lonergan's discussion of the operations of consciousness offers a framework for analyzing the transformation from a hermeneutics of hostility to a hermeneutics of respect and generosity, leading toward friendship. A hermeneutics of hostility distorts the perception of the other. False accusations, skewed perceptions, and outright lies provide a distorted basis for understanding the other, as in traditional Christian falsehoods about Jews and Muslims.

Ressentiment can poison perceptions, feelings, and actions in relation to other religions. Much of the history of Christian interpretations of the Bible in relation to other religions has proceeded within a horizon of systemic hostility, with ressentiment often lurking in the background. We have seen that in the second century Melito of Sardis accused the entire Jewish people of the horrible and unprecedented crime of attempted deicide. Scholars have speculated that Melito, a member of a new and small Christian community, felt threatened by the larger and more powerful Jewish population, which enjoyed the largest synagogue known from the ancient world (Taylor 1995, 53). We have also seen that in the early Middle Ages Christians often felt profoundly uneasy with Islam because of the success of Muslims in many aspects of learning and culture, as well as on the battlefield.

On the level of understanding and interpretation, Christians often interpreted other religions in the harshest terms, frequently interpreting them as works of the devil; they often interpreted the Bible in a framework of animosity toward other religious options. Most Christians traditionally projected tremendously negative stereotypes onto Jews and Muslims, seeing them as allies of the Antichrist and believing violence against them was the will of God. Based on often skewed or distorted data and hostile interpretations, Christians often made sharply negative judgments, for example, judging non-Christians to be condemned to eternal damnation if they did not repent before the end of their mortal lives. Given the hostile interpretations and judgments, discriminatory and violent decisions often followed. Preaching about alleged Jewish guilt for the death of Jesus during Christian celebrations of Holy Week often inspired fierce attacks on the Jews, including physical violence against Jews after the ceremonies were ended. Pope Urban II called for war against the Turks, whom he described as "more execrable than the Jebusites" (E. Peters 1971, 9).

Lonergan's analysis of bias and scotosis offers a helpful model for understanding the hermeneutics of hostility in the history of biblical interpretation. In a hostile environment, individuals and communities focus on claims, whether valid or not, that cast their adversaries in the worst possible light; the charges are then interpreted in a way that reinforces the guilt of the other religion as an enemy of God. Negative judgments and decisions follow. When dominated by bias and scotosis, communities resist information or insights that would challenge the negative view of the other religion. A hermeneutics of hostility can become a self-reinforcing system.

This description of conversion offers a way of understanding the process of change from a horizon of hostility to one of respect. Lonergan applies the traditional categories of Catholic spiritual life to the dynamic state of religious experience:

> Traditionally that dynamic state is manifested in three ways: the purgative way in which one withdraws from sinning and overcomes temptation; the illuminative way in which one's discernment of values is refined and one's commitment to them is strengthened; the unitive way in which the serenity of joy and peace reveal the love that hitherto had been struggling against sin and advancing in virtue. (1979, 289)

Lonergan assumes that all other religious traditions also experience the love of God and the call to authentic understanding, judging, deciding, and being in love without restriction. Lonergan believes that "from an experience of love focused on mystery there wells forth a longing for knowledge, while love itself is a longing for union; so for the lover of the unknown beloved the concept of bliss is knowledge of him and union with him, however they may be achieved" (1979, 109). Lonergan is aware that his categories come from Western philosophical reflection and the Catholic tradition, and he recognizes that other traditions have very different approaches. For him, the particular concepts used are not what is most important.

His language comes from the theistic tradition of Christianity. Even though not all traditions believe in God, Lonergan trusts that there may well be analogies. He suggests that the "alleged atheism" of Buddhists is not a barrier to communication but may be viewed as an alternative approach to religious experience, possibly arising from "the expression of a non-objectified experience" (Gregson 1985, 70). From the Buddhist tradition, Japanese philosopher Keiji Nishitani compares the nondiscriminating love of God described by Jesus (Matt. 5:43-48) to the nondiscriminating compassion of the Buddhist tradition. In response to Jesus' command to love one's enemies, Nishitani comments: "In Buddhism this is what is known as 'non-differentiating love beyond enmity and friendship'" (1982, 58). Regarding Jesus' description of God sending rain on the just and the unjust, he remarks, "It is a non-differentiating love that transcends the distinctions men make between good and evil, justice and injustice" (58). For some practitioners, the final stage of religious conversion leads to mystical union with God or a form of nondual experience. There could be interreligious analogies to be explored among Christian mystics, Jewish Kabbalists, Muslim Sufis, Hindu sannyasis and devotees to Vishnu and Shiva, and Buddhist practitioners.

Lonergan's call for a multilevel intellectual, moral, and religious conversion offers a framework for interpreting the turn away from traditional Christian interpretations of the Bible toward a more respectful, generous approach to the Bible in relation to other religious traditions. At its best, Christian theological reflection seeks to understand and be guided by the true, the good, and the beautiful, transcendental notions that are important for other religious traditions as well. John Haughey draws out the implications of Lonergan's perspective for interreligious relations in scholarship:

> Part of the mission of the Catholic intellectual tradition is to affect other intellectual traditions. Its mission is not to evangelize other traditions, but to complement them in their approach to interiority and transcendent meaning, assuming they value these, though in analogous ways. The Catholic intellectual tradition will accomplish its mission if it is attentive to the fact that "there are the prior transcendental notions that constitute the very dynamism of our conscious intending." These notions of being and the good intend the unknown that gradually becomes better known; they also seek to make meaning and a whole out of the known parts. (Haughey 2009, 103, quoting Lonergan 1979, 12)

Following Lonergan, Haughey assumes that all religious traditions, and indeed all people, use the operations of consciousness: experience, understanding, judgment, and decision. Haughey further agrees with Lonergan in believing that "all people seek the true, the good, and the beautiful, never abstractly but always concretely, and that all people need help discerning between true and false goods" (2009, 103). Haughey further notes the challenge posed to human intentionality by "pollution" from various sources.

Lonergan's approach to conversion, while inspired by the Bible as interpreted in the Catholic tradition, is open to revision in dialogue. Gregson comments, "It is precisely the flexibility of Lonergan's method in matters such as this which makes it valuable and which serves to encourage both collaboration and continual revision" (1985, 71). In interreligious and cross-cultural contexts, Lonergan's imperative to be attentive applies across religious boundaries. The first step in his model of theological reflection involves research, gathering data. Given the history of disinformation, partial views, and distorted perceptions in interreligious relations, this step is vital. Lonergan's imperative to be intelligent in understanding and interpreting other religions applies in cross-cultural hermeneutics. The imperative to be reasonable in judging demands careful scrutiny before making a final assessment in relation to another religious tradition.

The imperative to be responsible in making decisions shapes the actions that flow from the process. On this level the functional specialty that Lonergan calls "dialectic" explores fundamental clashes of values and discerns what is good and evil. Lonergan expects an openness to challenge from participants in this process: "Encounter is more. It is meeting persons, appreciating the values they represent, criticizing their defects, and allowing one's living to be challenged at its very roots by their words and by their deeds" (1979, 247). While Lonergan orients his discussion of dialectic in *Method in Theology* to the historical study of the past, the same principles can be applied to contemporary interreligious encounters as well. "Encounter is the one way in which self-understanding and horizon can be put to the test" (1979, 247). Dialectic prods investigators toward conversion: "It will make conversion a topic and thereby promote it. Results will not be sudden or startling, for conversion commonly is a slow process of maturation. It is finding out for oneself and in oneself what it is to be intelligent, to be reasonable, to be responsible, to love" (253). The challenge "can lead to a new understanding of oneself and one's destiny" (253).

René Girard

Like Lonergan, Girard believes that humans need to go through a conversion inspired by divine grace to escape from the patterns of systemic bias. However, his theory views other religious traditions in a profoundly different manner than Lonergan. Wolfgang Palaver has noted the intimate relation between the mimetic theory of René Girard and conversion: "I now think that mimetic theory is very closely connected to conversion" (Palaver 2009, 191). Palaver finds this not only in the great European writers from whom Girard learned so much, but also in Girard's own life: "But the close connection between mimetic theory and conversion is also true for Girard himself. It is not by chance that Girard experienced his own conversion as he was finishing his first book,

Deceit, Desire, and the Novel" (Palaver 2009, 191). Girard analyzes human conflicts in terms of mimetic rivalry and the surrogate victim mechanism. He also reflects on biblical revelation as a response to these dilemmas. Crossing the usual boundaries of academic disciplines, Girard proposes a wide-ranging theory that explores the intertwining of religion and violence and that finds a resolution in Jesus' nonviolent response to violence in his death and resurrection. My interest in this discussion is in how Girard's mimetic theory can illumine the transformation in Christian interpretations of the Bible in relation to other religious traditions.

Mimetic Rivalry and the Scapegoat Mechanism

Girard has developed a three-point theory that interprets the central dynamics of human conflict, the patterns of religiously motivated violence, and the significance of biblical revelation, especially Jesus' death. The first part of Girard's theory involves the construction of desire. Girard claims that from the time we are very young we learn what is desirable from other persons whom we take as models. Desire arises from an awareness of a lack within us, a lack not only of possessions but of being. In some way we feel we are not adequate as we are, and so we look to a model as an example of someone who really is. We desire to appropriate the model's possessions, prestige, in an effort to be someone in reality. As we grow up, we tell ourselves that our desires are spontaneously directed toward objects, but Girard warns that to an overwhelming degree we learn what to desire from models. Often the process of imitating someone else's desires is hidden from our conscious awareness, and so Girard uses the Greek word *mimēsis* to name it.

According to Girard, desire is triangular; we seek the object of longing through the mediation of a model. We desire possessions and persons because others have them and we do not. Girard comments on the structure of romantic desire: "The subject is unable to desire on his own; he has no confidence whatever in a choice that would be solely his own. The rival is needed because his desire alone can confer on the girl whatever value she has in the eyes of the subject" (1988, 66). This is the principle behind much competition and advertising, as well as much romantic rivalry, not to mention national and international conflicts driven by jealousy and envy of others. In some ways, this process resembles what Lonergan, Nietzsche, and Scheler mean by *ressentiment*, as Girard comments: "Many features of *ressentiment*, as Nietzsche describes them, resemble the consequences of the mimetic process. *Ressentiment* is really a thwarted and traumatized desire" (73). However, in his critique of Nietzsche and Freud, Girard insists strongly on the mimetic character of desire: "All desires say to each other 'imitate me' and 'do not imitate me' almost simultaneously, which is the same thing as saying that mutually frustrated desires generate and reinforce each other" (73).

When we imitate models from a distance and do not threaten them, all is well. If, however, we are in a position of power to challenge the model, we quickly find ourselves in a double bind: the model says, "Imitate me." If, however, we imitate the model's desires in a way that threatens the person, there arises a rivalry that will sooner or later lead to violence. Because the imitator seeks the being of the model, no amount of physical possessions can resolve the conflict. Girard explains: "The hero in the grip of some second-hand desire seeks to conquer the *being*, the essence, of his model by as faithful an imitation as possible. . . . The nearer the mediator, the more does the veneration that he inspires give way to hate and rivalry" (1988, 3).

Despite the growing animosity, the obstacle exerts a strange attractive power: "If the model keeps interfering with the subject's desire, ultimately it is this interference itself that will be actively sought, as a designation of the most desirable object, and the triangle will be there" (1988, 67). Over time, mimetic rivalry ensures that tensions will increase in any group. Violence erupts and is also mimetic, calling forth retaliatory violence and threatening to make common life impossible; however, early humans discovered a way to channel and limit violence.

Girard argues that from time immemorial the first humans learned that the most effective way to discharge tension and resolve the crisis of mimetic rivalry is to target a scapegoat, a surrogate victim who can be blamed for the crisis. Then others can direct their anger and animosity toward that individual or group. Girard proposes that "society is seeking to deflect upon a relatively indifferent victim, a 'sacrificeable' victim, the violence that would otherwise be vented on its own members, the people it most desires to protect" (1977, 4). Since the dawn of history, Girard argues, humans have formed unstable communities by targeting certain individuals or groups with responsibility for all the troubles. To a frightening extent, the lynch mob lurks behind cultural patterns. Girard goes so far as to assert of the primal sacred: "For in the final analysis, the sole purpose of religion is to prevent the recurrence of reciprocal violence" (55). Girard finds the only exception to this generalization in biblical revelation. This leaves in principle little room for acknowledging revelation in any other religious tradition.

According to Girard, it is essential to the effectiveness of the process that those targeting the scapegoat believe that the accusations are true. In the classic pattern, the victim receives all the violence of the community and is judged to be indeed guilty. Whether the charge is actually true does not matter for the effectiveness of the process, as long as people believe it. After the victim's expulsion or death, there is an eerie calm, at least for a while, which seems to confirm the person's guilt. In general, Girard assumes the victim is innocent.

When a victim of scapegoating is put to death, it is often done in a way that no one individual is clearly responsible, for example, by stoning or by being forced by a mob to walk ever closer to a cliff until the person falls off. A lynch mob offers anonymity. No one can be identified, and no one is be punished. Because the guilt seems so evident, the process of scapegoating is never apparent. Indeed, if we can use the term to describe the process as scapegoating, we have already seen through the central dynamics and it is no longer as effective.

The resolution, however, is never completely stable. The cycle of mimetic rivalry and violence starts up again, before long another scapegoat must be found. Ideally, it will be someone who is marginal to society, whether from being powerless and despised or from being extremely powerful and therefore envied, someone who will not have defenders who will fight back.

In time, the spontaneous pattern of murdering an innocent victim became ritualized and sacralized. Girard believes that primal religions justify the scapegoating process through mythologies that blame the victim and cover up the process. Thus, since prehistory, primal religions have demanded bloody sacrifices, whether human or animal. Sacralized violence lies at the root of religious and cultural patterns that target certain individuals or groups as the source of all problems, while denying the responsibility of those doing the violent deeds.

Girard and Biblical Revelation

Girard thinks that the process of mimetic rivalry and scapegoating has played itself out over and over again in myriad forms in human history, usually without being clearly understood. According to Girard, these dynamics dominate the religious life of humanity, except for the revelation offered in the Bible.

In the Bible, Girard finds God's response, repeatedly intervening on the side of innocent victims and exposing the scapegoating mechanism as a fraud. Abel is a victim of mimetic rivalry, a classic conflict between brothers, but he is presented as innocent. When God asks Cain, "Where is your brother Abel?" (Gen. 4:9), there is no justification for the murder (Girard 1987a, 147). In contrast to religions that justify the murder of the innocent victim and cover up the traces, the Bible condemns the murder and draws it out into the open. The blood of Abel cries out from the earth to God (Gen. 4:10). But God does not wish the cycle of violence to continue and places a sign on Cain, not to curse him but to protect him from vengeance (Gen. 4:15; Girard 1987a, 146).

For Girard, what is striking about ancient Israel is that many biblical authors recognized the primordial pattern of scapegoating, exposed it, and denounced it. Many psalms express the perspective of the victim surrounded by the hostile crowd. The book of Job presents the friends insisting that Job really is guilty, but Job protests his innocence, appealing to God. However, Girard believes: "The God of the final speeches remains the God of the persecutors but less visibly, in a more hypocritical manner than the general at the head of the celestial armies. He conceals his game cleverly, all the more so because he himself has no understanding of it" (1987b, 142). However, Job succeeds in finding the truth: "Only Job has spoken the truth about God, by apparently insulting him and denouncing his injustice and cruelty—whereas the friends, who always spoke in his favour, had spoken badly of him" (144).

In the poems of the Suffering Servant in the second part of the book of Isaiah, a crowd surrounds an innocent victim and heaps abuse upon him (Isa. 52:13-53:12). Girard comments, "This death, the murder of the great prophet rejected by his people, is the equivalent of the Passion in the Gospels. As in the Gospels, the collective lynching of the prophet and the revelation of Yahweh make up one and the same event" (2001, 30). The Psalms repeatedly present persons surrounded by hateful foes. The drama involves the ancient pattern of scapegoating, but the point of view has changed (115-17, 127-28). The biblical author does not accept the charges; the victim is indeed innocent and is vindicated by God.

For Girard, this sets the stage for the story of Jesus' life, death, and resurrection in the Gospels. In the Gospel of John, Jesus says, "They hated me without cause" (John 15:25; cf. Ps. 35:19). Girard comments, "It appears banal at first, but this sentence expresses the essential nature of the hostility against the victim. The hostility is without any specific reasons precisely because it is the poisoned fruit of mimetic contagion" (2001, 127). In Jesus, God enters into all the violence of human history. How can God end the cycle of violence? If Jesus calls down legions of angels to attack Pontius Pilate, what lesson will be learned? That God has more violent power than the Roman Empire? That violence resolves problems, if one only has enough force? Girard explains: "A nonviolent deity can only signal his existence to mankind by having himself driven out by violence—by demonstrating that he is not able to establish himself in the Kingdom of Violence" (1987a, 219).

On the cross, Jesus refuses to continue the cycle of mimetic violence; instead of blaming his persecutors and demanding vengeance, he looks at the situation from their point of view and asks God to forgive them because they do not understand the process in which they are participating: "Father, forgive them; for they do not know what they are doing" (Luke 23:34; Girard 2011, 82-83). In Jesus, God appears in history as the innocent victim who goes to his death as the scapegoat. "It requires the good news that God himself accepts the role of the victim of the crowd so that he can save us all" (Girard 2001, 130). Far from demanding victims, God identifies with the victim and thus exposes the scapegoat mechanism as a fraud and a deception. "The divinity of Christ is fully revealed when he is the victim of the mimetic event of all against one, but it owes absolutely nothing to this phenomenon of violent contagion and scapegoating" (2001, 131).

God responds to human violence with nonviolent love. The realization that God is on the side of the innocent victim is, for Girard, the center of biblical revelation. From a Girardian perspective, what the persecutors of Jesus do not know is that their victim is innocent. As long as they are caught up in mimetic rivalry and violence, they believe that the charges against the scapegoat are true and can claim they are doing the will of God or the gods. Trapped in a vicious cycle, they cannot see their own responsibility but project all blame onto an innocent victim. Girard comments, "Scandals are above all a kind of inability to see, an insurmountable blindness" (2001, 126).

The Bible unmasks the process of mimetic rivalry and scapegoating and responds with God's forgiving love, inviting humans to a conversion of attitudes, values, and actions. In the Acts of the Apostles, the young Saul believes he is doing the will of God by seeking to kill early followers of Jesus (Acts 9:1-2). This represents much of the dynamic of religiously motivated violence throughout history. When Saul encounters the risen Lord Jesus on the road to Damascus, the first thing that he learns is that Jesus is present in the intended victims of his fury, as he hears the words "I am Jesus, whom you are persecuting" (Acts

9:5). Instead of fulfilling God's will, Saul realizes that he has been persecuting God. It is this insight that opens up hope for the human community.

According to Girard, the revelation of God answers the problem of mimetic rivalry and scapegoating. Only by having a transcendent goal can humans move beyond the incessant double bind of mimeticism. In conversation with Wolfgang Palaver on this matter, Girard cites Dante's *Divine Comedy*:

> Because you make things of this world your goal,
> Which are diminished as each shares in them,
> Envy pumps hard the bellows for your sighs.
> But if your love were for the lofty sphere,
> Your cravings would aspire for the heights.
> And fear of loss would not oppress your hearts.
> (*Purgatorio* 15.49-54; Palaver 2009, 194)

Girard notes the paradox: as long as we deny that we are involved in mimetic rivalry and scapegoating, we continue the process and are like other persecutors. Once we acknowledge our complicity, however, we receive a new awareness and can be set free from the age-old patterns and live in a new horizon of grace. For Girard, the essential moment in the conversion is coming to see the processes in which we have been living. Once we understand the scapegoat mechanism, he trusts that it will lose its hold.

Girard and Interreligious Relations

Girard's mimetic theory has multiple implications for interreligious relations, and it sheds much light on interreligious conflicts. Religious traditions often appear as mimetic rivals, and persecutions dot the history of interreligious relations. Judaism, Christianity, and Islam all claim to be "children of Abraham," but they have been bitter rivals for centuries. The surrogate victim mechanism had a powerful role in shaping the history of Christian–Jewish relations. As an example, Girard cites Guillaume de Machaut, a French writer who maligned Jews during the time of the Black Death in the fourteenth century, as an example of the hermeneutics of scapegoating. According to Girard, Machaut is not consciously lying when he accuses Jews of being responsible for the plague, and yet contemporary readers do not believe his accusations against the Jews: "We reject without question the meaning the author gives his text. We declare that he does not know what he is saying" (Girard 1992, 4). It is essential for the success of the scapegoat mechanism that it remain hidden. "The perspective is inevitably deceptive since the persecutors are convinced that their violence is justified; they consider themselves judges, and therefore they must have guilty victims" (6). For Girard, the power of the gospel has undermined the effectiveness of the scapegoat mechanism.

Girard's analysis is helpful in many ways, but he proposes a new form of exclusivism, insisting on the radical differences between Christianity and other religions and maintaining that only the revelation of God in Jesus Christ can overcome mimetic rivalry and scapegoating. For Girard, there is no hope of salvation outside of Christ: "Violence is the controlling agent in every form of mythic or cultural structure, and Christ is the only agent who is capable of escaping from these structures and freeing us from their dominance" (1987a, 219). Girard argues, "Nowhere in the world, even in our time, can we find this description of the mimetic war of all against one and its effects as complete as the Gospels give. Moreover, they contain unique information about what makes this disclosure possible" (2001, 124). The narratives of the crucifixion of Jesus rupture the unanimity of mythology, making possible the revelation of the innocence of the victim. The resurrection vindicates the innocent victims: "Only the Resurrection, because it enlightens the disciples, reveals completely the things hidden since the foundation of the world, which are the same thing as the secret of Satan, never disclosed since the origin of human culture: the founding murder and the origin of human culture" (2001, 125). Girard asserts, "The resurrection of Christ crowns and finishes both the subversion and the unmasking of mythology, of archaic ritual, of everything that insures the foundation and perpetuation of human cultures. The gospels reveal everything that human beings need to understand their moral responsibility with regard to the whole spectrum of violence in human history and to all the false religions" (2001, 125). According to Girard, no other religious tradition can effectively respond to the challenge of mimetic rivalry and the surrogate victim mechanism.

There are many questions and problems with the all-encompassing character of Girard's theory; often he appears to know too much, making ungrounded assumptions about early human life at a time when there are no written records. His insight into the scapegoating mechanism and the dynamic of the biblical response is, however, worth serious consideration. One can read the history of Christianity's hostile relations with other religions as to a large degree the working out of bias and scotosis, of mimetic rivalry and the surrogate victim mechanism. For centuries Christians attributed enormous power and guilt to Jews, seeing them as responsible for wrongs beyond any realistic accounting. The Abrahamic religions compete for the status of children of Abraham and display the hallmarks of sibling rivalry and mimesis. Girard's analysis offers a way to understand how religions that are so close to each other can also be caught in such bitter conflicts.

Girard's exclusivism views all nonbiblically based religions as products of mimetic rivalry and scapegoating. As a result of this assumption, he looks assiduously to signs of mimetic rivalry and scapegoating in the sacrificial rituals of the Hindus (2011).

Perhaps the greatest difficulty with Girard's mimetic theory lies in its claim to explain the dynamics of all religion and culture. I have argued elsewhere that the Buddhist tradition has perspectives and practices that counter mimetic rivalry and the surrogate victim mechanism (Lefebure 1996a, 1996b). The *Brahma-viharas* ("The Noble Abodes") are virtues that directly counter the temptations of mimetic rivalry and scapegoating: loving-kindness, compassion, appreciative joy, and equanimity. If one is truly practicing these central Buddhist virtues, one is free from the curse of mimetic rivalry and one cannot scapegoat. Of course, Buddhists have difficulty in following the Buddha's path, just as Christians have difficulty implementing the teachings of Jesus. Nonetheless, the ideals of both traditions converge in rejecting mimeticism and scapegoating.

In his critique of Girard, Peter Phan maintains that Girard's view of God as rejecting scapegoating "is neither unique nor the only one present in the Bible. Girard has ignored or played down the many 'texts of terror' of both the Old and New Testaments" (Phan 2004, 199). Moreover, citing the virtue of harmony in Confucianism and Thich Nhat Hanh's practice of mindfulness, Phan argues cogently, "Nor can Girard's claim for the uniqueness of the Hebrew-Christian God's identification with victims and God's rejection of victimization and violence be sustained. Nonviolence and the call for peace are also present in non-Christian religions" (2004, 199). As we have seen, Mahatma Gandhi drew on the teachings of nonviolence (*ahimsa*) in the Jain and Hindu traditions in his interpretation of Jesus' Sermon on the Mount.

Conversion and Healing

Both Lonergan and Girard trust that, despite the entrenched power of scotosis and scapegoating, the love of God can call humans out of their blindness and invite them to a change of perception, understanding, and judgment. This involves looking at experience with different perspectives. In Lonergan's terminology, conversion calls humans to follow the transcendental precepts even when they are most uncomfortable and disagreeable. This means attending to data even when it threatens age-old prejudices. It means questioning earlier prejudices and searching for the best interpretations of other religious traditions in dialogue with their representatives. Conversion means judging in accord with the widest range of available evidence. As Lonergan comments, "Fears of discomfort, pain, privation have less power to deflect one from one's course. Values are apprehended where before they were overlooked. Scales of preference shift. Errors, rationalizations, ideologies fall and shatter to leave one open to things as they are and to man as he should be" (1979, 52). In Girardian terms, this means acknowledging the danger of mimetic rivalry and suspending the proclivity to blame others for our failings. In the process of conversion, the self-transcending process of human consciousness can critique itself, reform itself, and learn with God's grace to function properly.

For Christians, God offers an invitation to a far-reaching conversion involving all the levels of consciousness that Lonergan has analyzed: experience, understanding, judgment, and decision. The conversion demands self-criticism and self-transcendence. William Johnston reflects on what this path demands. He cites Ignatius of Loyola's principle for interpreting someone else's perspective: "It is necessary to suppose that every good Christian is more ready to put a good interpretation on another's statement than to condemn it as false" (*Spiritual Exercises of St. Ignatius*, "Presupposition"; Johnston 2000, 212). While Ignatius was thinking of Christians who could be suspected of heresy, the principle can be applied in a hermeneutics of respect and generosity to all partners in interreligious dialogue. Johnston notes the relevance of this principle for assessing interpretations from Asia and Africa:

> If Western theologians (particularly those who find themselves called to "investigate") insist that Asian and African theologians remain exclusively with the Western propositions, if they insist on the wording of Western theology and no other, if they threaten and condemn and punish the Asians and Africans who carry Christianity into a new world—they could make mistakes no less terrible than those of the inquisitors, and they could jeopardize the very existence of Roman Catholicism in Asia of the third millennium. (2000, 213)

Johnston hopes that Lonergan's discussion of intellectual conversion can assist in negotiating such issues. Johnston invokes Lonergan's analysis of moral conversion to support respect for human rights: "Here it is enough to say that in the practical order moral conversion leads to respect for the dignity of the human person and recognition of his or her human rights. It is clear to everyone that in this area the Roman Catholic Church is in dire need of conversion. The church must be careful lest, after preaching to others, she herself go astray" (2000, 213).

Finally, Johnston stresses the importance of Lonergan's religious conversion: "It is clear that this is the answer to all our problems, whether in our church or in the world. . . . Lonergan's religious conversion, however, is not for Christians alone. It is for all human beings" (2000, 214). Johnston closes by invoking the mystical: "Only through love can we transcend the little ego, thus becoming fully human and fully authentic. And this radical love leads to the sublime wisdom that we call mysticism. How extraordinary! Lonergan, probably unconsciously, calls not only for a mystical Christianity but also for a mystical world" (214-15). In the Catholic tradition, conversion does not end with the forgiveness of sins but leads into mystical union with God. The dialogue of spiritual experience explores the experience of oneness and nonduality in various traditions.

The steps taken toward biblical interpretation and interreligious understanding are merely a beginning, and clearly much remains to be done. Biblical interpretation in relation to interreligious dialogue and understanding is more necessary than ever in the current time of conflict. Despite the tragic and terrible history of Christian atrocities, the gospel message still rings out across the centuries, challenging each new generation of Christians to creative fidelity. Christians experience both the scriptures and tradition as ambiguous, as sanctioning violence against others, but also as mediating truth, goodness, beauty, and grace.

In reading the Bible in relation to other religious traditions, Christians can acknowledge that followers of other religious paths also seek and find the holy, the true, the good, and the beautiful. Humans do not have a "God's-eye" perspective from which to survey religious diversity. According to medieval

Catholic theology, our condition in this world is that of *viatores*, wayfarers. The condition of a wayfarer is in-between, on the road toward a destination that is anticipated but not yet reached. Christians since the early centuries have made pilgrimages to sacred places, often as penitents seeking God's forgiveness for the sins of the past and praying for absolution and a new start toward a better future. Christian wayfarers today can welcome Jews, Muslims, Hindus, Buddhists, and followers of other paths, as companions for the journey. While respecting the important differences between our traditions, we can hope that our journeys bring us close enough to each other that we are within the range of fruitful conversation. Interreligious partners and companions can give us hope and sustenance for the journey.

Bibliography

Abe, Masao. 1986. *Zen and Western Thought.* Edited by William R. LaFleur. Honolulu: University of Hawaii Press.

———. 1990a. "Kenotic God and Dynamic Sunyata." In *The Emptying God: A Buddhist-Jewish-Christian Conversation,* edited by John B. Cobb Jr. and Christopher Ives, 3-65. Maryknoll, NY: Orbis Books.

———. 1990b. "Kenosis and Emptiness." In *Buddhist Emptiness and Christian Trinity: Essays and Explorations,* edited by Roger Corless and Paul F. Knitter, 5-25. New York and Mahwah, NJ: Paulist.

———. 1995a. "Kenotic God and Dynamic Sunyata." In *Divine Emptiness and Historical Fullness: A Buddhist-Jewish-Christian Conversation with Masao Abe,* edited by Christopher Ives, 25-90. Valley Forge, PA: Trinity Press International.

———. 1995b. *Buddhism and Interfaith Dialogue,* Part 1 of a two-volume sequel to *Zen and Western Thought.* Edited by Steven Heine. Honolulu: University of Hawai'i Press.

Abhishiktananda [Henri Le Saux]. 1965. *Sagesse hindoue, mystique chrétienne: Du Védanta à la Trinité.* L'Église en son temps. Paris: Centurion.

———. 1979. *The Secret of Arunachala.* Delhi: ISPCK.

———. 1993. *Prayer.* New ed. Delhi: ISPCK.

———. 1998. *Ascent to the Depth of the Heart: The Spiritual Diary (1948–1973) of Swami Abhishiktananda (Dom H. Le Saux).* Selected and edited by Raimon Panikkar. Translated by David Fleming and James Stuart. Delhi: ISPCK.

Adams, Jad. 2011. *Gandhi: The True Man behind the Modern India.* New York: Pegasus.

Adso of Montier-en-Der. 1979. "Letter on the Origin and Time of the Antichrist." In *Apocalyptic Spirituality,* edited and translated by Bernard McGinn, 89-96. Mahwah, NJ: Paulist.

Albrektson, Bertil. 1967. *History and the Gods: An Essay on the Idea of Historical Events as Divine Manifestations in the Ancient Near East and in Israel.* Coniectanea Biblica, Old Testament Series 1. Lund: Gleerup.

Alexander, Paul Julius. 1985. *The Byzantine Apocalyptic Tradition.* Edited by Dorothy de F. Abrahamse. Berkeley: University of California Press.

Allaire, Gloria. 1996. "Portrayal of Muslims in Andrea da Barberino's *Guerrino il Meschino.*" In *Medieval Christian Perceptions of Islam: A Book of Essays,* edited by John Victor Tolan, 243-69. New York and London: Garland.

Amaladass, Anand. 1990. "Dialogue between Hindus and the St. Thomas

Christians." In *Hindu–Christian Dialogue: Perspectives and Encounters,* ed. Harold Coward, 13-27. Maryknoll, NY: Orbis Books.

Amaladass, Anand, and Francis S. Clooney. 2000. "Introduction." In Roberto de Nobili, *Preaching Wisdom to the Wise: Three Treatises by Roberto de Nobili, S.J., Missionary and Scholar in 17th Century India.* Translated and introduction by Anand Amaladass and Francis X. Clooney. St. Louis: Institute of Jesuit Sources.

Amaladoss, Michael. 1992. *Walking Together: The Practice of Inter-religious Dialogue.* Anand, Gujarat, India: Gujarat Sahitya Prakash.

———. 1997. *Life in Freedom: Liberation Theologies from Asia.* Maryknoll, NY: Orbis Books.

———. 2006. *The Asian Jesus.* Maryknoll, NY: Orbis Books.

———. 2011. "Swami Abhishiktananda's Challenges to Indian and Western Theology." In *Witness to the Fullness of Light: The Vision and Relevance,* edited by William Skudlarek and Bettina Bäumer, 47-62. New York: Lantern Books.

Ambedkar, B. R. 2002. *The Essential Writings of B.R. Ambedkar.* Edited by Valerian Rodrigues. Oxford and New York: Oxford University Press.

———. 2011. *The Buddha and His Dhamma: A Critical Edition.* Edited by Aakash Singh Rathore and Ajay Verma. New Delhi: Oxford University Press.

Andrews, Charles F. (1930) 2003. *Mahatma Gandhi: His Life and Ideas.* Reprint, Woodstock, VT: Skylights Paths Publishing.

Ansbro, John J. 2000. *Martin Luther King, Jr.: Nonviolent Strategies and Tactics for Social Change.* Lanham, MD: Madison Books.

Ariokasamy, Soosai. 1986. *Dharma, Hindu and Christian, According to Roberto de Nobili: Analysis of Its Meaning and Its Use in Hinduism and Christianity.* Documenta Missionalia 19. Rome: Gregorian University Press.

Armstrong, R. J., J. A. W. Hellmann, and W. J. Short, eds. 1999–2002. *Francis of Assisi: Early Documents.* 4 vols. New York: New City Press.

Arokiaraj, G. Cosmon. 2007. "God Beyond Space Enters Human Space." In *Dalit World—Biblical World: An Encounter,* edited by Leonard Fernando and James Massey. New Delhi: Centre for Dalit/Subaltern Studies and Vidyajyoti College of Theology.

Ashton, John. 1991. *Understanding the Fourth Gospel.* Oxford: Clarendon.

Assmann, Jan. 1997. *Moses the Egyptian: The Memory of Egypt in Western Monotheism.* Cambridge, MA, and London: Harvard University Press.

———. 2008: *Of God and Gods: Egypt, Israel, and the Rise of Monotheism.* George L. Mosse Series in Modern European Cultural and Intellectual History. Madison: University of Wisconsin Press.

Ateek, Naim Stifan. 1989. *Justice and Only Justice: A Palestinian Theology of Liberation.* Maryknoll, NY: Orbis Books.

———. 2008. *A Palestinian Cry for Reconciliation.* Maryknoll, NY: Orbis Books.

Attridge, Harold W. 2010. *The Acts of Thomas.* Edited by Julian V. Hills. Early Christian Apocrypha 3. Salem, OR: Polebridge Press.

Augustine. 1964. *Of True Religion.* Translated by J. H. S. Burleigh. Chicago: Henry Regnery.

———. 1992. *Confessions.* Translated by Henry Chadwick. Oxford and New York: Oxford University Press.

———. 1996. *Teaching Christianity: De Doctrina Christiana.* Translated by Edmund Hill. Edited by John E. Rotelle. Hyde Park, NY: New City Press.

———. 1998. *The City of God against the Pagans.* Edited and translated by R. W. Dyson. Cambridge Texts in the History of Political Thought. Cambridge: Cambridge University Press.

Avery-Peck, Alan J. 2011. "The Second Letter of Paul to the Corinthians." In *The Jewish Annotated New Testament,* edited by Amy-Jill Levine and Marc Zvi Brettler. Oxford and New York: Oxford University Press.

Baker, Alan. 2003. *The Knight.* Hoboken, NJ: John Wiley & Sons.

Barth, Karl. 1957a. *Church Dogmatics.* Vol. 2, part 2. Edinburgh: T&T Clark.

———. 1957b. *Church Dogmatics.* Vol. 4, part 1. Edinburgh: T&T Clark.

Baum, Gregory. 2005. *Amazing Church: A Catholic Theologian Remembers a Half-Century of Change.* Maryknoll, NY: Orbis Books; Toronto: Novalis.

Baumann, Chad M. 2010. "Identity, Conversion and Violence: Dalits, Adivasis and the 2007-08 Riots in Orissa." In *Margins of Faith: Dalit and Tribal Christianity in India,* edited by Rowena Robinson and Joseph Marianus Kujur. New Delhi: Sage Publications India; Thousand Oaks, CA: Sage.

Bäumer, Bettina. 2011. "Introduction." In *Witness to the Fullness of Light: The Vision and Relevance of the Benedictine Monk Swami Abishiktananda,* edited by William Skudlarek and Bettina Bäumer, 1-3. New York: Lantern Books.

Baumer, Christoph. 2006. *The Church of the East: An Illustrated History of Assyrian Christianity.* London and New York: I. B. Tauris.

Becker, Adam H., and Annette Yoshiko Reed, eds. 2007. *The Ways That Never Parted: Jews and Christians in Late Antiquity and the Early Middle Ages.* Minneapolis: Fortress.

Bell, Ian B. 2008. *The Relevance of Bernard Lonergan's Notion of Self-Appropriation to a Mystical-Political Theology.* American University Studies: Series 7, Theology and Religion 267. New York: Peter Lang.

Bellah, Robert N. 2011. *Religion in Human Evolution: From the Paleolithic to the Axial Age.* Cambridge, MA, and London: Belknap Press of Harvard University Press.

Benedict XVI, Pope. 2011. "Message for the Celebration of the World Day of Peace: Religious Freedom, The Path to Peace." http://www.vatican.va/holy_father/benedict_xvi/messages/peace/documents/hf_ben-xvi_mes_20101208_xliv-world-day-peace_en.html

Bergoglio, Jorge Mario, and Abraham Skorka. 2013. *On Heaven and Earth: Pope Francis on Faith, Family, and the Church in the Twenty-First Century.* Edited by Diego F. Rosemberg. Translated by Alejandro Bermudez and Howard Goodman. New York: Image.

Bernardin, Joseph Cardinal. 1995. *Antisemitism: The Historical Legacy and the*

Continuing Challenge for Christians. Fairfield, CT: Sacred Heart University.

Bernstein, Carl, and Marco Politi. 1997. *His Holiness: John Paul II and the History of Our Time.* New York: Penguin Books.

Bertaina, David. 2011. *Christian and Muslim Dialogues: The Religious Uses of a Literary Form in the Early Islamic Middle East.* Piscataway, NJ: Gorgias Press.

Béthune, Pierre-François de. 1998. "Prayer as Path." In *The Gethsemani Encounter: A Dialogue on the Spiritual Life by Buddhist and Christian Monastics,* edited by Donald W. Mitchell and James A. Wiseman, 82-88. New York: Continuum.

———. 2002. *By Faith and Hospitality: The Monastic Tradition as a Model for Interreligious Encounter.* Leominster, UK: Gracewing.

Betz, Hans Dieter. 1995. *The Sermon on the Mount: A Commentary on the Sermon on the Mount, including the Sermon on the Plain (Matthew 5:3-7:27 and Luke 6:20-49).* Hermeneia. Minneapolis: Fortress.

Bevans, Stephen. 1992. *Models of Contextual Theology.* Maryknoll, NY: Orbis Books.

Bielefeldt, Heiner. 2001. *Symbolic Representation in Kant's Practical Philosophy.* Cambridge: Cambridge University Press.

Bischoff, Bernard, and Michael Lapidge. 1994. *Biblical Commentaries from the Canterbury School of Theodore and Hadrian.* Cambridge: Cambridge University Press.

Blée, Fabrice. 2011. *The Third Desert: The Story of Monastic Interreligious Dialogue.* Translated by William Skudlarek and Mary Grady. Collegeville, MN: Liturgical Press.

Boguslawski, Steven C. 2008. *Thomas Aquinas on the Jews: Insights into His Commentary on Romans 9-11.* New York and Mahwah, NJ: Paulist.

Boyarin, Daniel. 1994. *A Radical Jew: Paul and the Politics of Identity.* Contraversions 1. Berkeley and Los Angeles: University of California Press.

———. 2004. *Border Lines: The Partition of Judaeo-Christianity.* Divinations. Philadelphia: University of Pennsylvania Press.

———. 2010. "Origen as Theorist of Allegory: Alexandrian Contexts." In *The Cambridge Companion to Allegory,* edited by Rita Copeland and Peter T. Struck. Cambridge: Cambridge University Press.

———. 2012. *The Jewish Gospels: The Story of the Jewish Christ.* New York: New Press.

Boyd, R. H. S. 1969. *An Introduction to Indian Theology.* Madras: Christian Literary Society.

———. 1974. *India and the Latin Captivity of the Church: The Cultural Context of the Gospel.* London: Cambridge University Press.

Boys, Mary C. 2000. *Has God Only One Blessing? Judaism as a Source of Christian Self-Understanding.* Mahwah, NJ: Paulist.

Boys, Mary C., and Sara S. Lee. 2006. *Christians and Jews in Dialogue: Learning in the Presence of the Other.* Woodstock, VT: Skylight Paths.

Branick, Vincent P. 2011. *Understanding the Historical Books of the Old Testament.* New York and Mahwah, NJ: Paulist.

Braverman, Mark. 2010. *Fatal Embrace: Christians, Jews, and the Search for Peace in the Holy Land.* Austin, TX: Synergy Books.

Brenner, William H. 1999. *Wittgenstein's Philosophical Investigations.* Albany: State University of New York Press.

Brinkman, Martien E. 2009. *The Non-Western Jesus: Jesus as Bodhisattva, Avatara, Guru, Prophet, Ancestor or Healer?* Translated by Henry and Luch Jansen. London and Oakville, CT: Equinox.

Broadhead, Edwin D. 2010. *Jewish Ways of Following Jesus: Redrawing the Religious Map of Antiquity.* Wissenschaftliche Untersuchungen zum Neuen Testament 266. Tübingen: Mohr Siebeck.

Brown, Brian A. 2007. *Noah's Other Son: Bridging the Gap between the Bible and the Qur'an.* New York: Continuum.

Brown, Judith M. 1989. *Gandhi: Prisoner of Hope.* New Haven and London: Yale University Press.

Brown, Raymond E. 1979. *The Community of the Beloved Disciple.* New York: Paulist Press.

———. 1986. *A Crucified Christ in Holy Week: Essays on the Four Gospel Passion Narratives.* Collegeville, MN: Liturgical Press.

———. 1997: *An Introduction to the New Testament.* Anchor Bible Reference Library. New York: Doubleday.

Brueggemann, Walter. 2003. *An Introduction to the Old Testament: The Canon and Christian Imagination.* Louisville and London: Westminster John Knox.

———. 2010. "Foreword." In Mark Braverman, *Fatal Embrace: Christians, Jews, and the Search for Peace in the Holy Land.* Austin, TX: Synergy Books.

Bruteau, Beatrice, ed. 1996. *The Other Half of My Soul: Bede Griffiths and the Hindu-Christian Dialogue.* Wheaton, IL, and Adyar, Madras, India: Quest Books.

Buber, Martin. 1968. *Between Man and Man.* Translated by Ronald Gregor Smith. New York: Macmillan.

Bulliet, Richard. 2004. *The Case for Islamo-Christian Civilization.* New York: Columbia University Press.

Bundy, David. 1996. "The Syriac and Armenian Christian Responses to the Islamification of the Mongols." In *Medieval Christian Perceptions of Islam: A Book of Essays,* edited by John Victor Tolan, 33-53. New York and London: Garland.

Burge, Gary M. 2010. *Jesus and the Land: The New Testament Challenge to "Holy Land" Theology.* Grand Rapids: Baker Academic.

Burghardt, Walter J. 1950. "On Early Christian Exegesis." *Theological Studies* 11:78-116.

Buri, Fritz. 1997. *The Buddha-Christ as the Lord of the True Self: The Religious Philosophy of the Kyoto School and Christianity.* Translated by and introduction by Harold H. Oliver. Macon, GA: Mercer University Press.

Burr, David. 1996. "Antichrist and Islam in Medieval Franciscan Exegesis." In

Medieval Christian Perceptions of Islam: A Book of Essays, edited by John Victor Tolan, 131-52. New York and London: Garland.

Burrell, David B. 1992. *Knowing the Unknowable God: Ibn-Sina, Maimonides, Aquinas.* Notre Dame, IN: University of Notre Dame Press.

———. 2011. *Towards a Jewish-Muslim-Christian Theology.* Malden, MA, and Oxford: Wiley-Blackwell.

Burrell, David B., and Bernard McGinn, eds. 1990. *God and Creation: An Ecumenical Symposium.* Notre Dame, IN: University of Notre Dame Press.

Burrows, William R., ed. 1993. *Redemption and Dialogue: Reading Redemptoris Missio and Dialogue and Proclamation.* Maryknoll, NY: Orbis Books.

Capetz, P. E. 2009. "Friedrich Schleiermacher on the Old Testament." *Harvard Theological Review* 102:297-326.

Carroll, James. 2001. *Constantine's Sword: The Church and the Jews.* Boston and New York: Houghton Mifflin.

Carter, Warren. 1998. "Response to Amy-Jill Levine." In *Anti-Judaism and the Gospels,* edited by William R. Farmer. Harrisburg, PA: Trinity Press International.

Cassell's Latin Dictionary. (1997) 2007. Edited by D. P. Simpson. London: Cassell.

Cassidy, Edward Idris Cardinal. 2005. *Ecumenism and Interreligious Dialogue: Unitatis Redintegratio, Nostra Aetate.* New York and Mawhah, NJ: Paulist.

Cavanaugh, William T. 2009. *The Myth of Religious Violence: Secular Ideology and the Roots of Modern Conflict.* Oxford and New York: Oxford University Press.

Chacour, Elias, with David Hazard. 1984. *Blood Brothers.* Tarrytown, NY: Chosen Books.

Chacour, Elias, with Alain Michel. 2008. *Faith beyond Despair: Building Hope in the Holy Land.* Norwich, UK: Canterbury Press.

Charbonnier, Jean-Pierre. 2007. *Christians in China: A.D. 600–2000.* Translated by M. N. L. Couve de Murville. San Francisco: Ignatius Press.

Chattanatt, John. 1991. "Two Paradigms of Liberative Transformation: Approaches to Social Action in the Theological Ethics of Gandhi and Gutiérrez." Ph.D. diss., University of Chicago.

Chilton, Bruce. 2008. *Abraham's Curse: Child Sacrifice in the Legacies of the West.* New York: Doubleday.

Claassens, Geert H. M. 1996. "Jacob van Maerlant on Muhammad and Islam." In *Medieval Christian Perceptions of Islam,* edited by John Victor Tolan, 211-42. New York and London: Garland.

Clarke, Sathianathan, Deenabandhu Manchala, and Philip Vinod Peacock. 2010. *Dalit Theology in the Twenty-First Century: Discordant Voices, Discerning Pathways.* Oxford: Oxford University Press.

Clement of Alexandria. 1991. *Stromateis: Books One to Three.* Translated by John Ferguson. Fathers of the Church. Washington, DC: Catholic University of America Press.

Clifford, Patricia Hart. 1994. *Sitting Still: An Encounter with Christian Zen.* New York and Mahwah, NJ: Paulist.

Clooney, Francis X. 1993. *Theology after Vedanta: An Experiment in Comparative Theology.* SUNY Series, Toward a Comparative Philosophy of Religions. Albany: State University of New York Press.

———. 1996. *Seeing through Texts: Doing Theology among the Srivaisnavas of South India,* SUNY Series, Toward a Comparative Philosophy of Religions. Albany: State University of New York Press.

———. 1998. *Hindu Wisdom for All God's Children.* Maryknoll, NY: Orbis Books.

Cobb, John B., Jr., ed. 2012. *Religions in the Making: Whitehead and the Wisdom Traditions of the World.* Eugene, OR: Cascade Books.

Cobb, John B., Jr., and Christopher Ives, eds. 1990. *The Emptying God: A Buddhist–Jewish–Christian Conversation.* Maryknoll, NY: Orbis Books.

Coda, Piero. 2003. *Il logos e il nulla: Trinità religioni mistica.* Rome: Città Nuova.

Coelho, Ivo. 2001. *Hermeneutics and Method: The 'Universal Viewpoint' in Bernard Lonergan.* Toronto: University of Toronto Press.

Collins, Adela Yarbro. 1979. *The Apocalypse.* New Testament Message 22. Wilmington, DE: Michael Glazier.

———. 1984. *Crisis and Catharsis: The Power of the Apocalypse.* Philadelphia: Westminster.

Collins, John J. 1984. *The Apocalyptic Imagination: An Introduction to the Jewish Matrix of Christianity.* New York: Crossroad.

———. 2000. *Between Athens and Jerusalem: Jewish Identity in the Hellenistic Diaspora.* Grand Rapids: Eerdmans.

———. 2004. *Does the Bible Justify Violence?* Minneapolis: Fortress.

Collins, Raymond F. 1999. *First Corinthians.* Sacra Pagina 7. Collegeville, MN: Liturgical Press.

Commission for Religious Relations with the Jews. 1998. *We Remember: A Reflection on the Shoah.* http://www.vatican.va/roman_curia/pontifical_councils/chrstuni/documents/rc_pc_chrstuni_doc_16031998_shoah_en.html.

Common Word, A. 2007. http://www.acommonword.com/the-acw-document/.

Connelly, John. 2012. "The Catholic Church and Mission to the Jews." In *After Vatican II: Trajectories and Hermeneutics,* edited by James L. Heft and John O'Malley, 96-133. Grand Rapids/Cambridge: Eerdmans.

Conze, Edward. 1988. *Buddhist Wisdom Books Containing The Diamond Sutra and The Heart Sutra.* London: Unwin Paperbacks.

Copeland, Rita, and Peter T. Struck, eds. 2010. *The Cambridge Companion to Allegory.* Cambridge: Cambridge University Press.

Corless, Roger, and Paul F. Knitter, eds. 1990. *Buddhist Emptiness and Christian Trinity.* New York and Mahwah, NJ: Paulist.

Correia-Afonso, John. 1997. *The Jesuits in India: 1542-1773: A Short History.* Anand, Gujarat, India: Gujarat Sahitya Prakash.

Cragg, Kenneth. 1977. "Legacies and Hopes in Muslim/Christian Theology." *Islamo-christiana* 3:1-10.

———. 1986. *Christ and the Faiths.* Philadelphia: Westminster.

———. 2000. *The Call of the Minaret.* 3rd ed. Oxford: Oneworld.

Crawford, S. Cromwell. 1987. *Ram Mohan Roy: Social, Political, and Religious Reform in Nineteenth-Century India.* New York: Paragon House.

———. 1988. "Raja Ram Mohan Roy's Attitude toward Christians and Christianity." In *Neo-Hindu Views of Christianity,* edited by Arvind Sharma, 16-65. Leiden: Brill..

Cronin, Vincent. 1959. *A Pearl to India: The Life of Roberto de Nobili.* New York: E. P. Dutton.

Crossan, John Dominic. 1996. *Who Killed Jesus? Exposing the Roots of Anti-Semitism in the Gospel Story of the Death of Jesus.* San Francisco: HarperSanFrancisco.

Crowe, Frederick E. 1980. *The Lonergan Enterprise.* Cambridge, MA: Cowley.

———. 1989. *Appropriating the Lonergan Idea.* Edited by Michael Vertin. Washington, DC: Catholic University of America Press.

Cunningham, Philip. 2003. *Sharing the Scriptures.* New York: Paulist Press.

———. 2012. "A Christian-Jewish Dialogical Model in Light of New Research on Paul's Relationship with Judaism." In *Paul and Judaism: Crosscurrents Pauline Exegesis and the Study of Jewish-Christian Relations,* edited by Reimund Bieringer and Didier Pollefeyt, 141-62. New Testament Studies. Edinburgh: T. & T. Clark.

Dalai Lama. 1991. *Freedom in Exile: The Autobiography of the Dalai Lama.* San Francisco: Harper & Row.

———. 1998. *The Good Heart: A Buddhist Perspective on the Teaching of Jesus.* Edited by Robert Kiely. Translated by Geshe Thupten Jinpa. Boston: Wisdom Publications.

Daly, Robert J. 1996. "Removing Anti-Judaism from the Pulpit: Four Approaches." In *Removing Anti-Judaism from the Pulpit,* edited by Howard Clark Kee and Irvin J. Borowsky. Philadelphia: American Interfaith Institute; New York: Continuum.

Daniel, David Mills. 2007. *Briefly; Kant's Religion within the Boundaries of Mere Reason.* London: SCM.

Daniel, Monodeep. 2007. "Finding Sources of the Living Water." In *Dalit World—Biblical World: An Encounter,* edited by Leonard Fernando and James Massey. New Delhi: Centre for Dalit/Subaltern Studies and Vidyajyoti College of Theology.

Daniel, Norman. (1960) 2000. *Islam and the West: The Making of an Image.* Reprint, Oxford: Oneworld.

Daniélou, Jean. 1977. *The Theology of Jewish Christianity: A History of Early Christian Doctrine before the Council of Nicaea.* Translated and edited by John A. Baker. London: Darton, Longman & Todd; Philadelphia: Westminster.

Davey, Nicholas. 2006. *Unquiet Understanding: Gadamer's Philosophical Hermeneutics.* SUNY Series in Contemporary Continental Philosophy. Albany: State University of New York Press.

Davids, Adalbert. 1994. "Is the Theology of the Assyrian Church Nestorian?" In *Syriac Dialogue* 1, 134-41. Vienna: Foundation Pro Oriente.

Dawson, Christopher (1955) 1995. *Mission to Asia*. Reprint, Toronto: University of Toronto Press.

Desideri, Ippolito. 2010. *Mission to Tibet: The Extraordinary Eighteenth-Century Account of Father Ippolito Desideri, S.J.* Translated by Michael J. Sweet. Edited by Leonard Zwilling. Boston: Wisdom.

De Silva, Lynn A. 1976. "Sri Lanka: Theological Construction in a Buddhist Context." In *Asian Voices in Christian Theology*, edited by Gerald H. Anderson, 37-52. Maryknoll, NY: Orbis Books.

———. 1979. *The Problem of the Self in Buddhism and Christianity*. New York: Barnes & Noble Books/Harper & Row.

———. 1980. "Christian Reflection in a Buddhist Context." In *Asia's Struggle for Full Humanity: Towards a Relevant Theology*, edited by Virginia Fabella, 96-107. Maryknoll, NY: Orbis Books.

Dhavamony, Mariasusai. 2002. *Hindu-Christian Dialogue: Theological Soundings and Perspectives*. Amsterdam and New York: Rodopi.

Dieker, Bernadette. 1999. "Merton's Sufi Lectures to Cistercian Novices, 1966-68." In *Merton and Sufism: The Untold Story. A Complete Compendium*, edited by Rob Baker and Gray Henry, 130-62. Louisville: Fons Vitae.

Dodd, C. H. 1965. *The Interpretation of the Fourth Gospel*. Cambridge: Cambridge University Press.

Donaldson, Terence L. 2010. *Jews and Anti-Judaism in the New Testament: Decision Points and Divergent Interpretations*. London: SPCK; Waco, TX: Baylor University Press.

Doniger, Wendy. 2010. *The Hindus: An Alternative History*. New York and Harmondsworth, UK: Penguin.

Douglass, James W. 1970. *The Non-Violent Cross: A Theology of Revolution and Peace*. New York: Macmillan; London: Collier-Macmillan.

———. 1991. *The Nonviolent Coming of God*. Maryknoll, NY: Orbis Books.

Dozeman, Thomas. 1996. *God at War: A Study of Power in the Exodus Tradition*. New York and Oxford: Oxford University Press.

"Dream of the Rood, The." 1986. In *The Norton Anthology of English Literature*, 5th ed., edited by M. H. Abrams, 1:23-25. New York: W. W. Norton.

Drevet, Camille. 1967. *Massignon et Gandhi: La contagion de la vérité*. Chrétiens de tous les temps 23. Paris: Cerf.

Drijvers, Hans J. W. 1985. "Jews and Christians at Edessa." *Journal of Jewish Studies* 36:88-102. Reprinted in *Early Christianity and Judaism*, edited by Everett Ferguson, 350-64. New York and London: Garland, 1993.

Du Boulay, Shirley. 1998. *Beyond the Darkness: A Biography of Bede Griffiths*. New York: Doubleday.

———. 2005. *The Cave of the Heart: The Life of Swami Abhishiktananda*. Maryknoll, NY: Orbis Books.

Dunn, James D. G., ed. 1999. *Jews and Christians: The Parting of the Ways*. Grand Rapids: Eerdmans.

———. 2005. *The New Perspective on Paul: Collected Essays.* Tübingen: Mohr Siebeck.

Dunn, Maryjane, and Linda Kay Davidson, eds. 1996. *The Pilgrimage to Compostela in the Middle Ages.* New York: Routledge.

Eckel, Malcolm David. 1987. "Perspectives on the Buddhist-Christian Dialogue." In *The Christ and the Bodhisattva*, edited by Donald S. Lopez Jr. and Steven C. Rockefeller. SUNY Series in Buddhist Studies. Albany: State University of New York Press.

Eisenbaum, Pamela. 2009. *Paul Was Not a Christian: The Original Message of a Misunderstood Apostle.* New York: HarperCollins.

Ellis, Marc. 2009. *Judaism Does Not Equal Israel.* New York and London: New Press.

Enomiya-Lassalle, Hugo. 1974. *Zen Meditation for Christians.* LaSalle, IL: Open Court.

———. 1988. *Living in the New Consciousnes.* Edited by Roland Ropers. Translated by Paul Shepherd. Boston and Shatesbury: Shambhala.

Ephrem the Syrian. 1989. *Hymns.* Translated by Kathleen E. McVey. New York and Mahwah, NJ: Paulist.

Eusebius. 1981. *The History of the Church from Christ to Constantine.* Translated by G. W. Williamson. Harmondsworth, UK: Penguin Books.

Evans, Craig A., and Donald A. Hagner, eds. 1993. *Anti-Semitism and Early Christianity: Issues of Polemic and Faith.* Minneapolis: Fortress.

Farmer, William R., ed. 1999. *Anti-Judaism and the Gospels.* Harrisburg, PA: Trinity Press International.

Faure, Bernard. 1991. *The Rhetoric of Immediacy: A Cultural Critique of Chan/Zen Buddhism.* Princeton, NJ: Princeton University Press.

Fernando, Leonard. 2007. "Preface." In *Dalit World—Biblical World: An Encounter*, edited by Leonard Fernando and James Massey, 5-9. New Delhi: Centre for Dalit/Subaltern Studies and Vidyajyoti College of Theology.

Fernando, Leonard, and G. Gispert-Sauch. 2004. *Christianity in India: Two Thousand Years of Faith.* New Delhi and London: Penguin Viking.

Fernando, Leonard, and James Massey, eds. 2007. *Dalit World—Biblical World: An Encounter.* New Delhi: Centre for Dalit/Subaltern Studies and Vidyajyoti College of Theology.

Firestone, Chris L., and Nathan Jacobs. 2008. *In Defense of Kant's Religion.* Indiana Series in the Philosophy of Religion. Bloomington and Indianapolis: Indiana University Press.

Firey, Abigail. 2010. "The Letter of the Law: Carolingian Exegetes and the Old Testament." In *With Reverence for the Word: Medieval Scriptural Exegesis in Judaism, Christianity, and Islam*, edited by Jane Dammen McAuliffe, Barry D. Walfish, and Joseph W. Goering, 204-24. Oxford and New York: Oxford University Press.

Fischer, Louis. 1983. *The Life of Mahatma Gandhi.* New York: Harper & Row.

Fitzgerald, Michael L., and John Borelli. 2006. *Interfaith Dialogue: A Catholic View.* Maryknoll, NY: Orbis Books.

Fitzmyer, Joseph A. 1998. *The Acts of the Apostles: A New Translation with Introduction and Commentary.* Anchor Bible 31. New York: Doubleday.

Flannery, Edward H. 1965. *The Anguish of the Jews: Twenty-three Centuries of Anti-Semitism.* New York: Macmillan; London: Collier-Macmillan.

Fleming, Kenneth. 2002. *Asian Christian Theologians in Dialogue with Buddhism.* Religions and Discourse 11. Oxford: Peter Lang.

Ford, David, and C. C. Pecknold, eds. 2006. *The Promise of Scriptural Reasoning.* Malden, MA: Blackwell.

Francisco, Adam S. 2013. "Luther's Knowledge of and Attitude Towards Islam." In *The Routledge Reader in Christian-Muslim Relations,* edited by Mona Siddiqui, 129-53. London and New York: Routledge.

Fredriksen, Paula. 2008. *Augustine and the Jews: A Christian Defense of Jews and Judaism.* New York: Doubleday, 2008.

Fredriksen, Paula, and Adele Reinhartz, eds. 2002. *Jesus, Judaism, and Christian Anti-Judaism: Reading the New Testament after the Holocaust.* Louisville and London: Westminster John Knox.

Frend, W. H. C. 1984. *The Rise of Christianity.* Philadelphia: Fortress.

Fretheim, Terrence. 2007. *Abraham: Trials of Family and Faith.* Columbia, SC: University of South Carolina Press.

Frey, Jörg. 2012. "The Jewishness of Paul." In *Paul: Life, Setting, Work, Letters,* edited by Oda Wischmeyer, 57-95. Translated by Helen S. Heron and Dieter T. Roth. London and New York: T&T Clark..

Frykenberg, Robert Eric. 2000. "India." In *A World History of Christianity,* edited by Adrian Hastings, 148-91. Grand Rapids, MI, and Cambridge, UK: Eerdmans.

———. 2010. *Christianity in India: From Beginnings to the Present.* Oxford and New York: Oxford University Press.

Frymer-Kensky, Tikva, David Novak, Peter Ochs, David Fox Sandmel, and Michael A. Signer, eds. 2000. *Christianity in Jewish Terms.* Boulder, CO: Westview.

Gabriele, Matthew. 2007. "Against the Enemies of Christ: The Role of Count Emicho in the Anti-Jewish Violence of the First Crusade." In *Christian Attitudes toward the Jews in the Middle Ages: A Casebook,* edited by Michael Frassetto, 61-82. New York and London: Routledge.

Gadamer, Hans-Georg. 1989. *Truth and Method.* Translation revised by Joel Weinsheimer and Donald G. Marshall. 2nd rev. ed. New York: Crossroad.

Gager, John G. 2000. *Reinventing Paul.* Oxford and New York: Oxford University Press.

———. 2007."Did Jewish Christians See the Rise of Islam?" In *The Ways That Never Parted: Jews and Christians in Late Antiquity and the Early Middle Ages,* edited by Adam H. Becker and Annette Yoshiko Reed, 361-72. Minneapolis: Fortress.

Gandhi, Mohandas K. 1983. *Autobiography: The Story of My Experiments with Truth.* Translated by Mahadev Desai. New York: Dover.

———. 1991. *Gandhi on Christianity.* Edited by Robert Ellsberg. Maryknoll, NY: Orbis Books.

———. 2000. *The Bhagavad Gita according to Gandhi.* Edited by John Stohm-
    eier. Berkeley, CA: Berkeley Hill Books.
———. 2001. *Non-Violent Resistance (Satyagraha).* Mineola, NY: Dover.
Garcia Turza, Javier. 2000. *El Camino de Santiago y la Sociedad Medieval.*
    Logroño: Ediciones Instituto de Estudios Riojanos.
Geertz, Clifford. 1973. *The Interpretation of Culture: Selected Essays.* New
    York: Basic Books.
Gernet, Jacques. 1985. *China and the Christian Impact: A Conflict of Cultures.*
    Cambridge: Cambridge University Press; Paris: Editions de la Maison des
    Sciences de l'Homme.
Gillman, Ian, and Hans-Joachim Klimkeit. 1999. *Christians in Asia before 1500.*
    Ann Arbor: University of Michigan Press.
Gillman, Neil. 2000. *The Way into Encountering God in Judaism.* Woodstock,
    VT: Jewish Lights.
Girard, René. 1977. *Violence and the Sacred.* Translated by Patrick Gregory.
    Baltimore and London: Johns Hopkins University Press.
———. 1987a. *Things Hidden since the Foundation of the World.* Translated by
    Stephen Bann and Michael Metteer. Stanford, CA: Stanford University
    Press.
———. 1987b. *Job, the Victim of His People.* Translated by Yvonne Freccero.
    Stanford, CA: Stanford University Press.
———. 1988. *"To Double Business Bound": Essays on Literature, Mimesis, and
    Anthropology.* Baltimore: Johns Hopkins University Press.
———. 1990. *Deceit, Desire, and the Novel: Self and Other in Literary Structure.*
    Translated by Yvonne Freccero. Baltimore and London: Johns Hopkins
    University Press.
———. 1992. *The Scapegoat.* Translated by Yvonne Freccero. Baltimore: Johns
    Hopkins University Press.
———. 1996. *The Girard Reader.* Edited by James G. Williams. New York:
    Crossroad.
———. 2001. *I See Satan Fall like Lightning.* Translated by James G. Williams.
    Maryknoll, NY: Orbis Books; Ottawa: Novalis; Leominster, UK: Grace-
    wing.
———. 2011. *Sacrifice.* Translated by Matthew Pattillo and David Dawson. East
    Lansing: Michigan State University Press.
Gnuse, Robert Karl. 1997. *No Other Gods: Emergent Monotheism in Israel.*
    Journal for the Study of the Old Testament: Supplement Series 241. Shef-
    field: Sheffield Academic Press.
Goddard, Hugh. 2000. *A History of Christian–Muslim Relations.* Chicago: New
    Amsterdam Books.
Golb, Norman. 1998. *The Jews in Medieval Normandy: A Social and Intellec-
    tual History.* Cambridge: Cambridge University Press.
Gorenberg, Goshem. 2002. *The End of Days: Fundamentalism and the Struggle
    for the Temple Mount.* Oxford and New York: Oxford University Press.
Goshen-Gottstein, Alon. 2012. "God between Christians and Jews: Is It the
    Same God?" In *Do We Worship the Same God? Jews, Christians, and Mus-*

lims in Dialogue, edited by Miroslav Volf, 50-75. Grand Rapids and Cambridge: Eerdmans.

Gow, Andrew Colin. 1995. *The Red Jews: Antisemitism in an Apocalyptic Age, 1200-1600.* Studies in Medieval and Reformation Thought 55. Leiden: Brill.

Graham, Dom Aelred. 1994. *Zen Catholicism.* New York: Crossroad; York: Ampleforth.

Grant, Robert M. 1986. *Gods and the One God.* Philadelphia: Westminster.

Grant, Robert M., and David Tracy. 2005. *A Short History of the Interpretation of the Bible.* 2nd rev. ed. Minneapolis: Fortress.

Grant, Sara. 1987. *The Lord of the Dance.* Bangalore: Asian Trading Corporation.

———. 2002. *Toward an Alternative Theology: Confessions of a Non-Dualist Christian.* Notre Dame, IN: University of Notre Dame Press.

Grayston, Kenneth. 1984. *The Johannine Epistles.* New Century Bible Commentary. Grand Rapids: Eerdmans; London: Marshall, Morgan & Scott.

Green, Arthur. 2006. *Seek My Face: A Jewish Mystical Theology.* Woodstock, VT: Jewish Lights.

Greer, Rowan, and James L. Kugel. 1986. *Early Biblical Interpretation.* Philadelphia: Westminster.

Gregory I, Pope. 2004. *The Letters of Gregory the Great.* Translated by John R. C. Martyn. 3 vols. Toronto: Pontifical Institute of Medieval Studies.

Gregson, Vernon. 1985. *Lonergan, Spirituality, and the Meeting of Religions.* Lanham, MD: University Press of America.

Griffith, Sidney H. 1999. "Merton, Massignon, and the Challenge of Islam." In *Merton and Sufism: The Untold Story. A Complete Compendium,* edited by Rob Baker and Gray Henry, 51-78. Louisville: Fons Vitae.

———. 2008. *The Church in the Shadow of the Mosque: Christians and Muslims in the World of Islam.* Princeton and Oxford: Princeton University Press.

Griffiths, Bede. 1976. *Return to the Center.* Springfield, IL: Templegate.

———. 1990. *A New Vision of Reality: Western Science, Eastern Mysticism and Christian Faith.* Edited by Felicity Edwards. Springfield, IL: Templegate.

Gritsch, Eric W. 2012. *Martin Luther's Anti-Semitism: Against His Better Judgment.* Grand Rapids and Cambridge: Eerdmans.

Gude, Mary Louise. 1996. *Louis Massignon: The Crucible of Compassion.* Notre Dame, IN: University of Notre Dame Press.

Guelich, Robert A. 1993: "Anti-Semitism and/or Anti-Judaism in Mark?" In *Anti-Semitism and Early Christianity: Issues of Polemic and Faith,* edited by Craig A. Evans and Donald A. Hagner, 80-101. Minneapolis: Fortress.

Guyer, Paul. 2007. *Kant.* London and New York: Routledge.

Habito, Ruben L. F. 1989. *Total Liberation: Zen Spirituality and the Social Dimension.* Maryknoll, NY: Orbis Books.

———. 1993. *Healing Breath: Zen Spirituality for a Wounded Earth.* Maryknoll, NY: Orbis Books.

———. 1994. "Maria-Kannon Zen: Explorations in Buddhist-Christian Practice." *Buddhist-Christian Studies* 14:150-51.

Hackett, David G. 1996. *The Silent Dialogue: Zen Letters to a Trappist Abbot.* New York: Continuum.

Hadot, Pierre. 1995. *Philosophy as a Way of Life.* Edited by Arnold I. Davidson. Translated by Michael Chase. Oxford and New York: Blackwell.

———. 2002. *What Is Ancient Philosophy?* Translated by Michael Chase. Cambridge, MA: Belknap Press of Harvard University Press.

Hanson, Craig L. 1996. "Manuel I Comnenus and the 'god of Muhammad': A Study in Byzantine Ecclesiastical Politics." In *Medieval Christian Perceptions of Islam: A Book of Essays,* edited by John Victor Tolan, 55-82. New York and London: Garland.

Hare, Douglas. 1979. "The Rejection of the Jews in the Synoptic Gospels and Acts." In *Anti-Semitism and the Foundations of Christianity,* edited by Alan T. Davies, 27-47. New York: Paulist.

Harkins, Franklin T. 2008. "Unwitting Witnesses: Jews and Judaism in the Thought of Augustine." In *Augustine and World Religions,* edited by Brian Brown, John Doody, and Kim Paffenroth, 37-69. Lanham, MD: Lexington Books.

Harnack, Adolf. (1904) 1961. *The Mission and Expansion of Christianity.* Translated and edited by James Moffatt. New York: Harper & Row.

Harrington, Daniel J. 2007. *The Gospel of Matthew.* Sacra Pagina 1. Collegeville, MN: Liturgical Press.

Harrington, Wilfred J. 2008. *Revelation.* Sacra Pagina 16. Collegeville, MN: Liturgical Press.

Harris, Elizabeth J. 1994. "A Case of Distortion: The Evangelical Missionary Interpretation of Buddhism in the 19th Century." *Dialogue* n.s. 21:19-42.

Hassner, Ron E. 2009. *War on Sacred Grounds.* Ithaca, NY, and London: Cornell University Press.

Haughey, John C. 2009. *Where Is Knowing Going? The Horizons of the Knowing Subject.* Washington, DC: Georgetown University Press.

He, Jianming. 2000. "Buddhist-Christian Encounter in Modern China: A Case Study of *Ren Jian Jue banyuekan.*" *Ching Feng* n.s. 1.2:121-42.

Heath, Peter. 2010. "Allegory in Islamic Literature." In *The Cambridge Companion to Allegory,* edited by Rita Copeland and Peter T. Struck, 83-100. Cambridge: Cambridge University Press.

Hertzberg, Arthur. 1968. *The French Enlightenment and the Jews.* New York: Columbia University Press.

Heschel, Susannah. 2010. *The Aryan Jesus: Christian Theologians and the Bible in Nazi Germany.* Princeton, NJ: Princeton University Press.

Hitchens, Christopher. 2009. *God Is Not Great: How Religion Poisons Everything.* New York: Twelve.

Hood, John Y. B. 1995. *Aquinas and the Jews.* Philadelphia: University of Pennsylvania Press.

Hoyland, Robert G. 2006. "New Documentary Texts and the Early Islamic State." *Bulletin of the School of Oriental and African Studies* 69:395-416.

Hsia, R. Po-Chia. 2010. *A Jesuit in the Forbidden City: Matteo Ricci, 1552-1610.* Oxford: Oxford University Press.

Hughes, Kevin L. 2005. *Constructing Antichrist: Paul, Biblical Commentary, and the Development of Doctrine in the Early Middle Ages.* Washington, DC: Catholic University of America Press.

Hvalik, Reidar. 1996. *The Struggle for Scripture and Covenant: The Purpose of the Epistle of Barnabas and Jewish-Christian Competition in the Second Century.* Wissenschaftliche Untersuchungen zum Neuen Testament 2/82. Tübingen: Mohr Siebeck.

Idel, Moshe. 2007. *Ben: Sonship and Jewish Mysticism.* New York: Continuum; Jerusalem: Shalom Hartman Institute.

Innocent III, Pope. 1208. *Ut Esset Cain.* http://www.cn-telma.fr/relmin/extrait30493/.

International Conference of Christians and Jews. 2009. *A Time for Recommitment: Jewish Christian Dialogue 70 Years after War and Shoa.* Berlin: Konrad-Adenauer-Stiftung.

Ipgrave, Michael, ed. 2004. *Scriptures in Dialogue: Christians and Muslims Studying the Bible and the Qur'an Together.* London: Church House Publishing.

———. 2005. *Bearing the Word: Prophecy in Biblical and Qur'anic Perspective.* London: Church House Publishing.

Isaac, Jules. 1964. *The Teaching of Contempt: Christian Roots of Anti-Semitism.* Edited by Claire Huchet-Bishop. New York: Holt, Rinehart & Winston.

———. 1971. *Jesus and Israel.* Edited by Claire Huchet-Bishop. Translated by Sally Gran. New York: Holt, Rinehart & Winston.

Israel, Jonathan. 2010. *A Revolution of the Mind: Radical Enlightenment and the Intellectual Origins of Modern Democracy.* Princeton and Oxford: Princeton University Press.

Ives, Christopher, ed. 1995. *Divine Emptiness and Historical Fullness: A Buddhist-Jewish-Christian Conversation with Masao Abe.* Valley Forge, PA: Trinity Press International.

Jackson-McCabe, Matt, ed. 2007. *Jewish Christianity Reconsidered: Rethinking Ancient Groups and Texts.* Minneapolis: Fortress.

Jahanbegloo, Ramin. 2013. *The Gandhian Moment.* Cambridge, MA, and London: Harvard University Press.

Jamieson, A. G. 2006. *Faith and Sword: A Short History of Muslim-Christian Conflict.* London: Reaction.

Jaoudi, Maria. 1993. *Christian and Islamic Spirituality: Sharing a Journey.* New York and Mahwah, NJ: Paulist.

Jeanrond, Werner G., and Aasulv Lande, eds. 2005. *The Concept of God in Global Dialogue.* Maryknoll, NY: Orbis Books.

Jenkins, Philip. 2008. *The Lost History of Christianity: The Thousand-Year Golden Age of the Church in the Middle East, Africa, and Asia—and How It Died.* New York: HarperOne.

John, E. C. 2007. "Dalit Biblical Theology." In *Dalit World—Biblical World: An Encounter,* edited by Leonard Fernando and James Massey. New Delhi: Centre for Dalit/Subaltern Studies and Vidyajyoti College of Theology.

John XXIII, Pope. 1963. *Pacem in Terris: Encyclical on Establishing Univer-*

sal Peace in Truth, Justice, Charity, and Liberty. http://www.vatican.va/
holy_father/john_xxiii/encyclicals/documents/hf_j-xxiii_enc_11041963_
pacem_en.html.

John Chrysostom. 1979. *Discourses against Judaizing Christians.* Translated
by Paul W. Harkins. Fathers of the Church 68. Washington, DC: Catholic
University of America.

John of Damascus. 1958. *Writings.* Translated by Frederic H. Chase. Washington, DC: Catholic University of America Press.

John Paul II, Pope. 1980. "Address to Representatives of the West-German Jewish Community." Mainz, West Germany, Nov. 17, 1980. In *Bridges: Documents of the Christian-Jewish Dialogue.* Vol. 1, *The Road to Reconciliation
(1945-1985),* edited by Franklin Sherman, 177-80. New York and Mahwah,
NJ: Paulist.

———. 1986. "Address at the Great Synagogue of Rome." April 13, 1986. http://
web.archive.org/web/20080708235855/http://www.bc.edu/research/cjl/
meta-elements/texts/cjrelations/resources/documents/catholic/john
paulii/romesynagogue.htm.

———. 1994. *Tertio Millennio Adveniente: Apostolic Letter on Preparation
for the Jubilee of the Year 2000.* http://www.vatican.va/holy_father/john_
paul_ii/apost_letters/1994/documents/hf_jp-ii_apl_19941110_tertio-
millennio-adveniente_en.html.

———. 1999. "Message to the Faithful of Islam at the End of the Month of
Ramadan, April 3, 1991." In *John Paul II and Interreligious Dialogue,* edited
by Byron L. Sherwin and Harold Kasimow. Maryknoll, NY: Orbis Books.

———. 1999. "To the Participants in the Symposium on 'Holiness in Christianity and in Islam' (Rome, May 9, 1985)." In *John Paul II and Interreligious
Dialogue,* edited by Byron L. Sherwin and Harold Kasimow, 59-60. Maryknoll, NY: Orbis Books.

———. 2001. "Address of the Holy Father." Meeting with the Muslim Leaders
at the Omayyad Great Mosque, Damascus, http://www.vatican.va/holy_
father/john_paulii/speeches/2001/documents/hf_jp-ii_spe_20010506_
omay.

John Paul II, Pope, and Catholicos Mar Dinkha IV. 1994. "Common Christological Declaration between the Catholic Church and the Assyrian Church of
the East." In *Syriac Dialogue: First Non-Official Consultation on Dialogue
within the Syriac Tradition,* edited by Alfred Stirnemann and Gerhard
Wilflinger, 230-31. Vienna: Foundation Pro Oriente.

Johnson, James Turner. 1997. *The Holy War Idea in Western and Islamic Traditions.* University Park, PA: Pennsylvania State University Press.

Johnson, Luke Timothy. 1989. "The New Testament's Anti-Jewish Slander and
the Conventions of Ancient Polemic." *Journal of Biblical Literature* 108
(1989): 419-41.

———. 2009. *Among the Gentiles: Greco-Roman Religion and Christianity.*
Anchor Yale Bible Reference Library. New Haven and London: Yale University Press.

Johnston, William. 2000. *"Arise, My Love . . .": Mysticism for a New Era.* Mary-knoll, NY: Orbis Books.

———. 2002. "Introduction." In J. K. Kadowaki, *Zen and the Bible.* Maryknoll, NY: Orbis Books.

———. 2006. *Mystical Journey: An Autobiography.* Maryknoll, NY: Orbis Books.

Jones, E. Stanley. 1925. *The Christ of the Indian Road.* New York: Abingdon.

———. 1968. "My Conversion to Non-Violent Non-Cooperation." In *Mahatma Gandhi 100 Years,* edited by S. Radhakrishnan, 171-79. New Delhi: Gandhi Peace Foundation.

Josephus. 1998. *The Complete Works.* Nashville: Thomas Nelson.

Justin Martyr. 2003. *Dialogue with Trypho.* Edited by Michael Slusser. Translated by Thomas B. Falls. Revised by Thomas P. Halton. Selections from Fathers of the Church 3. Washington, DC: Catholic University of America Press.

Kadowaki, J. K. 2002. *Zen and the Bible.* Translated by Joan Rieck. Maryknoll, NY: Orbis Books.

Kaegi, Walter E. 1997. *Byzantium and the Early Islamic Conquests.* Cambridge, UK: Cambridge University Press.

Kamenetz, Rodger. 1995. *The Jew in the Lotus: A Poet's Discovery of Jewish Identity in Buddhist India.* New York: HarperCollins.

Kant, Immanuel. 1965. *Critique of Pure Reason.* Translated by Norman Kemp Smith. New York: St. Martin's Press.

———. 1975. *On History.* Translated by Lewis White Beck, Robert E. Anchor, and Emil L. Fackenheim. Indianapolis: Bobbs-Merrill.

———. 1981. *Critique of Practical Reason.* Translated by Lewis White Beck. Indianapolis: Bobbs-Merrill.

———. 1987. *Critique of Judgment Including the First Introduction.* Translated by Werner S. Pluhar. Indianapolis: Hackett.

———. 2010. *Religion within the Boundaries of Mere Reason and Other Writings.* Translated and edited by Allen Wood and George DiGiovanni. Cambridge: Cambridge University Press.

Kearney, Richard. 2004. *On Paul Ricoeur: The Owl of Minerva.* Transcending Boundaries in Philosophy and Theology. Aldershot, UK, and Burlington, VT: Ashgate.

———. 2006. "Introduction: Paul Ricoeur's Philosophy of Translation." In Paul Ricoeur, *On Translation,* translated by Eileen Brennan. London and New York: Routledge.

Kedar, Benjamin Z. 1984. *Crusade and Mission: European Approaches toward the Muslims.* Princeton, NJ: Princeton University Press.

Kee, Howard Clark, and Irvin Borowsky, eds. 1996. *Removing Anti-Judaism from the Pulpit.* Philadelphia: American Interfaith Institute; New York: Continuum.

Keenan, John P. 1989. *The Meaning of Christ: A Mahayana Theology.* Mary-knoll, NY: Orbis Books.

———. 1995. *The Gospel of Mark: A Mahayana Reading.* Maryknoll, NY: Orbis Books.

——. 2005. *The Wisdom of James: Parallels with Mahayana Buddhism.* New York and Mahwah, NJ: Newman.

——. 2007. "The Limits of Thomas Merton's Understanding of Buddhism." In *Merton & Buddhism: Wisdom, Emptiness, and Everyday Mind,* edited by Bonnie Bowman Thurston, 118-33. Louisville: Fons Vitae.

Keenan, John P., with Sydney Copp, Lansing Davis, and Buster G. Smith. 2009. *Grounding Our Faith in a Pluralist World—with a Little Help from Nagarjuna.* Eugene, OR: Wipf & Stock.

Keenan, John P., and Linda K. Keenan. 2011. *I Am/No Self: A Christian Commentary on the Heart Sutra.* Christian Commentaries on Non-Christian Sacred Texts. Leuven: Peeters; Grand Rapids: Eerdmans.

Keller, Catherine. 2008. *On the Mystery: Discerning Divinity in Process.* Minneapolis: Fortress.

Kennedy, Robert. 1996. *Zen Spirit, Christian Spirit: The Place of Zen in Christian Life.* New York: Continuum.

——. 2000. *Zen Gifts to Christians.* New York: Continuum.

Kertzer, David I. 2001. *The Popes against the Jews: The Vatican's Role in the Rise of Modern Anti-Semitism.* New York: Alfred A. Knopf.

King, Coretta Scott. 2010. "Foreword." In Martin Luther King Jr., *Strength to Love.* Minneapolis: Fortress.

King, Martin Luther, Jr. 1958. *Stride toward Freedom.* New York: Harper & Brothers.

——. (1963) 2010. *Strength to Love.* Minneapolis: Fortress.

King, Richard. 1999. *Orientalism and Religion: Post-colonial Theory, India, and "The Mystic East."* London: Routledge.

Kirsch, Jonathan. 2005. *God against the Gods: The History of the War between Monotheism and Polytheism.* New York: Penguin Books.

Kiser, John W. 2002. *The Monks of Tibhirine: Faith, Love, and Terror in Algeria.* New York: St. Martin's Griffin.

Kissinger, Warren S. 1975. *The Sermon on the Mount: A History of Interpretation and Bibliography.* Metuchen, NJ: Scarecrow Press.

Klijn, A. F. J., ed. and trans. 2003. *The Acts of Thomas: Introduction, Text, and Commentary.* 2nd rev. ed. Supplements to Novum Testamentum 108. Leiden and Boston: Brill.

Klostermaier, Klaus. 2007. *A Survey of Hinduism.* 3rd ed. Albany: State University of New Press.

Kopf, David. 1979. *Brahmo Samaj and the Shaping of the Modern Indian Mind.* Princeton, NJ: Princeton University Press.

——. 1988. "Neo-Hindu Views of Unitarian and Trinitarian Christianity in Nineteenth Century Bengal: The Case of Keshub Chandra Sen." In *Neo-Hindu Views of Christianity,* edited by Arvind Sharma, 106-19. Leiden: Brill.

Koyama, Kosuke. 1974. *Pilgrim or Tourist: 50 Short Meditations.* Singapore: Christian Conference of Asia.

——. 1976. *No Handle on the Cross: An Asian Meditation on the Crucified Mind.* London: SCM.

———. 1979. *Three Mile an Hour God*. London: SCM.

———. 1984. *Mount Fuji and Mount Sinai: A Pilgrimage in Theology*. London: SCM; Maryknoll, NY: Orbis Books..

———. 1996. "How Many Languages Does God Speak?" *Cross Currents* 46:169-78.

———. 1997. "My Pilgrimage in Mission." *International Bulletin of Missionary Research* 21:55-59.

Krey, Philip. 1996. "Nicholas of Lyra and Paul of Burgos on Islam." In *Medieval Christian Perceptions of Islam: A Book of Essays*, edited by John Victor Tolan, 153-74. New York and London: Garland.

Küng, Hans. 1986. *Christianity and the World Religions*. New York: Doubleday.

———. 1990. "God's Self-Renunciation and Buddhist Emptiness: A Christian Response to Masao Abe." In *Buddhist Emptiness and Christian Trinity: Essays and Explorations*, edited by Roger Corless and Paul F. Knitter, 26-43. New York and Mahwah, NJ: Paulist.

———. 1995. "God's Self-Renunciation and Buddhist Emptiness: A Christian Response to Masao Abe." In *Divine Emptiness and Historical Fullness: A Buddhist-Jewish-Christian Conversation*, edited by Christopher Ives, 207-23. Valley Forge, PA: Trinity Press International.

———. 2007. *Islam: Past, Present, and Future*. Oxford: Oneworld.

———. 2013. "Christianity and World Religions: The Dialogue with Islam as One Model." In *The Routledge Reader in Christian-Muslim Relations*, edited by Mona Siddiqui, 242-55. London and New York: Routledge.

Küng, Hans, and David Tracy, eds. 1989. *Paradigm Change in Theology: A Symposium for the Future*. Translated by Margaret Köhl. New York: Crossroad.

Kuriakose, M. M., ed. 1982. *History of Christianity in India: Source Materials*. Madras: Christian Literature Society.

Kurikilamkatt, James. 2005. *First Voyage of the Apostle Thomas to India: Ancient Christianity in Baruch and Taxila*. Bangalore: Asian Trading Corporation.

Kyung, Chung Hyun. 1995. "Who Is Jesus for Asian Women?" In *Theology and Cultures: Doing Theology with Asian Resources*, vol. 2, edited by Yeow Choo-Lak. Singapore: Association for Theological Education in South East Asia.

LaFleur, William R. 1998. "Interpretation as Interlocution." In *Masao Abe: A Zen Life of Dialogue*, edited by Donald W. Mitchell, 75-88. Boston: Charles E. Tuttle.

Lai, Pan-chiu. 2000. "Influence of Chinese Buddhism on the Indigenization of Christianity in Modern China." *Ching Feng* n.s. 1.2:143-59.

———. 2004. "Christian-Confucian Dialogue on Humanity: An Ecological Perspective." *Studies in Interreligious Dialogue* 14.2:202-15.

———. 2005. "Typology and Prospect of Sino-Christian Theology." *Ching Feng* 6.2:211-30.

———. 2007. "Mahayana Interpretation of Christianity: A Case Study of Zhang Chunyi (1871-1955). *Buddhist-Christian Studies* 27:67-87.

———. 2009. "Timothy Richard's Buddhist-Christian Studies." *Buddhist-Christian Studies* 29:23-38.

Lai, Whalen, and Michael von Brück. 2001. *Christianity and Buddhism: A Multicultural History of Their Dialogue.* Translated by Phyllis Jestice. Maryknoll, NY: Orbis Books.

Lambrecht, Jan. 1999. *Second Corinthians.* Sacra Pagina 8. Collegeville, MN: Liturgical Press.

Lamoreaux, John C. 1996. "Early Eastern Christian Responses to Islam." In *Medieval Christian Perceptions of Islam: A Book of Essays,* edited by John Victor Tolan, 3-32. New York and London: Garland.

Langer, Ruth. 2012. *Cursing Christians? A History of the Birkat HaMinim.* Oxford: Oxford University Press.

Lankavatara Sutra, The: A Zen Text. 2012. Translation and commentary by Red Pine. Berkeley, CA: Counterpoint.

Lapide, Pinchas. 1967. *Three Popes and the Jews.* New York: Hawthorn Books.

Laven, Mary. 2011. *Mission to China: Matteo Ricci and the Jesuit Encounter with the East.* London: Faber & Faber.

Lederach, John Paul. 2003. *The Little Book of Conflict Transformation.* Intercourse, PA: Good Books.

Lee, Chwen Jiuan A., and Thomas G. Hand. 1990. *A Taste of Water: Christianity through Taoist-Buddhist Eyes.* Burlingame, CA: Mercy Center.

Lefebure, Leo D. 1996a. "Victims, Violence, and the Sacred: The Thought of René Girard." *The Christian Century* 113/36 (Dec. 11):1226-29.

———. 1996b. "Mimesis, Violence, and Socially Engaged Buddhism: Overture to a Dialogue." *Contagion: Journal of Violence, Mimesis and Culture* 3:121-40.

———. 1997. "Report of the Working Group on Buddhist-Catholic Dialogue: Conference of the Society of Buddhist-Christian Studies, July 30-August 2, 1996." *Pro Dialogo* 95:220-27.

———. 1999. "Christology in Ecumenical Dialogue: Expressing the Identity of Jesus Christ." *Chicago Studies* 39:154-64. Expanded version published in *The Anglican* 29/1 (2000): 5-10.

Lefebure, Leo D., and Peter Feldmeier. 2011. *The Path of Wisdom: A Christian Commentary on the Dhammapada.* Christian Commentaries on Sacred Non-Christian Texts. Leuven: Peeters; Grand Rapids: Eerdmans.

Leibig, J.E. 1983. "John and 'the Jews': Theological Anti-Semitism in the Fourth Gospel." *Journal of Ecumenical Studies* 20:209-34.

Leithart, Peter. 2009. *Deep Exegesis: The Mystery of Reading Scripture.* Waco, TX: Baylor University Press.

Lelyveld, Joseph. 2011. *Great Soul: Mahatma Gandhi and His Struggle with India.* New York: Alfred A. Knopf.

Levenson, Jon. 1985. *The Universal Horizon of Jewish Particularism.* New York: American Jewish Committee.

———. 1987. *Sinai and Zion: An Entry into the Jewish Bible.* San Francisco: HarperSanFranciso.

———. 2012. *Inheriting Abraham: The Legacy of the Patriarch in Judaism, Christianity, and Islam.* Princeton, NJ: Princeton University Press.

Levine, Amy-Jill. 1999. "Anti-Judaism and the Gospel of Matthew. In *Anti-*

Judaism and the Gospels, edited by William R. Farmer, 9-36. Harrisburg, PA: Trinity Press International.

———. 2002. "Matthew, Mark, and Luke: Good News or Bad?" In *Jesus, Judaism, and Christian Anti-Judaism: Reading the New Testament after the Holocaust,* edited by Paula Fredriksen and Adele Reinhartz. Louisville: Westminster John Knox.

Levine, Amy-Jill, and Marc Zvi Brettler, eds. 2011. *The Jewish Annotated New Testament.* Oxford and New York: Oxford University Press.

Lian, Xi. 1997. *The Conversion of Missionaries: Liberalism in American Protestant Missions in China, 1907-1932.* University Park: Pennsylvania State University Press.

Linafelt, Tod, ed. 2002. *A Shadow of Glory: Reading the New Testament after the Holocaust.* New York and London: Routledge.

Lincoln, Abraham. (1865) 1984. "Second Inaugural Address." In Abraham Lincoln. *Mystic Chords of Memory: A Selection from Lincoln's Writings.* Edited by Larry Shapiro, 76-78. New York: Book-of-the-Month Club.

Lipner, Julius J. 1999. *Brahmabandhab Upadhyay: The Life and Thought of a Revolutionary.* Delhi and New York: Oxford University Press.

Little, Lester K. 1991. "The Jews in Christian Europe." In *Essential Papers on Judaism and Christianity in Conflict: From Late Antiquity to the Reformation,* edited by Jeremy Cohen, 276-97. Essential Papers on Jewish Studies. New York: New York University Press.

Livingston, James C. 2009. *Anatomy of the Sacred: An Introduction to Religion.* 6th ed. Upper Saddle River, NJ: Pearson Prentice Hall.

Llull, Ramon. 2002. *The Book of the Gentile and the Three Wise Men.* Translated by Anthony Bonner. In Amador Vega, *Ramon Llull and the Secret of Life.* Translated by James W. Heisig. New York: Crossroad.

Lodahl, Michael E. 2010. *Claiming Abraham: Reading the Bible and the Qur'an Side by Side.* Grand Rapids: Brazos.

Lomax, John Phillip. 1996. "Frederick II, His Saracens, and the Papacy." In. *Medieval Christian Perceptions of Islam: A Book of Essays,* edited by John Victor Tolan, 175-97. New York and London: Garland.

Lonergan, Bernard J. F. 1967. *Collection.* Edited by F. E. Crowe. New York: Herder & Herder.

———. 1974a. *A Second Collection.* Edited by William F. J. Ryan and Bernard J. Tyrrell. Philadelphia: Westminster.

———. 1974b. *Grace and Freedom: Operative Grace in the Thought of St. Thomas Aquinas.* Edited by J. Patout Burns. London: Darton, Longman, & Todd.

———. 1979 [1972]. *Method in Theology.* New York: Seabury.

———. 1985. *A Third Collection: Papers by Bernard J. F. Lonergan, S.J.* Edited by Frederick E. Crowe. New York and Mahwah, NJ: Paulist; London: Geoffrey Chapman.

———. 1987 [1980]. *Understanding and Being: An Introduction and Companion to Insight. The Halifax Lectures.* Edited by Elizabeth A. Morelli and Mark D. Morelli. Lewiston and Queenston: Edwin Mellen Press.

———. 1997 [1957]. *Insight: A Study of Human Understanding.* Collected

Works of Bernard Lonergan 3. Edited by Frederick E. Crowe and Robert M. Doran. Toronto: University of Toronto Press.

Louth, Andrew. 2002. *St. John Damascene: Tradition and Originality in Byzantine Theology.* Oxford and New York: Oxford University Press.

Lubac, Henri de. 1998. *Medieval Exegesis.* Vol. 1, *The Four Senses of Scripture.* Translated by Mark Sebanc. Grand Rapids: Eerdmans; Edinburgh: T&T Clark.

———. 2007. *History and Spirit: The Understanding of Scripture according to Origen.* San Francisco: Ignatius Press.

Lüdemann, Gerd. 1997. *The Unholy in Holy Scripture: The Dark Side of the Bible.* Translated by John Bowden. Louisville: Westminster John Knox.

Luther, Martin. (ca. 1530) 1956. *The Sermon on the Mount.* Translated and edited by Jaroslav Pelikan. In *Luther's Works,* vol. 21. St. Louis: Concordia.

———. (1542) 2004. *The Jews and Their Lies.* York, SC: Liberty Bell.

Maharshi, Ramana. 1988. *The Spiritual Teaching of Ramana Maharshi.* Boston and London: Shambhala.

Martinez, F. J. 1985. "Eastern Christian Apocalyptic in the Early Muslim Period: Pseudo-Methodius and Pseudo-Athanasius." Dissertation, Catholic University of America. .

Massey, James. 1994. *Towards Dalit Hermeneutics: Rereading the Text, the History and the Literature.* Delhi: ISPCK.

———. 2007. "Introduction." In *Dalit World—Biblical World: An Encounter,* edited by Leonard Fernando and James Massey, 13-20. New Delhi: Centre for Dalit/Subaltern Studies and Vidyajyoti College of Theology.

Massignon, Louis. 1987. *L'hospitalité sacrée.* Edited by Jacques Keryell. Paris: Nouvelle Cité.

———. 1994. *The Passion of Al-Hallaj: Mystic and Martyr of Islam.* Abridged edition. Translated and edited by Herbert Mason. Bollingen Series 98. Princeton, NJ: Princeton University Press.

———. 1997. *Les trois prières d'Abraham: Patrimoines.* Paris: Cerf.

Matera, Frank J. 2007. *Galatians.* Sacra Pagina 9. Collegeville, MN: Liturgical Press.

May, John D'Arcy. 2003. *Transcendence and Violence: The Encounter of Buddhist, Christian and Primal Traditions.* New York: Continuum.

———. 2006. "Buddhists, Christians and Ecology." In *Buddhism, Christianity and the Question of Creation: Karmic or Divine?,* edited by Perry Schmidt-Leukel, 93-109. Aldershot, UK, and Burlington, VT: Ashgate.

McCarter, P. Kyle. 1997. "The Religious Reforms of Hezekiah and Josiah." In *Aspects of Monotheism: How God Is One,* edited by Hershel Shanks and Jack Meinhardt, 57-80. Washington, DC: Biblical Archaeology Society.

McDonald, Lee Martin. 2007. *The Biblical Canon: Its Origin, Transmission, and Authority.* Peabody, MA: Hendrickson.

McDonald, Lee Martin, and James A. Sanders, eds. 2002. *The Canon Debate.* Peabody, MA: Hendrickson.

McGinn, Bernard J. 1979a. *Visions of the End: Apocalyptic Traditions in the Middle Ages.* New York: Columbia University Press.

———. 1979b. *Apocalyptic Spirituality: Treatises and Letters of Lactantius, Adso of Montier-en-Der, Joachim of Fiore, The Franciscan Spirituals, Savonarola.* Translated by Bernard McGinn. New York: Paulist.

———. 1994. *Antichrist: Two Thousand Years of the Human Fascination with Evil.* San Francisco: HarperSanFrancisco.

McGinn, Bernard J., John J. Collins, and Stephen J. Stein, eds. 2003. *The Continuum History of Apocalypticism.* New York and London: Continuum.

McKnight, Scot. 1993. "A Loyal Critic: Matthew's Polemic with Judaism in Theological Perspective." In *Anti-Semitism and Early Christianity: Issues of Polemic and Faith,* edited by Craig A. Evans and Donald A. Hagner, 55-79. Minneapolis: Fortress.

McMichael, Steven J. 2012. "Francis and the Encounter with the Sultan (1219)." In *The Cambridge Companion to Francis of Assisi,* edited by Michael J.P. Robson, 127-42. Cambridge: Cambridge University Press.

Medlycott, A. E. (1905) 2007. *India and the Apostle Thomas: An Inquiry with a Critical Analysis of the Acta Thomae.* Whitefish, MT: Kessinger.

Meier, John P. 2001. *A Marginal Jew: Rethinking the Historical Jesus.* Vol. 3, *Companions and Competitors.* Anchor Bible Reference Library. New York: Doubleday.

Melito of Sardis. 1979. *On Pascha and Fragments.* Edited and translated by Stuart George Hall. Oxford: Clarendon.

———. 2001. *On Pascha, With the Fragments of Melito and Other Material Related to the Quartodecimans.* Translated by Alistair Stewart-Sykes. Crestwood, NY: St. Vladimir's Seminary Press.

Merton, Thomas. 1954. *The Last of the Fathers: Saint Bernard of Clairvaux and the Encyclical Letter Doctor Mellifluus.* San Diego: Harcourt Brace Jovanovich.

———. 1966. *Conjectures of a Guilty Bystander.* New York: Doubleday.

———. 1967. *Mystics and Zen Masters.* New York: Delta.

———. 1968. *Zen and the Birds of Appetite.* New York: New Directions.

———. 1973. *The Asian Journal of Thomas Merton.* Edited by Naomi Burton, Patrick Hart, and James Laughlin. New York: New Directions.

Meyendorff, John. 1964. "Byzantine Views of Islam." *Dumbarton Oaks Papers* 18:115-32.

Michael, Robert. 2006. *Holy Hatred: Christianity, Antisemitism, and the Holocaust.* New York: Palgrave Macmillan.

———. 2008. *A History of Catholic Antisemitism: The Dark Side of the Church.* New York: Palgrave Macmillan.

Michel, Thomas. 2010. *A Christian View of Islam: Essays on Dialogue.* Edited by Irfan A. Omar. Maryknoll, NY: Orbis Books.

Millar, F. 1993. "Hagar, Ishmael, Josephus, and the Origins of Islam." *Journal of Jewish Studies* 44:23-45.

Milodinow, Leonard. 2012. *Subliminal: How Your Unconscious Mind Rules Your Behavior.* New York: Pantheon Books.

Minj, Francis. 2011. "Jesus Christ *Paramadivasi*: An Indian *Adivasi* Construal of Jesus Christ." In *Jesus of Galilee: Contextual Christology for the 21ˢᵗ Cen-*

tury, edited by Robert Lassalle-Klein et al., 187-203. Maryknoll, NY: Orbis Books.

Mitchell, Donald W. 1991. *Spirituality and Emptiness: The Dynamics of Spiritual Life in Buddhism and Christianity.* New York and Mahwah, NJ: Paulist.

——, ed. 1998a. *Masao Abe: A Zen Life of Dialogue.* Boston: Charles E. Tuttle.

——. 1998b. "Dialogue and Unity." In *Masao Abe: A Zen Life of Dialogue*, edited by Donald W. Mitchell, 128-40. Boston: Charles E. Tuttle.

Mitchell, Donald W., and James Wiseman, eds. 1999. *The Gethsemani Encounter: A Dialogue on the Spiritual Life by Buddhist and Christian Monastics.* New York: Continuum.

Mitchell, Margaret M. 2010. *Paul, the Corinthians, and the Birth of Christian Hermeneutics.* Cambridge: Cambridge University Press.

Miyamoto, Ken Christoph. 2007. *God's Mission in Asia: A Comparative and Contextual Study of This-Worldly Holiness and the Theology of Missio Dei in M.M. Thomas and C.S. Song.* American Society of Missiology Monograph Series 1. Eugene, OR: Pickwick.

Moffett, Samuel Hugh. 1998. *A History of Christianity in Asia.* Vol. 1, *Beginnings to 1500.* 2nd rev. ed. Maryknoll, NY: Orbis Books.

——. 2005. *A History of Christianity in Asia.* Vol. 2, *1500 to 1900.* Maryknoll, NY: Orbis Books.

Moloney, Francis J. 1998. *The Gospel of John.* Sacra Pagina 4. Collegeville, MN: Liturgical Press.

Moltmann, Jürgen. 1990. *The Way of Jesus Christ: Christology in Messianic Dimensions.* San Francisco: HarperSanFrancisco.

Monchanin, Jules, and Henri Le Saux. 1956. *Ermites du Saccidananda: Un essai d'intégration chrétienne de la tradition monastique de l'Inde.* Tournai and Paris: Casterman.

Moniz, John. 1996. *"Liberated Society" Gandhian and Christian Vision: Comparative Study.* Documenta Missionalia 23. Rome: Gregorian Pontifical University Press.

Moorhead, John. 2005. *Gregory the Great.* London and New York: Routledge.

Morris, Benny. 2001. *Righteous Victims: A History of the Zionist-Arab Conflict 1881-2001.* New York: Random House.

Most, Glenn W. 2010. "Hellenistic Allegory and Early Imperial Rhetoric. In *The Cambridge Companion to Allegory,* edited by Rita Copeland and Peter T. Struck, 26-38. Cambridge: Cambridge University Press.

Moule, A. C. (1930) 1977. *Christians in China before the Year 1550.* New York: Octagon Books.

Moyaert, Marianne. 2010. "Absorption or Hospitality: Two Approaches to the Tension between Identity and Alterity." In *Interreligious Hermeneutics,* edited by Catherine Cornille and Christopher Conway, 61-88. Eugene, OR: Cascade Books.

Nagao, Gadjin. 1991. *Mādhyamika and Yogācāra: A Study of Mahāyāna Philosophies.* Edited and translated by L. S. Kawamura in collaboration with

G. M. Nagao. SUNY Series in Buddhist Studies. Albany: State University of New York Press.

Nagarjuna. 1995. *The Fundamental Wisdom of the Middle Way: Nagarjuna's Mulamadhyamakarika.* Translation and commentary by Jay. L. Garfield. New York and Oxford: Oxford University Press.

Nagl-Docekal, Herta. 2010. "Issues of Gender in Catholicism: How the Current Debate Could Profit from a Philosophical Approach." In *Church and People: Disjunctions in a Secular Age,* edited by Charles Taylor, José Casanova, and George McClean. Series VIII, vol. 1. San Antonio, TX: Council for Research in Values and Philosophy.

Narinskaya, Elena. 2010. *Ephrem, A 'Jewish' Sage: A Comparison of the Exegetical Writings of St. Ephrem the Syrian and Jewish Traditions.* Studia Traditionis Theologiae 7. Turnhout: Brepols.

Nedungatt, George. 2008. *Quest for the Historical Thomas Apostle of India: A Re-reading of the Evidence.* Bangalore: Theological Publications in India.

Neusner, Jacob. 1970. "The Jewish-Christian Argument in Fourth-Century Iran: Aphrahat on Circumcision, the Sabbath, and the Dietary Laws." *Journal of Ecumenical Studies* 7:282-90. Reprinted in *Early Christianity and Judaism,* edited by Everett Ferguson, 366-74. New York and London: Garland.

New Oxford Annotated Bible, with the Apocryphal/Deuterocanonical Books. 2007. Edited by Michael D. Coogan. Augmented 3rd ed. Oxford: Oxford University Press.

Nicholls, William. 1995. *Christian Antisemitism: A History of Hate.* Northvale, NJ, and London: Jason Aronson.

Nickelsburg, George W. E. 2003. *Ancient Judaism and Christian Origins: Diversity, Continuity, and Transformation.* Minneapolis: Fortress.

Niditch, Susan. 1993. *War in the Hebrew Bible: A Study in the Ethics of Violence.* New York and Oxford: Oxford University Press.

Niebuhr, H. Richard. 1970. *Radical Monotheism and Western Culture with Supplementary Essays.* New York: Harper Torchbooks.

Niebuhr, Reinhold. 1960. *Moral Man and Immoral Society: A Study in Ethics and Politics.* New York: Charles Scribner's Sons.

Niemoeller, Martin. 2000. "The Way of Peace." In *Peace Is the Way,* edited by Walter Wink. Maryknoll, NY: Orbis Books.

Nishida, Kitaro. 1992. *An Inquiry into the Good.* Translated by Masao Abe and Christopher Ives. New Haven: Yale University Press.

Nishitani, Keiji. 1982. *Religion and Nothingness.* Translated by Jan Van Bragt. Nanzan Studies in Religion and Culture. Berkeley, CA: University of California Press.

Nobili, Roberto de. 2000. *Preaching Wisdom to the Wise: Three Treatises by Roberto de Nobili, S.J., Missionary and Scholar in 17th Century India.* Translated and introduction by Anand Amaladass and Francis X. Clooney. St. Louis: Institute of Jesuit Sources.

Nock, A. D. 1998. *Conversion: The Old and the New in Religion from Alexander the Great to Augustine of Hippo.* Baltimore and London: Johns Hopkins University Press.

Noth, Martin. 1967. *The Laws in the Pentateuch and Other Studies.* Philadelphia: Fortress.

Novikoff, Alex. 2010. "The Middle Ages." In *Antisemitiusm: A History,* edited by Albert S. Lindemann and Richard S. Levy, 63-78. Oxford and New York: Oxford University Press.

Olivera, Bernardo. 1997. *How Far to Follow? The Martyrs of Atlas.* Petersham, MA: St. Bede's Publications.

Origen. 1973. *On First Principles.* Translated by G. W. Butterworth. Gloucester, MA: Peter Smith.

———. 1980. *Contra Celsum.* Translated with an introduction and notes by Henry Chadwick. Cambridge: Cambridge University Press.

———. 2002: *Homilies on Joshua.* Edited by Cynthia White. Translated by Barbara J. Bruce. Washington, DC: Catholic University of America Press.

Palaver, Wolfgang. 2009. "Drawn into Conversion: How Mimetic Theory Changed My Way of Being a Christian Theologian." In *For René Girard: Essays in Friendship and in Truth,* edited by Sandhor Goodhart, Jorgen Jorgensen, Tom Ryba, and James G. Williams, 189-97. East Lansing, MI: Michigan State University Press.

Palmer, Martin, Eva Wong, Tjalling Halbertsma, Zhao Xiao Min, Li Rong Rong, and James Palmer. 2001. *The Jesus Sutras: Rediscovering the Lost Scrolls of Taoist Christianity.* New York: Ballantine Wellspring.

Pannenberg, Wolfhart. 1995. "God's Love and the Kenosis of the Son: A Response to Masao Abe." In *Divine Emptiness and Historical Fullness: A Buddhist-Jewish-Christian Conversation with Masao Abe,* edited by Christopher Ives, 244-50. Valley Forge, PA: Trinity Press International.

Panikkar, Raimon. 1978. *The Intrareligious Dialogue.* New York: Paulist.

———. 1981. *The Unknown Christ of Hinduism: Towards an Ecumenical Christophany.* Rev. and enl. ed. London: Darton, Longman & Todd.

———. 1993. *A Dwelling Place for Wisdom.* Translated by Annemarie S. Kidder. Louisville, KY: Westminster/John Knox Press.

———. 2004. *Christophany: The Fullness of Man.* Maryknoll, NY: Orbis Books.

Parrinder, Geoffrey. 1964. *The Christian Debate: Light from the East.* London: Victor Gollancz.

Pathak, Sushil Madhava. 1967. *American Missionaries and Hinduism: A Study of Their Contacts from 1813 to 1910.* Delhi: Munshiram Manoharlal.

Paul VI, Pope. 1964. *Ecclesiam Suam: On The Church.* http://www.vatican.va/holy_father/paul_vi/encyclicals/documents/hf_p-vi_enc_06081964_ecclesiam_en.html.

Pelikan, Jaroslav. 1977. *The Christian Tradition: A History of the Development of Doctrine.* Vol. 2, *The Spirit of Eastern Christendom (600-1700).* Chicago: University of Chicago Press.

———. 2001. *Divine Rhetoric: The Sermon on the Mount as Message and Model in Augustine, Chrysostom, and Luther.* Crestwood, NY: St. Vladimir's Seminary Press.

Pellauer, David. 2007. *Ricoeur: A Guide for the Perplexed.* London and New York: Continuum.

Perdue, Leo G. 2007. *Wisdom Literature: A Theological History*. Louisville: Westminster John Knox.

——. 2008. *The Sword and the Stylus: An Introduction to Wisdom in the Age of Empires*. Grand Rapids: Eerdmans.

Perry, Marvin, and Frederick M. Schweitzer. 2002. *Antisemitism: Myth and Hate from Antiquity to the Present*. New York: Palgrave MacMillan.

Peters, Edward, ed. 1971. *The First Crusade: The Chronicle of Fulcher of Chartres and Other Source Materials*. Philadelphia: University of Pennsylvania Press.

Peters, F. E. 1985. *Jerusalem: The Holy City in the Eyes of Chroniclers, Visitors, Pilgrims, and Prophets from the Days of Abraham to the Beginnings of Modern Times*. Princeton, NJ: Princeton University Press.

Phan, Peter C. 2004. *Being Religious Interreligiously: Asian Perspectives on Interfaith Dialogue*. Maryknoll, NY: Orbis Books.

——. 2005. *Mission and Catechesis: Alexandre de Rhodes and Inculturation in Seventeenth-Century Vietnam*. Maryknoll, NY: Orbis Books.

Philo of Alexandria. 1981. *The Contemplative Life, The Giants, and Selections*. Translated by David Winston. Mahwah, NJ: Paulist.

——. 2008. *The Works of Philo: Complete and Unabridged*. Translated by C. D. Yonge. Updated ed. Peabody, MA: Hendrickson.

Pieris, Aloysius. 1988a. *An Asian Theology of Liberation*. Maryknoll, NY: Orbis Books.

——. 1988b. *Love Meets Wisdom: A Christian Experience of Buddhism*. Maryknoll, NY: Orbis Books.

——. 1996. *Fire and Water: Basic Issues in Asian Buddhism and Christianity*. Maryknoll, NY: Orbis Books.

Pius XI, Pope. 1937. *Mit brennender Sorge: Encyclical on the Church and the German Reich*. http://www.vatican.va/holy_father/pius_xi/encyclicals/documents/hf_p-xi_enc_14031937_mit-brennender-sorge_en.html.

Pomplun, Trent. 2010. *Jesuit on the Roof of the World: Ippolito Desideri's Mission to Eighteenth-Century Tibet*. Oxford: Oxford University Press.

Pontifical Biblical Commission. 1993. *The Interpretation of the Bible in the Church*. http://catholic-resources.org/ChurchDocs/PBC_Interp.htm.

——. 2001. *The Jewish People and Their Sacred Scriptures in the Christian Bible*. http://www.vatican.va/roman_curia/congregations/cfaith/pcb_documents/rc_con_cfaith_doc_20020212_popolo-ebraico_en.html.

Pontifical Council for Interreligious Dialogue. 1991. *Dialogue and Proclamation: Reflections and Orientations on Interreligious Dialogue and the Proclamation of the Gospel of Jesus Christ*. http://www.vatican.va/roman_curia/pontifical_councils/interelg/documents/rc_pc_interelg_doc_19051991_dialogue-and-proclamatio_en.html.

Prabhu, R. K., and U. R. Rao. 1967. *The Mind of Mahatma Gandhi*. 2nd rev. ed. Ahmedabad: Navajivan Publishing House.

Pritz, Ray. 1988. *Nazarene Jewish Christianity: From the End of the New Testament Period until Its Disappearance in the Fourth Century*. Studia Post-Biblica 37. Jerusalem: Magnes Press; Leiden: Brill.

Probst, Christopher J. 2012. *Demonizing the Jews: Luther and the Protestant Church in Nazi Germany.* Bloomington: Indiana University Press.

Pseudo Methodius. 1993. *The Apocalypse of Pseudo-Methodius.* In *The Seventh Century in the West-Syrian Chronicles.* Translated by Andrew Palmer and Sebastian Brock. Liverpool: Liverpool University Press.

Rad, Gerhard von. 1991. *Holy War in Ancient Israel.* Translated and edited by Marva J. Dawn. Grand Rapids: Eerdmans.

Rajkumar, Peniel. 2010. *Dalit Theology and Dalit Liberation: Problems, Paradigms and Possibilities.* Surrey, UK, and Burlington, VT: Ashgate.

Rao, K. L. S. 1988. "Mahatma Gandhi and Christianity." In *Neo-Hindu Views of Christianity,* edited by Arvind Sharma, 143-55. Leiden and New York: Brill.

———. 1990. *Mahatma Gandhi and Comparative Religion.* 2nd rev. ed. Delhi: Motilal Banarsidass.

Redford, Donald B. 1992. *Egypt, Canaan, and Israel in Ancient Times.* Princeton, NJ: Princeton University Press.

Reinders, Eric. 2004. *Borrowed Gods and Foreign Bodies: Christian Missionaries Imagine Chinese Religion.* Berkeley: University of California Press.

Reinhartz, Adele. 1988. "The New Testament and Anti-Judaism: A Literary-critical Approach." *Journal of Ecumenical Studies* 25:524-37.

———. 2002. "The Gospel of John: How 'the Jews' Became Part of the Plot." In *Jesus, Judaism, and Christian Anti-Judaism: Reading the New Testament after the Holocaust,* edited by Paula Fredriksen and Adele Reinhartz. Louisville: Westminster John Knox.

Renard, John. 2004. *Knowledge of God in Classical Sufism: Foundations of Islamic Mystical Theology.* Translated by John Renard. New York: Paulist.

———. 2011. *Islam and Christianity: Theological Themes in Comparative Perspective.* Berkeley: University of California Press.

Rende, Michael L. 1991. *Lonergan on Conversion: The Development of a Notion.* Lanham, MD: University Press of America.

Rensberger, David. 1998. "Anti-Judaism and the Gospel of John." In *Anti-Judaism and the Gospels,* edited by William R. Farmer. Harrisburg, PA: Trinity Press International.

Reventlow, Henning Graf. 2009-10. *The History of Biblical Interpretation.* 4 vols. Resources for Biblical Study 50, 61-63. Atlanta: Society of Biblical Literature. Vol. 1, *From the Old Testament to Origen,* translated by Leo G. Perdue. Vol. 2, *From Late Antiquity to the End of the Middle Ages,* translated by James O. Duke. Vol. 3, *Renaissance, Reformation, Humanism,* translated by James O. Duke. Vol. 4, *From the Enlightenment to the Twentieth Century,* translated by Leo G. Perdue.

Richard, Timothy. (1910) 2009. *The New Testament of Higher Buddhism.* Edinburgh: T&T Clark. Reprint, Ithaca, NY: Cornell University Press.

Ricoeur, Paul. 1966. *Freedom and Nature: The Voluntary and the Involuntary.* Translated by Erazim V. Kohák. Evanston, IL: Northwestern University Press.

———. 1967. *The Symbolism of Evil.* Translated by Emerson Buchanan. Boston: Beacon.

———. 1970. *Freud and Philosophy: An Essay on Interpretation.* Translated by Denis Savage. New Haven and London: Yale University Press.

———. 1974. *The Conflict of Interpretations.* Edited by Don Ihde. Evanston, IL: Northwestern University Press.

———. 1976. *Interpretation Theory: Discourse and the Surplus of Meaning.* Fort Worth, TX: Texas Christian University Press.

———. 1981. *The Rule of Metaphor: Multi-disciplinary Studies of the Creation of Meaning in Language.* Translated by Robert Czerny, Kathleen McLaughlin, and John Costello. Toronto: University of Toronto Press.

———. 1991. *From Text to Action: Essays in Hermeneutics, II.* Translated by Kathleen Blamey and John B. Thompson. Evanston, IL: Northwestern University Press.

———. 1992. *Oneself as Another.* Translated by Kathleen Blamey. Chicago and London: University of Chicago Press.

———. 1995. *Figuring the Sacred: Religion, Narrative, and Imagination.* Edited by Mark I. Wallace. Translated by David Pellauer. Minneapolis: Fortress.

———. 1996. "Reflections on a New Ethos for Europe." In *Paul Ricoeur: The Hermeneutics of Action,* edited by Richard Kearney. London: Sage.

———. 2004. *Memory, History, Forgetting.* Translated by Kathleen Blamey and David Pellauer. Chicago: University of Chicago Press.

———. 2006. *On Translation.* Translated by Eileen Brenna. London and New York: Routledge.

Riesebrodt, Martin. 2010. *The Promise of Salvation: A Theory of Religion.* Translated by Steven Rendall. Chicago and London: University of Chicago Press.

Robinson, Rowena, and Joseph Marianus Kujur, eds. 2010. *Margins of Faith: Dalit and Tribal Christianity in India.* New Delhi: Sage Publications India; Thousand Oaks, CA: Sage.

Rolandi, Luca. 2013. "Tauran on Interreligious Dialogue: 'We're Not Competitors but Pilgrims Searching for the Truth.'" http://vaticaninsider.lastampa.it/en/inquiries-and-interviews/detail/articolo/dialogo-dialogue-dialogos-interreligioso-interrelegious-24474/

Roth, Cecil. 1991. "The Medieval Conception of the Jew: A New Interpretation." In *Essential Papers on Judaism and Christianity in Conflict: From Late Antiquity to the Reformation,* edited by Jeremy Cohen, 298-309. Essential Papers on Jewish Studies. New York: New York University Press.

Ruether, Rosemary Radford. 1979. *Faith and Fratricide: The Theological Roots of Anti-Semitism.* New York: Seabury.

Rynne, Terrence J. 2008. *Gandhi and Jesus: The Saving Power of Nonviolence.* Maryknoll, NY: Orbis Books.

Sacks, Jonathan. 2002. *The Dignity of Difference: How to Avoid the Clash of Civilizations.* London: Continuum.

———. 2005. *To Heal a Fractured World: The Ethics of Responsibility.* New York: Schocken Books.

Sahas, Daniel J. 1990. "The Art and Non-Art of Byzantine Polemics, Patterns of Refutation in Byzantine Anti-Islamic Literature." In *Conversion and Continuity: Indigenous Christian Communities in Islamic Lands, Eighth to Eighteenth Centuries,* edited by Michael Gervers and Ramzi J. Bikhazi, 55-73. Papers in Medieval Studies 9. Toronto: Pontifical Institute of Medieval Studies.

Salenson, Christian. 2012. *Christian de Chergé: A Theology of Hope.* Translated by Nada Conic. Collegeville, MN: Liturgical Press; Trappist, KY: Cistercian Publications.

Sanders, E. P. 2002. "Jesus, Ancient Judaism, and Modern Christianity." In *Jesus, Judaism, and Christian Anti-Judaism: Reading the New Testament after the Holocaust,* edited by Paula Fredriksen and Adele Reinhartz. Louisville: Westminster John Knox.

Sarris, Peter. 2011. *Empires of Faith: The Fall of Rome to the Rise of Islam, 500-700.* Oxford History of Medieval Europe. Oxford: Oxford University Press.

Schäfer, Peter. 2007. *Jesus in the Talmud.* Princeton, NJ, and Oxford: Princeton University Press.

Schimmel, Annemarie. 1975. *Mystical Dimensions of Islam.* Chapel Hill: University of North Carolina Press.

Schleiermacher, Friedrich. (1821-22) 1976. *The Christian Faith.* Edited by H. R. Mackintosh and J. S. Stewart. 2nd ed. Philadelphia: Fortress.

———. 1977: *Hermeneutics: The Handwritten Manuscripts.* Edited by Heinz Kimmerle. Translated by James Duke and Jack Forstman. AAR Texts and Translations 1. Missoula, MT: Scholars Press.

———. (1799) 2000. *On Religion: Speeches to Its Cultured Despisers.* Translated by Richard Crouter. Cambridge: Cambridge University Press.

Schmidt-Leukel, Perry, ed. 2006. *Buddhism, Christianity and the Question of Creation: Karmic or Divine.* Aldershot, UK, and Burlington, VT: Ashgate.

Schneiders, Sandra. 1999. *The Revelatory Text: Interpreting the New Testament as Sacred Scripture.* 2nd ed. Collegeville, MN: Liturgical Press.

Schouten, Jan Peter. 2008. *Jesus as Guru: The Image of Christ among Hindus and Christians in India.* Translated by Henry Jansen and Lucy Jansen. Currents of Encounter 36. Amsterdam and New York: Rodopi.

Schramm, Brooks, and Kirsi Stjerna, eds. 2012. *Martin Luther, the Bible, and the Jewish People: A Reader.* Minneapolis, MN: Fortress.

Schreiter, Robert. 1985. *Constructing Local Theologies.* Maryknoll, NY: Orbis Books.

———. 2005. "The Possibilities (and Limitations) of an Intercultural Dialogue on God." In *The Concept of God in Global Dialogue,* edited by Werner G. Jeanrond and Aasulv Lande, 19-31. Maryknoll, NY: Orbis Books.

Schurhammer, Georg. 1977. *Francis Xavier, His Life, His Times.* Vol. 2, *India (1541-44).* Translated by M. Joseph Costelloe. Rome: Jesuit Historical Institute.

Sebeos, Bishop of Bagratunik. 1999. *The Armenian History Attributed to Sebeos.* Translated by R. W. Thomson. Historical commentary by James Howard-Johnston with assistance from Tim Greenwood. 2 vols. Liverpool: Liverpool University Press.

Sen, Keshub Chandra. 1879. *Lectures and Tracts*. Calcutta: Indian Mirror Press.

Senior, Donald. 1997. *The Gospel of Matthew*. Nashville: Abingdon Press.

Severus ibn al-Muqaffa, Bishop of el-Ashmunein. 1948. *History of the Patriarchs of the Coptic Church of Alexandria*. Edited and translated by B. Evetts. Paris: Firmin-Didot.

Shah-Kazemi, Reza. 2012. "Do Muslims and Christians Believe in the Same God?" In *Do We Worship the Same God? Jews, Christians, and Muslims in Dialogue*, edited by Miroslav Volf, 76-147. Grand Rapids/Cambridge: Eerdmans.

Shanks, Hershel, and Jack Meinhard, eds. 1997. *Aspects of Monotheism: How God Is One*. Washington, DC: Biblical Archaeology Society.

Sharma, Arvind. 1998. "A Chrysanthemum with a Lotus Stalk: Reminiscences from a Hindu Perspective." In *Masao Abe: A Zen Life of Dialogue*, edited by Donald W. Mitchell, 326-34. Boston: Charles E. Tuttle.

———. 2005. *Modern Hindu Thought: An Introduction*. Oxford: Oxford University Press.

Shepardson, Christine C. 2001. "Anti-Jewish Rhetoric and Intra-Syriac Conflict in the Sermons of Ephrem Syrus." *Studia Patristica* 35:502-7.

———. 2008. *Anti-Judaism and Christian Orthodoxy: Ephrem's Hymns in Fourth-Century Syria*. Washington, DC: Catholic University of America Press.

Sherman, Franklin. 1995. *Luther and the Jews: A Fateful Legacy*. Baltimore: Institute for Christian and Jewish Studies.

———, ed. 2011. *Bridges: Documents of the Christian-Jewish Dialogue*. Vol. 1, *The Road to Reconciliation (1945-1985)*. New York and Mahwah, NJ: Paulist.

Shweder, Richard. 1993. *Thinking through Cultures: Expeditions in Cultural Psychology*. Cambridge, MA: Harvard University Press.

Siker, Jeffrey S. 1991. *Disinheriting the Jews: Abraham in Early Christian Controversy*. Louisville: Westminster John Knox.

Simmer-Brown, Judith. 2007. "The Liberty That Nobody Can Touch: Thomas Merton Meets Tibetan Buddhism." In *Merton & Buddhism: Wisdom, Emptiness, and Everyday Mind*, edited by Bonnie Bowman Thurston. Louisville: Fons Vitae.

Simon, Marcel. (1964) 1986. *Verus Israel: A Study of Relations between Christians and Jews in the Roman Empire (AD 135-425)*. Translated by H. McKeating. Oxford: Oxford University Press.

Simonetti, Manlio. 1994. *Biblical Interpretation in the Early Church: An Historical Introduction to Patristic Exegesis*. Translated by John A. Hughes. Edited by Anders Bergquist and Markus Bockmuehl. Edinburgh: T&T Clark.

Skarsaune, Oskar. 2002. *In the Shadow of the Temple: Jewish Influences on Early Christianity*. Downers Grove, IL: InterVarsity.

Skarsaune, Oskar, and Reidar Hvalik, eds. 2007. *Jewish Believers in Jesus: The Early Centuries*. Peabody, MA: Hendrickson.

Slotkin, Richard. 1973. *Regeneration through Violence: The Mythology of the American Frontier, 1600-1860.* Norman: University of Oklahoma Press.

Smiga, George M. 1992. *Pain and Polemic: Anti-Judaism in the Gospels.* New York and Mahwah, NJ: Paulist.

Smith, Mark S. 2002. *The Early History of God: Yahweh and the Other Divinities in Ancient Israel.* 2nd ed. Grand Rapids: Eerdmans.

Smith, Wilfred Cantwell. 1991. *The Meaning and End of Religion.* Minneapolis: Fortress.

Soares-Prabhu, George M. 1994. "Two Mission Commands: An Interpretation of Matthew 28:16-20 in Light of a Buddhist Text." *Biblical Interpretation* 2–3:264-82.

———. 2003. *The Dharma of Jesus.* Edited by Francis X. D'Sa. New York: Maryknoll, NY: Orbis Books.

Song, Choan-Seng. 1960. "The Obedience of Theology in Asia." *South East Asia Journal of Theology* 2:7-15.

———. 1982. *The Compassionate God.* Maryknoll, NY: Orbis Books.

———. 1986. *The Compassionate God: An Exercise in the Theology of Transposition.* London: SCM.

———. 1991. *Third-Eye Theology: Theology in Formation in Asian Settings.* Rev. ed. Maryknoll, NY: Orbis Books.

———. 1994. *Jesus in the Power of the Spirit.* Minneapolis: Fortress.

———. 1999. *The Believing Heart: An Invitation to Story Theology.* Minneapolis: Fortress.

Soro, Mar Bawai. 2007. *The Church of the East Apostolic and Orthodox.* San Jose, CA: Adiabene.

Southern, R. W. 1962. *Western Views of Islam in the Middle Ages.* Cambridge, MA, and London: Harvard University Press.

Spector, Stephen. 2009. *Evangelicals and Israel: The Story of American Christian Zionism.* Oxford and New York: Oxford University Press.

Stark, Rodney. 2001. *The One True God: Historical Consequences of Monotheism.* Princeton, NJ, and Oxford: Princeton University Press, 2001.

———. 2003. *For the Glory of God: How Monotheism Led to Reformations, Science, Witch-Hunts, and the End of Slavery.* Princeton, NJ, and Oxford: Princeton University Press.

Steiner, George. 1998. *After Babel: Aspects of Language and Translation.* Oxford and New York: Oxford University Press.

Stendahl, Krister. 1989. *Paul among Jews and Gentiles and Other Essays.* Philadelphia: Fortress.

Stirnemann, Alfred, and Gerhard Wilflinger, eds. 1994. *Syriac Dialogue: First Non-Official Consultation on Dialogue within the Syriac Tradition.* 1994. Vienna: Pro Oriente Foundation.

———. 1996. *Syriac Dialogue: Second Non-Official Consultation on Dialogue within the Syriac Tradition.* Vienna: Pro Oriente Foundation.

———. 1998. *Syriac Dialogue: Third Non-Official Consultation on Dialogue within the Syriac Tradition.* Vienna: Pro Oriente Foundation.

Stowers, Stanley K. 1994. *A Rereading of Romans: Justice, Jews, and Gentiles.* New Haven: Yale University Press.

Strecker, Georg. 1971. "Appendix I: On the Problem of Jewish Christianity." In Walter Bauer, *Orthodoxy and Heresy in Earliest Christianity.* Philadelphia: Fortress. Reprinted in *Early Christianity and Judaism,* edited by Evertett Ferguson, 31-75. New York and London: Garland.

Stuart, James. 1995. *Swami Abhishiktananda: His Life Told through His Letters.* Delhi: ISPCK.

Stylianopoulos, Theodore. 1975. *Justin Martyr and the Mosaic Law.* Society of Biblical Literature Dissertation Series 20. Missoula, MT: Society of Biblical Literature and Scholars Press.

Synan, Edward A. 2010. "The Four 'Senses' and Four Exegetes." In *With Reverence for the Word: Medieval Scriptural Exegesis in Judaism, Christianity, and Islam,* edited by Jane Dammen McAuliffe, Barry D. Walfish, and Joseph W. Goering, 225-36. Oxford and New York: Oxford University Press.

Tang, Li. 2004. *A Study of the History of Nestorian Christianity in China and Its Literature in Chinese Together with a New English Translation of the Dunhuang Nestorian Documents.* 2nd rev. ed. Frankfurt am Main: Peter Lang.

Tanner, Norman, ed. 1990. *Decrees of the Ecumenical Councils.* London: Sheed & Ward; Washington, DC: Georgetown University Press: Vol. 1, *Nicaea I to Lateran V.* Vol. 2, *Trent to Vatican II.*

Tauran, Jean-Louis Cardinal. 2013. "Message to Buddhists for the Feast of Vesakh/Hanamatsuri 2013A.D./2556 B.E." http://www.vatican.va/roman_curia/pontifical_councils/interelg/documents/rc_pc_interelg_doc_20130502_festivita-buddista_en.html.

Taylor, Miriam S. 1995. *Anti-Judaism and Early Christian Identity: A Critique of the Scholarly Consensus.* Studia Post-Biblica 46. Leiden: Brill.

Thangaraj, M. Thomas. 1994. *The Crucified Guru: An Experiment in Cross-Cultural Christology.* Nashville: Abingdon.

Thatamanil, John J. 2006. *The Immanent Divine: God, Creation, and the Human Predicament.* Minneapolis: Fortress.

Thiselton, Anthony C. 1992. *New Horizons in Hermeneutics.* Grand Rapids: Zondervan.

Thomas Aquinas. 1947. *Summa Theologica.* Translated by Fathers of the English Dominican Province. 3 vols. New York: Benziger Brothers.

———. 2010. *Commentary on the Gospel of John.* Translated by Fabian Larcher and Thomas Weisheipl. 3 vols. Washington, DC: Catholic University of America Press.

Thurman, Howard. 1979. *With Head and Heart: The Autobiography of Howard Thurman.* San Diego: Harvest Book, Harcourt Brace.

Thurston, Bonnie. 1999. "Thomas Merton's Interest in Islam: The Example of Dhikr." In *Merton and Sufism: The Untold Story. A Complete Compendium,* edited by Rob Baker and Gray Henry, 40-50. Louisville: Fons Vitae.

Tiede, David L. 1993. "'Fighting against God': Luke's Interpretation of Jewish Rejection of the Messiah Jesus." In *Anti-Semitism and Early Christianity:*

    Issues of Polemic and Faith, edited by Craig A. Evans and Donald A. Hagner, 102-12. Minneapolis: Fortress.

Tillich, Paul. 1958. *Dynamics of Faith.* New York: Harper Torchbooks.

Todorov, Tristan. 1995. *Les Abus de la mémoire.* Paris: Editions Arléa.

Tolan, John V. 2008. *Sons of Ishmael: Muslims through European Eyes in the Middle Ages.* Gainesville, FL: University Press of Florida.

———. 2012. "Of Milk and Blood: Innocent III and the Jews Revisited." http://hal.archives-ouvertes.fr/docs/00/72/64/85/PDF/Of_Milk_and_Blood.pdf.

Trachtenburg, Joshua. 1943. *The Devil and the Jews: The Medieval Conception of the Jew and Its Relation to Modern Antisemitism.* Philadelphia: Jewish Publication Society of America.

Tracy, David. 1998. *The Analogical Imagination: Christian Theology and the Culture of Pluralism.* New York: Crossroad.

Trocmé, André. 2004. *Jesus and the Nonviolent Revolution.* Maryknoll, NY: Orbis Books.

Turner, Denys. 2010. "Allegory in Christian Late Antiquity." In *The Cambridge Companion to Allegory,* edited by Rita Copeland and Peter T. Struck, 71-82. Cambridge: Cambridge University Press.

Tweed, Thomas A. 1988. *The American Encounter with Buddhism 1844-1912: Victorian Culture and the Limits of Dissent.* Bloomington, and Indianapolis: Indiana University Press.

Tyerman, Christopher. 2006. *God's War: A New History of the Crusades.* Cambridge, MA: Belknap Press of Harvard University Press.

United Nations. 2006. *The Alliance of Civilizations: Report of the High-Level Group.* New York: United Nations. http://www.unaoc.org/repository/HLG_Report.pdf.

Unterseher, Lisa A. 2009. *The Mark of Cain and the Jews: Augustine's Theology of Jews and Judaism.* Gorgias Dissertations 39. Piscataway, NJ: Gorgias.

Vatican Council II. 2004. *Dogmatic Constitution on Divine Revelation, Dei Verbum.* In Vatican Council II. Vol. 1, *The Conciliar and Postconciliar Documents.* Edited by Austin Flannery. Rev. ed. Northport, NY: Costello; Dublin: Dominican Publications.

Vega, Amador. 2002. *Ramon Llull and the Secret of Life.* Translated by James W. Heisig. New York: Crossroad.

Vergote, A. 1996. *Religion, Belief and Unbelief: A Psychological Study.* Leuven: Leuven University Press; Atlanta, GA: Editions Rodopi Amsterdam.

Volf, Miroslav. 1996. *Exclusion and Embrace: A Theological Exploration of Identity, Otherness, and Reconciliation.* Nashville: Abingdon.

———. 2011. *Allah: A Christian Response.* New York: HarperOne.

———, ed. 2012. *Do We Worship the Same God? Jews, Christians, and Muslims in Dialogue.* Grand Rapids and Cambridge: Eerdmans.

Volf, Mirsolav, Ghazi bin Muhammad, and Melissa Yarrington, eds. 2009. *A Common Word: Muslims and Christians on Loving God and Neighbor.* Grand Rapids: Eerdmans.

Wahlde, Urban C. von. 1993. "The Gospel of John and the Presentation of Jews and Judaism." In *Within Context: Essays on Jews and Judaism in the New*

Testament, edited by E. P. Efroymson, E. J. Fischer, and L. Klenicki, 67-84. Collegeville, MN: Liturgical Press.

Waldenfels, Hans. 1980. *Absolute Nothingness: Foundations for a Buddhist-Christian Dialogue.* Translated by J. W. Heisig. New York and Ramsey, NJ: Paulist.

Waltz, James. 2013. "Muhammad and the Muslims in St. Thomas Aquinas." In *The Routledge Reader in Christian-Muslim Relations,* edited by Mona Siddiqui, 112-21. London and New York: Routledge.

Ware, Kallistos. 2002. "How Do We Enter the Heart?" In *Paths to the Heart: Sufism and the Christian East,* edited by James S. Cutsinger, 2-23. Bloomington, IN: World Wisdom.

Watt, W. M. 1991. *Muslim-Christian Encounters: Perceptions and Misperceptions.* London: Routledge.

Wei, Francis C. M. 1947. *The Spirit of Chinese Culture.* New York: Charles Scribner's Sons.

Weinrich, William C., ed. 2005. *Revelation.* Ancient Christian Commentary on Scripture: New Testament 12. Downers Grove, IL: InterVarsity.

Whalen, Brett Edward. 2009. *Dominion of God: Christendom and Apocalypse in the Middle Ages.* Cambridge, MA, and London: Harvard University Press.

Whitehead, Alfred North (1933) 1967. *Adventures of Ideas.* New York: Free Press; London: Collier Macmillan.

———. (1926) 1974. *Religion in the Making.* New York and Scarborough, ON: New American Library.

Wilfred, Felix. 2003. *Asian Dreams and Christian Hope at the Dawn of the Millennium.* Delhi: ISPCK.

Wilken, Robert L. 1983. *John Chrysostom and the Jews: Rhetoric and Reality in the Late Fourth Century.* Transformation of the Classical Heritage 4. Berkeley: University of California Press, 1983.

Wilkinson, Robert. 2009. *Nishida and Western Philosophy.* Farnham, UK, and Burlington, VT: Ashgate.

Williamson, Clark M. 1993. *A Guest in the House of Israel: Post-Holocaust Church Theology.* Louisville: Westminster John Knox.

Wink, Walter. 1992. *Engaging the Powers: Discernment and Resistance in a World of Domination.* Philadelphia: Fortress.

———. 2003. *Jesus and Nonviolence: A Third Way.* Minneapolis: Fortress.

Wittgenstein, Ludwig. 1965. *Preliminary Studies for the "Philosophical Investigations" Generally Known as the Blue and Brown Books.* New York: Harper Colophon Books.

———. 1968. *Philosophical Investigation: The English Text of the Third Edition.* Translated by G. E. M. Anscombe. New York: Macmillan.

Wolf, Kenneth Baxter. 1996. "Christian Views of Islam in Early Medieval Spain." In *Medieval Christian Perceptions of Islam: A Book of Essays,* edited by John Victor Tolan, 85-108. New York and London: Garland.

Wood, Susan K. 1998. *Spiritual Exegesis and the Church in the Theology of Henri de Lubac.* Grand Rapids: Eerdmans; Edinburgh: T&T Clark.

Wright, Tom. 2004. "On the Road to Emmaus." In *Scriptures in Dialogue: Christians and Muslims Study the Bible and the Qur'an Together.* Edited by Michael Ipgrave, 25-35. London: Church House Publishing.

Yoder, John Howard. 1983. *Christian Attitudes towards War, Peace, and Revolution.* Durham, NC: Duke University Divinity School.

———. 1994. *The Politics of Jesus.* 2nd ed. Grand Rapids: Eerdmans.

Yusa, Michiko. 2002: *Zen and Philosophy: An Intellectual Biography of Kitaro Nishida.* Honolulu: University of Hawai'i Press.

Yuval, Israel Jacob. 2006. *Two Nations in Your Womb: Perceptions of Jews and Christians in Late Antiquity and the Middle Ages.* Translated by Barbara Harshav and Jonathan Chipman. Berkeley: University of California Press.

Zaehner, R. C. 1970. *Concordant Discord: The Interdependence of Faiths.* Oxford: Clarendon.

Zupanov, Ines G. 1999. *Disputed Mission: Jesuit Experiments and Brahmanical Knowledge in Seventeenth-century India.* Oxford: Oxford University Press.

Index